Matthew Atmore Sherring

History of Protestant Missions in India

Matthew Atmore Sherring

History of Protestant Missions in India

ISBN/EAN: 9783337820824

Printed in Europe, USA, Canada, Australia, Japan

Cover: Foto ©ninafisch / pixelio.de

More available books at **www.hansebooks.com**

THE HISTORY

OF

PROTESTANT MISSIONS
IN INDIA,

FROM THEIR COMMENCEMENT IN 1706 TO 1871.

BY THE

REV. M. A. SHERRING M A LL.D., LOND.

MISSIONARY OF THE LONDON MISSIONARY SOCIETY; FELLOW OF THE CALCUTTA UNIVERSITY;
CORRESPONDING MEMBER OF THE BENGAL ASIATIC SOCIETY;
Author of "*The Indian Church during the Mutiny,*" "*The Sacred City of the Hindoos,*" "*The Tribes and Castes of India as Represented in Benares,*" &c. &c.

With an Illustrative Map of India.

LONDON:
TRÜBNER & CO., LUDGATE HILL.
1875.

TO

THE DIRECTORS

OF THE

LONDON MISSIONARY SOCIETY

This Book

IS

RESPECTFULLY INSCRIBED.

PREFACE.

AMONG the beneficent influences at work in India, not the least potent and pervasive is Christianity. The aim of this work is to show historically what Protestant Missions have accomplished in India since their commencement in the beginning of the last century. In pursuance of this object, I have collected together all the important events of these Missions, and have presented them in a succinct and consecutive narrative, thus striving to give a complete view, as in a panorama, of their operations and achievements. Notwithstanding the numerous reports which have been for many years issued by missionaries concerning their respective fields of labour, it has hitherto been wellnigh impossible to gain an adequate and distinct conception of the wonderful work which has been accomplished in the evangelisation of the people of India. While leaving matters of unnecessary detail, I have endeavoured to furnish an outline of the various methods, plans, and projects which have been pursued in the formation and growth of the Indian Protestant Church, sufficiently minute to be correct, and yet so compacted together and interwoven as to suffer neither in unity nor comprehensiveness. My desire, in short, has been to show how the wave of Christianity, commencing in one corner of the land, has gradually advanced until it has spread over the entire country.

The ancient creeds of India, which, like wild luxuriant plants, have brought forth pernicious fruit in abundance, nevertheless demand our profoundest study. Surely, therefore, we cannot withhold the same attention and consideration from another faith, which although in its influence upon India dates, as compared with the older ones, only from yesterday, yet seeks to attain what they never designed, namely, to make men pure and holy like God Himself, and has in some small degree, in many places, achieved its transcendent purpose.

I earnestly trust that this historical sketch will tend to stimulate the zeal of the Churches at home in behalf of the great enterprise of Missions in India.

I wish to render my warmest thanks to the Editors of the Report of the General Missionary Conference held at Allahabad in 1872-73, for permission to make use of their valuable Missionary Map of India in this work.

M. A. SHERRING.

BENARES, *April* 30, 1874.

CONTENTS.

MISSIONARY MAP OF INDIA   *Facing Title.*

CHAPTER I.

PAGE

PROTESTANT MISSIONS IN INDIA DURING THE EIGHTEENTH
    CENTURY 1

CHAPTER II.

MISSIONS IN CALCUTTA AND ITS VICINITY   . 60

CHAPTER III.

MISSIONS IN BENGAL, EXCLUDING CALCUTTA AND ITS VICINITY   133

CHAPTER IV.

MISSIONS AMONG THE KÔLS AND SANTALS   .   . 158

CHAPTER V.

MISSIONS IN THE NORTH-WESTERN PROVINCES, OUDH, AND
    ROHILKHAND 177

CHAPTER VI.

MISSIONS IN THE PUNJAB 214

CHAPTER VII.

MISSIONS IN CENTRAL INDIA, INCLUDING RAJPOOTANA, HOLKAR'S COUNTRY, THE CENTRAL PROVINCES, THE BERARS, AND THE NIZAM'S DOMINIONS 231

CHAPTER VIII.

MISSIONS IN THE CITY AND PRESIDENCY OF BOMBAY . 247

CHAPTER IX.

MISSIONS OF THE BASLE EVANGELICAL SOCIETY IN THE SOUTHERN MAHRATTA COUNTRY, CANARA, AND MALABAR 278

CHAPTER X.

MISSIONS IN BELLARY AND THE MYSORE . . 293

CHAPTER XI.

MISSIONS OF THE CHURCH MISSIONARY SOCIETY IN NORTH TRAVANCORE AND COCHIN 308

CHAPTER XII.

MISSIONS OF THE LONDON MISSIONARY SOCIETY IN SOUTH TRAVANCORE 320

CHAPTER XIII.

MISSIONS OF THE CHURCH MISSIONARY SOCIETY, AND OF THE SOCIETY FOR THE PROPAGATION OF THE GOSPEL IN FOREIGN PARTS, IN THE PROVINCE OF TINNEVELLY . 334

CHAPTER XIV.

MISSIONS IN THE PROVINCE OF MADURA, OF THE AMERICAN BOARD OF COMMISSIONERS FOR FOREIGN MISSIONS, AND OF THE SOCIETY FOR THE PROPAGATION OF THE GOSPEL IN FOREIGN PARTS 371

CHAPTER XV.

MISSIONS IN TANJORE, TRICHINOPOLY, POODOOCOTTAH, COIMBATOOR, AND THE NEILGHERRIES . . . 380

CHAPTER XVI.

MISSIONS IN THE PROVINCES OF ARCOT AND SALEM . 397

CHAPTER XVII.

MISSIONS IN THE CITY OF MADRAS AND ITS VICINITY, INCLUDING THE PROVINCE OF CHINGLEPAT . . . 400

CHAPTER XVIII.

MISSIONS IN THE PROVINCES OF CUDDAPAH, KARNOOL, AND NELLORE 438

CHAPTER XIX.

MISSIONS IN THE KISTNA AND GODAVERY DISTRICTS, AND IN VIZAGAPATAM AND GANJAM . . . 449

CHAPTER XX.

REVIEW OF THE PREVIOUS CHAPTERS—CONCLUSIONS DRAWN FROM THEM 459

THE HISTORY
OF
PROTESTANT MISSIONS IN INDIA.

CHAPTER I.

PROTESTANT MISSIONS IN INDIA DURING THE EIGHTEENTH CENTURY.

AMONG Protestant nations the Danes have the honour of first conceiving the idea of conveying the gospel to the races of India. Although occupying but a very limited tract in that country, yet the obligation of bringing the blessings of Christianity within the reach of its inhabitants was acknowledged by them twenty years before it was admitted by Great Britain. The Danes, however, hardly deserve much credit, for they were upwards of eighty years in possession of Tranquebar before they took any steps for the evangelisation of the natives. In the year 1705, at the instigation of Dr Lutkens, chaplain to the King of Denmark, two young men of learning and ability, Bartholomew Ziegenbalg and Henry Plutschau, were sent forth as missionaries to Tranquebar. They had been students at the University of Halle, and were singularly fitted for the great work they had under-

The Danes, the pioneers of Indian missions.

taken. Both had zeal; that of Plutschau was patient and calm; but that of Ziegenbalg was fiery. One followed; the other led. One had the gift of organisation, and enthusiasm to face and surmount all difficulties; the other, besides courage, had the faculty of labouring steadily and well. Both could endure much; but Ziegenbalg endured hardship longer than his fellow-labourer.

Soon their varied gifts and powers were put to the test. On arriving in India they met with little sympathy from European residents, who, like most persons in England and elsewhere, regarded the enterprise as visionary and absurd. In defiance of the King of Denmark's injunctions, opposition was shown to the missionaries and their work, especially by the Governor of the colony, a Norwegian by birth. Ziegenbalg was thrown into prison, and kept in close confinement for four months. There he pined in solitude, forbidden the use of pen and paper, and prohibited from holding intercourse with the outer world. On regaining his freedom, he found, to his dismay, that the small community of converts from the heathen which he and his colleague had gathered together, had been scattered to the winds by persecution and terror. Some were in prison; others were banished; and the mission seemed in ruins. Nothing daunted, Ziegenbalg, in spite of bodily weakness and disease, recommenced his work. Being in great need of money, four thousand crowns were sent to him from home in two ships, one of which was wrecked, and although the money was recovered, it was taken back to Copenhagen. The other ship reached Tranquebar in safety, but as the money was being brought to shore, the boat, which was in charge of drunken sailors, upset, and the whole was lost. Still, these two brave men kept at their post, undismayed by disappointment, hardship, and loss.

Now came a greater trial. Hitherto, troubles had been from without. But the two missionaries, having laboured together harmoniously, had upheld and comforted one another. The mission was replenished by the arrival of three new missionaries, one of whom from the outset vigorously opposed the plans and operations of the older brethren. Their dissension became a fruitful cause of heartburning. The Governor looked on with satisfaction, adding fuel to the fire by taking part with the young missionary. Schools, however, had been established; the slaves of the settlement were assembled for religious instruction two hours daily; the German residents were invited to Divine service held regularly in their behalf; a class of catechumens gathered from the heathen was being trained in the truths of the gospel preparatory to baptism; converts increased rapidly; a church had been erected for the native congregation; conferences had been held with Hindoos and Mahomedans; excursions had been made into the country as far as Negapatam; several Christian books had been written in Tamil, and the translation of the Scriptures, and the compilation of a dictionary, in the same language, had been commenced. Three years and a half after the arrival of the first missionaries the native Christian community numbered one hundred and sixty persons, an amount of success truly astonishing, considering the gigantic obstacles against which they had to contend.

Discussions.

Successes. 160 converts gathered in three years and a half.

The conversion of a young Tamil poet of some distinction was an incident of much importance, both on account of the interest it awakened among the natives generally, and of the essential aid he was able to render in translating Christian works into good Tamil verse, and in many other ways. Ziegenbalg endeavoured to introduce the gospel into the dominions of the Rajah of Tanjore, and actually undertook a journey into that country dressed in native costume; but was stopped before he had proceeded far, in consequence of an order of the Rajah prohibiting Europeans from entering his territories without his express permission, and was obliged to return. On account of the increasing expenditure of the mission, arising from the establishment of schools and the enlarged operations which were undertaken, attempts were made to raise money in Germany and also in England. An English translation of several letters of the missionaries having been presented to the members of the "Society for the Propagation of the Gospel in Foreign Parts," which had been established by royal charter in the year 1701, the society generously sent the missionaries a donation of twenty pounds, and a collection of books. This may be regarded as the beginning of that noble work of Christian enterprise and zeal which this venerable society has prosecuted with much perseverance and varying success in behalf of India.

Help from the Society for the Propagation of the Gospel in Foreign Parts.

From this time much interest continued to be cherished in England in the welfare of the Tranquebar Mission. It was thought, however, that as the object of the Propagation Society, according to its charter, was to administer to the spiritual necessities of the British colonies in North America and the West Indies, it would not be proper to extend its labours to the East Indies. But another society undertook the work. This was the "Society for Promoting Christian Knowledge," which had been established in the year 1699. Its purpose was somewhat more general than that of the other society, and yet its sphere of action was confined to Britain and her colonies. Hence a similar difficulty occurred as in the case of the Propagation Society; which was removed by opening a fund with special reference to the Danish Mission in India. Contributions came from all quarters. La Croze writes: "Nothing could be more gratifying than the liberality of the English who distinguished themselves on this occasion. People of all ranks, nobility and clergy, ladies and gentlemen, citizens and merchants, contributed to a large amount, some without wishing it to be known."

Sympathy in England for the Tranquebar Mission. Labours of the Christian Knowledge Society.

The translation of the Bible into the languages of India has ever been considered an imperative and primary duty of missionaries labouring in that land. And it should never be forgotten that, independently of the good thus accomplished in promoting a knowledge of Christianity, and so spreading the religion of the gospel among its inhabitants, a work of incalculable importance, in the social progress and civilisation of the people, has been achieved, such as ought not to be overlooked by statesmen and historians in estimating the mental and moral advancement of Hindoo races under the influence of Western enlightenment. The intimate connection between a revival in national literature and a free circulation of the Bible, between a country's highest and greatest prosperity and the

Translation of the Bible into Tamil.

widespread prevalence of the Sacred Scriptures, is clearly seen in the history of Britain and of other Protestant countries of Europe. The same connection is visible just as plainly in the history of India since the commencement of the last century. Every Protestant missionary recognises the living power of the Word of God; and rests not until it is translated into the language of the people among whom he dwells. A little more than two years after reaching India Ziegenbalg began the translation of the New Testament into Tamil, and finished it on the 21st March 1711. By 1719, the year of his death, he had translated as far as Ruth, in the Old Testament.

The incessant disputes between the Danish Governor and the missionaries at last became so threatening that Plutschau determined on returning home and laying their common grievances before the King of Denmark. After much vexatious opposition on the part of the Governor, he was able to accomplish his purpose. About the same time, M. Bövingh, the missionary who, as already stated, from the moment of his arrival in India had studiously thwarted the efforts and plans of the other missionaries, quitted the country from ill-health, yet bound also to the King with the object of representing to his Majesty his own views, and those of the Governor, on the other side of the question. By a strange coincidence they both together presented themselves to the King, who was in camp with his army. The result of the interview may be conjectured from the circumstance that M. Bövingh walked away on foot through the deep mire caused by the heavy rains which had deluged the country, while Plutschau was sent away in the royal carriage.

Although the latter had fully stated his case to the Monarch in a long conversation lasting for several hours, yet before his coming the King had displayed such sympathy towards the missionaries, and such interest in their work, that he had already given orders for the sum of three hundred pounds a year to be given from the revenue for the support of four missionaries. In future, regular reports of the mission were sent to the King, who, together with the princes and princesses of the royal family, exhibited the keenest eagerness in all its affairs, the latter even personally corresponding with the indefatigable though worn-out Ziegenbalg.

The King of Denmark gives £300 a year to the mission.

In 1712 the converts had increased to two hundred and fifty-five, but the loss by death had been thirty-four, making the aggregate number of native Christians two hundred and twenty-one. In the schools there were seventy-eight children under instruction, fifty-nine of whom were supported by the missionaries. The method adopted was evidently that designated in India, and so well known, as the Boarding School system, which has worked in some places well, and in others very badly, and which we shall have frequently to refer to in the progress of this history. In addition to the translation of the New Testament, the missionaries had by this time compiled and written thirty-three works in the Tamil language, including a dictionary. In 1714 Ziegenbalg being compelled to seek a change of air and scene, and to rest from his labours for a while, returned to his native land. Before starting, the Governor sought reconciliation with him, and in the true spirit of Christian charity Ziegenbalg consented to forgive and forget all the

Commencement of the Boarding School system.

Ziegenbalg returns home.

wrongs which himself and the mission had received. It so happened that on reaching Europe, Ziegenbalg found the nations at war with one another. The King of Denmark was at the siege of Stralsund, in Pomerania, taking part in the great struggle with Charles XII. "One evening there was evidently a profound movement among the Danish troops. A stranger of note had had an audience of the King, who had shown him singular favour, and for hours, it was said, they had been closeted together. The soldiers who had gathered round may have been disappointed when they saw that he was only a clergyman, a man indeed of commanding presence, of a wonderful dignity and fire, resolute and calm, with a keen eye, a bronzed and almost swarthy face seamed with deep lines of care, and a winning courtesy and lovableness of manner; but when he opened his lips and preached to them, and they heard it was Mr Ziegenbalg, the missionary from Tranquebar, there were some at least who ceased to wonder at his welcome from the King. To the camp Ziegenbalg had hurried with all speed. Letters had given no warning of his journey; and he seemed to have dropped out of the clouds. He was accustomed to rapid movement, and the mission had no time to spare; but he got his story told to the King, and he was content. Some days were snatched from war for this work of peace; changes and arrangements were proposed in the management of the mission; Ziegenbalg was informed that his patent of Superintendent had already been sent to India; and for details he was referred to Copenhagen. Thither he journeyed with restless speed; and then into Germany, to Francke and Halle, halting little at any place, but preaching to vast crowds who filled the churches and swayed out into the street, 'very weak,' we are told, yet kindling by his presence the zeal of all the mission friends, and moving his audiences as he would, by his glowing appeals."*

Proceeding to England, Ziegenbalg was everywhere received with enthusiasm. George the First, the Prince and Princess of Wales, the Archbishop of Canterbury, the Bishop of London, and many other persons of rank and influence, were eager to express their sympathy and goodwill to the zealous, self-denying missionary. Returning to India early in 1716, he found that his colleague, M. Grundler (Plutschau having remained in Germany), had opened a new school, which already contained seventy children, and had made preparations for erecting a new church, as the old one was "too small for the increasing congregation." This building was completed and opened in 1717, during which year the missionaries addressed a letter to the King of England, giving an account of the condition and progress of the mission; to which his Majesty graciously sent the following reply:— "George, by the grace of God King of Great Britain, &c., to the reverend and learned Bartholomew Ziegenbalg, and John Ernest Grundler, missionaries at Tranquebar: Reverend and beloved—Your letters, dated the 20th of January of the present year, were most welcome to us, not only because the work undertaken by you, of converting the heathen to the Christian truth, doth, by the grace of God, prosper; but also because that, in this our kingdom, such a

Returns to India.

Letter from King George I. of England to Ziegenbalg and his colleague Grundler.

---

* "The Last Years of Ziegenbalg," by the Rev. W. Flaming Stevenson; in *Good Words* for December 1872.

laudable zeal for the promotion of the gospel prevails. We pray you may be endued with health and strength of body, that you may long continue to fulfil your ministry with good success; of which, as we shall be rejoiced to hear, so you will always find us ready to succour you, in whatever may tend to promote your work, and to excite your zeal. We assure you of the continuance of our royal favour. George R. Given at our palace of Hampton Court, the 23d August, A.D. 1717, in the fourth year of our reign."

<small>Death of Ziegenbalg and Grundler</small>

But dark days were near. Ziegenbalg had overstrained his powers, and had spent himself before he had attained to middle age. In the autumn of 1718 he was smitten by disease, from which he rallied for a time, but which reappearing, he sank to rest on the 23d February 1719. Three hundred and fifty-five converts, and a numerous body of catechumens, mourned over his loss. He had been the guiding spirit of the mission, every department of which, through all the vicissitudes which it had undergone, having felt the influence of his enthusiasm, his patience, and his love. He laboured with the inspiration of an apostle, and with the elasticity of a man determined to rise above every obstacle. A little more than a year after the death of Ziegenbalg, he was followed by his fellow-labourer, Grundler, who had joined the mission in 1709, had been associated with him on terms of closest intimacy, and had been animated by his earnestness and zeal. Bereft of its two distinguished leaders, the mission was left to the judgment and skill of young and untried men, at a time when it needed the help and counsel which experience alone could give. We shall presently see that, in its hour

of desolation and trial, the spirit of its holy founders
pervaded their successors, and that they were
prompted by the same Divine impulse.

In reality, there was no cause for apprehension, for
the mission was well organised, and needed only
sound judgment and thorough Christian principle for
its proper management. These are qualities, however,
not always associated together in missionaries any more
than in other Christian men. The predominance of
the latter over the former is an evil as great, and, in
some cases, greater than that of the former over the
latter. Indeed, it is a fact too frequently illustrated
in the history of Indian missions, that men of a
demonstrative piety, and of little wisdom and knowledge, have, though with the best intentions and
unconsciously to themselves, done much mischief,
and retarded the great work in which they were
engaged. The methods of procedure marked out by
men of large minds and much experience have sometimes been ruthlessly abandoned for whimsical plans
by men of narrow views newly arrived in the country.
It was predicted by the opponents of the Tranquebar <small>Ability and zeal of their successors.</small>
Mission, that now that the firm hands of Ziegenbalg
and Grundler no longer guided its affairs, the mission
would fall to pieces. Fortunately for its life and
vigour, the three new missionaries, Schultze, Dahl,
and Keistenmacher, who had come to India only in
the middle of 1719, were men of the same noble cast
and character as their predecessors. Keistenmacher
died in less than two years; but in this brief period
he laboured with assiduity and success. The others
remained, devoting themselves with unflagging energy
and with wonderful wisdom to the development

of those schemes which had been already set on foot.

Animosity of the Rajah of Tanjore gives place to friendship. Schultze completes the translation of the Bible in 1725.

The Rajah of Tanjore, who had hitherto cherished bitter animosity against the missionaries, was won over by their earnestness and address, and threw open the whole of his kingdom to the preaching of the gospel. Schultze resumed the translation of the Bible at the Book of Ruth where Ziegenbalg had left off, and finished it, including the Apocrypha, in the year 1725. He was a scholarly man, like all those sent out at this period, and was well acquainted with the principal European languages as well as with Hebrew. The Christian community suffered at this time from two causes, a disastrous fire which destroyed many of their houses, and a terrific hurricane, which, breaking upon the coast, swept away the greater part of their dwellings, not only the old ones but also those which had been rebuilt after the fire. Moreover, so many misrepresentations had been made against the missionaries and their labours, that Christian people in Europe had lost confidence in the mission. But faithful and steady performance of duty met with its reward. In spite of the continued hostility of many Europeans in India, the confidence of Christians at home was gradually restored. The Society for Promoting Christian Knowledge, under the presidentship of the Archbishop of Canterbury, deliberated on the best means of rendering help to the mission. The King of Denmark appointed three young men of education and piety to the work, who were ordained by the Bishop of Worms. The Princess Charlotte Amelia gave them money and kind words of encouragement, promising them her prayers, and intrusted them with a letter which she sent by their hands to Schultze. Proceeding to England, the King admitted them to his presence, and placed at their disposal the sum of one hundred and eighty crowns. Collections were made at the German Chapel Royal and the Savoy Church, after sermons preached by them, amounting to no less than one hundred and twenty pounds. A free passage was obtained for them on a ship of war, and they left for India laden with presents, taking with them a pastoral letter from the Archbishop of Canterbury addressed to Schultze. So popular and exciting had the Tranquebar Mission become among the Protestants of Denmark, Germany, and England!

<small>Popularity of the Danish missions in England and on the Continent.</small>

Public opinion among the small Danish community at Tranquebar, though slow in forming, at last became sufficiently strong to produce an effect upon the Government in favour of the education of the natives. Schools were established, and, strange to say, the missionaries were placed in charge of them, with the approbation of both Hindoos and Mahomedans, who had come to regard them as sincere and disinterested friends. Soon twenty-one schools were in operation, seventeen of which were supported by the Government, and the remainder by the mission. The missionaries were permitted to place Christian teachers in four of the Government schools at their own expense, in which the truths of Christianity were expounded to the pupils; but they were not taught in the rest of the Government schools. The missionaries, however, soon retired from the management of these institutions; and they languished. By the year 1726, that is, seven years after the death of

<small>Establishment of Government schools at Tranquebar. The missionaries placed in charge of them.</small>

<small>678 converts baptized in twenty years.</small>

Ziegenbalg, so steadily had been the progress of the mission that it numbered six hundred and seventy-eight converts. This closed twenty years of missionary labour in Tranquebar. The result will seem small or large as viewed by different persons. To us living in India, and knowing by experience the nature and extent of the obstacles which caste, idolatry, Brahmanism, and Islamism, oppose to the gospel, they appear considerable; to those who look at the matter from the distance of England or America, they may, and doubtless will, appear otherwise.

<small>Schultze's journey to Madras; and establishment of a mission there in 1726.</small>

Having completed the translation of the Scriptures, Schultze undertook a journey to Madras in 1726, preaching the gospel to the towns and villages on the road. There he spent several months in the same work, re-established a school for the instruction of native children which had been in existence several years before,* and commenced the mission of which, at his suggestion, the Christian Knowledge Society undertook the charge a few years afterwards. The mission was situated in Black Town, and was placed under the management of Schultze. An English church was already in existence in Madras, built in 1680, sixty years after its occupation by the East India Company. The Governor and members of his council showed their interest in the enterprise by assisting in its establishment. As for Schultze himself, his zeal seems to have received a fresh

---

* This school, and another at Cuddalore, were originally established through the instrumentality of Ziegenbalg and Grundler, and the assistance of the Rev. Mr Stevenson, chaplain of Madras, as early as 1716. But they were left to themselves without proper superintendence; and fell to ruin.

stimulus, for he at once entered upon a multitude of varied labours in connection with the responsible and important post which he occupied. He preached to the people in various languages in vogue in the city, Tamil, Telugu, and Portuguese; he translated portions of the Bible into Telugu, and the entire Bible into Hindustani; he watched over the progress of several schools; he wrote religious tracts; in these and other ways he exhibited the intense earnestness which inflamed his soul. The result was soon seen; for converts were gathered in, and a Christian church was formed. Schultze was sustained by his brethren at Tranquebar in the formation of the Madras Mission, with whose advice he had established it, which, until it came under the control of the Christian Knowledge Society, was regarded as an integral portion of the Danish missions in India. As an evidence of the eagerness with which the people welcomed the gospel in those days, in one year, 1729, Schultze baptized in Madras one hundred and forty persons. By the end of 1736 there were four hundred and fifteen converts in this mission, the result, it should be observed, of less than ten years' labour.

[margin: Translation of the Bible into Telugu and Hindustani. Manifold labours of Schultze.]

[margin: 415 converts in Madras in 1736.]

Although the Danish Mission was confined to a small district, yet its influence began to be felt over an extensive tract of country. The books published by the mission press found their way to Bombay, on the opposite coast, to the Northern Circars, in the north, and to Ceylon, in the south. Thus gradually the minds of the people were becoming prepared for that wide evangelistic effort to be put forth in a future generation. A small Christian community was formed at Marawar, a state governed by a native prince; and in the year 1729 the missionaries were successful in establishing another congregation in the district of Wedarnionsen, through the instrumentality of a native juggler or magician who had embraced Christianity. A visit was paid to the city of Ramnad, a considerable distance to the south, where scriptural instruction was imparted and books were distributed to the people. But it does not appear that the missionaries were able at present to occupy the station permanently. Other agents continued to arrive from Europe from time to time; and in 1730 the Christian Knowledge Society appointed Mr Sartorius to their station in Madras. It is a matter of great interest to observe that, at this early period, the importance of uniting the healing of the sick with direct spiritual labour was distinctly recognised, for we find that one physician was sent out in 1730, and another in 1732, for the Tranquebar and Madras Missions. The influence of the medical agents of the Tranquebar Mission seems to have been very great, and to have been one of the chief reasons of the large increase of its converts. In the latter year as many as three hundred and eighty-one persons were added to the native Christian community. Throughout the entire province the people were affected more or less favourably by the gospel; and Christian converts continued to multiply in the neighbouring kingdom of Tanjore. Some of the most earnest and eminent of the Christians were proselytes from the Roman Catholic faith. The Madras Mission derived much strength and encouragement from the steady support of the English governors, first of Mr Macrae, and next of his successor, Mr Pitt. The Archbishop of

Appointment of Sartorius to Madras. Medical missionaries sent out in 1730 and 1732.

Canterbury gave substantial proof of the interest he cherished in it by the present of four hundred and twenty pagodas (one hundred and sixty-eight pounds), which was sent to Schultze, accompanied by a letter expressive of his warm sympathy in his labours.

It is singular that, although the Tranquebar Christians now amounted to about one thousand five hundred individuals, yet that up to the present time not one of them had been ordained to the office of the Christian ministry. This is doubtless one of the most manifest errors committed by the devoted pioneers of Protestant Christianity in India—an error which was copied and perpetuated for many years, and which is only now giving place to a wiser, not to say more scriptural, system. Had the Christian communities, as they were established, been placed under the control of native pastors, they would long ago have acquired that independency, strength of character, and power of reproduction, so strikingly seen among the Christian churches of primitive ages, and so necessary to the permanence of Christianity in India. The Tranquebar missionaries were left to themselves in many things; but their ecclesiastical organism was inelastic and stiff. Before they could venture to ordain one of their most distinguished native brethren, they were compelled to obtain the consent of their superiors at Copenhagen, of the Mission College, and also of the King of Denmark, which it took five years to gain. His ordination was not only beneficial to the native agents of the mission and to the Christian community in general, but also had a good effect on the heathen population in the neighbourhood. The spirit of union existing among the missionaries of these earlier

Obstacles to the ordination of the first native pastor.

times was beautifully illustrated in the ordination; for the missionaries of Tranquebar, and of Madras, and also the Danish chaplains, took part in it.

<small>Mission stations formed at Negapatam, Madras, and Fort St David.</small>

At the invitation of the Dutch chaplain of Negapatam, to the south of Tranquebar, the Danish missionaries sent a catechist to that city in 1732, and in the course of a few years three others were added, who were the means of establishing a Christian church in that district. Thus step by step the truth spread abroad, and congregations of believers were formed in the country around. Moreover, from the Dutch colony of Negapatam a catechist proceeded to the English station of Sadras on the sea-coast, with the view of imparting Christian instruction to the natives there. The work was afterwards taken up by the missionaries from Madras under the direction of the Christian Knowledge Society. A mission was also established at Fort St David, to the north of Cuddalore, on the representation of Mr Sartorius, who, having visited the place, had received the promise of aid from the Governor in the event of missionary labours being commenced there. This information being communicated to the Christian Knowledge Society, its directors at home with promptitude and liberality determined on the establishment of a mission on this spot, and requested Schultze to make all necessary arrangements for carrying out their wishes. A church and two schools, with the consent of the Court of Directors, were at this time erected in Madras under the superintendence of the same missionary. In the year 1737 Cuddalore was occupied by Mr Sartorius and Mr Geister; but the health of the former giving way, he died in the following year. He

<small>Cuddalore occupied in 1737. Death of Sartorius in 1738.</small>

PROTESTANT MISSIONS IN INDIA.

was an accomplished scholar, spoke Tamil like a Brahman, and was impelled with intense ardour; his loss therefore was great. Mr J. L. Kiernander joined the mission in 1740, having been introduced to the Christian Knowledge Society by Professor Franck, of Halle, a man of great zeal and generosity in the cause of missions, who occupied at this period a very prominent position in Europe as one of their chief promoters and defenders. By 1743 the mission had ninety-seven converts, forty-four of whom were communicants. When the fort was besieged by the French in 1746, Mr Kiernander remained at his post, but sent his family, together with much of the mission property, to the Danish settlement at Tranquebar. Notwithstanding the dangers into which he was thrown, he continued steadily in his labours so far as was practicable; and his congregations greatly increased, for we find that in the year of the siege there were two hundred and twenty-nine Christians attached to the mission, and ten years later, six hundred and twelve. An instance of the sympathy and liberality of the Tranquebar Christians is recorded at this time; for, hearing of the distresses of their brethren at Cuddalore occasioned by war and famine, they contributed the large sum of two hundred dollars towards their relief.

Meanwhile, several congregations of Christians had grown up in the kingdom of Tanjore, which were placed under the charge of two native pastors. In 1736 the country congregations were divided into six districts containing eleven hundred and forty members, while the Tranquebar congregations numbered eleven hundred and eighty-nine persons.

Kiernander's Arrival, 1740.

Siege of Cuddalore by the French in 1746.

Eleven hundred and eighty-eight Christians had died since the commencement of the mission in 1706. There were six hundred and thirty-six communicants in the city and country congregations, or nearly two-sevenths of the entire number. During the next ten years three thousand eight hundred and twelve persons were baptized. This period is interesting for the quiet and steady growth of the mission. It exhibits nothing of a remarkable character demanding special attention; but the increasing influence of Christianity upon the minds of the native population becomes strikingly manifest. The entire community was affected by its plastic energy, for everywhere in India, as in other countries, Christianity has softened and purified, to some extent, the hearts of all who have lived within its reach, even though many may not have accepted it as their religion, or have submitted themselves consciously to its sway. It is found to be a transforming, and even revolutionising power, when coming in contact with the peculiar social customs and feeble morality of the Hindoo races. As a humanising agent, purifying the inner consciousness, and developing the intellectual life of a nation, its potency has been nowhere more strongly felt than in India. Its direct triumphs may not have been numerous in that land; yet its indirect victories, in imparting new virtue and a higher form of religious thought to the people, have not been surpassed elsewhere. Such was the kind of illumination now elevating the native inhabitants of Tranquebar, of portions of Tanjore, of other districts in its vicinity, and of cities, towns, and villages on the Coromandel coast, as far north as Madras, and as far south as Ramnad.

3812 converts in ten years.

The antagonism of Roman Catholicism and Protestantism, which sometimes, as at this period, became very active, perhaps ought not to be overlooked in a history of the Protestant religion in India; but as my object is to show how this form of Christianity became firmly rooted in the soil of India, and by degrees became a widespreading tree yielding abundant fruit, and not to discuss the dissensions of Christians themselves, I shall avoid the subject entirely, as a course most pleasant to my own feelings, and I trust also to those of my readers.

In the year 1742 Schultze returned to his native land, and retired from missionary pursuits, to which he had devoted twenty-three years of his life, of which fifteen had been spent in Madras, the Christian congregation in which amounted to about seven hundred persons at this time. For his many labours, his steady perseverance, his great learning, his humble piety, and his entire consecration to the work, he deserves more than a passing remark. During these most critical years in the history of Protestant missions in India, he had acted with surpassing wisdom, and been the leading spirit in the enterprise. The high-toned spiritual life of the missions existing at this period was, so to speak, a reflection of his own mind guided and overruled by the Divine Spirit Himself. The Christian Church everywhere, and in all ages, has been powerfully affected both in feeling and action by individuals, who have been apparently media through which much spiritual influence has flown, whereby the Church has increased in zeal and in love.

The mission in Madras was thrown into great straits in the autumn of 1746, in consequence of the war between France and England. A French fleet entered the roads, and bombarded Fort St George, which at the end of five days, being defended by only three hundred men, capitulated. Thus both city and fort fell into the hands of the victors. The mission-house was destroyed, and the church became a magazine. In the meantime, Mr Fabricius, who was then in charge of the mission, removed with the children of the school to Pulicat, then a Dutch settlement, where he assembled together the Christians who had fled from Madras, and with the assistance of a catechist and two schoolmasters commenced a work of evangelisation among the surrounding villages. He remained there until 1748, when peace was proclaimed, and Madras was restored to the English. The Roman Catholic missionaries having been expelled through their disloyal attachment to French interests during the late war, their church at Vepery, and the houses and gardens belonging to it, were presented to the mission. The Governor of Fort St David also gave over to the mission at Cuddalore, of which Mr Kiernander was the head, the Roman Catholic church at that station. It is difficult, in the light of modern times, to judge of such gifts. If, as seems to have been the case, the Romish missionaries of these towns proved treacherous to the British Government, and played into the enemy's hands, they must have lost their property in consequence, on the return of peace. It may appear to us that it would have been more magnanimous, on political grounds, and more just, on religious grounds, had the missionaries not received such questionable presents. But it is hard to judge of the matter unless we rightly apprehend the political struggles and animosities in India during the middle of the last century.

At Pulicat a native Christian community had gradually been formed. It was visited occasionally by missionaries from Madras; but it was chiefly under the management of a reader or unordained native preacher, who had been brought up in the Madras Mission. In 1744 it numbered one hundred and fifty persons. During the troubles at Madras, alluded to above, the mission had the advantage of the direct superintendence of Mr Fabricius.

We are now approaching an event of great moment, not merely to the mission at Tranquebar, but also to all other Protestant missions which at various periods were subsequently established in the country. This was the arrival in India of Christian Frederic Schwartz, which occurred on the 30th of July 1750. Thenceforward, for many years, the missionary enterprise in that land, in its progress and development, was intimately associated with the life and labours of this distinguished man. Both Protestant and Roman Catholic missions are able to boast of a long list of earnest and zealous men, from their first establishment in India down to the year in which this testimony is recorded; and they are especially proud of individual men, who by their transcendent ability and devotion shone with brilliant lustre, reflecting a divine light far and near, and who for a long period were powerful centres of attraction and influence, and on finally passing away, left a long line of light behind them. The history of the British possession of India is remarkable for great names. Men of uncommon force as soldiers, civilians, and statesmen, rising far above mediocrity into the regions of true genius, have never been wanting. They have not only imparted imagination and vivacity to this otherwise dull tropical life, but have likewise contributed largely to the success of those stupendous movements which the Government has occasionally undertaken. Each period of British Indian history is connected with great names, which figure conspicuously in its foreground, give to it its brightest colours, and prevent it from becoming uninteresting and tame. In like manner, in the history of Christian missions in India, the eye rests with pleasure on celebrities like Schwartz, Carey, Martyn, and Duff, and others of equal rank, whose varied talents and accomplishments have elevated the missionary body in India to a position of intellectual greatness inferior to none.

Schwartz's first labours

In the year 1751 we find this zealous labourer busily engaged in missionary work as though he had been for years accustomed to it. He sets an excellent example to all young missionaries by commencing with a daily catechetical class attended by children of tender age. He says characteristically: "Soon after the commencement of the new year, I began a catechetical hour in the Tamil, or Malabar, school, with the youngest lambs; and thus I learned to stammer with them. At the same time, I made almost daily excursions, and spoke with Christians and heathens, though, as may be easily conceived, poorly and falteringly."* Yet in the course of this year he prepared two separate classes of converts for baptism, to whom he administered the holy rite. In 1751 four hundred persons, old and young, were added by

* Memoirs of Schwartz, by Dr Pearson, Dean of Salisbury, vol. i. p. 77.

baptism to the Tamil congregation alone. This preparation of candidates for baptism, at certain periods of the year, was an important feature of the Tranquebar Mission, and was, it seems, usually imposed, though for what reason it is hard to see, on the junior missionaries. Great fidelity and discrimination, as well as much plainness of speech, were required to be exercised on such occasions; and doubtless these junior missionaries, although strangely called to discharge the most responsible duties, were enabled thereby quickly to develop their talents for the important spiritual work which they had undertaken. In India too little responsibility is a much greater evil than too much; for although a man's powers may be overtasked thereby, yet he retains his mental vigour and elasticity, to weaken which ten thousand ungenial influences are constantly working.

Great attention paid in the Tranquebar Mission to the preparation of candidates for baptism.

At the commencement of the Tranquebar Mission, Ziegenbalg had established two weekly conferences. The first was of a devotional character. The missionaries met together for prayer and meditation on the Scriptures. This excellent custom exists in Benares and in other parts of India at the present time. The object of the second conference is thus explained by Ziegenbalg himself: "The weekly conference which we hold every Friday with all the labourers, is of the greatest utility in keeping the mission work in order; for on that day, in the forenoon, we pray to God for wisdom and counsel, and each relates how he has been employed, or what has occurred in the congregations and schools, and in the printing and bookbinding offices, and in the private houses. Here everything which might occasion disorder or detriment is adjusted; and those means are adopted which may best

Two devotional conferences held in the mission weekly. Continued for 100 years.

promote the general good. The conference being ended, the Portuguese and Tamil assistants make a report of their labours, and of whatever may be wanting, that as far as possible it may be supplied."* This conference was kept up for nearly one hundred years, when it was abolished.

Failure of an attempt to plant a mission on the Nicobar Islands.

The missionaries at Tranquebar, ever ready to extend their field of operations, cordially fell in with a proposal of the Danish Government to send one of their number in the company of some colonists to the Nicobar Islands, where a commercial settlement was established, in the hope that a permanent mission might be formed among the aborigines. But their purpose was frustrated by the death of the missionary a few weeks after his arrival at the settlement. The year 1756 was important to the Tranquebar Mission, as it then had been in existence fifty years. Special services were held to commemorate the event, at which the missionaries, now increased to eight, took a review of this period of the mission's history. Their efforts had been crowned with considerable success, for during the half century about eleven thousand persons in this one mission had abandoned idolatry and superstition, and had embraced the gospel of Christ. Such a result was ground for much thankfulness to God; and was also a stimulus to increased faith and zeal.

11,000 Christians in the Tranquebar Mission at the end of fifty years.

A knowledge of the Lord's Prayer, the Ten Commandments, the Creed, and the words of the institution of the sacraments, required of converts.

It had been the custom in this mission, apparently from the commencement, for converts to be taught to repeat the Lord's Prayer, the Ten Commandments, the Creed, and the "words of the institution of both the sacraments." The advantage of this was seen in many ways, not the least of which was in the inter-

* Memoirs of Schwartz, vol. i. pp. 91, 92.

course of native Christians in outlying villages with the heathen in their neighbourhood; for having in their memories certain great Scripture truths and doctrines, which had been well explained to them, they could always enforce them on their friends and acquaintance, even though they might be unable to read the sacred volume which contained them. Missionaries in India, at the present day, pursue very diverse plans in this respect. Some trust to a mere exposition of the truth to inquirers and catechumens; and are not at all anxious that any portion of Scripture should be actually learned and remembered. Others rely much on the knowledge of a catechism containing a condensed account, frequently in the form of question and answer, of the distinguishing facts and principles of the Bible. Others, again, adopt a method much like that pursued by the Tranquebar missionaries. My strong conviction, derived from long observation, is, that in regard to beneficial results, this last method of training candidates for baptism is to be preferred to all others.

In spite of the war raging in the Carnatic at this period, the Tranquebar missionaries prosecuted their labours over extensive tracts of country, for they still regarded themselves as pioneers in the evangelisation of India. They not only visited new regions, but also the mission stations which had been established, whether in connection with the Danish Society, or with the Christian Knowledge Society of England. In this way we find two or more of them travelling, mostly on foot, to Madras, Cuddalore, Negapatam, Tanjore, Seringham, and Trichinopoly, and to towns and villages between these places. One peculiarity

The system pursued in the gathering in of converts.

of these itinerations was, that they were very careful to gather up and husband the fruit of such labours, by the establishment of schools or the appointment of catechists, in order to collect converts together into Christian congregations, and to foster the growth of religious principles among them. In this way ramifications of the mission spread about in all directions. A church was built at Negapatam; a school was commenced at Trichinopoly, where persons were also baptized, and a small Christian community was formed. Moreover, such visits conducted upon system tended to comfort and strengthen catechists, schoolmasters, and other native Christian labourers, as well as the congregations, scattered about the country. This kind of spiritual oversight was of great utility and importance to the infant churches.

For some years the missionaries had cast their eyes on Calcutta, with the intention of establishing a mission there whenever a favourable opportunity offered. Such an opportunity now occurred, and was occasioned by the capture of Cuddalore by the French troops under Lally, whereby many of the Christians were dispersed, mission work was suspended, and the missionaries were compelled to employ themselves elsewhere. After much deliberation it was determined to add Calcutta to the list of Danish missions; and Mr Kiernander was requested to proceed thither; which he did in September 1758. There he laboured with diligence and earnestness for many years; and we shall have, in the course of this historical sketch, to speak of his doings there from time to time. The early missionaries conceived the true idea of spreading out over the country, until it should be covered by a

The Calcutta Mission commenced by Kiernander in September 1758.

network of missions. Moreover, they were in this matter wisely left much to themselves as the best judges of their own ability, unfettered by home legislation, which in these days is so prone to direct missionaries in their plans and enterprises, in opposition sometimes to their matured views and counsels, whereby their enthusiasm becomes weakened, and their usefulness seriously impaired. Were the responsibility, often so unnecessarily, not to say imprudently, taken up by home boards and committees, more frequently, as formerly, thrown upon the missionaries themselves, who are, for the most part, quite willing to bear it, the stimulus imparted to them would be increased, and they would be preserved from sinking down to a dead matter-of-fact level, which is the bane of missionary life, and one of the chief obstacles to progress. *Responsibility should be borne by missionaries rather than by home boards and committees.*

In the year 1758 Madras was once more besieged by the French, who imagined that, in the absence of the English fleet, they would be able to take the city and fort as easily as they did in 1746; but they reckoned badly. Native troopers actually entered the town, and plundered the houses both of the missionaries and the Christians. A day was observed for fasting, humiliation, and prayer. Mr Fabricius found his way to Lally, the French general, under the charge of a friendly Roman Catholic trooper, and represented to him the straits to which the Christians were reduced. Lally most generously granted him a soldier as his own representative in the protection of himself and the Christian community. While much of the mission property was destroyed, yet the most valuable portion of it was preserved. Fabricius first retired to Vepery, *A.D. 1758. Madras again besieged by the French. Lally's kindness to Fabricius and the Christians.*

and afterwards to Pulicat, the safety of himself,
native Christians, and friends being secured by a
passport from Lally. The garrison behaved gallantly,
and the French suffered a good deal; but they prosecuted the siege vigorously, and at last made such
considerable breaches in the walls that they had
intended to make a direct assault on the 17th February
1759. On this very day, just as their preparations
were completed, the English fleet suddenly hove in
sight, and the aspect of affairs instantaneously changed.
The French abandoned the siege, and sought safety
in flight. The native Christians remained steadfast
throughout this hour of trial, and not one of them
apostatised. The hour of trial tested their faith, and
strengthened and purified it.

During the occupation of Cuddalore by the French
the mission buildings were preserved, although the
city was for the most part in ruins. The work of
the mission, however, was suspended; but the
Christian community remaining behind was kept in
safety. The city was retaken by the British army,
and the fortunes of the French, which had been for a
time so bright, were beclouded; and at last, being
driven into Pondicherry, the French were closely
blockaded there, and on the 15th January 1761 the
citadel was taken by the British. The weak condition of the Cuddalore Mission, in consequence of
losses arising from the war, was represented to the
Christian Knowledge Society at home, which endeavoured to excite public attention in England to the
circumstance, but with little success. A donation of
one hundred pounds from one person was the principal
result. The almost complete apathy on the subject of

missions to the heathen pervading the Christian community of England at this time, may be seen from the fact that no more than eighty pounds a year was usually subscribed towards all the missionary operations carried on in India.

In preaching in the streets of Cuddalore, the missionary, Mr Hutteman, found that two circumstances interfered with these ministrations in such places; one was their heat and bad ventilation, the other was the great noise of people in transacting their business. These two hindrances to missionary operations in crowded streets and bazaars, exist, for the most part, all over India. Mr Hutteman got rid of these difficulties by abandoning the bazaar and holding religious services in a schoolroom. A bell was rung, giving notice to the surrounding population of the service about to be held, and the people assembled accordingly. From long examination of various methods of conveying the gospel to the densely inhabited cities and towns of India, I am persuaded of the wisdom of the course pursued by Mr Hutteman. In the great thoroughfares, chief bazaars, and wherever the heathen are assembled in large numbers, and make a considerable noise, it is impossible to speak so as to be heard distinctly, and consequently to be properly understood. Retired spots, private streets, and corners, where there is freedom from noise and from direct traffic, are much more favourable for this work. The room open to the frequented road or street, provided there is no noise in the immediate neighbourhood, is perhaps best of all.

System of street-preaching Methods considered.

Having received a special invitation from the Christians of Ceylon, Schwartz visited that island in

Schwartz visits Ceylon

the spring of 1760. He first proceeded to Jaffna, where he was cordially received by the Dutch residents, and by the two native ministers in charge of the Christian congregation. Thence he journeyed on to Colombo. Here he commenced a series of earnest ministrations among both Christians and heathen; but his labours were cut short by a severe illness, which lasted for nearly a whole month. On recovering, he preached twice, and administered the sacrament to four hundred persons. He next paid a visit to Point de Galle, at the request of the Christians there, preached to the people, and admitted one hundred and twenty-six persons to the communion. In this way Schwartz spent three months in Ceylon, and then returned to Tranquebar. In 1761 he and his friend Kohlhoff undertook a missionary tour to Cuddalore and Madras; and in the following year he went on foot to Tanjore and Trichinopoly. Thus did he display a perpetual activity and unflagging enthusiasm as a missionary desiring to tread in the footsteps of his Divine Master. From this time forward he devoted much more of his time and energy to the two latter places than to the mission in Tranquebar. In Trichinopoly a room was built for the purpose of Divine worship and as a school for children. Major Preston, the commandant of the place, entered heartily into Schwartz's plans of usefulness. He requested Schwartz to accompany him to the siege of Madura in 1764, which was in the hands of the rebel, Mahomed Tsuf, who for two months successfully resisted the attacks made upon the fort. He was afterwards betrayed by one of his men, but not until a considerable loss had been occasioned among the besieging force, Major Preston himself having been killed in one of the assaults. In the two following years, with the assistance of the new commandant, Colonel Wood, a man of Christian zeal like his predecessor, and the contributions of the garrison, a spacious church was erected, holding nearly two thousand persons, which was opened on the 18th May 1766, by the name of Christ's Church. Representations were made to the Christian Knowledge Society respecting the good work which had been accomplished in Trichinopoly, and the promising field which it presented for missionary labour; to which that society, in a true spirit of religious enterprise, lent a willing ear, and in the next year a mission was established under its auspices. Here, on an income of forty-eight pounds a year, dressed in dimity dyed black, eating rice and vegetables cooked in native fashion, and living in a room of an old building just large enough to hold himself and his bed, Schwartz devoted himself, with the utmost simplicity, combined with an enthusiasm which consumed him, to his apostolic duties among the inhabitants of the city and neighbourhood.

Church for 2000 persons erected in Trichinopoly, and opened May 18, 1766.

Schwartz establishes a mission at Trichinopoly in connection with the Christian Knowledge Society.

At Tranquebar the mission lost two of its missionaries within a few days of each other. One of these had recently arrived in the country; the other, Mr Wiedebrock, had seen thirty-one years' service, and was reverenced as the father of the mission. All persons, both Christians and Hindoos, bore testimony to his worth, and lamented his death. During the ten years ending with 1766 the Christian community of this mission had been augmented to the extent of two thousand persons. The first thirty years of its history

Progress of the Tranquebar Mission.

c

had yielded three thousand five hundred and seventeen converts; the second thirty had yielded nine thousand six hundred and eighty. A new church was erected at Negapatam by the Governor, both for Europeans and native Christians; and two missionaries, Messrs Kohlhoff and Koenig, presided at its consecration, and returned to Tranquebar laden with contributions from the Dutch residents for the benefit of the Danish Mission.

<small>Madras saved from the Mahrattas.</small>

Madras was a prey to all the vicissitudes of war for many years in the middle of the last century. The French had twice besieged the city, and once taken it. In 1767 it was threatened by the Mahrattas, who desolated the country in all directions. Having reached St Thomé, a short distance to the south of the city, they were making their way to Vepery, in the suburbs, when they were met by an English force, which put them to flight, and thus saved the city from their barbarities. While the danger lasted, the missionaries and some of the Christians were permitted to reside in the fort.

<small>Churches erected at Cuddalore and Pelham.</small>

The Government of India, in these early times, did not hesitate to show its approval of Christian work performed by missionaries among the native population, by contributing towards its support in one shape or another. For instance, the Madras Government helped the missionaries to erect a new church at Cuddalore in 1767, intended for the use both of the native Christian community and also of the British troops stationed there. The Christians in the country districts around Cuddalore had so much increased that they needed a separate church for themselves. Accordingly, a few years after, one was built at

Pollam, twelve miles distant from that city, and was visited constantly by missionaries and catechists. In it an earnest Christian congregation met together, and gave encouraging signs of spiritual life and vigour.

The Governor of Fort St George requested Schwartz to discharge the duties of chaplain to the garrison at Trichinopoly on a salary of one hundred pounds a year. The first year's sum he appropriated entirely to the mission; and ever after this gave fifty pounds of his salary to the native congregation, retaining the remaining fifty for his own use, but this, it is said, was mostly devoted to works of charity. Although regarding himself as specially sent to make known the truth to the heathen tribes of India, yet this man was too zealous to confine his labours simply to them, and not to avail himself of every opportunity of imparting religious instruction to the numerous Europeans of various nationalities who came within his reach. Indeed, he was very anxious that they should live according to the gospel, not merely for their own sakes, but also for the sake of the example they would thus set to the Hindoo population. One gentleman expressed his gratitude to Schwartz, by leaving him a legacy at his death; which, however, he declined to accept.

The unchristian life led by many European Christians in India, is an old question dating back to a period long before that of Schwartz, and is one of immense importance. The glaring forms of vice rife in his day, and for long afterwards, are happily now of rare occurrence. It is questionable, however, whether the dead weight of religious apathy among our fellow-countrymen in India was ever greater than in this year of grace 1874. There is a general decent attention to the Christian duties of the Sabbath; and the obligations of morality are perhaps more acknowledged than at any previous period; and yet it is quite certain that, in proportion to the increase of the European population in the country, they never displayed less zeal in the service of God, and were never less concerned either for the destruction of idolatry or for the conversion of the Hindoo races. Even many religious persons seem to distrust their religion, or to be ashamed of it; and consequently shrink from any active representation of their sentiments. To them, I have no doubt, the missionary appears a fanatic, far too demonstrative for the easy and fastidious Christianity which sits so lightly upon their shoulders, forgetting that a religious man must be impassioned and enthusiastic, and if not so, he is recreant to his principles. The cause of this lack of interest in the spread of the Christian faith on the part of a professedly Christian people, lies most probably in that absence of restraint and freedom from criticism in religious matters felt by every young man on commencing life in India. Not a few Europeans, however, to their honour be it said, are conspicuous for the manly resistance they offer to this common tendency to suppress spiritual convictions, and to avoid all sign of religious animation. It is manifest, therefore, that to preserve the flame of religion from languishing, and to fan it into increased intensity and brightness, among their own countrymen, is the duty not merely of chaplains appointed by the Government, but also of all missionaries labouring in the land, who should feel that a living and fruitful

Christianity is as much a blessing to Europeans as to Hindoos.

A third native Christian was now ordained to the pastoral office in connection with the Tranquebar Mission. There is some discrepancy as to the exact date of the ordination, one account representing it to have been in 1770, while another states it to have occurred on the 28th December 1772. It was considered to be an event of much importance, as it undoubtedly was. The Danish Governor, and other gentlemen, were present at the ceremony, together with a large concourse of native Christians.

In spite of the unsettled state of the country, of the prevalence of great scarcity in the Carnatic, and of other trials, the growth of this mission continued steady and rapid. Year by year large numbers were added to it. In 1772, the addition was two hundred and forty; in 1773, three hundred and sixty; in 1774, four hundred and sixty-eight; in 1775, four hundred and thirty; and thus in ten years, namely, from 1767 to 1776, the increase was upwards of two thousand five hundred. The numerical progress of the Tranquebar Mission throughout the whole of the last century was eminently satisfactory. Had all the missions which have been established in other parts of India advanced as quickly, the aggregate results would have been very far different from what they have been. It must be remembered, however, that in India, where there are so many nationalities, so many social distinctions, and so vast a population, some parts of the country are found by experience to be much more susceptible to the influences of Christianity than others. At the same time, great allowance must

Increase of 2500 Christians to the Tranquebar Mission in ten years.

Methods of procedure in mission work productive of varied results.

be made for the difference of method adopted by missionaries and their societies. It is a startling fact that the plans of action existing in one mission will secure scarcely a dozen converts in as many years, while other plans in another mission similarly situated, and among the same class of people, will produce a multitude of converts every year. This subject will be discussed further on. It is of vital interest in regard to missionary labour in India, and should be fully expounded and understood.

The mission established in Madras endeavoured to extend its influence to Poonamallee westward, and thence southwards to Conjeveram. The country had been devastated by Mahratta marauders, but was now free from their incursions; and, consequently, the missionaries and their native assistants could prosecute their labours among the towns and villages without fear of molestation. Yet, as is often the case, war was followed by pestilence in the form of cholera. Many of the Hindoos were carried off, and the small Christian community lost fifty-two of its members in one year. This was the year 1773. Nevertheless, the prosperity and progress of the mission continued undiminished, for we find that in the space of four years as many as five hundred and twenty-four converts were added to the native congregation.

Speckled Christians.

The vigilance and honesty of the missionaries were both displayed in their treatment of some of the catechumens who had come forward to embrace Christianity under the influence of improper motives, and had been suspected, if not detected in acts of dishonesty. The missionaries wisely and candidly acknowledged the imposition which had been practised

on them; and took the opportunity of representing to
the people more clearly than ever that Christianity
was a spiritual reformation, involving a complete
change of heart and life. Yet the same difficulty
which arose in the Madras Mission in the last century,
finds its way in these more modern times into all the
missions of India, and doubtless also of all other
pagan lands on which the light of the gospel is
beginning to shine. Converts in name only, converts
with mixed motives, converts with bad and disreput-
able motives, in spite of the utmost watchfulness,
sometimes are introduced into the native Christian
communities, to which they presently prove an occasion of mortification and scandal. The worst of the
matter is, that the outside world, captious and cynical,
rejoices over these speckled Christians, and makes up
its mind to regard the entire native Church as of the
same feeble and unworthy character.

Vellore, being a strategical position of great impor- <small>Mission at Vellore.</small>
tance, was at this time occupied by a strong body of
English troops. Thither a catechist of experience
was sent. He had formerly belonged to the Trichinopoly Mission, but with the approval of Schwartz he
now proceeded to Vellore under the auspices of the
mission at Madras. The enterprise succeeded, like
all similar enterprises of that period. A few persons
of the city and adjacent villages were infected by the
earnestness of the catechist Tasanaik, and recognised
the Divine power of the gospel. Soon a Christian
community was formed. Several British officers took
great interest in the work; and the Commandant,
Colonel Lang, promised Mr Fabricius, on his visiting
Vellore, that a suitable building should be placed at

the disposal of the catechist for holding public religious services. This kindness on the part of the Commandant was of considerable moment, as the town belonged entirely to Mahomedans, who altogether refused to allow any house or land to be made use of for Christian purposes. The principle of non-interference in the religious prejudices of a people may sometimes be carried to excess. It is certain, that from the commencement of British rule in India down to the present time, we have shown greater forbearance towards the religious scruples of the races of India than they ever showed towards one another, or than any other power ever displayed in its treatment of a conquered nation.

Attention to the religious scruples of the natives.

Extensive excursions were made far into the country by Mr Gerické, the missionary at Cuddalore, who seemed like the sower in the parable going forth to sow, and scattering the seed broadcast in every direction on the good soil, and also on the bad. He does not appear, however, to have been satisfied with the measure of success which attended these wearisome ministrations. And yet in ten years there were five hundred baptized in Cuddalore alone, exclusive of those in the outlying villages to whom he administered the rite.

Labours of Gerické in Cuddalore and its neighbourhood.

Among the noble band of catechists which Schwartz had gathered together in his mission at Trichinopoly, was Satyanâdan, a young man of great promise, who for many years was a most zealous and distinguished preacher of the gospel. It was the custom of Schwartz to send his catechists forth two and two together, a custom observed very generally in the Indian missions of the present day. It not only has the highest

The catechists labour in pairs.

authority and sanction, but is proved by experience to be sound and wise.

It is instructive to mark the personal influence exerted by Schwartz on all persons who came within his reach. His plain common sense, his winning manner, his intense earnestness, and his purity and simplicity of life, charmed and fascinated every one. English soldiers, officers of the army, civilians of high position, felt alike a glow of excitement and a subtle pleasure which his presence inspired. Natives of all classes acknowledged his wonderful power. The Rajah of Tanjore, although he might not fully trust other Europeans, had the greatest confidence in Schwartz, and entertained towards him sentiments of friendship and regard, which continued unbroken as long as he lived. And yet he boldly expounded the truth to the Rajah, and to the people of his court, in the face of Brahmans and priests who endeavoured to withstand him, and to destroy the effect of his words. The Rajah even requested him to remove from Trichinopoly, and to reside in Tanjore.

Personal influence of Schwartz.

One obstacle to his immediately complying with the Rajah's request was the conflict which now ensued between the latter and the British Government. The Rajah having broken treaty with the Nawab of the Carnatic, in which the honour of the English was concerned, as having guaranteed its fulfilment, a force was sent from Trichinopoly to bring the Rajah to reason. The fortress of Vellam was captured, and Tanjore was besieged. A breach being made in the walls, the Rajah perceived that further opposition was useless, and signed a treaty of peace. After this Schwartz took three catechists with him to Tanjore,

Tanjore besieged by the British.

but these latter being assaulted in the streets by some of the Rajah's servants, he concluded that the time had hardly yet come to establish a mission in that city. He was, however, able to occupy Vellam in the neighbourhood, where he placed a catechist, and also two more in a village about twenty miles from Trichinopoly. In six months the Christian congregation at Vellam numbered eighty persons. A chapel was erected with the assistance of the Commandant and the officers of the garrison.

The vicissitudes through which the kingdom of Tanjore passed a hundred years ago, illustrate, on the one hand, very forcibly the uncertainty of the tenure of native princes in those eventful times, and, on the other, the unscrupulousness and absence of principle occasionally manifested by British rulers in India.

The Nawab of Arcot plans the ruin of the Rajah of Tanjore, and is supported by the Madras Government. The Nawab of Arcot planned the ruin of the Rajah, and obtained the support of the Madras Government in the nefarious enterprise. Professing that the Rajah had neglected to pay him tribute, he determined to attack him in his capital with an overwhelming force, consisting of his own troops united to those sent from Madras.

The Rajah seeks advice from Schwartz. The Rajah foreseeing the impending storm, sent for Schwartz, that he might render him assistance by undertaking a political mission in his behalf. Greatly compassionating the Rajah, Schwartz went to see him, but, although it is evident that his sympathies were on his side, had the great good sense not to interfere. The Rajah paid him a high compliment at the interview, by saying to him, "Padre, I have confidence in you, because you are indifferent to money."*

* Schwartz's Memoirs, vol. i. p. 263.

It was no difficult matter to crush the Rajah; and his destruction was soon completed. The united army marched from Trichinopoly in August 1773, and entered the Rajah's territories, halting at length a short distance from the capital. In spite of the remonstrances of the doomed man, the siege was commenced, breaches were made in the wall, and on the 16th of September the English troops assaulted the city, and took it. The kingdom was forthwith handed over to the Nawab together with the royal treasures; and the Rajah and his families became prisoners. To the honour of the Court of Directors, this ruthless act was disavowed and repudiated by them, and an order was sent to the Madras Governor to restore the Rajah to his kingdom, which was carried out in April 1776. Meanwhile, the effect of the Rajah's captivity was to destroy the influence of Christianity in Tanjore. Schwartz had built a small church there, but this was destroyed in the siege, and the Nawab was most emphatic in forbidding him to erect another. But, on the restoration of the Rajah, the obstacles to the spread of Christianity were removed, and friendship was renewed between the Rajah and Schwartz. The members of the Madras Government were now desirous that Schwartz should render help in bringing forward in the court of the Rajah some political matters which they were anxious about. But he showed the same wisdom in declining to assist the Government, which he had exhibited in refusing to aid the Rajah. The next year, that is, in 1776, Schwartz took up his abode in Tanjore; and the mission there may be regarded as commencing from that date.

Christian church erected in Tanjore in 1779.

As the number of Christians increased rapidly in Tanjore, Schwartz determined on the erection of a suitable church, which appears to have been commenced in 1779. He found it no easy matter, however, to raise money for the purpose. But his indomitable zeal overcame all difficulties in this respect. He obtained bricks and lime as a present from the Government at Madras, he sold some gold cloth presented to him by the Rajah, he received contributions from friends, and thus was enabled to complete the work. In a letter written to a friend at the close of the following year, Schwartz says he has two churches in Tanjore.

Successes of Hyder Ali. Schwartz sent on a political mission to him by the Governor of Madras.

The country was now in much agitation on account of the successes of Hyder Ali, who, having taken possession of the kingdom of Mysore, spread terror in every direction. The entire Carnatic was in confusion, and Madras itself was thrown into considerable danger. The British Government conceived the idea of employing Schwartz as an arbitrator between themselves and Hyder. The usurper altogether distrusted the English, and refused to receive an embassy from them; but stated his willingness to receive Schwartz in their name. "Let them send me the Christian," he said, meaning Schwartz; "he will not deceive me."* At the request of the Government, the missionary proceeded to Madras, in entire ignorance of the object of his journey. On arriving, he was astonished to learn from Sir Thomas Rumbold, the Governor, that the Government was desirous that he should visit Hyder Ali at Seringapatam, " to endeavour to ascertain his actual disposition with respect to the English, and to assure him of the pacific intentions of

* Hough's History of Christianity in India, vol. iii. p. 567.

the Madras Government."* This mission he thought
it his duty to undertake; and commenced his journey
to Seringapatam on the 1st July 1779, accompanied
by his catechist Satyanâdan. He had several inter-
views with Hyder Ali, by whom he was treated with
the highest respect. But Hyder, although he received
the ambassador with much consideration, well knowing that he was a disinterested and upright envoy,
paid little heed to the representations of the Madras
Government, and returned a letter by Schwartz,
couched in strong, if not defiant, language. Each, indeed, suspected the other; and Hyder was not slow
to conjecture that the Madras Governor had sent the
peace-loving missionary to him as a blind to his own
hostile intentions.

While at Seringapatam, Schwartz observed the character of Hyder, marked the powerful will and overbearing tyranny he displayed, and came to the conclusion that he was making preparations for a war of gigantic dimensions. The next year saw the fulfilment of his anticipations, for Hyder fell like a tem-
pest on the Carnatic, and for a time seemed as though
he would sweep everything before him. He pursued
his conquests, taking Negapatam from the Dutch, and
capturing one fort after another, until he reached
Arcot, of which he took possession. Although it was
plain that a large portion of the population were glad
of the change, and welcomed Hyder as a deliverer
rather than as a conqueror, yet the devastations
which he committed produced great poverty and distress. Hyder, with a hundred thousand men, and
assisted by his French allies, sustained a great check

Progress of Hyder in the Carnatic.

* Schwartz's Memoirs, vol. i. p. 303.

at Porto Novo, where he was defeated by General Caste, with a small force of only eight thousand troops, English and native. Schwartz had sufficient foresight of the coming calamities to lay up abundant stores for the native Christians before their price had increased; indeed, he was able not only to provide for them, but also for many Hindoos who were in a state of destitution. Multitudes, panic-stricken, fled from the country districts to Tanjore. It is very singular to perceive that, in the universal distrust—distrust of the British Government, distrust of the native governments, distrust of Hyder—complete confidence of the natives generally was placed in Schwartz. He had won the hearts of the people, who recognised in him their wisest and truest friend. On two occasions, when the Fort of Tanjore was threatened with famine and the Rajah was powerless to obtain supplies, Schwartz, at his urgent request, united with that of the Company, undertook to relieve it; and by the excellent commissariat which he established, and the promise to pay for everything with his own hands, succeeded in saving its inmates from starvation at a most critical period, when the enemy was every moment expected to make a fresh attack, and was ravaging the country on all sides. Schwartz, however, moved about with impunity; for Hyder, deeply impressed with the sanctity of his character and life, had issued orders throughout his army to allow him to proceed wherever he wished. And thus it came to pass that the missionary went from post to post without molestation, among the ranks of one of the most cruel and bloodthirsty armies that ever spread ruin upon the earth.

On the death of Hyder Ali in the year 1782, Lord

Macartney, Governor of Madras, requested Schwartz to act as interpreter to the commissioners he was sending to Tippoo Sultan, son of Hyder. The missionary reluctantly consented, commenced his journey, and proceeded to the borders of Coimbatoor; but difficulties arising, he was obliged to return to Tanjore, and, on their removal, Lord Macartney begged him to set out afresh. But Schwartz was now suffering in health, and therefore was obliged to decline joining the mission altogether. Moreover, it is manifest that his judgment was opposed to it, and that, in his opinion, Tippoo's hatred to the English was far too deadly to be removed or diminished by any pacific words which he might be able to utter. Without the consummate ability of his father, Tippoo was as headstrong and as haughty. He could only be brought to reason by defeat and humiliation. And these he had soon to endure, when he was despoiled of his conquests, was driven back to his own kingdom, and was in danger of losing even that. He was then glad to accept a peace, which was concluded with him on the 11th of March 1784.

Tippoo Sahib's humiliation.

During this period of peril and alarm the missions at Tranquebar, Trichinopoly, and Madras had been more or less exposed to danger, and to the calamities incident to a widespread war. Moreover, in Tranquebar a severe hurricane had produced great mortality and distress. To add to their numerous troubles, the missionaries were unable to receive their usual pecuniary assistance from home. But, on the conclusion of peace, supplies once more came, and they restored the buildings which had been injured by the war. The work of the mission had been carried on with unre-

The work of the missions not stopped by the war.

mitting ardour, and the ten years of labour, when the country was, on several occasions, seething in the horrors of war, produced the fruit of fourteen hundred and eleven converts, making a total since the establishment of the mission of seventeen thousand seven hundred and sixteen.

When the Carnatic was overrun by Hyder Ali, his troops threatened Madras itself, and actually came to St Thomas's Mount in sight of the city, so that the smoke of the burning houses could be seen by its inhabitants. Many of the Christians fled in terror, but the missionaries remained behind, and endeavoured by their presence to render what assistance they were able, and to lessen the general consternation. A detachment of troops from Bengal took possession of the mission church and other buildings; and consequently the missionaries were obliged to retire into Fort St George. Soon after quietness was restored, one of the two missionaries, Mr Breithaupt, was removed by death, having devoted thirty-eight years faithfully and zealously to the service of the mission, which was now left in the sole charge of the aged Fabricius. Madras was at this time visited with a severe famine, which carried off multitudes of the people, and was felt in every grade of society. Even the Governor, it is said, "found it necessary to discharge his palankeen-bearers, and to dispose of all his bearers but two."* The catechist, Tasanaik, stationed at Vellore, joined the mission, having been compelled to abandon his own sphere of labour for a time, owing to the dangers by which he was surrounded.

Cuddalore having surrendered to Hyder Ali, the

* Hough's Christianity in India, vol. iii. p. 449.

very existence of the mission there was imperilled. *Disastrous effect of the war on mission work* The French took possession of the town, and turned the church into a powder-magazine. Nevertheless, Mr Gerické continued his labours in the face of the enemy, and while they were in occupation. But he finally retired to Negapatam; and Cuddalore no longer remained one of the chief stations of the Christian Knowledge Society. In Trichinopoly the war had scattered many of the Christians, so that in 1784 their numbers were reduced to three hundred and ninety-four, of whom, however, two hundred and seven were communicants. The pernicious influence of constant dangers and hostilities extending over several years is seen in the fact, that although in six years two hundred and forty-seven converts were added to the Christian community, yet that so few remained attached to the mission, the rest having been dispersed about the country. Mr Pohle, a man of much earnestness but of a quiet temperament, was in charge of the mission, and continued to be so for a number of years subsequently. Little of a striking character occurred in its history during the next ten years. The native congregation grew steadily, for at the end of this period we find that no less than six hundred and twenty-nine had been added to it. Yet, strange to say, an unusual mortality, and a roving spirit engendered by the war, so far counteracted the numerical increase by conversions that the actual number in the mission was only three hundred and five.

The Rajah of Tanjore gained little wisdom by his troubles. While under their pressure, and for some time afterwards, he treated his subjects with consideration, and seemed desirous of promoting their welfare; but gradually the old spirit of harshness and tyranny returned, until his rule became intolerable. As one of the conditions of his restoration to the government of Tanjore was, that he should be just in his administration, and should extend a generous protection to the people, the British authorities of Madras resolved that he had broken his covenant, and that they would therefore take temporary charge of his dominions, in order to remove the disorders which had been introduced, and to tranquillise the minds of his subjects. Accordingly, a Committee of Inspection, as it was called, was appointed for undertaking the management of his country, consisting of two gentlemen. But, at the urgent request of the Resident, a third was added, in the person of the venerated Schwartz. "He grounded his application on his personal knowledge of the consummate ability and inflexible integrity of this humble missionary; adding, 'It is, and will be, as long as I live, my greatest pride, and most pleasing recollection, that, from the moment of my entering on this responsible station, I have consulted with Mr Schwartz on every occasion, and taken no step of the least importance without his previous concurrence and approbation; nor has there been a difference of sentiment between us in any one instance.'"* The Governor of Madras cordially sanctioned this appointment in these words: "Such is my opinion of Mr Schwartz's abilities and integrity, that I have recommended to the Board that he should be admitted a member of the committee, without any reservation whatever; and my confidence in him is

* Hough's Christianity in India, vol. iii. p. 586.

such, that I think many advantages may be derived therefrom."* As member of this committee Schwartz rendered very important services, into which I will forbear to enter, although much tempted to do so.

The Resident of Tanjore, Mr Sullivan, in consultation with Schwartz, had established several schools among the natives, with the chief object of imparting knowledge to Hindoo children through the medium of the English language. On returning to England, Mr Sullivan communicated to the East India Company the course he had pursued in this matter, and received from them their unqualified approval of it. Moreover, the Company determined on rendering substantial support to the enterprise, and sent out orders that the sum of two hundred and fifty pagodas, or one hundred pounds, should be given yearly from the public funds towards the support of each of the three schools then existing in Tanjore, Ramanadapuram, and Shevagunga, and of other schools also which might be established. This liberal measure was adopted in the hope that native princes would imitate the generosity of the Government. Schwartz took an active part in carrying out the intentions of the Court of Directors, and was personally responsible for much that was done. Although most of the children were of Hindoo families, not a few being Brahmans, yet Schwartz and his colleagues did not hesitate to enjoin, and the Court to sanction, a thorough training in Christian principles. Prayer was offered twice a day, and two hours daily and upwards were consumed in imparting Christian instruction. It is evident that the Company was not then either afraid of, or ashamed of, its Christianity.

The East India Company orders support to be rendered to the native schools. Schwartz responsible for their management.

* Schwartz's Memoirs, vol. ii. p. 35.

The political labours of Schwartz. Missionaries are not politicians; yet may occasionally render essential services to the State.

During the remaining years of his life, until its close, in addition to his labours in the mission, which he never neglected, Schwartz always cherished great interest in the prosperity of the kingdom of Tanjore. No important matter in connection with its government was undertaken without consultation with him. Not that he sought the anxiety and burden of such duties; but as his judgment, experience, and integrity were alike trusted by all parties, the British Government, the Rajah, and the people, it was difficult, nay, impossible, for him to withhold his counsel and aid at a period when the country was occasionally exposed to violence and danger both from without and from within, and was sometimes brought to the verge of rebellion by tyranny and misrule. Nor would it have been right for him to do so. Missionaries are seldom called upon to diverge from their own proper duties, and to associate with officers of Government for the purpose of rendering assistance in times of political strife and emergency. Yet they are not always bound to keep quiet, when by timely advice they are able to further the cause of order and peace. In India, in ordinary times, missionaries are not required to be active politicians, although it may be quite right for them to be so at special seasons, when they may be in a position to perform important services in behalf of the State.

Schwartz appointed guardian to the Rajah's adopted son.

The Rajah of Tanjore, a few hours before his death, requested Schwartz to act as guardian to his adopted son. He refused the important trust, well knowing the difficulties attending its due performance. Afterwards, however, when it was found that the poor boy was exposed to the cruel severity of his uncle, at the earnest solicitation of the Government of Madras, he accepted the post. He also was placed in charge of the court of justice in Tanjore ; and a weekly report of its proceedings was submitted to him. An attempt was made to reform the administration of justice in the principality, and Schwartz wrote a letter on the subject to the Governor of Madras, accompanied by an elaborate plan or scheme representing his views on the subject. He was likewise the "active intermediate agent between the Government and the Rajah relative to the adjustment of the revenue accounts;" and addressed two letters to the Madras Government on the proper system to be adopted in the administration of the revenue of Tanjore, for which, and for the letter on the administration of justice, he received the thanks of the Board. In an investigation into the conduct of several servants of the Company at Tanjore, against whom complaints had been made, he was appointed by the Government to ascertain the truth of certain important charges. When it was determined to deliver the adopted son of the late Rajah from the grievous surveillance of the reigning Rajah, and to send him and the widowed Ranees to Madras, the delicate and difficult task of removal was accomplished by a detachment of troops under the superintendence of Schwartz, who accompanied them all the way to Madras. The child adopted by the late Rajah, to whom Schwartz was guardian, had not succeeded to the rule of Tanjore, but had been put aside with the direct sanction of Sir Archibald Campbell, Governor of Madras, in favour of the brother of the late Rajah. Some years afterwards, however, Schwartz thought it his duty to reopen the subject in a communication to

Lord Cornwallis, the Governor-General, when the whole question was reconsidered *de novo*. Finally, after a lengthened investigation, the Court of Directors reversed the decision of Sir Archibald Campbell, and placed the adopted son upon the throne.

Opinion of Lord Teignmouth on Schwartz.

On this last transaction, Sir John Shore, afterwards Lord Teignmouth, who succeeded Lord Cornwallis as Governor-General, in a minute sent to the Court of Directors, says of Schwartz, that "he has never heard his name mentioned without respect, who is as distinguished for the sanctity of his manners as for his ardent zeal in the promulgation of his religion; whose years, without impairing his understanding, have added weight to his character; and whose situation has enabled him to be the protector of the oppressed, and the comforter of the afflicted; who as a preacher of the Christian faith, and a man without influence except from character, was held in such estimation by the late Rajah, a Hindoo prince, approaching to his dissolution, that he thought him the fittest person he could consult concerning the management of his country during the minority of his adopted son, Serfojee."*

Character of Schwartz. His death in 1798. Forty-eight years a missionary.

Much more might be written respecting the public political life of this eminent missionary. Less than has been written would have left his history incomplete and unsatisfactory. But it is time that I draw this sketch of his labours to a close. He was revered as a father by the people as well as by the Rajah of Tanjore. Mainly through his wisdom the state had been remodelled, and entirely through his conscientiousness and skill the succession had been

* Memoirs of Schwartz, vol. ii. p. 267.

changed. The Tanjore Mission was founded by him, and he continued its guiding spirit to the end. Yet he imparted a stimulus to all the other missions of the Presidency, and either occasionally visited them personally or communicated with them by letter. The religious welfare of the people far and wide was a thought ever uppermost in his mind. All other enterprises and toils in which he engaged were subordinated to this, and were embraced in the broad views of Christian duty which he entertained. He lived as a celibate, that he might devote himself unreservedly to the service of his Master. The qualities of his mind and heart were depicted in his venerable and impressive figure; and his features were those on which men loved to look, and which stirred their souls with a subtle spiritual influence. Few men have lived to sway human hearts so strongly. In his last illness, a transient improvement in his condition enabled him to visit the church at the Christmas festival. The congregation was wild with excitement, and he could scarcely make his way through the crowd. At his death in February, a long and bitter cry of lamentation arose from multitudes, and the Rajah shed a flood of tears over his body, and covered it with a gold cloth. Thus died this Apostle of India, in the year 1798, after forty-eight years spent uninterruptedly in the mission-field.

With the death of this great and distinguished man ends the first period of Protestant missions in India. We shall find the next period, extending on to our own times, of a very different cast. The one prepared the way for the other. At the close of the last century, public attention in England was on a sudden powerfully excited in regard to the obligation resting on religious people to send the gospel to the heathen of India and of other lands; in the production of which excitement, the earnest self-denying labours of Schwartz, Gerické, Schultze, and many others, together with the great successes which they had achieved, had taken a prominent part. Before entering on the second period, and unfolding its characteristics, let us endeavour to understand the work which had been accomplished by Protestant missions in India during the eighteenth century.

Review of the work accomplished. When we bear in mind the fewness of the agents, and the very limited tract of country which they occupied, it is a matter of considerable astonishment that so many converts were every year baptized in the various missions. In Tranquebar alone, in nineteen years, there were nineteen thousand three hundred and forty persons baptized; and during the century, the entire number of converts was nearly, if not quite, double of this amount. In Madras, as many as four thousand natives were received into the Christian Church. The Cuddalore Mission, notwithstanding its great troubles, yielded between one and two thousand converts; the Trichinopoly Mission, more than two thousand; the Tanjore Mission, about fifteen hundred; the Calcutta Mission, under the charge of Kiernander, of whose labours an account will be given in another chapter, upwards of twelve hundred; and the mission established at Palamcottah in Tinnevelly in 1785, to *50,000 converts.* be spoken of hereafter, also a few. Altogether, not less than fifty thousand natives of India had abandoned heathenism and embraced Christianity within this period. Most of them had died; and what proportion were still living at the end of the century, is difficult to ascertain.

That many of the converts were sincere and genuine, we cannot doubt. Yet it is certain that the permission to retain their caste customs and prejudices throws considerable suspicion on the spiritual work accomplished among them. The Danish and German missionaries soon perceived the formidable influence of caste as an opponent of the gospel, unless they were ready, like the Roman Catholics, to enlist it on their side, by permitting it to be retained in the Christian churches established by them. They chose to make caste a friend rather than an enemy. In doing this, however, while they made their path easier, they sacrificed their principles. They admitted an element into their midst which acted on the Christian community like poison. They embraced an adversary, which could never become a friend. They sowed the seeds of pride, distrust, and alienation in their native congregations, which brought forth abundant crops of rank and vexatious weeds. Although this terrible evil seems never to have been so potent among the Christians as among unbelieving Hindoos, yet it wrought mischief in numberless ways, chiefly in preventing the full display of Christian graces and virtues, by forbidding that social intercourse and union which are the very life of a Christian community. Doubtless, this repression of Christian principle, and this compromise with the worst foes of Christianity, facilitated conversions, if they are worthy of the name. To this circumstance, I apprehend, may be mainly attributed the large number of baptisms in so few missions in the course of the last century.

Caste allowed in the native churches.

Its pernicious influence upon them.

Still, of what value were these Christians; and how are we to regard them as compared with the Christians converted from heathenism nowadays under a directly opposite system — namely, that of the complete abandonment of caste, and of every other principle and custom opposed to humility and brotherly love, and to the virtues of a pure Christianity?

<small>Comparison of mission work in the last century and in this.</small> A sufficient answer to these questions may be given in the reply to another, How have they stood the test of time? It might be fairly supposed that missions established from one hundred to one hundred and sixty years ago, if originally sound and true, would in the present day be the largest and most flourishing of all the missions in India. But what do we actually find? Instead of thousands of converts which the Tranquebar Mission possessed for many years in the last century, there were in 1850 only seven hundred and seventeen Christians, and twenty years later, only seven hundred and seventy-one. Again, Tanjore, the principal scene of Schwartz's labours, contained, in 1850, fifteen hundred and seventy Christians. In the same year, Trichinopoly had six hundred and thirty-eight; Cuddalore, three hundred and twenty-five; and Madras probably not more than a thousand. It should also be remembered that many of these converts, perhaps the greater portion, were not descendants of the earlier Christians, but were the fruit of labours performed during the first half of the present century, through the instrumentality of a continuous series of missionaries connected with several societies. The truth is, there is strong reason for believing that the earlier Christians died off, leaving but an exceedingly small number of

natural successors; and that, had it not been for modern efforts, by this time little would have been seen of the great results of former times.

Yet compare the instability of earlier results with the stability of later. In the year 1857 many of the missions in Northern India were temporarily scattered by a malignant enemy. Multitudes of Christians were exposed to great and prolonged peril, and not a few fell into the hands of the foe. Nevertheless, with only here and there an exception, they remained faithful to their creed. On the cessation of hostilities, the wanderers returned to their homes, and every one of these missions has since then increased in numbers, while some have doubled and even trebled. The difference lies in this, that although the work in modern times is slower in progress, and stricter in principle, yet it is more thorough and trustworthy, more genuine and satisfactory, and more grounded on real conviction, than the work achieved by the distinguished missionaries of the previous period.

CHAPTER II.

MISSIONS IN CALCUTTA AND ITS VICINITY.

Religious reaction in England. THE apathy of England concerning the spiritual condition of heathen countries, and the rigid, exclusive selfishness which characterised its religion, continued almost unchanged until the eighteenth century was dying out, when suddenly the Christian Church awoke to the conviction of its gross neglect of duty. That it should have been so long heedless of the fact that more than one-half of the human race were worshippers of idols, and slaves of the most debasing superstitions, and then should have been so thoroughly transformed, as, in the course of a few short years, to be found devising practical schemes for the spiritual regeneration of pagan races of every country on the face of the earth, is a curious phenomenon in the history of mankind. The burden of the world's errors and sins, no doubt, had become heavier from year to year; but why Christian people should have been able to gaze upon the increasing burden with comparative calmness, and even cheerfulness, for many generations, and in the fading years of a worn-out century should have with strange abruptness set themselves to the gigantic task of removing it from the earth, is a question not easy of solution. The Danish missions in India had produced some excitement in Denmark and Germany, and had aroused some small attention in England. But the religious heart of Britain continued dull and cold. It was not yet warmed by genuine enthusiasm.

True, the religious movements inaugurated by Wesley and Whitefield had imparted an electric influence to all the sections of the Christian Church. The frivolity and scepticism of Rousseau, Voltaire, and their numerous followers on the Continent, had shocked the feelings of Christian men in Great Britain, and had caused a reaction of religious loyalty throughout the nation generally. Moreover, the conservatism of the past was giving way before the revolutionary struggles then fiercely raging in France. New ideas on human society, politics, and religion, were fast spreading among the nations of Europe. Men perceived that they had new responsibilities to share, and new labours to undertake, for the benefit of one another. These, doubtless, were some of the reasons, though not all, which led Christian people in England to become suddenly inspired with a singular zeal for the spiritual welfare of their fellow-men in remote regions of the earth, and for the establishment of so many societies for carrying out their newly-formed purpose.

Some of its causes.

The founders of our missionary societies, as is often the case with originators of great enterprises, set out with timidity and caution. They knew not, in fact, their own aims with any degree of distinctness. They were irresolute, were afraid of going too fast. They were held back by pious souls still more irresolute and faint-hearted. When Mr Carey, afterwards the famous Dr Carey, the distinguished pioneer of modern mis-

Timidity of the founders of the first missionary societies in England.

sions in India, was endeavouring to awaken sympathy for his missionary project, the only minister in London who gave him countenance was "the venerable John Newton, who advised him with the fidelity and tenderness of a father."* At first most persons cherished the idea, that all schemes for the evangelisation of pagans were visionary, the result of a heated imagination, and of something akin to fanaticism. Afterwards, as they became popular, people changed their opinions, and suffered themselves to recognise the genuineness of the devotion which had prompted them. The intense earnestness of the Christian Church in these days, displayed in a thousand ways, was at that time unknown, or, if known, was confined to small bodies of Christians, and to certain special labours in which they were engaged.

Missions established at the end of the last, and during the present century, have produced many apostles, men of the fiery zeal of St Paul, ready to lay down their lives for the gospel. A man of this sublime stamp was Dr Carey. Of humble origin, yet consumed by an inward flame, he manfully faced and overcame enormous difficulties, until he had thoroughly aroused the Baptist denomination to which he belonged. Through his unwearying enthusiasm many members of that religious body became excited with his own fervour, and united together in endeavouring to establish a mission in India, of which he was to be the leader. Forbidden to proceed thither by a mercenary and godless Company, he nevertheless went; bound on the wonderful enterprise of converting the mighty population of India to Christianity, and of

Dr Carey; his wonderful enthusiasm

* Carey, Marshman, and Ward, by Mr John Marshman, pp. 12, 13.

translating the Bible into its numerous tongues. Smuggled into the country, exposed to poverty, almost to starvation, with scarcely a single friend to sympathise with him, left to his own resources, he still trusted in God, commenced the translation of the Scriptures, clearing away from his path one obstacle after another, and gradually won an honourable position for himself in the country both among natives and Europeans, and, what is more, inspired multitudes of Christians with that transcendent spirit of enthusiasm which animated his own breast.

On reaching Calcutta, Carey found the mission of Kiernander already in existence. This, as stated in the previous chapter, had been established by that missionary in 1758, on occasion of the capture of Cuddalore in the Madras Presidency, when, being obliged to abandon his mission, he proceeded to Bengal, to commence a mission there. This was the year after the battle of Plassey, that famous battle which gave to England its first firm footing in India. Still excited with the sense of his great success, Clive was earnestly endeavouring to bring the newly-acquired territory into order, and to make practical use of his victory. He, and the other members of Council, received Kiernander cordially, fell in with his benevolent plans, and were not ashamed to acknowledge him as a Christian missionary. Though not avowedly a religious man himself, Clive was free from prejudice and narrow-mindedness, and at once perceived the importance of the object which Kiernander had in view. Unlike some of his successors, he saw no harm in Christianity being introduced into India. His mind was, on this subject, not tortured with the

The views of Clive on the introduction of Christianity into India.

sophistries of a later period. And he was far too frank and plain-spoken to assert, in opposition to his convictions, that Hindooism, if not an unmixed good, was at least good enough for Hindoos.

Kiernander's labours and successes. Smiled upon by the Government, Kiernander entered upon his labours with ardour; and his mission soon became one of the fixed institutions of the metropolis. He started a school, which in the course of a year numbered nearly two hundred scholars. He preached to the natives; he preached to the Portuguese; he preached to the English troops. By the end of the first year he had baptized fifteen persons. As his congregation and school increased, a suitable building was placed at his disposal by the Governor, Mr Vansittart, which was transformed into a chapel. In ten years the native community consisted of one hundred and eighty-nine converts. After a time, the chapel being required for the public service, Kiernander built a church chiefly at his own expense, the cost of which was seven thousand five hundred pounds. Conversions continued to occur from year to year. From 1767 to 1776 the large number of four hundred and ninety-five appear to have been made. A German missionary was sent out to the assistance of Kiernander in 1773; and, strange to say, together with two of Kiernander's children returning from Germany, received a free passage from the East India Company in one of their ships.

His fidelity. From the more or less detailed accounts which we have of the course pursued by Kiernander, it is very manifest that he was a man of great energy and perseverance; and although living in the midst of a corrupt city, where Europeans seem to have forgotten their religion, and to have accepted, if not the idolatry, at least the immorality, of the Hindoos, he kept steadily to his great work, and set a noble example of piety and zeal. His later years were somewhat beclouded by pecuniary difficulties, in which he became involved through the improvidence of his son; but this indiscretion ought not to dim the lustre of the reputation which he had acquired as a true and faithful missionary. The seeds of Protestant missions in Northern India were first sown by him; and by him were the first-fruits gathered in. He baptized hundreds of converts; he established important mission schools; he proclaimed the gospel to the people, both European and native; he built a spacious church; and by these and other labours proved his earnestness and efficiency.

It was fortunate for the growth of the mission in Calcutta that a small knot of devoted Christian men was assembled there. Among them were Mr Charles Grant, Sir Robert Chambers, and his brother, Mr William Chambers, Mr Udny, and the Rev. David Brown, chaplain to the Military Orphan School. Some of these were anxious to promote the religious welfare of the heathen population, and not only showed strong sympathy in the Christian work already in progress, but strove laboriously and long to establish a mission, not for Calcutta merely, but also for the whole of Bengal. Their plan was to divide Bengal into eight districts, each of which should be in the charge of a clergyman of the Church of England, who should preach to the people, superintend schools, and in other ways act the part of a zealous missionary. In their simplicity, they imagined that the Government

Mr Charles Grant, Mr Udny, the Rev. David Brown, and others. Their scheme for Christianising Bengal.

might be induced to sanction and liberally support the scheme. Their own minds were not embarrassed with the political difficulties which surrounded it. They did not see why the Government should not educate the people over whom they ruled, and also make them acquainted with the principles of that religion which they themselves professed, and from which their own country had derived so much good.

The opposition it met with. They reckoned in ignorance of the cold indifference with which their project would be received by some, and of the determined opposition with which it would be assailed by others. Lord Cornwallis, the Governor-General at the time, imagined that no benefit could possibly accrue to the people from any such schemes. The East India Company, perceiving the blow aimed at the supremely selfish theory of government then in vogue, that India was to be ruled for the advantage, not of herself, but of England, denounced it in the strongest terms. The British Parliament, notwithstanding the eloquence of Wilberforce, refused its patronage, and lent a willing ear to the antagonistic declamations of the Company's directors. Thus the scheme was bandied about, and at last fell to the ground, not, however, before it had awakened a spirit of bitter resentment in the minds of many persons interested in the success of British rule in India.

One grievous result of this controversy was, that for a number of years English missionaries found it extremely difficult to gain admission into the Company's territories. If they ventured to proceed thither, they did so either surreptitiously, or in some other capacity, or with the knowledge that on landing in the country they ran the chance of immediate de-

PROTESTANT MISSIONS IN INDIA. 67

portation therefrom. Kiernander and his confederates had been left for a long time to the undisturbed performance of their Christian duties in Calcutta. The Indian Government regarded their work with favour, and never dreamt that they were called upon to thwart them in the smallest degree. But when Carey came to India the dispute had produced much virulence, and was not yet settled. He found it impossible to procure a licence permitting him to embark for India; and after being removed from one ship which had actually set sail with him on board, he finally took a passage in a Danish vessel, which reached Calcutta on the 11th November 1793, and landed quietly and unobserved. With him was associated Mr Thomas, a surgeon, who had resided in Bengal for several years, and was now a missionary of the Baptist Society like himself.

Dr Carey and Mr Thomas land in Calcutta, November 11, 1793.

Although unmolested, their anxieties were great. Their funds being originally very limited, were soon exhausted. Carey set about learning the language, but penury stared him in the face. He removed for a short time to the Soondarbuns, a tract scantily populated, and notorious for pestilence and wild beasts, thinking that he might farm the land and instruct the people. From this unpromising place he was invited by Mr Udny to the superintendence of a factory at Malda, which he gladly accepted; his colleague, Mr Thomas, being placed in charge of another. Carey spent five years in Malda, during which time he translated the New Testament into Bengalee, held daily religious services with the servants on the estate, preached among the neighbouring villages, and superintended a school which he had established.

Carey's difficulties. He proceeds first to the Soondarbuns, and then to Malda.

In the declining years of Kiernander, and when he was obliged to retire from Calcutta on account of the pecuniary troubles which befell him, as already described, Mr D. Brown undertook many of the duties of the mission; and such was his zeal, that when the managers of the asylum called upon him to abandon the mission, and to devote himself exclusively to their own institution, he nobly threw up his appointment, and for a time gave himself entirely to missionary labour. Meanwhile, the Christian Knowledge Society sent out the Rev. Mr Clarke, who is sometimes spoken of as the first English missionary of the Church of England that went out to India. He, however, was hardly worthy of the designation, as he soon, though still employed in the service of the mission, accepted the post of Superintendent of the Free School Society, and subsequently, and very abruptly, left the mission altogether, and became a chaplain of the East India Company. In this fresh emergency Mr Brown once more stepped forward to save the mission from ruin, and carried on the religious services of the church. In 1797 the society was enabled to relieve Mr Brown by despatching a German missionary, the Rev. W. T. Ringletaube, to Calcutta, who in a fit of impatience and despondency suddenly abandoned the mission two years afterwards, and returned to England, much to the surprise and disappointment of the directors of the society. It is plain that at that period there was little or no enthusiasm in the Church of England in favour of the missionary enterprise, and that very few persons were willing to incur the odium as well as danger of being directly engaged in it. Men of earnest piety and great zeal like the Rev. D. Brown, the Rev. Dr Buchanan (who arrived in Calcutta from England in March 1797), and the Rev. Henry Martyn and others, manifested a warm interest in the conversion of the natives to Christianity, but these eminent men entered the country as chaplains, not as missionaries. Without disparaging in the smallest degree their unwearied energy and abundant labours in the cause of missions, still it is indisputable that the time for the dedication of the best sons of the Church of England solely to this grand and self-denying work, had not yet come.

In the autumn of 1799 four English missionaries arrived in the Hoogly in the American ship *Criterion*. Carey was still at Mudnabutty in Malda, having purchased an indigo-factory in the neighbourhood. He at once made arrangements for their reception, little realising the opposition from the Government which awaited him. Before landing his passengers, the captain of the ship was required to state in writing their occupation and object. After some consultation the missionaries concluded that it would be best to acknowledge their missionary purpose; but having done so, they proceeded without delay to the Danish settlement of Serampore, fifteen miles from Calcutta, where they placed themselves under the protection of the Governor, an old friend of Schwartz, and a man full of sympathy for their great object, and therefore ready to give them all the assistance in his power. When the ship's papers were presented to the Government official in Calcutta, it was at once determined to send the missionaries back to England, and to seize the ship until they should comply with the demand of the Government by returning to their native land. Fortunately, Colonel Bie, the Danish

Fruitless attempt of the Government of India to deport four new missionaries who sought the protection of the Danish Governor of Serampore.

Governor of Serampore, was not the man to yield to an unjust interference with his authority; and as he had taken the missionaries under his protection, he was not inclined to give them up. The Marquis of Wellesley, who was then Governor-General, after some hesitation, let the matter drop, and the missionaries were left to themselves. Their purpose, however, was to join Carey in his mission to the north of Bengal, and not to remain in Serampore. But they soon found that it was not only impossible for them to proceed thither, but also to quit the Danish territory, without exposing themselves to the risk of instant deportation. The Rev. D. Brown and others endeavoured to have the rules relaxed in their favour; but the Governor-General and his Government were invincible in their determination to prohibit the establishment of an English mission in their territories. The Danish Governor, on the other hand, increased his kindness and offers of assistance in proportion as the illiberality and harshness of the British Government became more manifest. He in fact proposed that they should establish themselves permanently in Serampore, should start schools for the education of Hindoo youths, and a printing press for the publication of the Scriptures and other books, and should carry on such other missionary labours as they might choose to engage in. Carey was written to on the subject, and Mr Ward, one of the new missionaries, under the safeguard of a passport from Colonel Bie, proceeded to Malda, and laid the whole matter before him.

Carey proceeds to Serampore. Establishment of the mission there. Perceiving the great advantages of the Governor's proposal, Carey at length resolved on quitting his present position, and uniting with the other missionaries in the prosecution of their scheme. And thus it came to pass that the Baptist Mission was established in Serampore.

A week had not passed after Carey's arrival in this town, before the missionaries had purchased a large house and spacious grounds for their own accommodation, and for the numerous purposes which they had in view in connection with the mission. Rules were framed for their mutual guidance. They agreed to have all things common, and with their wives and children to dine at a common table. "Their first attention," says Mr J. C. Marshman, in his interesting and graphic "Story of Carey, Marshman, and Ward," "was given to the printing-office. With the exception of two books of the Old Testament, the translation of the whole Bible in the Bengalee language was completed. Mr Ward set the first types with his own hands, and presented Mr Carey with the first sheet of the New Testament on the 18th of March. The feeling of exultation with which it was contemplated, and the great prospects which it opened up, may be more easily imagined than described. While Mr Ward was thus working the press, Mr Carey and Mr Fountain were engaged morning and evening in preaching to the heathen in the town and its neighbourhood. These addresses in all places of public resort brought a constant succession of inquirers to the mission-house; and no small portion of Mr Carey's time was occupied in answering their questions and explaining the doctrines of Christianity to them. The 24th of April was selected as a day of thanksgiving for the establishment of the mission in circumstances so favourable. At this meeting the missionaries voted

Printing of the Bengalee Bible commenced on March 18, 1800.

an address to the King of Denmark, expressing their warmest gratitude for the generous protection which his servants had extended to their undertaking, and soliciting his permission to continue in the settlement, and prosecute their labours. In the ensuing year, his Majesty, Frederick the Sixth, signified the gratification he felt at the establishment of the mission in his dominions; and informed the missionaries that he had taken their institution under his special protection. On the 18th of May 1800 Mr and Mrs Marshman opened two boarding schools for the support of the mission, which, before the close of the year, brought in an income of £860 a year, and secured the mission from pecuniary destitution. Under their able management the school rose in public estimation, and soon became the most flourishing and remunerative in the country."*

The Marquis of Wellesley dreads the influence of the Serampore press. As the printing of the Bengalee New Testament involved considerable expense, the missionaries courageously invited Europeans of Calcutta to assist in its publication, little dreaming of the consternation this would produce among the members of the Government. The Marquis of Wellesley dreaded the influence of the press of Serampore, and rightly conjectured that to stifle public opinion in Calcutta would be useless if perfect liberty were allowed to a press only fifteen miles off. And no doubt complications would have arisen between the Governor-General and the Governor of Serampore, had not the former been plainly assured by the Rev. David Brown, a friend of the mission, and a person also in whom the Governor-General had great confidence, that the sole

* Carey, Marshman, and Ward, pp. 60, 61.

object of the missionaries was of a religious character, and that they had no intention to enter into political discussion or strife. How much was to be learned on this subject by our politically brave, though religiously timid, rulers of India in the earlier years of British occupancy of the country! It is difficult to comprehend their feelings judged by the light of the present day. Why were they alarmed at the free thoughts and keen criticism of Englishmen? Why were they afraid of Christianity? of its friendship with civilisation? and of its antipathy to idolatry and superstition? How curiously warped must their Christian instinct have become before they could have indulged in such sentiments of anxiety and alarm!

The first convert was baptized in the presence of the Governor and a vast multitude of Hindoos and Mahomedans, Portuguese and English. Its effect upon Mr Thomas, who was present at the ceremony, was such that his mind lost its balance from sheer thankfulness and joy, and he remained as one insane for the space of a month. He died in the autumn of 1801 at Dinagepore, where he and the Rev. Mr Fountain, sent out by the Baptist Society in 1796, had lived, partly engaged in secular pursuits, and partly in preaching the gospel to the people. Mr Fountain died before him, on the 20th August 1800.

On the establishment of Fort William College, Carey was appointed to the chair of Sanskrit and Bengalee, on a salary at first of six hundred pounds a year, which was shortly increased to fifteen hundred pounds a year, sums which being thrown into the mission funds were of great importance in the development of the projects which the missionaries had started and were then vigorously carrying out. The publication of the Bengalee New Testament was completed on the 7th February 1801. A copy was presented to the Marquis of Wellesley, who expressed his gratification at this important result of missionary labours. The good feeling between the British Government and Denmark, which had existed so long, having come to an end, and been followed by hostilities between the two countries, the small territory of Serampore was taken possession of by the Governor-General on the 8th May of the same year, and remained in his hands for fourteen months. It would have been quite feasible for his Excellency to break up the mission, and to scatter the missionaries during this period of occupation, had he chosen to do so. But by this time the mission had become consolidated, had proved itself to be free from factious and political purposes, and had shown itself to be simply actuated by the desire to promote the spiritual welfare of the people. Yet the danger was considerable, for all the Government officials were not then, as they are not all now, men of sufficiently strong mind to keep themselves out of mischief. Some of the Christian tracts which had been printed in the Serampore press having fallen into the hands of a Hindoo of high position in Calcutta, in his indignation he laid them before one of the principal judges of that city, a weak man who was foolish enough to bring them to the notice of another weak man, Mr George Barlow, the Vice-President of the Council, then wielding authority in the capital, in the absence of the Governor-General, who was far away in the North-Western Provinces.

These sages might have proceeded to extremities but for the fortunate suggestion of Mr Buchanan, that they should make themselves acquainted with the contents of the tracts. These being translated, were found to be so exceedingly harmless that the Vice-President and judge were compelled to keep silence about them.

When Carey commenced his lectures in Bengalee there was not a single prose work existing in that language. "After a lapse of sixty years" (now upwards of seventy), says Mr Marshman, "when thousands of volumes are annually poured forth from the native presses in Calcutta, it is interesting to trace the germ of Bengalee literature to the missionary press at Serampore, at the beginning of the century. Mr Carey compiled a grammar of the language for the use of his students."* About this time the horrid practice of offering children in sacrifice at great public festivals was abolished by the Governor-General, at the instigation of Mr Udny, who had become a member of the Supreme Council. *[margin: Commencement of Bengalee literature.]*

A bold step was now taken by the missionaries in extending their operations to Calcutta, first by the distribution of Christian tracts among the native inhabitants, and then by hiring a house for the purpose of imparting religious instruction to them. Since the days of Kiernander the Government had become very jealous of Christianity, and therefore it required no ordinary courage to commence a work of this nature. As the converts in Serampore increased, the question of polygamy soon presented itself. The missionaries decided that a convert with more than *[margin: Polygamy of Christian converts allowed.]*

* Carey, Marshman, and Ward, p. 76.

one wife should not be compelled to put any away.

Caste not permitted. On the subject of caste, they adopted the safe though stringent rule, that it should not be permitted in any shape; and at the first sacramental service after the baptism of a Brahman, the cup was given to a Sudra before it was handed to him. A short time after this the Brahman was married to the daughter of the Sudra.

Missionary tours to Jessore and other places. Occasionally tours were made to distant places, such as Jessore, Ganga, Saugor, and elsewhere; and thus was commenced that all-important work of itinerating among the towns and villages of the country, which has been prosecuted from that time to the present, and, although attended with varying success, has doubtless been an efficient means of spreading Christian truth far and wide, and of causing vast multitudes of the people to become more or less acquainted with it.

The London Missionary Society sends its first missionary to India in 1798. The London Missionary Society, established in 1795, sent its first missionary to India in the year 1798. This was the Rev. Mr Forsyth, who came in the first instance to Calcutta, but finally settled at Chinsurah, twenty miles to the north of that city. He seems for a time to have divided his labours between the two places, but finally devoted himself entirely to Chinsurah. He continued alone in the work until 1812, when he was joined by the Rev. Mr May and his wife from England. Although earnest and diligent, and truly devoted to his mission, he does not appear to have met with any direct success. In the early stage of a mission, it is proved to be commonly a fatal mistake to leave a missionary to encounter all the difficulties of his position single-handed. Isolated, without sympathy, opposed by the heathen, he is apt to become despondent, and to lose that faith in God, and that elasticity of spirit, so absolutely necessary to success. I know not what was the experience of Mr Forsyth in this respect; but judging from the various instances which have come under my own observation, I am convinced that the policy of intrusting a new mission to one European is a bad one, and is liable to end in failure. On the other hand, when a mission is well established, and especially when it is connected with others in its neighbourhood, it may be, and often is, advisable for it to be placed in the charge of one man; or even for a number of strong and healthy stations to be committed to his care, provided that he has the support and help of qualified native brethren.

It is impossible not to be impressed with some features of the noble ambition of the Serampore missionaries. They not only translated the Bible or portions of it into Bengalee, Sanskrit, Persian, Ooriya, Mahratta, and Chinese, but contemplated undertaking its translation into several other Oriental languages. Mr Buchanan fell in heartily with their great scheme; and drew up a paper, in which he proposed that the Bible should be translated into fifteen Oriental tongues; which was signed by himself and by the missionaries at Serampore, and was presented to the Governor-General. Copies were sent to England for the Court of Directors, the bishops of the English Church, the universities, and other public bodies. Large contributions were made towards this splendid enterprise; and Mr Buchanan alone subscribed the sum of five hundred pounds. For fifteen years did Mr Marshman devote

Scheme for translating the Bible into fifteen Oriental languages.

all his hours of leisure to his Chinese version of the Bible until it was completed. But this is only a specimen of the ardour of them all. They seem to have worked as though the conversion of all India, and the translation of the Bible into all its languages, depended on themselves.

<small>Unstable character of the first converts.</small>

In six years ninety-six adult natives were received into the Christian Church by baptism, of whom nine were Brahmans, and six Mahomedans. This represented a Christian community of probably upwards of three hundred persons. They were not all of the same spirit. Some indeed flagrantly disgraced their Christian character; others were weak and difficult to manage. "Sometimes," says Carey in his journal, "we have to rebuke them sharply; sometimes to expostulate; sometimes to entreat; and often, after all, to carry them to the throne of grace, and to pour out our complaints before God. Our situation, in short, may be compared to that of a parent who has a numerous family. He must work hard to maintain them; is often full of anxiety concerning them; and has much to endure from their dulness, their indolence, and their perverseness. Yet still he loves them, for they are his children, and his love towards them mingles pleasure with all his toil."*

<small>Opposition of the Government, and of the Court of Directors, to missionaries and their work.</small>

The mission at Serampore, with its out-stations in Calcutta and elsewhere, was now to pass through a fiery trial. The opposition of the Indian Government and of the Court of Directors to missionaries and their work had been gradually increasing in intensity until it at last attained to fever-heat. The former came to be regarded as firebrands who were sowing the seeds

* Hough's Christianity in India, vol. iv. p. 129.

of discontent in the country, and jeopardising British rule and authority; the latter as a mischievous attack upon time-honoured institutions, which as conquerors of India we should take under our protection. First, the famous temple of Jugaunath was by special Act placed under the charge of the State, and became, so to speak, one of the Government institutions of the day. This deference to idolatry could only have been shown by a feeble, time-serving Governor-General, afraid to act on the highest principles, and quite willing to sacrifice them, if, as he imagined, he could secure thereby the greater attachment of the people whom he governed. When the question was first mooted in the Council, it was received by the Marquis of Wellesley with the utmost abhorrence. But his Lordship was now gone from India, and his temporary successor was Sir George Barlow, the same that took fright, it will be remembered, at the circulation of Mr Ward's tracts in Calcutta.

The temple of Jugaunath placed in charge of the State by special Act.

The Government next proceeded to prohibit the circulation of tracts and public preaching in Calcutta. And its opposition reached a climax when, on the arrival of two new missionaries from England in August 1806, they were peremptorily ordered to quit the country immediately. The Vellore mutiny, which happened at this time, greatly excited Government officials, and in looking about for a scapegoat, instead of finding it in their own neighbourhood, they discovered it in the missionaries, of all men the most peace-loving in the land. The spirit then exhibited has been displayed at intervals from that day to the present, by rulers prone to annexation, unwise laws, and irritating regulations, who, after taxing the

The Government prohibits the circulation of tracts and public preaching.

The Vellore mutiny. The effects it produced in India.

loyalty of the people to the utmost, have been unwilling to trace the connection between the evil consequences which have ensued and their own acts. The two newly-arrived missionaries, like others who had preceded them, promptly placed themselves under the special protection of the Danish Governor of Serampore; and, although the Governor-General and his Council tried hard to enforce their threat of expulsion, yet they were finally overawed by the firm stand made by the captain of the American vessel which had brought the missionaries, and Colonel Krefting, the Governor of Serampore, both promising that the governments which they represented would call the British Government to account for the tyrannical course its agents in India were adopting. Then it was that Sir George Barlow, dreading such a complication, withdrew from the controversy. Meanwhile, all missionary work beyond the frontier of the small Serampore territory was temporarily suspended.

And in England.

In England the Vellore mutiny produced the same effect upon many members of the Court of Directors and of the Board of Control which it had produced on Government officials in India, in inspiring them with the strange hallucination that the missionaries were responsible for it. The matter was discussed at their meetings with great warmth and prejudice. The Marquis of Wellesley, when referred to, at once frankly and fully exonerated the missionaries from the blame of the Vellore disaster. Nevertheless, so violent was the antipathy excited against missions in India, that more than six years elapsed before the missionaries could gain permission to renew their Christian labours in the Company's territories.

For a few months the spirit of mischief was stayed in India, and the missionaries were left to themselves, though stripped of much of their former liberty. Unfortunately for them, a tract on the Mahomedan controversy, written by a Christian convert from Islamism, containing strong remarks against Mahomed, was issued from the Serampore press, without apparently any oversight or correction from the missionaries. This falling into the hands of the Government in Calcutta, reopened the discussion, and fanned the flame of opposition to mission work, which was beginning to lull. In addition, spies were sent to attend the meetings of the missionaries, to report on the purport of their addresses, and to procure copies of religious tracts in circulation among the natives. The Supreme Council met to deliberate on the entire question, and came to the determination to forbid the Serampore missionaries to carry on their labours in Calcutta, "as contrary," says Mr Marshman, who has given a full account of the matter, "to the system of protection which Government was pledged to afford to the undisturbed exercise of the religions of the country. The Governor-General," he adds, "moreover, directed that the Serampore press should be immediately removed to Calcutta, where alone the necessary control could be exercised over it; and the missionaries were directed to use every effort in their power to withdraw from circulation the pamphlets and treatises they had distributed."* _{The Seram-pore missionaries ordered to remove their press to Calcutta.}

An order embodying the sentiments of the Council was sent by Lord Minto, the new Governor-General, to Carey and his coadjutors, and a communication _{The order resisted by the Danish Governor of Serampore and the missionaries.}

* Carey, Marshman, and Ward, p. 139.

was also made to Colonel Krefting, the Governor of Serampore, by the same authority, requesting his Excellency to render his assistance in carrying it out. But the Danish Governor was not to be made a cat's paw after this fashion. He stood upon his rights with manly firmness. The missionaries, with hearts full of anxiety, yet bravely trusting in God, held a meeting for prayer, at which Carey "wept like a child." They then went to the Governor, and "received the assurance that he could not permit the removal of the press without incurring the serious displeasure of his sovereign; and that if the British Government thought fit to resort to compulsory measures, he would strike his flag, and leave the settlement in their possession."* At the suggestion of Mr Ward, the missionaries sought an interview with Lord Minto, to whom they explained their objects and motives, and afterwards drew up a memorial to him on the plans and operations of the Serampore Mission since its first establishment. When this document was read before the Council, together with the reply of Colonel Krefting, Lord Minto himself proposed a resolution revoking the late order, and only "requiring the missionaries to submit works intended for circulation in the Company's territories to the inspection of its officers." The Court of Directors, on hearing all the circumstances of this famous controversy, praised and blamed the Supreme Council of Calcutta in the following significant words: "The Court approved of their having refrained from resorting to the authority vested in them by law against the missionaries; and relied on their discre-

The order revoked.

* Carey, Marshman, and Ward, p. 141.

tion to abstain from all unnecessary and ostentatious interference with their proceedings in future."*

On the completion of the translation of the New Testament into Chinese, Mr Marshman found no little difficulty in printing it. At length clever workmen were procured, who carved the Chinese characters on wooden blocks, which were then used for printing. The first sheet of the Gospel of St Matthew was presented to the Governor-General, who, as the Serampore press was greatly in want of funds, was requested to head a subscription list for the printing of the Chinese version of the Sacred Scriptures. After some deliberation, and fearing that such an act would be misinterpreted, he declined to do so; but readily subscribed for ten copies of a translation of the writings of Confucius which Mr Marshman had made. His example was followed by many persons who would have hesitated to contribute towards the printing of the Bible in the Oriental languages, yet were quite willing to help the missionaries in this indirect manner.

Mr Marshman completes his translation of the New Testament into Chinese.

Protestant missions in India are much indebted to the labours of Brown, Buchanan, and Henry Martyn, three distinguished chaplains of the East India Company, whose piety, zeal, and influence enabled them to render the greatest assistance in promoting the good work in Calcutta, and other places in the Bengal Presidency, at a time when missions were not only unpopular but elicited the strongest opposition from the British Government. These fearless men were true missionaries, and were ready to brave the rebukes of the Government, in their love to Christ

Brown, Buchanan, and Henry Martyn.

* Carey, Marshman, and Ward, pp. 147, 148.

and to the souls of men. I have already spoken of the two first. The last, Henry Martyn, displayed the same spirit of earnestness which they exhibited. In coming to India, his longing desire was to make known the gospel to the heathen. While diligent as a chaplain, he devoted all his leisure hours, which often hang heavily on chaplains in India, to the prosecution of this purpose. He arrived in India in May 1806. Before the end of the year he was busily engaged in acquiring Persian, Sanskrit, and other languages, in translating the New Testament into Hindustani, and in conversing with all classes of the people on the subject of Christianity. Proceeding to Dinapore, he opened five schools for the instruction of the natives, and translated portions of the Common Prayer-Book into Hindustani sufficient for the purposes of public worship. In 1807, that is, less than two years after reaching the country, he had completed his Hindustani version of the New Testament, which, although too Persianised in style, is upon the whole an excellent idiomatic rendering of the original; and had also written a brief commentary on the parables of our Lord in the same language. During this year he commenced the translation of the New Testament into Persian; and in 1809 he undertook to render that portion of the Scriptures into Arabic, for which, in his own judgment, he had been somewhat prepared by his Persian studies. From Dinapore Martyn proceeded to Cawnpore, where through his exertions a large church was built, which was opened for Divine service in March 1809. But his severe studies and heavy labours began to tell upon his health, and in the autumn of 1810 he returned to

Calcutta, his frame so enfeebled that it became necessary for him to leave the country for a milder climate. Early in January 1811 he quitted the shores of India, never to return, bound for Shiraz, taking with him his Persian Testament, in order that, on reaching Persia, he might thoroughly prune it of the Arabic idioms which he had introduced into it, and adapt it to ordinary readers. Martyn reached Shiraz, remodelled and completed his Persian translation, and thence proceeded to Gebriz, near the Caspian Sea, with the object of presenting a copy of it to the King. This excellent version was published in the following year by the Russian Bible Society, and soon obtained a wide circulation in Persia. Shattered in health, Martyn determined to return to his native land by way of Constantinople, and commenced his long journey. He travelled about six hundred miles, until he came to Tokat, which was only two hundred and fifty miles from Constantinople. But the fatigue was beyond his endurance, and he could go no farther. And there, on the 16th of October 1812, at the age of thirty-one, he died. In less than seven years he had begun and terminated his missionary labours, leaving a character for holy enthusiasm and unquenchable zeal in the Master's service, on which Christians in all lands will love to meditate, so long as missions to the heathen shall continue to excite their interest.

 In no country in the world, and in no period in the history of Christianity, was there ever displayed such an amount of energy in the translation of the Sacred Scriptures from their originals into other tongues, as was exhibited by a handful of earnest men in Calcutta and Serampore in the first ten years of the present century. By their own industry, and that of other persons in various parts of India, who had caught from them the inspiration for the work, during this short period, portions of the Bible, chiefly of the New Testament, had been translated, and actually printed, in thirty-one Indian languages and dialects. One is amazed, and almost overwhelmed, at the stupendousness of this undertaking. It cannot be supposed that these first attempts are to be compared with the versions which have been subsequently made in these languages. But this must not diminish the intense admiration we ought to feel towards men of such boldness of design, and such astounding energy of execution. Not content with their labours in this direction, they also published a great multitude of tracts, the Serampore press alone issuing them in twenty languages, and, in addition, books for schools and colleges.

<small>700 converts baptised up to 1816.</small> Nor were the Serampore missionaries less active and successful in their more direct evangelistic labours. Up to the end of 1816 they had baptized about seven hundred native converts. Their schools had imparted Christian instruction to more than ten thousand heathen children. They had preached the gospel to the people wheresoever they could get the opportunity of doing so, and had distributed among them portions of the Scriptures and Christian tracts. Thus the moral power of Christianity was beginning to be felt and recognised; and Hindooism was already shaken, not to say confounded, by its aggressive spirit, when brought into close contact with it.

Fitful as the wind, the British Government was at times favourable to missionary enterprise in India, and at times violently opposed to it. For the most part, the Governors-General were men secretly wishing it God's speed; but they were so much in the hands of high officials who were utterly opposed to it, and saw in it only an influence for evil, if not an active cause of disord and rebellion, that occasionally they became openly hostile to it, and endeavoured to thwart the missionaries in every possible manner. In 1810 Lord Minto suffered the missionaries to open a station in Agra, and gave them a passport to proceed thither. In 1812 the Government first ordered two missionaries to be expelled the country, and then all others brought to their notice, excepting, as they always did, the brethren at Serampore. Two missionaries from the United States, the Rev. Messrs Judson (afterwards the "Apostle of Burmah") and Newell, having reached Calcutta, proceeded to the police-office, and stated to the presiding magistrate their purpose to establish a mission to the east of Bengal; at the same time presenting the passports which they had received from the Governor of Massachusetts. Presently six more missionaries arrived, three of whom were British subjects, and three American. Of the five Americans, three, including Messrs Judson and Newell, were forthwith expelled, but permission, obtained after great entreaty, was allowed them to proceed to Mauritius. The other two escaped to Bombay, having secretly left Calcutta through the connivance of the European residents, who felt outraged at the despotic course the Government was pursuing. But thither they were followed by a peremptory despatch, ordering their immediate deportation to England. Two of the three English

Violent opposition of the Government. Expulsion of missionaries.

missionaries were residing in Serampore, and the third was in the Dutch settlement of Chinsurah. The two former, together with Mr Robinson, a missionary who had been in India six years, after a long discussion, and after the Serampore brethren had exhausted every effort in trying to overcome the scruples of the Government, and to retain them, were ordered to quit the country. Mr Robinson baffled the authorities, however, by leaving for Java, where he founded a mission, on the invitation and under the express sanction of Mr, afterwards Sir Stamford, Raffles, the Governor. A second was permitted to remain, as it was shown that he could be useful in the literary work of the press. But the third, Mr Johns, in spite of all protestations, was sent home to England, at an expense to the mission of five hundred pounds. This was the last of the missionary expulsions; for the same year, 1813, on which Mr Johns was banished from India, was also the year of the new charter, which was to remove all restrictions on missionaries entering the country.

The harshness of the British Government, both in India and at home, in its pertinacious attempt to close the door of India against Protestant missions, was accomplishing more than the Government intended. Liberty-loving Englishmen, although they might have their own ideas of the prospects of missions in India, began to feel it intolerable that any portion of the British dominions should be closed to any of their own nation. From the violence which had been adopted they recoiled, under the conviction, which had been steadily strengthening in their minds, that those dominions were not the right of one class more

PROTESTANT MISSIONS IN INDIA. 89

than another, but were equally the right of all, and were equally open to all. The charter of 1793, which had enabled the local Government to withstand the missionaries, and to wage constant hostilities with them, with more or less virulence, for twenty years, was about to expire. The opportunity, therefore, was seized by all lovers of religion, and of liberty, to move the Supreme Government to an entire reversal of its policy. And they were successful. But the struggle was great; and the opposition was fierce. After a prolonged discussion in the House of Commons, sustained chiefly by Wilberforce on the one side, and retired old Indians on the other, the famous clause in the new charter, introduced by Lord Castlereagh, under pressure from without, and overpowered by the immense multitude of petitions with which every night both Houses were inundated, was carried. The clause stated that "it was the duty of this country to promote the introduction of useful knowledge, and of religious and moral improvement, in India, and that facilities be afforded by law to persons desirous of going to and remaining in India, to accomplish these benevolent designs."* The charter also provided for the establishment of an Indian bishopric, with three archdeacons for the three Presidencies, and came into effect on the 10th April 1814.

Expiration of the charter of 1793. Change of public opinion in England.

The new charter in favour of missions came into effect April 10, 1814.

The charter, in its provisions for the promotion of Christianity in India, soon began to bear fruit. By the month of June, the first bishop, Dr Middleton, with two of his archdeacons, was on his way to India. The missionary societies already existing in England had felt the depressing influence of the restrictions on

Dr Middleton the first bishop.

* Carey, Marshman, and Ward, pp. 226, 227.

their efforts to propagate the gospel in India. Some of them, as shown above, had endeavoured to evade these restrictions by the adoption of various artifices, more or less humiliating. But now that the country was virtually thrown open to Christianity, the societies began to stimulate one another by that spirit of friendly rivalry and emulation which, free from sinister and sectarian motives, has, from that time to the present, so distinguished them in their noble efforts to reclaim the Hindoos from the darkness of heathenism, and to shed upon them the light of the glorious gospel of the blessed God. The Church Missionary Society had hitherto sent no missionaries to India, although it had for several years taken part indirectly in mission work in several places in the country, which will be noticed in subsequent chapters. It had no mission in Calcutta; but a Corresponding Committee, in connection with it, had been appointed in that city as early as 1812, for the purpose of affording assistance to the mission stations about to be established in the North-Western Provinces; and even in 1807 we find the society sending a considerable sum of money to the Rev. Messrs Brown and Buchanan, and Mr Udny, to be appropriated to the translation of the Scriptures into the Eastern languages. It was not until 1815 that the society planted a mission in Calcutta. This was at Kidderpore, in the suburbs, where the site for a school had been given by a friendly Brahman. A school was formed here, and also another at Dum Dum, seven miles from Calcutta, which was superintended by the Rev. Mr Robinson, acting secretary of the Correspondence Committee, who was stationed there.

The first two missionaries sent out by the society to Bengal were the Rev. Messrs Greenwood and Schrœter, who reached Calcutta in June 1816. About the time of their arrival, the local committee purchased, in behalf of the society, an estate of seven acres of land for the mission, situated at Garden Reach, four miles below the city, and in the neighbourhood of several large villages.

Notwithstanding the almost overwhelming difficulties in its way, the London Missionary Society had been successful in introducing a missionary into Bengal in 1798, as already described in this chapter, who, unable to obtain a place for missionary labour in the Company's territories, had established himself in Chinsurah under the protection of the liberal Government of the Dutch, where the mission became firmly established. Mr Forsyth, the first missionary, was succeeded by Mr May, who devoted most of his time to the work of education. How eminently successful he was in this branch of labour may be gathered from the fact, that at the end of 1815 he had twenty schools under his charge, in which instruction was imparted to sixteen hundred and fifty-one children, of whom as many as two hundred and fifty-eight were the sons of Brahmans, a remarkable circumstance in those times. The scheme of education was highly approved by Mr Gordon Forbes, the Commissioner of Chinsurah, and was by him recommended to the Supreme Government. The Marquis of Hastings readily complied with the request of Mr Forbes, that the scheme should be aided from the imperial funds, and with great liberality appropriated a monthly grant of six hundred rupees, about sixty pounds, for the purpose.

The London Society's Mission at Chinsurah.

THE HISTORY OF

Its thirty schools with 2600 scholars.

By the aid of the grant, in the course of the next year, the schools and scholars were still further multiplied; so that at its close Mr May had under his superintendence as many as thirty schools, in which two thousand six hundred children received instruction. The Government, on hearing these rapid results, forthwith increased its grant to eight hundred rupees monthly. Mr May found himself unable to attend to this great work alone, and was soon joined by a missionary, the Rev. J. D. Pearson, sent out from England, and by Mr Hasle, a European who had resided for several years in India. The mission continued in the hands of the London Society for a period of fifty years; but although it commenced so auspiciously, and was prosecuted with much zeal, yet at the end of this long term its direct results were very meagre. One of the most diligent missionaries of this society, the Rev. Mr Mundy, laboured in Chinsurah for a great many years, but with little apparent fruit.

Mission of the London Missionary Society in Calcutta; commenced in 1816. Rev. Messrs Townley and Keith the first missionaries.

Meanwhile, the London Society, having determined on the establishment of a mission in the capital city of India, secured the services of the Rev. Henry Townley, a popular minister at Paddington in London, and of the Rev. Mr Keith, formerly a student at Gosport, who arrived in Calcutta early in September 1816, and proceeded at once to the formation of a mission in that city. They first preached in the Freemasons' Hall, but as it was too small for their congregation, the Presbyterian minister, Dr Bryce, kindly offered them the use of the temporary building he then occupied while a Presbyterian church was being erected, when not needing it himself. They also held religious services at Howrah, on the opposite side of the Hoogly; and established three schools in Calcutta for the instruction of native children. Day by day, likewise, as soon as they had obtained sufficient knowledge of Bengalee, they went among the people and conversed with them on the truths and claims of the Christian religion, distributing among them portions of the Scriptures and other Christian works. A printing press, for printing English and Bengalee books, was procured, and was first of all set up at Chinsurah, and afterwards in Calcutta, as being more favourable for this branch of labour. It was superintended by an English printer sent out by the society.

On the arrival of Bishop Middleton in Calcutta, the first measure of importance in which he was engaged was the formation of the "Calcutta Diocesan Committee in connection with the Christian Knowledge Society," which "soon entered on an active career of usefulness," says the Rev. J. Long, "in distributing Bibles, tracts, prayer-books, school-books, in hospitals, prisons, schools, and among that abandoned class, European sailors."* It also established native schools in the neighbourhood of Calcutta. In his eagerness to promote the higher education of the people, both in secular and Christian knowledge, the Bishop drew up a splendid scheme of a college, the foundation-stone of which was laid by him on the 15th of December 1820. A noble building was erected, but several years elapsed before it was finally completed. Its object was to prepare native Christian youths for the offices of preachers, catechists, and schoolmasters; to impart useful knowledge in the English language to

Formation of the Calcutta Diocesan Committee.

Bishop's College commenced in December 1820.

* Handbook of Bengal Missions, by the Rev. J. Long, p. 20.

Mahomedans and Hindoos; to translate the Scriptures, Liturgy, and moral and religious tracts; and to receive English missionaries on their first arrival in India. The college was placed under the control of the Society for the Propagation of the Gospel in Foreign Parts. From circumstances difficult of explanation this magnificent conception of Bishop Middleton, although carried out so far as the erection of the college was concerned, has been otherwise, for the most part, unfulfilled. Education in Calcutta, and in India generally, has since those days made rapid strides, but "Bishop's College" has never been really successful at any period during the fifty years that have passed away since its erection. It is no breach of charity to affirm, what everybody acknowledges, that it has been a failure. We suspect that its distance from Calcutta, and its situation on the opposite side of the Hoogly, are not, as some have imagined, the chief causes of its scanty success. In our opinion, the rules of the college need to be fundamentally remodelled, so that the institution may be brought into closer accord with the advanced thought and liberality of modern times. It would greatly rejoice, not merely the residents of Calcutta, but likewise all persons interested in the moral and religious progress of the natives of this country, were this handsome structure made to accomplish at last the great educational purpose for which it was erected.

Establishment of "The School Book Society," and of "The Calcutta School Society." In consequence of the rapid growth of schools in Calcutta and its neighbourhood, especially in the Dutch settlement at Chinsurah, where there were in 1817 thirty-six schools containing nearly three thousand scholars, a society was formed in Calcutta during this year for the express purpose of providing suitable class-books in various languages for use in them. This was "The School-Book Society," an institution which has proved an immense boon to the country, in bringing into circulation a multitude of books and tracts in many tongues, both of a secular and religious character. It is still in a most flourishing condition, and is conducted with great energy, liberality, and skill. The year following saw the establishment of "The Calcutta School Society," which was originated by the same persons. Its object was to improve indigenous schools, to found new ones, and to prepare native teachers for the work of education.

The missionaries now in Calcutta, representing the societies which had sent them forth, were actuated by a common desire to enlighten the natives by direct preaching, by schools, and by the press; and in prosecuting this desire they laboured together in the city and suburbs in harmony and love. The Church Society in 1821 established its headquarters in Mirzapore, a quarter of the city, where it purchased a suitable house with extensive grounds attached to it. Here a central school was opened, which was intended to be of the nature of a college. Other schools were possessed by the society in other parts of the city. The missionaries of the London Society erected a spacious church in Dhurrumtollah Street, and gave it the name of "Union Chapel." Of the large sum expended on it, nearly four thousand pounds were collected in India. It was dedicated to the service of God both when the foundation-stone was laid in May 1820, and when it was completed in April 1821. We

Harmony of missionaries in Calcutta.

gain some idea of the diligence and zeal of the early missionaries of this society from the fact, that at this time they occupied twenty-one stations in and about the city, in which they preached every week in Bengalee, and had charge of thirteen schools, eight for the instruction of boys, and five for the instruction of girls. The girls' schools were in the hands of a generous and noble-hearted lady, Miss Piffard, who not only personally superintended them, but defrayed all the charges connected with them.

Female education. The work of female education had already secured the earnest attention, not merely of missionaries, but also of many other persons anxious for the removal of the dense ignorance enveloping all classes of native society. The missionaries at Serampore paid great attention to this subject; and year by year increased the number of their girls' schools, until in 1826 they had twelve in connection with the mission, in which three hundred girls received a plain secular education, and were also instructed in the doctrines and precepts of Christianity. Through the exertions of the Rev. W. Ward, one of the Serampore missionaries, and other gentlemen from India then in England, the British and Foreign School Society in London was induced to render its aid in this great work, and succeeded in obtaining the services of Miss Cooke, a lady of education and piety, well acquainted with the instruction of the young, who arrived in India in the year 1821. The Calcutta School Society having on its committee at that time native gentlemen as well as Europeans, was so influenced by the presence of the former as to resist the efforts of the latter to secure Miss Cooke as its agent on her arrival in Calcutta, although she had come out recommended more especially to this society. In those days very few natives cherished the smallest desire for the education of the female sex. Hence the evil arising from the early connection of native gentlemen with the Calcutta School Society. Arrangements, however, were soon made with the Corresponding Committee of the Church Missionary Society, whereby Miss Cooke became associated with this society. She learned the colloquial Bengalee quickly, entered heartily on her work, and with such spirit that in the course of a few months, she established ten schools containing two hundred and seventy-seven girls. She displayed great tact in her intercourse with native ladies, and exercised a winning influence both over them and their children. These schools early received the aid and patronage of the Marchioness of Hastings, who, in her zeal, traversed the gullies and back streets of the city, in which some of them were situated, and thereby produced a great impression on the natives of all classes. Nor was such distinguished and disinterested patronage without its fruit. In 1823 the schools had increased to twenty-two, and the pupils to four hundred. The year following, "The Ladies' Society for Native Female Education in Calcutta and its Vicinity" was established, to which the Corresponding Committee surrendered its girls' schools. Female education had already become popular in Calcutta, and European ladies of the highest rank deemed it an honour to have their names connected with it. The schools had so far multiplied in 1826, that the Ladies' Society had thirty on their list, with an attendance of six hundred children. During this year a central school was erected, the

Labours of Miss Cooke.

The Ladies' Society for Female Education established in 1823.

G

foundation-stone being laid by Lady Amherst, wife of the Governor-General. On this occasion many native gentlemen and ladies with their daughters were present. Rajah Badinoth Roy, who had contributed twenty thousand rupees to the undertaking, "addressed Lady Amherst in terms of deep gratitude, for the obligation bestowed on his countrywomen, and congratulated her and the other ladies on the success attending their exertions."*

Meanwhile, the Serampore Mission continued its manifold enterprises with undiminished vigour. Cordially welcoming all other labourers into the mission-field, it set an example to them of lofty enthusiasm mingled with the highest ability—an example of self-denial, patience, and persistency, the magical influence of which was felt far and wide. A discussion had arisen between the Serampore brethren and the Baptist Missionary Society respecting the property of their mission, which was destined to extend over several years. I shall leave the merits of this great controversy with the simple observation, that it ended in a breach between the Serampore missionaries and the Home Society, and in the declaration of entire independence on the part of the former. The society established a mission in Calcutta with branches in the country, and with the concurrence of the Serampore brethren, relieved them of some of their outlying stations. A large chapel was erected in Calcutta in 1821, at a cost of three thousand pounds. the society succeeded in establishing a strong mission in this city. Its missionaries were men of talent and zeal; among whom the name of Dr Yates is prominent.

[margin note: Breach between the Serampore missionaries and the Home Society.]

* Hough's Christianity in India, vol. v. p. 264.

They laboured on both sides of the river. At Howrah, opposite to Calcutta, they had two chapels and a school; while in the city they held twenty services with the natives every week. They translated books, wrote commentaries and tracts in Bengalee, printed them in the press which they had established, and circulated them among the people.

Life in the Serampore Mission seems ever to have been at fever-heat. Every department of labour was carried on with the strength of a giant and the zeal of an angel. I have already repeatedly spoken of the extraordinary literary achievements of the missionaries, yet their other successes were just as wonderful. With the progress of education manifest in every direction, they conceived the idea of establishing a college, in which knowledge was to be imparted in English, Hebrew, Greek, Sanskrit, Arabic, Chinese, and a multitude of Indian languages; and lectures were to be delivered by qualified professors in mathematics, medicine, jurisprudence, ethics, and theology. And this brilliant conception they fully carried out. The Governor-General of India and the Governor of Serampore gave the scheme their sanction and support; and the King of Denmark, with his accustomed generosity, presented the missionaries with a valuable estate, the rent of which was to be appropriated to the expenses of the college, and also granted them a royal charter of incorporation, giving to the college the privilege and authority of conferring literary and honorary degrees. In addition to this central institution for affording a high-class education to the natives, numerous schools were formed in the villages and towns of the neighbourhood, containing

The Serampore College founded in 1818.

Mr John Marshman undertakes the charge of numerous schools containing 10,000 pupils.

the enormous number of ten thousand children, under the superintendence of Mr John Marshman, eldest son of the missionary of that name. Moreover, they established a savings-bank at Serampore, with the view of teaching the people habits of saving, in contradistinction to the universal custom of extravagant expenditure prevalent among all classes. Carey also founded in Calcutta an Agricultural and Horticultural Society, which has grown to be one of the great institutions of the country, and still cherishes with reverence the memory of its distinguished originator.

Carey establishes the Calcutta Agricultural and Horticultural Society.

I have now given a cursory view of the results which immediately followed on the renewal of the Company's charter in 1813, when an entirely new policy was inaugurated in regard to Christianity and education in India. In twelve years a moral revolution had been effected in many parts of the country, culminating in the metropolis. The fears of the timid, the hopes of the scoffer, had alike vanished. It was proved to demonstration that the principles of Christianity did not lead to anarchy, and that the missionaries of that religion were neither abettors of discontent nor promoters of confusion. On the contrary, it was abundantly shown, that wherever it had been introduced, the religion was an influence for good, and its advocates were messengers of peace and goodwill to men. In Calcutta and elsewhere, European society was already changed for the better; and as to the native community, it was no longer stagnant and unprogressive, but had begun to exhibit signs of life, and of recovered intelligence. New thoughts on religion, new thoughts on education, new thoughts on social manners, had entered the minds of

Changes produced by the new policy.

many, and, like good seed sown in good ground, were showing signs of coming fruit. The Brahmans were beginning to shake off their lethargy; and, writhing under the perpetual attacks made upon Hindooism, had established a periodical in 1821, in defence of their religion, entitled *The Brahmanical Magazine, or the Missionary and Brahman*. The English rulers of the country now threw their weight into the scale of progress, as it was fitting they should; and showed at last that they could be efficient rulers and good Christians at the same time.

One of the most prominent results of Christian influence working on the native mind, was seen in the effect which it produced on Rajah Ram Mohun Roy, who became famous for the zeal with which he renounced the old idolatrous creeds, and for the eagerness he displayed in searching after the truth, which indeed, though he sought after it long and with apparent sincerity, he never thoroughly embraced in its completeness and fulness. His new religious belief varied with the additional knowledge which he obtained, and the associations which he formed. At one time, it was thought that he would avow himself a Christian; and he actually did so; but the Christianity which he acknowledged was soon found to be of a spurious type. It was a Christianity without a Divine Christ, and without an atonement. He published "The Precepts of Jesus, the Guide to Happiness and Peace," setting forth the moral lessons of the gospel; and "A Defence of the Precepts of Jesus," in which he opposed the doctrine of the Trinity, and the incarnation and sacrifice of Christ. In writing this latter treatise he seems to have

<small>Ram Mohun Roy.</small>

obtained the assistance of a Baptist missionary, who, to the great distress of his colleagues, departed from the Christian faith, and joined the society established by Ram Mohun Roy, which was called " The Friendly Society." Moreover, while discarding Hindooism in almost all its phases, he presently reverted to its most ancient form, as presented in the Vedas and the first commentaries upon them, and sought in them for the unity of the Godhead. The principles of Ram Mohun Roy spread among some intelligent Bengalees, while he himself, as the champion of free thought as opposed to the despotism of idolatry and superstition, soon became famous. At the height of his celebrity he visited England, where he died, not however before he had been much courted and honoured. At his death, his followers being left to themselves, and destitute of the enthusiasm of their teacher, languished for years. But after several years, new life was imparted to the society, which, passing through a number of transitional stages, at length reached the peculiar form of development now known as the Brahmo Somaj, which has already split into two branches, at the head of one of which is the eloquent and distinguished Keshub Chunder Sen.

Missionary spirit of the English bishops, and of some of their chaplains.

In this review of missionary labour accomplished in India, it would indicate a want of truthfulness as well as great ingratitude were I not to record occasionally the conspicuous efforts of the bishops of the English Church who have been appointed to Indian sees, and of some of their chaplains, in promoting the spread of Christianity in the country. All the bishops of Calcutta, without a single exception, though some more than others, have exhibited their interest in this work; and while preferring, as was natural, their own ecclesiastical organisations, have, in a true spirit of catholicity, extended the right hand of Christian fellowship to missionaries of all denominations. They have been missionary bishops; and, in their day and generation, have been a spiritual power in the land. Who is there who does not thank God for the earnestness of Middleton, the devoutness of Heber, the practical sense and shrewdness of Wilson, the sweetness and large-heartedness of Cotton? Who is there who does not thank God likewise for the calm wisdom of David Brown, the high enthusiasm of Buchanan, the fiery zeal of Henry Martyn, the unwearied energy of Thomason, the love and labour of Corrie and of Dealtry, the sagacity and self-sacrifice of Pratt, who, while discharging faithfully their important duties as chaplains, devoted themselves assiduously to the evangelisation of the heathen around them? May successors to such apostolical men ever be found in the English Church in India!

We are now approaching a momentous period in the history of Indian missions. Hitherto, the schools established by missionaries had been chiefly of an elementary character, with the exception of the college at Serampore, and Bishop's College in Calcutta. Now a new system was to be tried, which was that of imparting the highest forms of knowledge, including sound Christian instruction, through the medium of the English language. The idea was a novel one, and in those days, when the Government and Europeans generally were still orientalised, and from prejudice and habit, as well as from a nervous dread of the too rapid advance of Christianity and enlightenment among Hindoos, violently attached, as every

Inauguration of a new educational system—Dr Duff.

one knew, to ancient usages, required no small amount of boldness, approaching to audacity, for any one to attempt to carry it out. But a man of wonderful intrepidity, equal to the emergency, had now arrived in India, possessing a dauntless will, consummate eloquence, impassioned piety, and great self-reliance. This was the Rev. Alexander Duff, who was sent out to India by the Church of Scotland as its first missionary, a society having been formed in connection with that Church at the instigation of the Rev. Dr Bryce, senior chaplain of the Scotch Kirk in Bengal. Dr Duff left England in October 1829, and after nearly an eight months' voyage, during which he was twice shipwrecked, reached Calcutta at the end of May 1830. One of the chief objects of this society was the establishment of a collegiate institution, which should confer the highest education on native youths. But the language in which they were to be instructed, as well as all details, were left to the judgment of Dr Duff. He soon ascertained that Bengalee, the language of the people, "could not possibly supply the medium for all the requisite instruction; nor, even if it had a sufficiency of adequate terms, had it any adequate supply of the necessary apparatus, in the form of appropriate books." It appeared, therefore, that, "as regarded the communication of a course of knowledge in any of its higher departments to a select portion of Hindoo youth, the choice could only lie between two, namely, the Sanskrit, or learned language of the natives, and the English, the language of their rulers. The determination of this choice," Dr Duff remarks, "involved the decision of one of the momentous practical questions connected with the ultimate evangelisation of India, a question which has ever since convulsed nearly the whole world of Orientalists and Christian philanthropists. The question was, Which shall hereafter be established as the language of learning in India? Which will prove the most effective instrument of a large, liberal, and enlightened education?"*

This question Dr Duff discusses with much ability. "It would seem at first view," he says, "that there could be no room for hesitation. All argument and authority not only preponderated in favour of the Sanskrit, but seemed exclusively to favour it. The Supreme Government had decided in its favour. Their schemes of education were essentially based on the assumption that, as a matter of course, and without the possibility of dispute, it must be the best. All learned Orientalists, whose opinion had hitherto been despotic and uncontrollable law, were enthusiastically and exclusively in its favour. And what was most silencing of all, the theory and practice of some of the oldest and most experienced missionaries in Bengal were decidedly in its favour. Against such a formidable array of authority who could have the hardihood to contend? Yet it was in the face of the highest authorities,—in the face of Government enactments, and learned dissertations, and the practices of Christian philanthropists, that the resolution was taken, after the maturest consideration, wholly to repudiate the Sanskrit and other learned languages of India as the best instruments of a superior education,—and openly and fearlessly to proclaim the English the most effective medium of Indian illumination, the best and amplest channel for speedily let-

Discussion of the merits of Sanskrit and English as the chief medium of communicating knowledge. Duff decides in favour of English.

* Duff's India and India Missions, pp. 517, 518.

ting in the full stream of European knowledge on the minds of those who by their status in society, their character and attainments, their professional occupations as teachers and preachers, were destined to influence and direct the national intellect and heart of India."*

In spite of the denunciation of distinguished Orientalists and others, who stigmatised the proposition "as the result of some new species of mental affection, to be henceforward known under the appellation of Anglomania," Dr Duff determined on carrying out his scheme in all its simplicity. Nor was he deterred by some "zealous friends of Christianity, who, looking at the Government Hindoo College and its fruits, could not help associating a superior English education with infidelity." The scheme was regarded by these timid people as an "infidelising" process, which would retard instead of promote the evangelisation of India. Without enlarging any further on the various points of this interesting controversy, which are given in full in Dr Duff's book already quoted, it is sufficient to state, that his institution was opened on the 12th July 1830. He commenced with five young men, but before the end of the first week he had more than three hundred applicants. Others daily came pouring in, and consequently, on account of the narrowness of the hall, he was obliged to make a selection from among them. The number selected amounted to two hundred and fifty, with whom the institution was actually opened. A simple yet thorough course of instruction in the English language for all the classes was laid down, and an hour was devoted daily to the

Duff opens his institution, July 12, 1830.

* Duff's India and India Missions, p. 518.

study of the Sacred Scriptures in the same language. Strict discipline was also enforced, which was at that day a novelty in native schools. The success of the institution, and of its peculiar system of tuition, soon became a common topic of conversation in Calcutta, both among Europeans and natives. With the latter it achieved a wonderful popularity, which indeed it never lost. Rigid Hindoos, however, soon began to perceive that it was making ruinous assaults upon their ancient superstitions and dogmas; and, in their anxiety for the consequences, strove to resist its influence to the utmost. Incited by them, one morning a panic seized the students, so that when the doors of the institution were opened as usual, about half-a-dozen pupils only presented themselves. But in a few days nearly all returned, the panic having done good rather than evil, and rendered the institution more popular than ever.

At the end of the first year a public examination of the scholars was held in a large hall in Calcutta, and was attended by a large number of European gentlemen and ladies, besides several natives of high rank. The result was eminently satisfactory. The novelty of the system pursued, and the effective instruction which had been evidently imparted, excited great interest in the minds of all present, and formed the subject of glowing articles in the Calcutta journals of the day. Dr Duff comments with natural pride on the important change in public sentiment which in this short time had been accomplished. "The favourable opinion so decidedly expressed by influential members of the British community, reacted powerfully on the native mind at large. The interest manifested on the part of so many magnates of the ruling caste in the progress and welfare of the pupils, poured fresh animation and vigour into all their onward endeavours after the attainment of the English language, and the incalculable wealth of knowledge, human and divine, that is treasured up in it. In a word, to the no small delight and surprise of the founder, the general impression then produced at once dragged the infant seminary from a humble obscurity, and thrust it forth into public favour and notoriety. On the reopening of the seminary, the number of new applications for admission was more than trebled. Additional accommodation was provided. Every year thereafter the character and credit of the system were progressively augmented in the estimation both of natives and Europeans. Elementary tuition was gradually advanced into an academical or collegiate course, somewhat similar to that pursued at one of our Scottish universities." Writing on the subject in 1839, nine years after the establishment of the institution, Dr Duff adds, "The five who entered on the day of its first commencement have since swollen into an average attendance of eight hundred. And the Governor-General, the fount of all power, honour, and influence, at length did homage to it by publicly proclaiming, in the face of all India, that it had produced 'unparalleled results.'"*

Importance of the method of instruction pursued.
I have devoted so much space to this subject because of its vast importance. It is impossible to form too high an estimate of the extraordinary results which have been attained during the last forty years, in the elevation and enlightenment of native society,

* Duff's India and India Missions, pp. 584, 585.

by the instrumentality of the English language. Copying the excellent example set by the eminent founder of the Scotch Institution in Calcutta, the Government of India, and many of the leading missionary societies, in their missions in the country, by degrees adopted the principle, that their colleges and superior schools should impart instruction mainly through the English language. So that at length the desire to acquire English has become wellnigh universal in the land. By the study of English an intellectual reformation is being wrought among the people. European ideas on every subject are by its means rapidly spreading in all directions. The native mind is being moulded on a new model. Although, as was to be expected, many sceptical, as well as good, principles, have found their way through English books into native society, yet incontrovertibly the good principles have immeasurably exceeded the bad, and the light which has been everywhere diffused has produced beneficent and glorious results, hardly bedimmed by the few streaks of cloud and darkness occasionally associated with it. Let it never be forgotten, that the first promoter of this magnificent enterprise was the great champion of Indian education, Dr Duff.

In addition to the extensive work of a Christian and educational character which was by this time being prosecuted in the city of Calcutta, the suburbs and neighbourhood for many miles around were receiving more or less attention from the various missionary bodies established in the capital. The Society for the Propagation of the Gospel in Foreign Parts took a prominent share of this labour. Its mission

Labours of the Propagation Society's Mission.

may be said to have been founded in Calcutta when Bishop's College was erected, which was placed in the hands of its agents. Their chief sphere of duty, however, was rather in the suburbs and surrounding district than in the city itself. They had a station at Howrah as early as 1824, and thence stretched out among the villages to the south. They also superintended several schools made over to them by the Christian Knowledge Society in 1828. Soon Tallyganj was occupied; and in 1833 other villages, such as Barripur, Khari, Bosor, Mogru Hat, and Jangira. The village of Meerpur, still further south, was taken up in 1841.

Christian work done in the outlying villages.
The London Society's missionaries had also their stations in the southern villages; and Ramakalchoke, and contiguous places, were taken under their charge in 1826, and have been held ever since. The Church Mission engaged in the same excellent work of evangelising this tract of country, and established itself in Thakarpukar in 1830. Not only in this direction were efforts made to bring the gospel within the reach of the country-people, but the villages in the north likewise were visited by the missionaries. The Serampore missionaries had early perceived the importance of village-preaching, and had by no means neglected it. In 1809 they had several stations among the villages in their district, one of the principal of which was Gandalpara, eight miles north-west of Serampore. Their schools, as already shown, were very numerous. In fact, they regarded the outlying country as a field which they were bound to cultivate to the extent of their ability.

Having described somewhat in detail the various

missions of Calcutta and the district around, including Serampore, in their establishment and first stages of development, little remains to be explained on this subject, further than to present at intervals, extending on to the present time, the progress they severally made, and the aggregate results which they attained. It would be unedifying to give an account of the yearly proceedings of each mission, especially as such proceedings are, and must necessarily be, characterised by much sameness.

It is of importance, however, to observe carefully the mental activity awakened in Calcutta and elsewhere by the influence of Christianity and education. Since the firm establishment of these institutions in the land, the natives have undergone miraculous changes in their views on many topics. It is impossible that it should be otherwise. Sound knowledge, in all its forms, is in direct opposition to superstition. It is not remarkable, therefore, but is what might à *priori* have been anticipated, that the powerful apparatus then at work in Calcutta for stimulating the intellect and arousing the moral sense of the natives, should speedily have accomplished vast results. The civilisation and religion of the West were assailing with extraordinary violence every phase of heathenism in the land—its idolatry, its mythology, its caste, its absurdities, and immoralities. All were submitted to a scathing criticism, to a merciless exposure; and at the same time a more rational system of human society and purer principles of human conduct were presented to them in a great variety of attractive lights. What wonder, therefore, that the smothered anxiety of Brahmans, and other strict

Spirit of Inquiry awakened in Calcutta.

Hindoos, for their religion, should occasionally have burst forth into general excitement!

Excitement produced by the delivery of public lectures on Christianity. One of these instances I may refer to. Four missionaries of Calcutta—namely, Archdeacon Dealtry, Dr Duff of the Scotch Kirk, and Mr Adam and Mr Hill of the London Mission—having agreed to deliver a course of public lectures on Christianity, a large number of native gentlemen, principally students, assembled to hear them. The effect produced was magical. The first lecture was delivered by Mr Hill, and was of considerable eloquence and power. "Instantly," says Dr Duff, "the report spread through the native community with the rapidity and violence of the beacon-blaze of feudalism. The whole town was literally in an uproar. Like a garrison taken by surprise, and suddenly awakened out of a long sleep, every one sprang to arms, resolved to defend himself from this unexpected attack of an inveterate foe. It is impossible to conceive or describe the wide and simultaneous sensation produced."* Two native papers were already existing in the vernacular, one the organ of the idolatrous party, the other of the purely pantheistic party. They had been recently discussing the question of Suttee, the former paper defending the horrid rite with intense fanaticism. Now, however, they unitedly directed their attention against Christianity, which was felt to be an opponent threatening the existence of both parties. Paine's works were at this time devoured by young Bengalees, who were in raptures at the possession of this armoury of arguments against Christianity. But native papers in English now sprang into existence. The first of

* Duff's India and India Missions, p. 610.

these was the *Reformer*, the organ of the fraternity of which Ram Mohun Roy was the recognised head. In politics, it was characterised by extreme violence towards the British Government. In religion, it was decidedly inimical to the prevailing idolatry, and yet not in favour of existing forms of Christianity. Two others, one in English, called the *Enquirer*, and the other in Bengalee, were conducted by men of liberal sentiment, and were the organs of the advanced educated natives. Both these levelled their attacks at Hindooism, and at the Brahmanical order, on which they dealt terrible blows. These efforts of educated Hindoos were received by the rest of the community with unbounded execration; and a strife of words was thus commenced among the two sections of natives in Calcutta, sometimes intensely heated and acrimonious, of a most important and interesting character. The liberal party, although threatened with excommunication, held fast to their principles.

<small>The reformed party oppose idolatry.</small>

The editor of the *Enquirer* was at length disowned by his family, and "as he and his friends were retiring, the infuriated populace," says Dr Duff, "broke loose upon them, and it was with some difficulty they effected their escape." Still this man was far from being a Christian, and seems then to have had no positive belief in any religion at all. The effect of this persecution, however, was to cause him to denounce Hindooism more strongly than ever. As he and his friends had been excommunicated, they determined to enter upon a crusade against idolatry, and were only restrained by judicious Europeans from adopting the most extreme measures. By this time native society in the metropolis was rent in twain on

<small>Agitation and earnestness manifest in native society.</small>

the most vital of all topics that can possibly engage the attention of man, whether blindly to follow old errors, or to search honestly after the truth with the intention of following its guidance. These signs of mental agitation were significant of the deep impression Western ideas had already made on native society. Such signs have since become visible in all the great cities of India, and have manifested themselves over extensive tracts of country. The educated classes in all directions are revolting from ancient superstitions, much to the dismay of Hindoos of the old school, who are determined, in spite of the odds against them, to fight the battle of paganism to the last. What the end will be, no one can foretell. The landmarks of ancient Brahmanical thought are being abandoned one after another, and nothing positive is taking their place except as here and there a few find a home and rest in Christianity. Mental distraction and disorder have taken the place of mental stagnation, and at present the intellectual condition of the educated classes is that of chaos and doubt.

<small>Negative character of Brahmoism.</small>

The Brahmo Somaj, which of late years has gradually developed itself out of the society instituted by Ram Mohun Roy, is negative throughout, and satisfies none of the highest aspirations of the human spirit, as it offers no clear and unambiguous propositions to the logical deductions of the human intellect. One of the two sections into which it is divided, seems to have some lingering desires towards the superstitions which it professes to have rejected; while the other will make no terms with the old enemy, but courageously avows its utter detestation of idolatrous usages of every form and colour. Yet both signally fail on the subject of a basis for religious belief, for they confessedly have no basis; and therefore we may rest perfectly sure that the Brahmo Somaj will never gain the affections of large masses of the people; and, judging from the religious history of the world in past ages, must, in the absence of all divine authority and inspiration, and of pretension to a supernatural origin and foundation, die out in the course of time, perishing from inanition and exhaustion. Even now, in the opinion of the Rev. S. Dyson, Principal of the Cathedral Mission College, connected with the Church Society, Calcutta, "the religious agitation, which resulted in the establishment of the Brahmo Somaj, is subsiding; but still," he adds, "it has left permanent marks on the face of Hindoo society. The Somaj has created institutions, and set on foot enterprises, which, if not animated by the same spirit of religious devotion as they were in their initiation, are a manifest advance upon the previous state. All the machinery of the Brahmo Somaj is well sustained; its organisation is being extended; new enterprises are being planned; and, in many respects, the spirit of reformation is progressing on all sides; but I think there is unmistakable evidence of a change in that spirit. All the recent movements have been in the direction of social and political amelioration, while the strictly religious element which, in the beginning, was the prime motive, and foremost object, seems to be falling into the background. One indication of this abatement of Brahmic fervour, as well as a practical confession of the inherent poverty of the creed, is the recent institution of classes for instruction and examination in religious

Opinion of the Rev. S. Dyson on the Brahmo movement.

philosophy. Examinations are held periodically in certain selected books, such as Tulloch's 'Theism,' Morell's 'History of Modern Philosophy,' and Hamilton's 'Metaphysics.' Of course, one likely result of this procedure will be the possession by the Brahmos of some theological and philosophical ideas."*

Conversion of Krishna Mohan Banerjea, editor of the Enquirer.

Among the converts to Christianity of the educated and influential classes in Calcutta, in those days of intellectual excitement just depicted, one was Baboo Krishna Mohan Banerjea, the intrepid editor of the *Enquirer*. A Kulin Brahman of high social position, well known and much respected throughout Calcutta, his baptism created no little stir. "What man, woman, or child in Calcutta," says Dr Duff, "had not heard of the name, and some of the doings, of Krishna Mohan Banerjea? Hence his baptism, in particular, became the theme of conversation and discussion with every group that met on the street or in the bazaar—in every snug coterie reposing under shade from the mid-day sun—in every school—and in every family circle." † This gentleman has been from that time to the present one of the noblest champions of Christianity among his fellow-countrymen. Some years after his baptism he saw it right to attach himself to the Society for the Propagation of the Gospel, and to receive ordination in the English Episcopal Church. He was at one time a distinguished professor at Bishop's College. In all the positions he has occupied in the Christian Church, he has steadily adhered to the principles of the gospel; his influence

* Report of the Cathedral Mission College for the year 1871, p. 50.
† Duff's India and India Missions, pp. 655, 656.

upon natives of all classes, especially the intellectual and well educated, has always been very great; and his conscientiousness and spirituality have made him one of the most conspicuous ornaments of the native Christian community in India. Another convert was Baboo Gopi Nath Nundy, who for many years displayed great earnestness and zeal in the service of Christ. In the mutiny of 1857 he was the pastor of a native congregation at Futtehpore, in the North-Western Provinces, in connection with the American Presbyterian Missionary Society; and in the time of danger fled with his family to Allahabad, where they fell into the hands of the rebels, and for eight days were in the greatest danger and distress. But, although exposed to insult and privation, they one and all held fast their profession, the children being animated by the steadfastness of their father.

And of Gopi Nath Nundy.

When in the year 1844 the Disruption occurred in the Church of Scotland, the missionaries of that Church in Calcutta quitted its communion, and connected themselves with the Free Church. Soon a new institution was erected; and now both the Church of Scotland and the Free Church have two noble institutions or colleges in the capital, in which upwards of seventeen hundred youths receive instruction. Both institutions have been favoured with men of the highest efficiency, men of profound learning, men of unusual mental vigour, men who have left behind them in Calcutta footprints of their labours which will not easily be effaced. The names of Dr Duff, their great founder, and of Dr Mackay, Dr Ewart, Dr Thomas Smith, and Dr Ogilvie, are indissolubly associated with

Effects of the Disruption in the Church of Scotland.

the history of that city at one of the brightest periods of its development and prosperity.

<small>Intangible nature of the indirect results of Indian missions.</small>

It is absolutely impossible to form any proper estimate of the indirect results of missions at any stage of their progress. These are, for the most part, intangible, and incapable of representation by figures. Suffice it to say, that in the great work of civilisation and general enlightenment which has been prosecuted in Calcutta, and throughout a large portion of India, during the last fifty years, by far the most efficient agency which has been employed has been that of Protestant missions. Leaving the indirect results, however, I will only speak of those which are of a direct character, and are susceptible of figuration. The following table of statistics will show what was the numerical condition of the missions in Calcutta and its neighbourhood in the year 1850 :—

NUMERICAL STATEMENT OF RESULTS OF MISSIONARY LABOUR IN CALCUTTA AND ITS ENVIRONS FOR THE YEAR 1850.

Number of Native Christian Congregations,	26
Number of Protestant Native Christians,	6410
Number of Native Communicants,	1972
Number of Ordained Native Ministers,	3
Number of Unordained Native Christian Preachers,	47
Number of Schools in the charge of Missionaries,	76
Number of Scholars in them, Male and Female,	8174

These are mainly the results of Christian missions established in 1816 and subsequently, after the termination of the old restrictive charter of the East India Company in 1813. With the exception of the Serampore Mission, and the mission of the Christian Knowledge Society in Calcutta, the work here represented extends over thirty-five years. It should be borne in mind that the missions which chiefly produced these results had to be organised in the midst of the greatest difficulties, arising from inexperience on the part of the missionaries, from coldness and sometimes contempt on the part of the Government, from scorn and derision on the part of most Europeans, and from the violent opposition, and hitherto unbroken prejudice, on the part of all classes of natives. During this period the missionaries had to feel their way to the methods of labour which they gradually selected; and, at the end of it, their missions had become compact, well arranged, and instinct with life and vigour.

In Calcutta greater attention has always been paid by missionaries to the work of education than to the preaching of the gospel. Not that the latter has really been neglected; but it has not been prosecuted to the extent of the former. Many missionaries, however, have been exclusively devoted to it, one of whom, the Rev. Mr Lacroix, of the London Mission, was considered to be one of the most eloquent and effective vernacular preachers in India. He laboured for many years in the metropolis and neighbouring villages, and could always secure a large audience by the charm of his manner and voice, and by a felicitous use of idiomatic Bengalee in enunciating his well-arranged ideas, often associated with beautiful imagery, which delighted his hearers, and sometimes attracted them to himself by a peculiar fascination. The most important, and perhaps the largest, numerical results achieved by missions in Calcutta, have, it must be acknowledged, been obtained by the agency

The Rev. A. Lacroix.

of a Christian education rather than by the direct preaching of the gospel.

Effect of the Educational Despatch of 1854. The celebrated Educational Despatch of 1854, establishing universities in India with the power of conferring degrees, gave an extraordinary impulse to education throughout the country. The desire to obtain degrees and honours has become in many places an intense passion. Education has consequently advanced in all directions; and has increased in quality as well as in extent. The eagerness to acquire a university distinction rather than the knowledge, of which it should be a genuine symbol, often causes university candidates to cram themselves with learning, instead of obtaining it gradually by steady labour and perseverance. Nevertheless, it is beyond all question that the good effected by the system immeasurably transcends the evil. When the Calcutta University was opened, the chief missionary institutions in the city became affiliated with it. Among *The London Missionary Society's Institution.* them was the Bhowanipore Institution of the London Mission, which has not been hitherto referred to. This college is situated in the suburbs of Calcutta. It was established in a rudimentary state as early as 1837, on the model of Dr Duff's Institution, and has expanded from year to year until it is now one of the great educational seminaries of the capital. The building itself is massive and imposing, and was erected in 1853, at a cost of six thousand eight hundred pounds. Six of the students have been *Superior influence of educated native Christians.* ordained to the Christian ministry since 1850. It may be stated as a general rule, that Christian converts who have received before conversion a good education in mission institutions or elsewhere, especially when there has been superadded to it a thorough study of the principles and precepts of Christianity, render far more effective service in the propagation of the gospel among their fellow-countrymen than converts of little or no education. It is on this account that the great educational work achieved by mission colleges in Calcutta has been of so much importance and assistance, in a Christian point of view, to many of the missions throughout the whole of Northern India, inasmuch as educated converts have gone from Calcutta to these missions as head-masters and superior teachers of their schools, and thus have rendered to them valuable service of a truly Christian character. This observation applies with peculiar force to the Free Church Institution, which has most generously supplied a multitude of missions in Bengal, the North-Western Provinces, the Punjab, and Oudh, with accomplished Christian men.

The following table represents the occupations of forty-eight highly-educated Christian converts of the Free Church Mission, Calcutta :—

Ordained Ministers,	8
Probationer,	1
Catechists,	10
Professors and Higher Grade Teachers,	17
Higher Grade Government Servants,	8
Assistant Surgeons and Doctors,	4
	48

Another feature of the Despatch was the appropriation of grants to non-Government schools and colleges. These grants have been of great help to many missionary institutions, not only in the capital, but also in almost every other city and important town in

Government grants to mission colleges and schools.

India. Yet their distribution has so much depended on the tentative and fickle views of Directors of Public Instruction and their inspectors, as well as on the similar views of Governors and Lieutenant-Governors, eager to do something useful and striking in the cause of education during their period of office, that missionaries have often felt themselves hampered with the grant, and their work retarded.

Female education — girls' schools and zenanas.

Of late years strenuous efforts have been made to bring education within the reach of native girls and women. Two methods have been extensively adapted to the accomplishment of this end, one that of schools, the other that of rendering instruction to native ladies assembled in the private apartments or zenanas of their own houses. The first of these has been in existence, to some extent, a good many years. The second is comparatively of recent origin. This twofold form of labour for the welfare of the female portion of the community has been established in many missions, and may be found in efficient operation in them. But it was commenced in Calcutta; which, in all educational movements in the country, has ever been conspicuous for priority in such enterprises, and for the success attending them. In addition to the very important work in this direction carried on by the various missions, four societies exist for this special department of labour, namely, the Society for Promoting Female Education in the East, the Indian Normal School and Female Instruction Society, the American Women's Union Zenana Mission, and the Baptist Ladies' Society. Where so many devoted Christian ladies are expending their time and talents in this loving enterprise, it seems invidious to speak of any by name, especially as it impairs that unostentatiousness which is the special charm of their labour. And yet I trust I may be pardoned, if I refer to two ladies, one from England, the other from America, who, by general confession, have attained to a position of eminence in this pursuit. The first is Mrs Mullens, who by her zeal and ability gave fresh life to female education in Calcutta, both in schools and zenanas. She had at one time under her own personal direction zenanas and girls' schools, containing eighty native ladies and seventy girls. But her day was short. "She had lived to enter on a sphere so long desired, to draw attention to its capabilities, to give the cause of zenana education a new and powerful impulse, to attract to it the regard of willing friends and coadjutors, to secure for it henceforth a fixed place among missionary agencies in India; and then, ripened in character, most consecrated in labour, purified by recent suffering, suddenly she was called from the toils of earth to the joyous rest of the 'better country.'"*

[margin: Labours of Mrs Mullens.]

The other is Miss Brittan, a lady of great tenacity of purpose, of much skill in organisation, and of wonderful energy and persistency. She is at the head of an establishment consisting of nineteen foreign and East Indian ladies, and fifty-three native Christian fellow-helpers, who have under their charge in Calcutta and its suburbs a normal school of thirty young Christian women training as teachers, twenty-one girls' schools with seven hundred and ninety-four scholars, an orphanage of twenty-one girls, and one hundred and fifty zenanas. These are the statistics for the year 1871, since which time the numbers have

[margin: And of Miss Brittan.]

* Ten Years' Missionary Labour in India, p. 147.

increased. The native Christian women, says Miss Brittan, "visit each house every day, and give all the secular teaching. The lady missionaries follow, visiting every house once a week, examining into the lessons of the whole week, and explaining them thoroughly, and giving a good Bible lesson. By this means the native teacher does all the first teaching of rudiments, which takes so much time; and the lady is enabled then to give her whole time to that which will be far more profitable."*

Her sentiments on the influence of religious teaching in zenanas.

On the subject of the influence of religious teaching on the women and girls secluded in the zenanas, Miss Brittan observes that it is hard to get at their true feelings upon the matter. "Yet," she says, "one thing is certain—a great stride has been made during the last ten years. Among the young women you do not find one really bigoted Hindoo, where ten years ago you found a hundred. Their faith in their own religion is very much shaken; they have many doubts; and now laugh at many of the things they used formerly to respect and admire. When I think of them, I am constantly reminded of Ezekiel's vision of the dry bones. Ten years ago they were dry, withered, dead, utterly dead. Now there is a shaking, and a very great shaking, among these dry bones; and if, like the prophet, we only have patience to wait the Lord's will, I believe we shall yet see them, gradually and slowly, but surely, step by step, being prepared, till at last, when the breath from the Lord shall blow on them, they will suddenly arise a great army. Here and there, thank God, we have been permitted to

* Report of the Missionary Conference at Allahabad: Paper by Miss Brittan on Zenana Missions in Calcutta, p. 161.

see one and another feeling the first touch of that mighty though gentle wind, and awaking, and trying to stand on their feet—and some who already have enrolled themselves as soldiers in that great army that shall be. But with the most, it is merely as yet the shaking of the dry bones. Still, we do thank God for this; anything is better than the stagnation of death. Everywhere now the strong desire among all the native gentlemen is for the education of their women. They say it is the hope of India; and many of the young men refuse to marry girls that cannot read. Let female education progress the next twenty years as it has the last ten, and I believe the missionaries will find, instead of here and there a stray convert, they will come as 'doves flock to their windows,' a great army."*

The following summary will show the nature and extent of the work of female education carried on by missionary agencies in this city and neighbourhood during the year 1871:—

STATISTICS OF FEMALE EDUCATION IN CONNECTION WITH THE MISSIONS IN CALCUTTA AND ITS ENVIRONS FOR YEAR 1871.

Number of Girls' Schools, ... 56
Number of Female Pupils, ... 2795
Number of Zenanas under Visitation, . . . 487
Number of Normal Schools for the Training of
    Christian Women, ... 3
Number of Young Women in them, . . . 85
Number of Girls in Orphanages, ... 221

A great improvement has been lately effected in the working of schools for the instruction of native

* Report of the Missionary Conference at Allahabad: Paper by Miss Brittan on Zenana Missions in Calcutta, pp. 162, 163.

Christian girls, the daughters of converts; and a spirit of independence has been evoked, contrasting in a striking manner with the former condition of the native community. This may be illustrated by the changes in female education which have been effected in the London Society's Mission. The Rev. J. E. Payne, in a communication to the writer, remarks that "the Christian girls' school has altered in character. In place of from sixty or seventy boarders, who were fed, clothed, educated, and provided with husbands, when husbands could be got for them, the number of boarders has been reduced to about a dozen; and the daughters of Christians have commenced to pay from four to ten annas (from sixpence to one shilling and threepence) a month for their education as day scholars; and buy their own books too. All matters connected with food, clothing, lodging, and things matrimonial, now rest with the parents and guardians. That this is now possible, shows that the Bengalee Christian community of Bhowanipore has grown from childhood to maturity in social matters during the last twenty years." In regard to the management of non-Christian female schools, likewise, Mr Payne makes some interesting observations. "The three Hindoo girls' schools have all been commenced during this period. There were bazaar schools before, to which the lowest class of girls were induced to come daily by an adequate supply of sweetmeats, and periodical presents of clothing. But in 1856 the first girls' school of respectable Hindoo girls was established, by means of a young Hindoo widow, whose father, a native doctor, had taught her to read. The girls that now attend these schools are from the middle and well-to-do classes. They leave school at from ten to thirteen years of age."

The mission press, established by the London Missionary Society in Calcutta, was afterwards abandoned. But its place has been well supplied by that founded by Mr W. H. Pearce, and now in the possession of the Baptist Society. This press has been conducted on a very extensive scale, and with distinguished ability, under the superintendence, first of the Rev. J. Thomas, and subsequently of the Rev. C. B. Lewis; and has brought into circulation a great multitude of books of a religious and secular character, not merely in English but also in many other languages. *The Baptist Mission press*

For many years the Church Missionary Society in Calcutta remained contented with the numerous lower class schools of which it had charge. Nor while we express our admiration at the noble mission colleges in Calcutta, is it at all necessary to speak lightly, much less disparagingly, of the great and important work accomplished in inferior schools. The Rev. J. Long, a missionary of varied talents, who delighted in antiquarian and historical researches, collected the proverbs prevalent in Bengal, and read with avidity all kinds of native literature, had charge of many excellent village schools in connection with the Church Mission in the metropolis, which, from personal observation of some of them, were, I know, while under his care, in a condition of high efficiency. One peculiar feature of these schools is, that knowledge is imparted to the pupils, for the most part, orally, and with signal success. But the mission rightly thought that with the advancement of education in Calcutta, it ought to have an institution of its own equal to the *The Rev. J. Long.*

128   THE HISTORY OF

Establishment of the Cathedral College by the Church Missionary Society.

best then existing there. And consequently, in the year 1865, it established the Cathedral College, which has no school department, but is purely a college, and only admits students who have passed the matriculation examination of the University of Calcutta. The missionary professors in the college are, it is needless to say, men of ripe scholarship in their various departments. The college already occupies a most honourable position in Calcutta, and has been very successful in passing its students at the higher examinations in the university.

The table below will show the number of graduates and under-graduates who have passed their examinations at the Calcutta University in connection with the mission institutions of Calcutta and its neighbourhood, during ten years, namely, from 1862 to 1871.

TABLE SHOWING THE NUMBER OF GRADUATES AND UNDER-GRADUATES OF MISSION SCHOOLS AND COLLEGES IN CALCUTTA AND ITS ENVIRONS, FROM 1862 TO 1871.

Number of Masters of Arts,	18
Number of Bachelors of Laws,	6
Number of Bachelors of Arts,	134
Number of Students who have passed the First Arts' Examination,	340
Number of Matriculated Students,	659

Fully one-half of these results have been achieved by two institutions, one belonging to the Free Church of Scotland, the other to the Scotch Kirk.

Between 1850 and 1871 not only was great progress made by the missions in Calcutta in the number of youths instructed, but also in the quality of the education imparted to them. By comparing the following table with that given for 1850, it will be seen what the actual numerical progress was.

STATISTICS OF EDUCATION IN CONNECTION WITH THE MISSIONS IN
CALCUTTA AND ITS ENVIRONS FOR THE YEAR 1871.

Number of Colleges and Schools, ... 199
Number of Scholars in them, Male and Female, . 12,744
Of these, the Number of Colleges and Schools for Males, 140
Number of Male Pupils, ... 9,864
Number of Girls' Schools, ... 59
Number of Female Pupils, ... 2,880

If the statistics of the direct results of missionary labour be added to this statement, a fair idea will be gained both of the moral and intellectual influence which Protestant missions were exerting over Calcutta and its neighbourhood in the year 1871; and by comparing these aggregate statistics with those given for 1850, it will be manifest at a glance what was the amount of progress made between the two periods.

STATISTICS OF DIRECT RESULTS OF MISSIONARY LABOUR IN
CALCUTTA AND ITS ENVIRONS FOR THE YEAR 1871.

Number of Native Christian Congregations, . . 72
Number of Protestant Native Christians, . . . 10,071
Number of Native Communicants, ... 3,653
Number of Ordained Native Ministers, . . . 15
Number of Unordained or Lay Preachers, . . 102
Number of Native Christian Teachers, Male and Female, 219

Much might be written on the internal relations of the native Christian Church of Calcutta, on its increasing vigour and earnestness, on the gradual development in its midst of a spirit of independence and self-reliance, and on its real and manifest progress in piety and enlightenment. But this forms a distinct subject of great interest and moment, yet into which the writer conceives it is not necessary for him to

Internal progress in native churches. Example of the Bhowanipore native church.

enter. He cannot refrain from recording, however, the earnest and, in the main, successful efforts which some of the native Christian congregations have been making of late years towards self-support. This may be illustrated by the Bhowanipore native church of the London Society. In 1861 the members of this church selected a native pastor, the Rev. Surjoo Koomar, and contributed nine hundred rupees, or ninety pounds, towards his support and the general expenses of their community. Two years afterwards they subscribed fifty rupees, or five pounds, a month of the pastor's salary; and when, in 1868, he became Bengalee editor of the Calcutta Tract and Book Society, the contributions of his flock, united with the proceeds derived from his literary labours, were entirely sufficient for his support. Moreover, a new building was erected by the Christians for public worship in 1867, and was paid for chiefly by themselves.

Also of six Baptist churches, to the south of Calcutta.
The native churches of the Baptist Society, to the south of Calcutta, have become almost independent. "There are now six churches having their own pastors, and managing their own affairs in all matters relating to their organisation as churches of Christ. Five of the pastors were receiving, three years ago, an allowance of eight rupees (sixteen shillings) a month from the society. This allowance has been reduced year by year, so that each pastor only receives five rupees from the society, with the understanding that in a few years more the society will cease altogether from sustaining the pastors." This undoubtedly is progress of the most satisfactory character.

Such, then, is what the Calcutta missionaries have

to show as the fruit of their varied labours. Some one may ask, "Is the result worth the means employed to obtain it?" meaning thereby the expenditure of large sums of money, and the earnest and unwearied devotion of thirty-six missionaries. In reply, it may be affirmed that, intellectually, the missionary agency in the metropolis and its vicinity, is, to say the least, accomplishing as much, in the general enlightenment of the people, as all other agencies of an educational character combined, whether in connection with, or separate from, the Government. Morally and religiously, in changing for the better the tone of native society, in scattering broadcast among all classes of the community the purest principles of human life and conduct, both as to the relations subsisting between man and man, and between man and his Maker, in breaking the bonds of superstition, in destroying idolatry and other erroneous conceptions of the Deity, in exciting the natives to seek after virtue and truth, they have exerted an influence far and wide which but for them would never have been felt, have already effected moral changes which but for them would never have been produced, have awakened a desire for knowledge among the wives and daughters of Bengalees which but for them would never have been experienced, and have inspired the breasts of multitudes with the ambition to become more honest, and more like God Himself, which but for them would have remained base and grovelling for ever. To sneer at missionaries is pitiful; but to ignore the sublime results of their labours is monstrous. Let their legion detractors show what they have done for the public welfare,

Results, religiously and socially, of missions in Calcutta.

before they resort to the miserable habit, which they have acquired, of shutting their eyes to the wonderful work of social reformation already accomplished through the instrumentality of missionaries, a habit which is doubtless blended with a sense of shame and dissatisfaction with themselves at not having taken an adequate part in it.

CHAPTER III.

MISSIONS IN BENGAL, EXCLUDING CALCUTTA AND ITS VICINITY.

THE aggressive spirit of Christianity has never been more strongly exhibited than in its conflict with the various forms of Hindooism in India during the present century. It has had a wide field to exercise itself upon, and it has entered upon the struggle with its numberless foes with pertinacious eagerness. It has combated superstition in its wildest forms. It has attacked Brahmanism in its famous seats of learning. It has contended with bloody rites, with foolish customs, with caste prejudices. It has followed idolatry to its most sacred spots. The silver sound of the gospel has been heard wherever the pundit has chanted his Shastras, and the priest has blown his shell. Within these seventy years the hills and valleys of India have been made to echo and re-echo with the praises of Christ the Son of God and Saviour of the world. Under the persistent assaults of Christianity, continued with sustained vigour from year to year, Hindooism has become fairly wearied; and as the range of its attacks and the directness and potency of its strokes increase, the ancient systems of paganism are in all directions showing signs of feebleness and decay. At one time strenuous resistance was shown,

Conflict of Christianity with Hindooism.

and controversy raged throughout the land. But that day is past. Idolatry is not an active foe; and any unusual energy which it may occasionally put forth, is necessarily impulsive and transitory. Christianity is looked upon as a young giant with whom it is dangerous to contend, and whom it is best to leave alone.

I have traced the spread of Christianity in Southern India through the last century, and also in Calcutta and its neighbourhood, from its introduction to the present time. I have now to show particularly how it advanced from province to province, and from country to country, until the great tidal wave reached from the eastern to the western shore, and penetrated to the remotest corners of the land. And first I shall endeavour to give a picture of the work accomplished in Bengal and the outlying provinces of Orissa, Assam, and Behar, excluding Calcutta and its precincts already described.

Spite of the obstacles in the way which would have daunted men of feebler calibre, the Baptist missionaries, soon after their arrival in India in 1793, finding it difficult to carry out their project in Calcutta, determined on its prosecution in the outlying districts of Bengal. Nor were they unsuccessful. Carey's scheme of evangelising the swamps of the Soondarbuns was fortunately of short duration. Yet he risked his life in the fruitless enterprise, because of his unquenchable eagerness to commence his great undertaking. It was to him, therefore, no vagary that he did this in the most unpromising and deadly spot in all India. To him, consumed with enthusiasm, it was everything that he had made a beginning. He soon, however, as already shown in the previous chapter, quitted the region of pestilence for the more congenial climate of Malda, to which district he had been invited by Mr Udny, then in charge of the East India Company's factory there. Carey became the manager of the indigo-factory of Mudnabutty, thirty miles distant from the chief station; and his colleague, Mr Thomas, had a similar post in another factory at Moypauldiggy, seventeen miles farther on. Here, while attending to their secular duties, they really began their missionary labours. Carey exhibited the wonderful zeal with which he was animated, and devised many schemes for the spiritual good of the people. But although much was accomplished, yet the two stations, after some years, were abandoned. However, the sphere of operations of the missionaries was extensive. They made frequent excursions among about one hundred villages, "going from place to place to publish the gospel." In September 1796 they were joined by the Rev. John Fountain, who reported favourably of what he saw. "The education of native youth was well begun; the translation of the New Testament was nearly completed; and they had conciliated the regard of the natives who attended their public worship."

<small>Labours of Carey and Thomas in the district of Malda.</small>

The missionaries cast their eyes towards the hilly country to the north, inhabited by strange tribes, and to Tibet lying beyond; and in 1797 paid a visit to Bhutan, and expounded the truths of the gospel to the Buddhists of that region. In the same year a mission was established under their auspices in the city of Dinagepore, through the instrumentality of Mr Fernandez, a gentleman of Portuguese descent, whose influence was great in the neighbourhood. He erected a building for Christian worship, and at the dedicatory

<small>Mission established in Dinagepore.</small>

services many natives of respectability were present. The history of the mission is one of vicissitudes. Of late years a steady and rapid progress is manifest in its numbers. In 1850 it had sixty-eight Christians; but in 1861 it had one hundred and thirty-five; and in 1871 one hundred and ninety-seven, with sixty-one communicants. At that date the church was under the charge of a native preacher. The idea of forming a mission in the Bhutan country was revived a few years after the visit above alluded to. From 1809 to 1811 vigorous efforts were made to acquire a permanent footing there, and a settlement at Burbari, on the borders, was actually made. A night attack, however, on the mission by an armed band of some sixty bandits, in which two natives were killed, a third was mortally wounded, the missionaries, Messrs Robinson and Cornish, were seriously injured, and a large amount of property was taken away, led to its being broken up. Mr Robinson was not deterred from making another attempt to establish a mission in Bhutan; but finally relinquished the scheme, which, so far as I am aware, has never been renewed since.

And at Jessore.

In the year 1802, on the invitation of a Mahomedan, Mr Marshman of the Serampore Mission paid a visit to Jessore. Such was the eagerness displayed by the people of some of the villages to become acquainted with Christian truth, that a native Christian was sent to Suksagar, on the borders of the Jessore district, for the purpose of imparting to them the instruction they desired. "He experienced the most determined opposition from the Brahmans, who were resolved to prevent his settlement among them; but a wealthy and liberal-minded Roman Catholic gentleman, Mr

Joseph Barrotto, one of the most eminent merchants in Calcutta, accommodated him with a piece of ground near his own princely residence, and offered him all the assistance in his power."* This may be regarded as the first stage in those interesting missionary labours which have been carried on in Jessore. At the end of the following year, when Mr Marshman again visited the district, while preaching in the market-place of Jessore, the chief city of the district, he was suddenly summoned into the presence of the English judge, at the instigation of some influential Brahmans, and was severely lectured on the impropriety of the course he was adopting. On receiving a quiet statement from Mr Marshman of the object he had in view, the judge cooled down, and inviting the stranger to dinner, drank success to his enterprise. The mission at Jessore does not seem to have been thoroughly established by the Baptist missionaries, however, until the year 1804; and for years after this, the suspicious attitude of the Government kept it in a state of depression. It has now upwards of five hundred Christians inhabiting thirteen villages, together with thirty-nine schools, in which thirteen hundred and eight native children are instructed. In addition to the large Baptist Mission, there is also a small one of the English Episcopal Church.

I have already spoken of the brief but eminent services performed by Henry Martyn in India. His career as a missionary properly commenced at Dinapore in Behar, to which station he was appointed as chaplain in 1806. Near to this military station is the large Mahomedan city of Patna, where fanaticism has

Henry Martyn commences missions in Dinapore and Patna.

---

* Carey, Marshman, and Ward, pp. 81, 82.

ever been rampant. In both places, as well as elsewhere in the neighbourhood, Martyn established Christian schools, which were under his immediate superintendence. He also preached to the natives in Hindustani. In less than two years and a half he was removed to Cawnpore, not, however, until he had exerted a sweet Christian influence upon the people with whom he had held intercourse. Thus, in the simplest manner, were laid the foundations of missions in Behar.

Chittagong occupied in 1812. The first missionary killed by a Mug.

Chittagong, to the east of Bengal, in Arracan, was occupied as a mission station in 1812. The missionary, the Rev. Mr De Bruyn, laboured mostly "among a people of the Mug tribe, who, in manners, language, and habits, resembled the Burmans."* A pupil in one of his schools having been punished for some offence, stabbed the missionary in revenge. The mission, however, has continued to the present moment, and is now in the hands of the Baptist Missionary Society. The same society has an important station in the great manufacturing city of Dacca, and in villages in the neighbourhood, commenced in 1816. One of the most flourishing missions in India of this distinguished society is situated at Barisal, in the Backergunj district, which is separated from the district of Jessore by one of the chief mouths of the Ganges. The Serampore missionaries established a school there in 1829, in which instruction was imparted in English. From this small beginning a very prosperous and extensive mission has been gradually elaborated. At one time a strong desire to become Christians manifested itself among a certain

Missions in Dacca and Barisal.

---

* Christianity in India, vol. iv. p. 411.

class of the people, the chief of whom was a Mahaut, or head of a Hindoo monastery. But undue haste was shown in their baptism, one missionary alone having baptized nearly three hundred adults in two years. The consequence was, that many of the converts afterwards relapsed to their old religion, to the disgrace of themselves and the dishonour of Christianity. Nevertheless, the work, though faulty, was in many respects good and true. The influence of the Rev. Messrs Page and Sale, two prudent and earnest missionaries, has been of great service in consolidating the native Christian communities, in developing their Christian principles, and in establishing them in the faith. The growth of the mission has been of late years exceedingly satisfactory. There were in 1871 three thousand six hundred and twenty-two converts occupying thirty-two villages, and separated into twenty-nine congregations. Of these, eight hundred and sixty-six were communicants. In the present year (1873), however, the mission has four thousand converts, and one thousand communicants, a large proportion, proving the high state of religious feeling existing among them. The mission sustains upwards of forty native preachers and teachers, only one of whom, however, is ordained. "Its present position," writes the Rev. Dr Mullens in 1862, "is the result of quiet, steady labour on a favourable soil. No special causes of increase have been at work. The faithful preaching of evangelical truth; the personal conversation of missionaries; the labours of consistent native catechists; the steady maintenance of a kind but strict discipline; the observance and employment of all public ordinances:

these alone have been the instrumentalities employed on this interesting field of labour."* The Society for the Propagation of the Gospel has also a very useful mission in the same city, numbering about five hundred Christians, who are divided into seven congregations, and have seven native preachers attached to them.

<small>The Church Society's Mission in Burdwan. Weitbrecht and Linke.</small>

The Church Missionary Society has taken a prominent part in diffusing the truths of the Christian religion in Bengal. As early as 1816 it laid the foundations of a mission in Burdwan, in which men of great devotedness, such as the Rev. J. Weitbrecht and the Rev. J. Linke, whose names have become known far beyond their own neighbourhood, and many others like-minded, have laboured. In 1834 the Christian community suffered from a terrible calamity, in the bursting of the embankment of the Damuda river, flowing by Burdwan, whereby all their houses were swept away. The entire district of Burdwan has a population of upwards of a million, and contains more than six thousand villages. It is particularly favourable for direct missionary work in the way of preaching and personal intercourse with the people; and many of these villages have been frequently visited by missionaries and their native brethren, so that in this manner they have become more or less acquainted with the leading truths of the gospel. And here it may be remarked that a similar work of evangelisation has been accomplished over extensive tracts of country throughout the whole of Northern India. In most of the larger missions,

<small>The gospel preached throughout large portions of the country.</small>

---

* Ten Years' Missionary Labour in India, by the Rev. Dr Mullens, pp. 55, 56.

missionaries have divided their labours, some being devoted chiefly to education, while others have given their main strength to preaching the Word daily to all classes of natives. The result is that the gospel has been made known far and wide, and a large number of both Hindoos and Mahomedans have become accustomed to a consideration of its claims.

The most important mission of this society in Bengal is that found at Krishnagar, in the district of Nuddea. In the year 1804 we hear of the gospel having been preached to the people by Mr Chamberlain; but no mission was established there till 1831. In the following year the Rev. Mr Deer took up his residence there. He was a man of great zeal and of many labours, not easily affected by disappointments or thwarted by difficulties. Numerous schools were planted in various places, and the truths of Christianity were expounded from village to village. The method itself was very simple, although the results have been great. At first a few persons only in the year were baptized; and indeed the opposition of friends and kindred was so strong, that only those who had powerful convictions and genuine faith could resist it. A singular sect was existing in the neighbourhood, called Karta Bhoja, consisting of a blending of Hindooism with Mahomedanism. While, on the one hand, professedly abandoning Hindooism, its members observed many of its ceremonies; yet, on the other, they conformed to Islamism, held religious services on a Friday, ignored caste, and ate together without distinction. One of this sect came to the missionaries as an inquirer; but his clan persecuted him savagely, and poisoned his food, so that his organs of speech

Method pursued in establishing the Krishnagar Mission.

were curiously affected, and he was unable to move his tongue for four days. In the next year, however, thirty of the sect, in spite of the most violent persecution that was raised against them, embraced Christianity. Two years subsequently, the head men of ten villages of the Karta Bhojas presented themselves for Christian instruction, and after a time were baptized. Respecting these, Archdeacon Dealtry, afterwards Bishop of Madras, gives the following interesting information: "They straightway confessed Christ before the heathen, and established public worship in the villages. This created great excitement and curiosity among their relatives and connections. They attended the worship to know what it all meant. More violent opposition and persecution was the result; and every one that attended the worship was considered a Christian. In one village the excitement was so great, that when the missionary began to preach, they anxiously inquired, 'What, has the pestilence reached us also?' An inquirer had two brothers who fled from their homes for fear of catching the infection. The man before whose house the preacher stood was turned out by the villagers, because they thought he had been the means of bringing the missionaries to the village. But, as is usual in persecutions, the truth spread, inquirers multiplied, and the Word of God prevailed."*

Bishop Dealtry's narrative.

The same excellent authority, in his "Brief Account of the Krishnagar Mission," states that "about the end of the year 1838 a remarkable movement took place in favour of Christianity among the natives, on the east side of the river Jellinghi, when, within the

* Handbook of Bengal Missions, by the Rev. J. Long, pp. 181, 182.

course of a few months, not less than six hundred families, comprising about three thousand souls, came forward to embrace the gospel."* On occasion of the Bishop of Calcutta visiting Krishnagar the following year, nine hundred persons were at one time admitted into the Christian Church by baptism. During this year it was ascertained, after complete investigation, that as many as fifty-five villages were more or less affected by Christianity. It is very remarkable that the good work, which bore such abundant fruit at the outset, should have been suspended for a number of years afterwards, and that, moreover, many of the converts should have continued to manifest a very low standard of Christian principle. At one time the hope was cherished, that considering the rapidity with which the original conversions had been effected, a large part of all that tract of country would speedily be evangelised. It is not my purpose to discuss this important topic, especially as it would demand an intimate acquaintance with all the circumstances which led to hundreds and thousands of Hindoos and Mahomedans suddenly avowing their belief in Christianity. The event is of great moment in the history of missions in India; and should serve as a warning not to be too sanguine from great and speedy success, inasmuch as such success may, from unforeseen causes, be arrested, and the fruit that looked so bright and fair never come to maturity.

Baptism of 900 persons in the presence of the Bishop of Calcutta.

Slow progress of late years.

The Krishnagar Mission numbered, in 1850, four thousand four hundred and seventeen Christians. Since then they have increased by four hundred and fifty-three; and at the end of 1871 there were four

Present condition.

* Handbook of Bengal Missions, by the Rev. J. Long, p. 184.

thousand eight hundred and seventy converts, scattered over forty-eight villages, and forming forty-one separate congregations. They possessed twenty-three native preachers, and sixty Christian teachers. They had forty-seven schools attended by two thousand one hundred and sixty-seven children. With proper oversight and extended education we may predict a prosperous future for this mission. And, in answer to earnest prayer, we may hope, and believe, that the spiritual life of former years, already beginning to manifest itself, will return in fulness and power.

The London Society's missions at Chinsurah and Culnah are surrendered to the Free Church of Scotland and Church Missionary Societies.

The London Society's Mission, with its numerous schools, in the old Dutch settlement of Chinsurah, passed in 1849 into the hands of the Free Church of Scotland, which also occupies Mohanad and Bansbaria, other important stations in the neighbourhood, all which, it is right to add, are at the present time under the control of two native ordained pastors. The same society had a station formerly in the city of Culnah, twenty miles farther north. This was surrendered to the Church Society, on its establishing a mission there under the superintendence of the Rev. Mr Deer, who, before this, was at Burdwan, and afterwards, as already shown, entered the Krishnagar Mission. In 1826 the schools had so increased that there were more than one thousand boys under instruction, exclusive of three girls' schools. Much important work was quietly done by the mission, especially by the instrumentality of schools, from year to year. In 1842 the mission was made over to the Church of Scotland; and on the Disruption, to the Free Church, which still retains it.

In the district of Moorshedabad the London Society

has an old mission in the city of Berhampore, estab- [Mission at Berhampore.] lished just fifty years ago. Its course has been a steady one. Although unable to show any brilliant results, it has exerted a powerful influence on the public mind, which it has greatly elevated and improved, both by education and preaching. The Government College at Moorshedabad, the abode of the Nawab Nazim of Bengal, no doubt has contributed greatly to the increased enlightenment of the people; yet the chief transforming influence is due far more to the moral teaching of the mission, in its constant enunciation and enforcement of the highest ethical principles, in contact with the natives of all classes, both in the cities and country villages, than to the training, for the most part purely intellectual, of the Government institutions. The Christians of the mission, one hundred and twenty-two in number, are chiefly employed in the cultivation of the soil. In the [At Rampore Bauleah, Rev. Bihari Lal Singh.] neighbouring district of Rajshye, across the river Ganges, is a small but flourishing mission newly established at Rampore Bauleah, under the auspices of the English Presbyterian Missionary Society. It is in charge of the Rev. Bihari Lal Singh, formerly of the Free Church, Calcutta, a man of high reputation for ability and zeal, and for his entire consecration to the great work in which he is engaged.

It is needless to refer to the numerous small stations of various societies, in addition to the larger and more important ones scattered over Bengal, already described, except to remark that each exercises its share of influence in the production of the aggregate result. [The Welsh Calvinistic Methodist missions in the hilly districts.] I must, however, direct special attention to the labours of the Welsh Calvinistic Methodists in the hilly districts of Sylhet, Cherrapunji, Laitkynseu, and Jiwaipunji, who are diligently occupied in becoming acquainted with, and instructing, the interesting aboriginal tribes of those regions, in baptizing converts, and in forming them into Christian churches. The language of the Khasia mountaineers was, previously to the coming of the missionaries, unwritten, and therefore without a literature. They have reduced it to writing, have compiled a grammar and a dictionary, and have translated several books into the language. The same kind of work is also being performed among the Garos of Cooch Behar by the American Baptist Missionary Union; and the Church of Scotland and the English Baptist Society both have stations at Darjeeling, the sanatarium of Bengal. Translations of portions of the Bible have been made, and grammars, vocabularies, and educational books have been written in some of these hill dialects, while schools have been established for the instruction of the young. In this way both secular and religious knowledge is being conveyed to tribes which until recently were plunged in darkness and ignorance. Here I must not omit to mention the self-denying labours of the Rev. W. Start, a clergyman of the Church of England, and a gentleman of fortune. He has at various times brought to India at his own expense no less than twenty missionaries. He commenced a mission among the Lepchas, and with the assistance of the Rev. W. Niebel, translated the Gospels into the Lepcha language, and published it with his own means. He has also translated a portion of the Scriptures into Nepalese. His missionaries have connected themselves with several societies, and many of them have been most useful and successful. The Rev. Mr Page, of the English Baptist Society, has been a zealous labourer among the Lepchas, by whom he is greatly loved and respected. He has erected a neat little church for them at Darjeeling. The Rev. Mr Macfarlane, of the Scotch Kirk, has paid much attention to their instruction, and has established schools for the education of their children both at Darjeeling and at other places in the neighbourhood.

<small>The Lepchas.</small>

Assam lies to the north-east of the Khasia hills, is about five hundred miles in length, and is divided into two portions by the Brahmaputra river. It is a most fruitful country, producing tea, sugar, rice, indigo, cotton, silk, lac, indiarubber, gold, coal, petroleum, and many other things. The inhabitants are a mixed race; but the religion is Hindooism. The genuine Assamese is a man of sluggish intellect, and is destitute of the vivacity and acuteness which are seen so strikingly in the Bengalee. In 1836 the American Baptist Union commenced its mission among this people. A sad catastrophe attended some of the first missionaries on their voyage up the Brahmaputra to Assam. One of them, the Rev. M. Bronson, being taken ill of cholera, his colleague, the Rev. J. Thomas, hastened in a small boat to procure medical assistance. He had come within sight of the new mission, when two trees fell together from the loosened soil of the bank, crushing the boat and drowning the missionary. The missionaries have laboured among the Garo, Kanari, Michi, Naga, Cachari, and other tribes of Assam. They have at present nearly three hundred converts. At Sibsaugor the mission issues a monthly

<small>Mission of the American Baptist Union among the Assamese and hill tribes.</small>

paper in the Assamese language, and has also printed in the same tongue a dictionary, the New Testament, parts of the Old, a hymn-book, and other works. The missions among the Nagas and Mikers are superintended from this station. Several men of the Garo tribe have proved most effective preachers. But other missionaries have also laboured among the Assamese. The Society for the Propagation of the Gospel has had a station at Tezpore since 1850. Forty schools have been established, and much labour has been expended in this and in other Christian efforts. The natives are intensely ignorant, and even many of the Brahmans are unable to read. There are already nine separate Christian communities among them, which are spread over twenty-eight villages. These are ministered to and taught by five missionaries, fourteen native preachers, and sixteen Christian teachers.

Not only Bengal Proper, but also the outlying provinces, within the jurisdiction of the Bengal Government, on all sides, are step by step being reached by Christianity. I have already shown the truth of this statement in regard to several of these provinces; but not in regard to all, or even the most important. Orissa, on the south, connecting Bengal with the Madras Presidency; Behar, on the west, connecting Bengal with the North-Western Provinces; Chota Nagpore and the Santal country, inhabited chiefly by aboriginal tribes; are all ramified by Christian missions with their separate elaborate organisations; for each mission in India accomplishes its work by various methods and a multiplicity of instruments, which in their combination exert, so to speak, a massive power, and produce a vast and many-sided effect upon the natives brought within its reach. The aboriginal tribes just mentioned have undergone an astonishing change under the influence of Christianity of late years, and will form the subject of the succeeding chapter. There remain the two provinces of Orissa and Behar.

The province of Orissa has its separate language, but its inhabitants are, for the most part, Hindoos, and observe their religion. Indeed, this country boasts of being one of the most ancient and honoured seats of Hindooism. It possesses beautiful temples, some of great antiquity; and contains within itself the famous temple of Jagaunath, of undoubted Buddhist origin, though now transformed into a Hindoo shrine. The first visit to Orissa with a missionary object seems to have been made by Dr Buchanan, in the beginning of the present century. Afterwards, the Serampore missionaries, true to their sacred instinct of planting the gospel wherever it was possible to do so, established a mission in Midnapore, in the northern division of the province; and also at Balasore, in the vicinity of Jagaunath. These were sustained for some years with success; but eventually were abandoned in favour of other societies, the first of which was the General Baptist Society, which was established in England in 1816, as distinct from the Baptist Missionary Society, and commenced its labours in Orissa in 1822. The horrid Meriah sacrifices early engaged the attention of the missionaries. These were practised on children who had been stolen, and who were nourished from year to year with the express object of being slaughtered. Many of these children being saved by the Government, were placed under the care of the missionaries, and were trained in the Christian religion. These children were from the Khoonds, yet not a few converts also have been made from the Hindoo Uriyas. Cuttack, the first station, was commenced in 1822 by the Rev. Messrs Bampton and Peggs, both men of unflagging energy and zeal. The former removed to Pooree in the following year. Here, living close to the temple of Jagaunath, he had an opportunity of witnessing the terrible scenes which were enacted there. He continued at Pooree for nine years, striving with all the earnestness that a profound conviction of the truth of Christianity, and of the gigantic evil of gross idolatry, could inspire, to guide into the paths of purity and righteousness the myriads of deluded pilgrims who flocked to the shrine; and then, full of hope, though, like many other apostolic men before him, not having received the promise, died. These missions had in 1850 five hundred and forty converts; in 1871 they had sixteen hundred and twenty-nine. But of these, as many as six hundred and seventy-one belonged to the male and female orphanages. There were also seven ordained native ministers, besides unordained native preachers and teachers, helping the missionaries in their work.

A third mission was established at Balasore, in the early part of 1827, by the Rev. Mr, afterwards Dr, Sutton, who had for some time resided at Cuttack. He laboured with conspicuous zeal for a long period in Orissa, preaching the gospel to the natives, writing and translating books, and in many other ways, directly and indirectly, endeavouring to lead the people to a knowledge of Christ. This station was afterwards given up; but a new mission was formed there by the American Free-Will Baptists in 1836, and is still in existence. It is worthy of remark, that a peculiar mode of itinerating was adopted by the missionaries of this society. Their object being to visit the same villages and towns frequently over a certain limited tract of country, they thought that it could be best attained by the erection of a few bungalows in a circle round some central point. This being done, they went at intervals from one to another throughout the circuit, visiting the same villages and people, who thereby became by degrees fairly instructed in Christianity.

The progress which the missions of the General Baptist Society have made in Orissa since their establishment will be manifest from the following figures. In 1850 they numbered five hundred and sixty-four Christians; but in 1871, twenty-one years afterwards, they had increased to two thousand one hundred and sixty-nine, of whom five hundred and forty were communicants. They had nine native ordained pastors; and their schools were twenty in number, in which thirteen hundred and twenty-three children were instructed.

Numerical results of the General Baptist Society's missions in Orissa.

As yet only one-half of the Orissa missions have been described. The second half are as important and extensive, so far as their operations are concerned, as the first, though possessing fewer converts. These missions are in the hands of the American Free-Will Baptist Society. Its first station was Balasore. Afterwards, others were formed at Jelasore, Midnapore, Santipore, and elsewhere. An able missionary, the Rev. B. B. Smith, has lately died, while the Rev. J. Phillips, one of the two who founded these missions, is still labouring with undiminished fervour and ability. Midnapore is now permanently occupied by this society, and a few native Christians in connection with the Church of England are also found there; but it has passed through somewhat strange vicissitudes, inasmuch as three separate societies endeavoured to establish a mission in this city, but after a time were obliged to abandon it for want of missionaries to carry it on. In the northern part of the province the Santals are scattered about, and have naturally attracted the attention of the missionaries, who have established schools among them, brought many under Christian influence, written several works in Santali, and translated portions of the Bible into the same language. But their chief literary labour has been the compilation of books in Uriya. Dr Carey translated the entire Bible into this tongue; but a new version was made by Dr Sutton, which is that now in use in the province. The American Baptists have nine separate native Christian communities occupying thirteen villages. Their schools are very numerous. They have in all seventy-eight, with sixteen hundred and seventy-nine pupils of both sexes. From a recent report of these missions I find that in the beginning of the present year, 1873, the Midnapore station had forty-nine Santali schools, in which eight hundred and ninety-seven Santali children, of whom sixty-two were girls, were being educated. A very useful institution is what is termed the Santal Training School, in which Santali boys are taught various arts and trades. A somewhat similar institution, but much more elaborate, exists at Balasore. It is called "The Industrial School." Only Christian youths, apparently, are trained in it. It is with much interest that I gather from the same report that, in March 1873, of these lads, there were six carpenters, five blacksmiths, four weavers, five tailors, five washermen, ten gardeners, and four house servants.

In the Santipore district is a mission farm, which affords means of support to the Christian families, and, in addition, to about thirty families of Santals. This is under the charge of the Rev. J. Phillips, to whom allusion has already been made. The annual report to Government of Mr Beames, the Magistrate and Collector of the district, makes an important reference to the working of this farm, and to the general influence of Mr Phillips upon the inhabitants. "Rev. Mr Phillips' Mission at Santipore, in the extreme north of the district, is a nucleus of good influence for the wild, rude people round him. Mr Phillips is quite a little chief in those parts. The people come to him on all occasions for advice and assistance; and his farming operations, assisted by the aunicut he has constructed, and the canal leading from it, are gradually converting the wild forest country into a fertile, agricultural tract."

The Santipore Mission farm. Report of Mr Beames, Magistrate of the district, upon it.

The large and fertile province of Behar possesses ten central missions, with their usual accompaniments of out-stations and schools. The societies to which they belong are Gossner's Evangelical Mission (of Berlin), the Baptist, Church, and Propagation Societies. It has been already stated that, during the brief period of his residence in Dinapore, Henry Martyn endeavoured to make known the gospel to the natives of that town, of the large city of Patna, and of other places in their vicinity. These seem to have

Missions in Behar.

been the first missionary efforts undertaken in Behar; and several years elapsed, after the departure of this distinguished man, before a mission was actually established in the province. In 1816 the Baptist Society occupied both Monghyr and Patna, which they continue to hold. The Rev. Mr Chamberlain, who had formerly lived in Agra, the inhabitants of which city first heard the gospel from his lips, resided in Monghyr for a number of years until his death in 1821, after a missionary career of nearly twenty years. "He was eminent for decision of character, for an inflexible adherence to truth, and for such an ardent attachment to the missionary work as led him often to exert himself beyond what his frame could well sustain."* At the suggestion of Bishop Heber the Propagation Society sent a missionary, the Rev. T. Christian, as early as the year 1825, to Bhagalpore; but he was carried off by jungle fever at the close of 1827. On the abandonment of the station by this society, the city remained without a missionary for many years. But in 1850 the Church Society sent there the Rev. E. Droese, a laborious German missionary of charming address, who has continued almost alone at his post for twenty-three years, at the end of which he finds himself at the head of a native Christian community numbering three hundred and twenty-one persons, divided into three congregations, and inhabiting five villages. The mission has six schools with three hundred and twenty-two scholars.

The Baptist missions in Behar, although so early established, have made little progress, and have had but scanty success in direct conversions among the

* Christianity in India, vol. v. pp. 171, 172.

people. Doubtless, the great and efficient work which the missionaries have performed in the direct preaching of the gospel, in which they have been chiefly occupied, has had the effect of making large numbers of the natives living in towns and remote villages acquainted with Christian truth; yet it is remarkable that their missions in Behar, two commenced in 1816, and the third, that at Gya, founded in 1857, should have yielded so little fruit, for we find that in 1871 they only possessed one hundred and thirty-three converts. Perhaps the principal reason to be assigned for this result is the studied limitation of the missionaries' labour to preaching. The three missions contain only three schools with one hundred and twenty-one children of both sexes. The Baptist Mission at Patna, with two missionaries, men of well-known earnestness and experience, has no mission school at all; and has a community of only thirty native Christians after fifty-five years' missionary labour. The Propagation Society has also a mission in the city with ninety Christians, although established only in 1860. Strange to say, this too has no schools connected with it. So that the anomaly exists of two important missions in the heart of a great native city without a single school attached to them, and without therefore displaying the smallest interest in the education of the rising generation. *Reason suggested*

The Berlin Society, commonly known as the Evangelical Mission established by Father Gossner of Berlin, has four stations in Behar, one just beyond at Ghazipore, in the Benares division of the North-Western Provinces, and others of great strength in Chota Nagpore. Were I giving an account of the *Gossner's missions at Mozaffarpore, Chuprah, Buxnr, and Durbhangah.*

progress of each society's missions in India, it would be proper to consider them as a whole. But such is not the object of this work, which is simply to give a general picture of the growth of Christianity in India, no matter by what section of the Protestant Church it may be produced. I shall therefore speak here merely of Gossner's missions existing in Behar, with the purpose of showing how far they have aided in promoting the religious welfare of that province. The first of these was commenced at Muzaffarpore in 1840; the second at Chuprah in 1842; the third at Buxar in 1852; and the fourth at Durbhangah in 1863. The satisfactory advance which these missions have made will be at once seen by comparing the results of one period with those of another. In 1850, ten years after the foundation of the first mission, the converts numbered ninety-two. In 1861 they had increased to one hundred and sixty-one; while in 1871 they amounted to three hundred and ninety-seven, an augmentation of one hundred and forty per cent. in the space of ten years. There were also at that time eleven schools with two hundred and ninety-eight pupils sustained by all the missions.

Summarising the mission work in Bengal together with all the provinces within the jurisdiction of the Bengal Government, as represented by the statistics on this subject collected for the year 1871, we have before us the following results:—

STATISTICS OF MISSIONARY LABOUR IN BENGAL, INCLUDING CALCUTTA, FOR THE YEAR 1871.

Number of Native Christian Congregations, .	383
Number of Protestant Native Christians, .	46,968
Increase in Ten Years, ...	26,450

Number of Native Communicants,	13,502
Increase in Ten Years,	8,783
Number of Towns and Villages containing Christians,	1,205
Number of Ordained Native Ministers,	35
Number of Unordained or Lay Preachers,	398
Number of Mission Colleges and Schools,	693
Number of Pupils, Male and Female,	27,950
Number of Native Christian Teachers, do.,	548

During the last ten years, Protestant native Christains in Bengal have more than doubled, and native communicants have nearly trebled, in number.

CHAPTER IV.

MISSIONS AMONG THE KÔLS AND SANTALS.

Greater readiness of the aboriginal races to accept the gospel.

THE two missions which form the subject of this chapter have an interest peculiar to themselves. Their singular success proves the greater readiness of some of the aboriginal tribes of India to receive the gospel than the old caste-ridden Hindoo races exhibit. The decennial statistics of Indian missions show, indeed, that throughout India the original tribes, the low castes, and the out-castes, furnish at the least four-fifths of all the converts gained to Christianity. Ignorant, without a literature, and free from many of the prejudices fostered by the elaborate superstitions and idolatrous practices of the Hindoos, they have fewer obstacles preventing them from considering the claims and tenets of the gospel.

The Chota Nagpore Mission.

The history of the Chota Nagpore Mission is a bright phase of Indian missions, and contributes greatly to relieve them of the necessarily prosaic character which they generally assume. Missionary life anywhere is anything but romantic; and yet, sometimes, in most missions, events occur in the highest degree sensational and romantic. The Chota Nagpore Mission furnishes an unusual number of such events, and therefore is unusually interesting to all Christian people, but especially to those who are perpetually seeking after wonders, and live on sensation.

The physical aspect of the country is graphically portrayed by one of our best writers on Indian missions. "About two hundred miles from Calcutta, on the western borders of the great plain of Bengal, and south of the neighbouring province of Behar, lies the broad tableland of Chota Nagpore. Raised on the shoulders of a long line of granite hills, on the east it looks down upon the vast rice-fields of Bancoorah and Midnapore, which its many streams richly fertilise; and on the west, buried in its dense impassable jungles, lies the beautiful valley of the Upper Soane. Though a tableland, its surface is far from level. It presents to the eye an endless succession of undulations, a rolling country, formed of gravelly hills with swampy hollows at their base; while on every side lofty detached hills, covered with brushwood to the top, stand sentinels, as if to guard the land from harm. The province is richly wooded in every part. All the Indian trees are found in its deep jungles, with the gigantic creepers that mount the loftiest; but the mango-trees are peculiarly fine. They appear at times in long avenues lining the tracks, which form the only roads; at others, they are found in vast shady groves, with enormous trunks and mighty arms; and, again, they stand singly in wide open glades, and give to the scenery the rich and peaceful aspect of an English park. The coffee plant, the orange, the shaddock, and the citron grow readily in gardens, and tea has also been produced, while rice is grown in all the swamps, and oil-seeds are most abundant. The approaches to Chota Nagpore are exceedingly interesting to the observer of physical geography. On its east side a steep pass leads up its hilly face from the plains of Pachete and Ramgurh. On the north, the traveller passes a series of broad terraces, the earliest being several miles wide, and having in its centre the healthy military cantonment of Hazareebaugh. Passing southwards from this station, terrace after terrace, ridge after ridge, and stream after stream are crossed, till seven have been numbered; and, finally, after a steady ascent of five miles through shady jungle, where birds of varied plumage are met with, where monkeys swing from bough to bough, where at night tigers and bears abound, we reach the undulating plain, with its great fruit-trees and broad fields of eorn. The climate of the province is more temperate than that of the Bengal plain. Spreading out at a height of two thousand feet above the sea, though not in the dry summer months, it is cool and pleasant in the rains; while in the cold season, with the thermometer at forty-four degrees, and a cloudless sky of pale blue overhead, there is a sheen in the atmosphere unknown to the heated plains, and at early morn the joyous lark pours forth his song upon the dewy air."* The entire province of Chota Nagpore extends over an area little less than that of England; and the subdivision of it, known as Chota Nagpore Proper, has a population of one million and a half, and is principally inhabited by aboriginal Kôls. This tribe is, in this tract, divided into two great branches, the Mundaris and Oraons; and, in all its seats, is said to embrace fully a million of persons.

* Dr Mullens' Ten Years' Missionary Labour in India, pp. 37, 38.

The Kóls are small in stature—"sometimes so small *The Kóls.* as to seem almost dwarfs beside the martial *physique* of a Rajpoot of Oudh, or the muscular frame of a stalwart Pathan of the Punjab frontier; yet well proportioned, many of them almost to symmetry, all well knit, muscular, and 'active as monkeys;' their faces darker than the average Hindoo; their thick prominent lips and broad flat noses contrasting strikingly with the fine chiselled features of the Brahman, or the classic *contour* of the Mahomedan."* They are a light-hearted people, fond of music and dancing, ignorant, and licentious.

The mission among the Kóls was commenced at Ranchee early in 1846, by six German missionaries sent out by the society established in Berlin through the instrumentality of Pastor Gossner, a man of singular faith and devotion, then upwards of seventy years of age. They visited the people in their villages; they laboured in their own gardens; they erected their own buildings; they were heedless of the changes of the climate and of the intense heat of an Indian sun. They were sustained by their wonderful ardour; but undue exertion, and constant exposure, diminished their numbers rapidly. One after another, four fell a sacrifice. Left alone, with sad regrets at their heavy losses, the zeal of the remainder did not flag. But they were neither cheered by conversions nor even by any inquirers coming to them, only by the consciousness that their work was Divine, and must eventually be successful.

The mission established in 1846 by six German missionaries, four of whom soon fell a sacrifice to toil and exposure.

In 1850 the first-fruits were gathered. That year *First-fruits. Persecutions.*

* The Chota Nagpore Mission, by the Rev. J. Cave-Browne, p. 2.

they baptized eleven adults, the next, twenty-seven, and every year the number increased until 1856, when ninety-six persons were baptized. In the year following, the Christian community had increased to upwards of eight hundred, who were scattered over a great many villages. This result had not been obtained without much opposition on the part of the landholders of the province. False charges were brought against the converts in the courts, " their houses were plundered by armed bands, the large rice-stores carried off, the very roofs of their houses taken away, and money and the women's ornaments forcibly seized. Most patiently did they bear the outrages from which they so deeply suffered; grace was given them to 'take joyfully the spoiling of their goods;' elders and people remained firm in their faith, and the trial only gave tone and strength to the principles which were so rudely tested. When the mutiny cast loose all the bonds of political authority, these persecutions broke out with fresh virulence. The Ramgarh battalion that held the country mutinied; and every Englishman, civil and military, of all ranks, fled for his life. Before many hours had passed, every bungalow was in flames; the mission-houses being tiled, were stripped of their furniture and books; the church was gutted, and the organ pulled to pieces; cannonballs were fired into the tower, but disfigured without harming it. The converts were hunted from their houses, and lost all their property of every kind; all their village chapels were unroofed and stripped; and at last, when nothing else remained, a price was set upon the converts' heads. They were compelled to hide in the jungles, and sought, though in vain, to

The mutiny of 1857. Danger and destruction.

descend the passes, which they found guarded, in order to escape into the plains. Many stories are told of hairbreadth escapes. At times they met with singular kindness from strangers, especially from women; nevertheless, a few were killed, and their persecutors had seriously planned to exterminate the Christians from the province, when the English soldiers marched up from Hazareebaugh, put an end to disorder, and captured the rebel delinquents. Their chief persecutor was hanged in the middle of Ranchee. The missionaries speedily returned; work was resumed; the congregations were regathered; and a strange measure of prosperity was henceforth granted. New life seemed given to the Christians; and their enemies saw with amazement that the dispersed and despised race came forth more numerous than ever."*

Thenceforward the trophies of the gospel became yearly more numerous. The villages in all directions felt the purifying and elevating power of the new ideas and emotions which Christianity produces. By 1863 there were three thousand four hundred and one baptized Christians, of whom seven hundred and ninety were communicants. I cannot forbear inserting another extract from the excellent narrative of Dr Mullens, on the subject of the peculiar festivity held at the New Year, which will furnish the reader with a clear conception of the simplicity and beauty of their religious services. It is prefaced by a reference to the gathering of the Christians for their Sunday services.

"A large number of the Christians," he observes, "come in from their villages to Ranchee every week

* Dr Mullens,' Ten Years' Missionary Labour in India, pp. 41, 42.

for the Sabbath services. They are so numerous that a special *serai* has been erected for their use, which, with its broad verandahs and inner court, can accommodate six hundred visitors. They bring all their food, and are merely supplied with firewood at the expense of the mission. They hold special festival at Christmas; and on the first Monday of the year they gather to celebrate their harvest feast, and hold an annual missionary meeting. It was a pleasant sight last year to contemplate the happy faces of the multitude, men, women, and children, as they collected in the square near the mission-house, with their offerings in their hands, prepared to march in procession to the station-house. As the gong sounded ten o'clock, the procession moved off, headed by Mr Brandt, with the boys' school; followed by Mrs Frederick Batsch, with the girls; the children all singing a hymn of praise to the tune of Kiel. Next came a number of women with large baskets on their heads; then the men, leading their children, or carrying other loads; all marching up the noble avenue of Pontianas to the church, which stands on the slope at its further end. Arrived at the church, they passed up the centre aisle, ascended the stairs into the deep chancel, and marched round the communion-table, which stood out in the centre, every one presenting an offering. In the front had already been raised a small stack, about six feet high, of sheaves of 'first-fruits.' Small boxes for money stood on the table; but the rice offered was poured upon the floor. None came empty-handed; every one, men, women, and children, presented money; but the chief gift was the cleaned rice that had been gathered in their fields. For half an hour the people came slowly on—old men and women, strong men and children, women with children at their sides, or slung upon their backs, the prosperous farmer, the poor day-labourer, all, and every one, brought their gifts. Some brought a handful in a cup; a few brought large baskets with half a hundred-weight; others a more moderate quantity. Meanwhile the children in the gallery sang a variety of hymns, accompanied by an organ, played by the school-teacher, one of their own people; and sang them with a clearness and precision, taking the different parts, which it was most delightful to hear. So the procession passed on, the money increasing in the boxes, and the rice-heaps growing higher on the floor, till all were seated in the church for worship. Those 'heaps' brought the old Temple to mind, with the promises of blessing to those who founded and maintained them; and could not fail to suggest the prayer, that, like the Jews of old, these temple-worshippers might grow in faith, and love, and gratitude, and that they too might receive showers of blessing from above."*

In the year 1864, Bishop Cotton happening to be at Ranchee, attended the Sunday service in the mission church, at which one hundred and forty-three persons, adults and children, received the rite of baptism. He was particularly impressed with this portion of the service, which was performed with great solemnity. During its celebration the Te Deum was chanted in Hindi at the west end of the church, while the service itself was being performed in the chancel. "As he drove away from the church," says Mr Cave-

Impressions of Bishop Cotton.

* Dr Mullens' Ten Years' Missionary Labour in India, pp. 43, 44.

Browne, "Colonel Dalton, the Commissioner, broke a long silence by asking him what he thought of the service. The Bishop did not answer for a few seconds, and then, with quivering lip, said, 'Sublime —the only word to describe it.' They who know," adds Mr Browne, "the undemonstrativeness of Bishop Cotton's manner, will appreciate the value of such testimony to the simple, solemn beauty of that service." *

A Sunday service.

The same writer gives a most striking account of a Sunday service, showing the great earnestness of these Kóls in the worship of God. It is taken from the Calcutta *Christian Intelligencer*. The quotation is important if only to silence those cavillers who, having never witnessed native Christians in India in their religious services, are prone to deny them that devoutness and reverence which are commonly exhibited by Christian people in England. "The lively ringing of church bells, with tones familiar to those who have been in foreign towns, gathered a punctual congregation of some six hundred persons within the substantial and ecclesiastical-looking building, which is seen to rise up in the landscape for miles around. The men seated themselves in the open sittings on one side of the church; the women glided into those on the other side; and the school-children, some seventy or eighty in number, ranged themselves in a gallery in front of a harmonium. While wondering at the orderly crowd, you are surprised to see a native organist commence his voluntary, as the black-robed officiating minister comes out of the vestry, and mounts the steps which lead up into the ample

* The Chota Nagpore Mission, by the Rev. J. Cave-Browne, p. 26.

chancel. You are at once struck with the taste and skill of the musical performance. At the minister's announcement of a hymn, a familiar tune strikes up, in which presently the children above, and the people below, heartily join.

"The elders of the church proceed to move about the nave and aisles for the collection of an offertory, to which every one contributes every Sunday, and which is set apart for the temple service, and for the erection of village chapels. Next, there is a prayer, and then the minister stands up to read portions of Scripture recognised as those appointed for the Epistle and Gospel of the day in the Church of England. After the alternate verses of a psalm have been read by the minister and the people, he ascends the pulpit. As you look at the congregation, you are a little ashamed of your inattention, for you find yourself to be the only one with wandering eyes. There is a quiet expression of ready watchfulness and self-possession in the countenances. As the animated preacher goes on, those who feel sleepy keep rising from their seats, and stand until they have recovered sufficient wakefulness to listen to the close. Some of the elders move quietly about the church to preserve order in the congregation; and also among the heathen strangers, who are generally seated near the door, and who occasionally call forth the preacher's rebuke. Such may even be peremptorily told by him, in the middle of his sermon, to leave the church. Now and then the office-bearers are concerned with the mothers of noisy infants, or they are quietly reminding by a touch a drowsy brother, that he should not lose the good words spoken. No wonder they are tired; some have come forty and even fifty miles during the previous twenty-four hours, and they will have to walk home next morning! Such earnestness would be disappointed if the preacher did not fill up his full hour. His uplifted arms at last announce the delivery of the blessing, which is received with lowly bended heads. And the people remain thus in private devotion while the minister descends from the pulpit, unrobes in the vestry, and comes out before the chancel steps, and gives the salutation, with which all Christians address one another here—'Isa Sahai,' Jesus, Helper. The whole congregation then rises, and quickly disperses. But first those in the front seats, who are evidently the elders, and the oldest converts, press forward to the missionary, to take his hands before they retire, disappointed should he quit the church without first according to them that honour."*

The catechists of the mission were alternately taught and sent forth on long tours among the villages, for the purpose of giving instruction to all classes, and of bringing back inquirers. These inquirers were kept at least a year on probation before baptism. Every village containing many Christians had its elder, who regularly taught them the truths of the gospel, held religious services with them in their own houses, or in the village church. The elder was also responsible for the order and decorum of the Christians of the village. Every candidate for baptism was obliged to present to the missionary a certificate of good conduct from the elder of his village before he could be admitted to the rite. In short,

Duties of Elders

* Calcutta *Christian Intelligencer*, June 1863, p. 168.

the elder was a man of great influence and importance in carrying out the mission scheme which had been set on foot. It was an honorary post for which he received no remuneration.

Before the baptism of any candidate the elder of his village is solemnly enjoined in the presence of the congregation not to hide anything which, in his judgment, should be a hindrance to his baptism. The candidate is then questioned as to his faith, his motives, and his readiness to abandon evil and sin in every form. But as a fact the missionary knows every candidate personally, for he has had him under his eye, imparting instruction to him, for several weeks previously. Those who have been baptized are taught that baptism is only a stepping-stone to the communion, and that they are not received into full church-membership until they have become communicants. Before, however, they can become communicants they have to receive further teaching in the Word of God. *[Ceremonies observed before baptism.]*

Thus the mission increased wonderfully, and produced a very perceptible change for the better in the moral and social condition of the Kôls over whom it had exerted its influence. In the midst of all this prosperity it is sad and painful to learn that dissensions sprang up between the Berlin Committee and the missionaries; but I shall refrain from saying a word upon them, as it is far from the purpose of this dissertation to discuss such matters. I shall only remark, as a warning to home committees, in venturing and presuming to interfere in the internal organisation and management of intricate and extensive mission stations, which their own missionaries have established, that the agent whom the Berlin Committee *[Dissensions.]*

sent to this country, in order to settle the differences between themselves and the missionaries, widened the breach and destroyed for ever all hope of harmony.

The mission divided. The mission divided itself into two portions, one, under the direction of the junior missionaries, continuing its connection with the Berlin Society; the other, with the senior missionaries at its head, entirely separating itself from that society, and uniting with the Society for the Propagation of the Gospel in Foreign Parts. It should be observed that this very important step was taken by the senior missionaries of their own freewill; and that they and their people earnestly solicited the bishop of the diocese to admit them into communion with the Church of England.

The division of the mission occurred in 1869, since which time the two missions have expanded and multiplied greatly. This will be seen from the enormous number of baptisms which have taken place. In 1871 these amounted to two thousand three hundred and forty-one, of which nineteen hundred and fifty-seven occurred in the German missions, and three hundred and eighty-four in the Propagation Society's missions. At the end of 1861 there were, as already stated, two thousand four hundred Kôl converts. At the end of 1871 there were twenty thousand seven hundred and twenty-seven, distributed as follows:—

STATISTICS OF THE KÔL MISSIONS IN CHOTA NAGPORE IN 1871.

Number of Native Christians of the German Mission, 14,107
Number of Native Christians of the Propagation
    Society's Mission, ... 6,620
Number of Communicants in both Missions, . . 6,233
Number of separate Congregations in do., . . 143

Number of Towns and Villages containing Christians,   811
Number of Native Preachers, ...   105
Number of Native Christian Teachers, .   .   .   56
Number of Schools, ...   62
Number of Scholars, Male and Female,   .   1,297

The missionaries of the two societies in Chota Nagpore, together with Colonel Dalton, the learned and philanthropic Commissioner of the province, are now engaged on the translation of portions of the Sacred Scriptures into the Kôl language, which, it is hoped, will soon be in circulation among the people.

Missions among the Santals are of recent origin. The first was established by the Church Missionary Society in 1862; the second in 1867, by two missionaries, one a Dane, the other a Norwegian, who have designated their society, of which they are the sole members, the Indian Home Mission; the third in 1870, by the Free Church of Scotland; and the fourth in 1871, by two gentlemen, the Rev. Messrs Johnson and Body. It is manifest, therefore, that great attention is being paid to the enlightenment of these aborigines. Their condition, relations with the British Government, and history in modern times, are sketched with much force by Dr Hunter in his "Annals of Rural Bengal." They differ in many respects from the Kôls; but are, however, like them in ignorance, licentiousness, and simplicity of manners.

The Santals. Four missions established among them.

The missions are separate from one another. The stations of the Church Society are numerous, and have many schools connected with them, and also a training institution. Two missionaries, the Rev. G. Puxley, a man of great self-denial and of calm enthusiasm, and the Rev. W. T. Storrs, devoted themselves

Mission of the Church Society. Rev. G. Puxley and Rev. W. T. Storrs.

for several years to the evangelisation of the Santals; and their patient and earnest labour has been richly rewarded. These aborigines have a keen perception of character, and may be said to fall in love with those philanthropists who show persistent and disinterested love to them. The missionaries having won their affections and their confidence, have induced them by hundreds to place themselves under religious instruction. This mission, commenced in 1862, had in 1871 no less than eight hundred and sixty-eight Christians; while its schools numbered twenty-seven, with five hundred and eight pupils.

<small>Visitation of the Bishop of Calcutta</small>

The Bishop of Calcutta visited Taljhari, the principal station of this mission, in the beginning of 1872, and speaks enthusiastically of what he saw and heard. "Here," says his Lordship, "the new church, though unfinished, was sufficiently advanced to use in an Indian climate, and, at the request of Rev. A. Hœrnle, I confirmed sixty-nine Sonthalee candidates. Mr Starke interpreted my addresses into Sonthalee very ably and fluently. There was a very large and crowded congregation. The church is beautifully situated, and is a striking object from the railway. It is very solidly built. I afterwards confirmed twenty-eight candidates in Hindee, chiefly pupils from the normal school. On Sunday there were more than sixty Hindee, and more than one hundred and seventy-six Sonthalee communicants. The normal and other schools are in excellent order, and well taught. In the evening we had a very picturesque *burra khana* (great feast), at which about eight hundred guests sat down wonderfully good-tempered and orderly. The singing was sweet. The mission flourishes, but has lost a great power by the departure of the Rev. W. Storrs, who is now in England, and whose return is doubtful. This mission, established by Rev. G. Puxley, has had a remarkable success. The people are a merry, cheerful, and truthful race; and among such races Christianity makes comparatively rapid progress."*

The Indian Home Mission has been equally successful. Its method of procedure is peculiar. The Rev. L. Skrefsrud, one of the missionaries, in an address delivered by him before the recent General Missionary Conference at Allahabad, gave the following outline of the method adopted. "The Santal country," he observed, "extends from Bhagulpore to Orissa, a district of two hundred and fifty miles in length, and one hundred miles in breadth. The mission to which I belong exists through Indian agency. A congregation has been gathered solely through the instrumentality of preaching. They did not begin by establishing schools: they simply went about from village to village preaching the gospel. We have no native preachers; and do not believe in them. We have a preaching Church. All the Christians are preachers. They preach without pay, and without being told to preach. When they are converted, they go off themselves, and say to their friends, 'Come, we have found something good.' One single man has thus brought five villages to Christ. The converts have got the gospel in their hearts—not simply in their heads. Last year eight Christian villages were

Success of the Indian Home Mission.

Method adopted described by the Rev. L. Skrefsrud.

* Report of a Visitation Tour of the Bishop of Calcutta, to the Lieutenant-Governor of Bengal: dated, Calcutta, 14th April 1873.

formed by the native Christians, not by us. The most suitable convert in a village is made pastor. They support their own pastor. Their pastor is a ploughing pastor. Morning, noon, and evening, he prays with his people; and ploughs his land in the intervals. They pray for certain villages; then go to them, and speak to the inhabitants; and then pray again. The gospel is preached to a small circle, accompanied with much prayer on its behalf. The result is, that nearly all the persons within the circle become Christians. They have no endowments; but the pastor gets the piece of land which formerly heathen priests received. From the commencement, they endeavoured to make converts depend upon themselves, and not trust to foreign aid. They had no trouble about salaries, for there were no native preachers paid by the mission. The missionaries intend to work, as far as possible, through the village system. In every village there are seven officers. As several of the head men have become Christians, it is hoped that many of the village councils will formally abandon idolatry; and the piece of land that now belongs to the priests will be devoted to the support of the pastor and schoolmasters. The aim kept in view is, to retain all the innocent customs of the people, and to let their Christianity, in its outward manifestations, take a Santali form. The Santals have no caste, properly speaking. They are divided into twelve tribes, each of which is further divided into twelve families. They never marry within their sub-tribe. The custom facilitates intercourse among the tribes, and the spread of Christianity. But it is manifest that it is an exclusiveness amounting to caste. The Christians pray for the breaking down of this caste. A man does not become an outcast by embracing Christianity."

This mission baptized two hundred and twenty persons during the year 1872, and has now about sixteen hundred native Christians among the Kól population, who are separated into eleven congregations. The communicants are two hundred and eighty-five. It has lately opened thirty additional vernacular schools. It has an important training school, in which eighty young men and thirty young women are instructed. The Rev. L. Skrefsrud, the learned Norwegian missionary, has just completed a Santali grammar, a work of four hundred and ten pages. His colleague, the Rev. Mr Boerresen, was formerly Principal of the Royal Engineering College for sons of noblemen in Berlin, but surrendered his high and responsible post from the irrepressible desire to devote his life to the greater work, as he imagined it to be, in which he is at present engaged. The missionaries have likewise brought out a hymn-book and a catechism in the Santali language.

Some Bengalees of Calcutta, incited by the support which the Government of Bengal has rendered to missionaries in their efforts to educate and civilise the rude aboriginal races, have requested the Government to grant them the same assistance, so that they too may labour in the good enterprise. Their principal object is known to be, to introduce Hindooism among these degenerate tribes. Still the Government, occupying a neutral position in religious matters, has wisely promised to aid these Bengalees in establishing and sustaining schools for the enlightenment of the

Efforts of Bengalees to introduce Hindooism among the Santals.

Santals, whom they have especially singled out as the first objects of their philanthropy. The Government stipulates, however, that they shall raise a fund for the purpose in view, whose contributions it will supplement. The movement is an interesting one. It might be supposed that it was indicative of vitality still remaining in Hindooism. But at present the project is too young for any opinion whatever to be formed of it.

CHAPTER V.

MISSIONS IN THE NORTH-WESTERN PROVINCES, OUDH, AND ROHILKHAND.

THE North-Western Provinces, lying between Behar on the east and the Punjab on the west, is inhabited by a people in many respects very different from the races found in Bengal. Ethnologically, the province of Oudh must not be separated from the North-Western Provinces, as their tribes and families are for the most part the same. In place of the stunted, dark races of Bengal, of great vivacity, and of considerable keenness of intellect, you have a fine stalwart people, tall, strong-limbed, often powerful, of noble presence, ready to fight, independent, of solid rather than sharp understanding, and of somewhat duller brain than their neighbours of Bengal. By reason of the contrariety between the two nationalities, there is no friendship between them, nor is ever likely to be. The Bengalee is proud; but it is because he is subtle and quick-witted, and thinks he is capable of overreaching you. The Hindustanee is proud; but it is because of his trust in his strong arm, because of his long pedigree, because of his well-cultivated manly habits. The Bengalee has no royal tribes to be compared for an instant with the Rajpoot clans of the north-west, with lineages stretching back for a thousand or even two thousand years. The

Bengalees and Hindustanees contrasted.

Bengalee has his polygamist Koolin Brahmans, of high local sanctity undoubtedly, but of little account elsewhere, and completely lost in the shade when brought into competition with the purest sections of the great Kanoujiya family. The Bengalee boasts of his ability, of his money, of his skill in a thousand ways. The Hindustanee does not undervalue these things; but he thinks much more of good breed, and good blood, and of all the associations of antiquity, which are intensely sacred in his eyes.

Hindooism most powerful in the North-Western Provinces.

Bengalees would naturally question the statement, which I believe to be quite true, that, in the Hindoo sense, they are much less devout and religious than Hindustanees. In fact, Hindooism, in all its phases, is more strongly professed and followed by the latter than the former. Where is there any place in all Bengal in which caste, idolatry, and Brahmanism are as powerful as in Benares, and throughout the province of that name? While, unquestionably, Hindooism exerts an enormous influence in Bengal, and in every other country in India—of which circumstance many Europeans in the land, who never investigate the matter, are in profoundest ignorance, and the force of which most people in England fail to comprehend—it is in the fulness and maturity of its strength in those Upper Provinces, where it has acquired a stony compactness and solidity of an almost impenetrable character. Hence the greater difficulty of the progress of Christianity in the north-west than in Bengal, and indeed than elsewhere in India. Humanly speaking, it is the last tract in India which will submit to the gospel. It is not changeable and progressive in the same way, and to the same extent, as Bengal, although of late years it is undeniable that it has made rapid strides in knowledge and enlightenment. And it will be slow in accepting any such radical reform as that introduced by the Brahmo Somaj movement, which, so far as I am aware, has made no proselytes among its inhabitants.

The vacillating and timid policy of the British Government of India, in regard to the introduction of Christianity among the people, before the passing of the charter of 1813, was never more strikingly illustrated than in its dealings with the Baptist Mission in Agra, established in the year 1811 by the zeal and enterprise of the Rev. Messrs Chamberlain and Peacock, of the distinguished band of Serampore missionaries. Before the mission had been eighteen months in existence, Mr Chamberlain fell into a dispute with the Commandant of the fort, the result of which was that he was sent back to Serampore under a guard of sepoys. But, shortly after, he returned to the north-west, and took up his residence at Sirdhana, having been invited thither by Colonel Dyce for the purpose of superintending the education of his child, afterwards the famous Dyce Sombre. "Here," says Mr Marshman, "three or four hours were daily devoted to his education; but the rest of Mr Chamberlain's time was left at his own disposal, and was passed in preaching, and superintending schools, and translating the New Testament."* But in 1814 Mr Chamberlain was again removed by the Government from the North-Western Provinces. The same writer gives the reasons for his removal in a short narrative, which, not only for the immediate subject

Establishment of the Baptist Mission in Agra in 1811.

* Carey, Marshman, and Ward, p. 241.

in hand, but as affording an insight into the nature of missionary labour at that time, is of too great interest and importance to be omitted.

The great fair at Hurdwar.

"In the month of April," says Mr Marshman, "the Begum proceeded from Sirdhana to the great fair at Hurdwar, the most renowned '*tirth*,' or holy place, in Hindostan. A particular conjunction of the heavenly bodies in the present year was supposed to enhance indefinitely the merit of bathing in the sacred stream at that place, and more than a hundred thousand pilgrims were attracted to it. Mr Chamberlain, who accompanied the Begum, was employed, without intermission for twelve days, in preaching to the devotees at the ghauts, or landing-stairs, and to the crowds who surrounded his elephant, or pressed into his tent, to hear this new and strange doctrine, which was now for the first time announced at this great seat of Hindoo superstition. The most profound tranquillity pervaded the multitude, though in a high state of religious excitement, while they listened to discourses which impugned the efficacy of the holy Ganges. An eyewitness thus described the scene : 'During the greater part of the fair a Baptist missionary, in the service of her Highness, daily read a considerable portion from a Hindee translation of the Sacred Scriptures, on every part of which he commented. He then recited a prayer, and concluded by bestowing a blessing on all assembled. His knowledge of the language was that of an accomplished native; his delivery was impressive; and his whole manner partook of much mildness and dignity. No abuse, no language which could in any way injure the sacred service he was employed in, escaped his lips.

His congregation eventually amounted to thousands. They sat round and listened with attention which would have reflected credit on a Christian audience. On his retiring, they every evening cheered him home with, "May the *padre* live for ever!" Towards the close of the year, Lord Moira made his first progress through the North-Western Provinces, accompanied by the secretary, Mr Ricketts, who had taken the most prominent part in the expulsion of missionaries eighteen months before. Some gentlemen, unfriendly to the cause of missions, brought the subject of Mr Chamberlain's labours at Hurdwar to the notice of Mr Ricketts, who made an alarming report on the subject to Lord Moira. Without any investigation, or any request for an explanation, a peremptory requisition was immediately made to the Begum to discharge Mr Chamberlain from her service, and he was at the same time ordered to return to the Presidency. On leaving Sirdhana he proceeded to the Governor-General's encampment, and solicited an audience, in the course of which he appealed to the testimony of Lady Hood and Colonel Mackenzie, who were present at Hurdwar, and had assured him of the pleasure they derived from witnessing the peaceable demeanour of the people, and more particularly the Brahmans, and the great interest which had been manifested in his addresses. But Lord Moira had been impressed with the danger of preaching to a large concourse of pilgrims, and refused to revoke the order, remarking that one might fire a pistol into a magazine and it might not explode, but no wise man would hazard the experiment. This was the only instance," adds Mr Marshman, "of any unfriendly feeling towards

Timidity of the Government.

missionaries during his long administration; and it may be sufficiently accounted for by reference to the prejudices of his secretary."*

Rev. D. Corrie's labours in Agra. The Church Society obtains a footing there.

The Baptist Mission in Agra was re-established in 1834, and has continued with fluctuations of prosperity to the present time. The Church Society obtained a permanent footing there in 1813, on occasion of the Rev. Daniel Corrie, afterwards Bishop of Madras, being appointed as chaplain to that station, taking with him Abdul Masih, a catechist, and several Christian youths, from Calcutta. Corrie remained sixteen months at Agra, when, his health failing, he was obliged to resign his post, and to return to England. In this short time, however, a great preparatory work had been accomplished in that city, and seventy-five natives, one-half Mahomedans and the other half Hindoos, had been baptized. Mean-

Mission to Meerut. Mr Bowley.

while, in the large military station of Meerut, fifty miles from Delhi, some families were receiving Christian instruction from Mr Bowley, a young East Indian, who had established several schools from his own resources, in which many native children were instructed. Mr Corrie gave him the assistance of a native Christian catechist, and himself proceeded thither in the beginning of 1814, and baptized one convert, and, a few weeks afterwards, two others in Agra, who could not be baptized in Meerut because of the violent opposition of their friends. Shortly, the native congregation in Meerut numbered between twenty and thirty Christians. On the departure of Mr Corrie from Agra, Mr Bowley was requested to take charge of the mission there in conjunction with Abdul Masih. Thus it came to pass that the two

* Carey, Marshman, and Ward, pp. 253, 254.

missions in Agra and Meerut, now large and influential, were established.

Previously to these labours, however, some work of a missionary character had been done by Mr Corrie when stationed in Chunar in 1807, and by Henry Martyn in Cawnpore in 1809. But unfortunately the labours of these eminent men in those cities were short-lived; and several years had to elapse before they were permanently occupied as mission stations. In 1815 Mr Bowley was transferred to Chunar, where he remained for many years. He published a translation of the New Testament into Hindee, which remained in circulation for a long time, but has been superseded by more correct versions, coming nearer to the original, though not superior in point of idiom. The Baptists had already commenced a mission in Allahabad as early as 1816 or 1817, under the Rev. Mr Mackintosh, who in 1818 despatched his catechist, Naripat Singh, to Cawnpore, on the invitation of a few Christians there. But this tentative effort, from the absence of a missionary, came to nothing. Mr Mackintosh continued in Allahabad for some ten or twelve years, labouring, together with his native Christian helpers, with conspicuous zeal, yet it does not appear that in ten years they were able to rejoice over a single convert. Nor is this surprising, considering the supreme sanctity of the spot in the opinion of all Hindoos. Here, as they imagine, is the junction of three rivers, the Ganges, Jumna, and Saraswatee. The inhabitants of Allahabad, and the numerous pilgrims resorting thither, are peculiarly influenced by prejudice and superstition. Eventually the mission was given up, though for what reason I am

He commences a mission in Chunar in 1815

Rev Mr Mackintosh's labours in Allahabad.

unable to say. Perhaps it was because of the barrenness of results achieved—a very poor reason for a missionary or for a missionary society to assign. Yet societies, and some missionaries too, are getting tired of labouring from year to year without abundant fruit, as though they expected all soils to be alike, and all to yield at the same time the same measure of fruit. The Baptist Society, which has set so noble an example of enterprise and perseverance to all other societies in India, has nevertheless been prone above all others to relinquish its missions, and to commence new ones. After an interval of thirty-five years, or more, it renewed its mission in Allahabad.

Benares.

It was a day of much importance in the history of Christianity in India when missionary operations were commenced in the sacred city of Benares. This famous seat of Hindooism is still as much venerated by Hindoo sects of all shades, from the slopes of the Himalayas throughout the entire peninsula, as it was twenty-five centuries ago. Humanly speaking, were the city to abandon its idolatrous usages, and to embrace the gospel of Christ, the effect of such a step upon the Hindoo community would be as great as was that produced on the Roman empire when Rome adopted the Christian faith. The special sanctity and influence of Benares constitute a gigantic obstacle to all religious changes within it. The Baptist Society was the first to introduce a mission into the holy city. This was in 1816, and the Rev. William Smith, then appointed, continued at his post for a period of forty years. Quiet and unassuming, he won the esteem of everybody; so much so, that it is a well-known fact that on occasion of a great disturbance

A Baptist mission established there in 1816.

and riot in the city, when the Magistrate durst not expose himself to the rage of the populace, on the approach of Mr Smith, the crowd separated and allowed him to pass harmlessly through. On Mr Corrie's proceeding as chaplain to Benares in 1817, he seems to have commenced missionary operations in behalf of the Church Society. One of the most important results of his labours was, that he acted as medium between a rich native, Rajah Jay Narain, and the Calcutta Corresponding Committee of that society, in the transfer of a school which that native gentleman had started, together with a valuable endowment which he attached to it. The school, which had been in existence several years under the direct supervision of the Rajah, was made over to the society by deed of gift on the 21st October 1818. The same year the society appointed Mr Adlington to be its head-master. But no ordained English missionary came to Benares in connection with this society until January 1821, when the Rev. Thomas Morris arrived. The school has developed into a college, called after the name of its founder; and is now one of the largest and most efficient educational institutions of that society in India. It has six hundred and fifty students, all of whom receive Christian instruction. A third mission exists in Benares, founded by the London Society, whose first missionary, the Rev. M. T. Adam, entered on his labours there in August 1820.

All these three missions have continued uninterruptedly from the date of their establishment to the present time. The Baptist Mission has been mostly a preaching mission. For many years it possessed several useful schools; but eighteen years ago, Dr Underhill, one of the secretaries of the society, visited Benares and other stations on deputation; and, at his suggestion, the schools of this and various other missions were closed, a retrograde step, the result of a mistaken theory, that greater proportionate good would be accomplished by simple preaching than by endeavouring also to educate the people. The numerical condition of the Baptist Mission in Benares in 1871, as compared with that which existed twenty years before, certainly gives no testimony in favour of such a theory, or in favour of the hopes entertained by the secretary, and by others like-minded. Almost the only additions which have been made to the mission during this period have been orphan children received into the excellent orphanage, which one of the ladies of the mission, in spite of great difficulties and of no little opposition, has established. Yet the mission has had its earnest and very able preachers. I have already mentioned its founder, the Rev. W. Smith, a man of singular simplicity and of unflagging devotion. I might also refer to the late Rev. John Parsons, a man intimately acquainted with the natives, and with the idioms of their language, whose apostolic fervour was known throughout the whole of Northern India; to the Rev. H. Heinig, who has passed thirty years in Benares as a diligent preacher of the gospel; to the Rev. W. Etherington, the author of a popular Hindee grammar; and to other faithful men. One entire quarter of the city is in great need of schools. Let the Baptist Society reverse its policy, which has been so clearly unsuccessful in Benares—and also in other places that might be mentioned—and, while paying due attention to direct evangelistic labours, take a fair share with the two other missions in imparting sound Christian and secular instruction to the vast population inhabiting the city.

The Church Mission has taken a very distinguished part in promoting the religious and intellectual welfare of the natives of Benares. It has always had a considerable staff of vernacular preachers engaged almost exclusively in this branch of labour. The oldest member of the mission, the Rev. W. Smith— the same name as that of the Baptist missionary alluded to above—has spent the greater part of forty-two years in unceasingly proclaiming the gospel in the streets and bazaars of the city, and in the villages in the neighbourhood. His colleague, the Rev. C. B. Leupolt, of only two years' less service, has also been largely occupied in this great work. Both are looked up to by younger missionaries of all societies in Northern India, without distinction of denomination or country, as noble examples of sustained zeal and holy enthusiasm. The mission has likewise its large college, to which reference has just been made, besides many schools. Moreover, it has extensive girls' schools, a large orphanage, a normal institution for the education of Christian young men and women for positions of usefulness in this and other missions, an infant school, two Christian villages, one for the residence of Christians, the other for the training of young men to become farmers and agricultural labourers, a lace-manufactory, and two churches, which are in the charge of two ordained native pastors. It is manifest from this enumeration of the various institutions of the mission, that it has undertaken a very broad range of philanthropic and Christian labour, and is influenced by no narrow views of duty. I must here add that the Female Normal School Society has as many as four ladies engaged entirely in the instruction of native women and girls in the zenanas of the city.

And of the London Mission. The London Mission, though inspired with the same sentiments as those influencing the members of the Church Society in Benares, has never been in a position to attempt the multiform labours which they have undertaken, and in which they have been so successful. It has confined itself to two branches of mission work, namely, preaching and teaching; which it has prosecuted with considerable energy. One of the two missionaries, with several native preachers, is daily engaged in the former branch; while the other missionary devotes himself to the latter. There is a large collegiate institution in the mission with five hundred scholars, besides boys' schools and girls' schools. Formerly there was also an orphanage, but the number of orphans is now very small. This mission, like those just mentioned, has had the advantage—the importance of which can hardly be over-estimated—of the continued labours, extending over many years, of several able missionaries. The Rev. W. Buyers, a man of diverse gifts, and the Rev. Mr Shurmann, a distinguished translator of the Bible into Hindustanee, spent their lives in the mission. The Rev. James Kennedy, now of Rance Khet, a hill-station lately established by him in behalf of the London Society, was a loving and effective agent of the mission for upwards of twenty-five years. He has published in Hindustance a useful commentary on the Epistle to the Romans.

What, then, are the results which these missions have to show? To what extent have they made their influence felt on the dense heathenism of the sacred city? How far have they succeeded or failed? These are questions which it is impossible to answer fully, because a sentimental influence not amounting to conversion to Christianity is a very intangible property to deal with. Yet such results as can be placed on record are as follows:—

STATISTICS OF MISSIONARY LABOUR IN BENARES.

Number of Native Christians in 1850,	390
Number of do. in 1871,	641
Increase (nearly 61 per cent.),	251
Number of Native Christian Communicants in 1871,	168
Number of Colleges and Schools in 1871,	29
Number of Scholars, Male and Female, in 1871,	2220
Number of Native Preachers in 1871 (of whom three are ordained),	19
Number of Native Christian Teachers in 1871,	48

These results, however, are no proper criterion of the great work which has been accomplished among the natives of Benares by Christian truth, education, just government, and the general civilising elements in operation in their midst. It is no exaggeration to affirm that native society in that city, especially among the better classes, is hardly the same thing that it was a few years ago. An educated class has sprung into existence, which is little inclined to continue in the mental bondage of the past. The men composing it may be compared to the bud ready to burst into the blossom under the united influence of

Intellectual and religious progress in Benares.

light and heat. The religion of idolatry, of sculptures, of sacred wells and rivers, of gross fetichism, of mythological representations, of many-handed, or many-headed, or many-bodied deities, is losing, in their eyes, its religious romance. They yearn after a religion purer and better. They want to know God as He is, not as symbolised in these mystical associations. English education based on the Bible has thus produced a revolution of thought in their minds. In the Government college and schools the Bible is not permitted as a text-book; yet it is none the less true that the English education they impart is, in no slight degree, Biblical. Thus it has come to pass, that the light which precedes and accompanies conviction, has been shed upon many minds in this seat of Hindooism. A new era of intellectual freedom and religious life has already commenced. Of not a few it may be said, that "old things have passed away;" and of the mass of the people, that "all things are becoming new." Such a change as has been wrought is full of promise and encouragement; and is of a much more satisfactory and genuine character than an addition of some scores or hundreds of mere nominal converts would be. On the other hand, stern and persistent opposition must be expected by the advocates of Christianity in a city like Benares, in which old creeds and customs exist, penetrating through and through the social and personal life of the people, and associated with their history for ages past; in which a powerful priesthood is ever on the alert to keep them attentive to their duties, and to mystify them by their magical charms and ceremonies; in which multitudes of persons read the sacred books, and reverence the mingled philosophy and religion they contain; and in which sensuous forms and symbols of the indigenous faith meet the eye in every direction. What wonder if in such a city a new and better religion, though derived from Heaven, and bearing on its front the glory of its Divine original, should meet with special, unwonted, and determined opposition? To reckon on the hasty and sudden downfall of the old religion, which harmonises so completely with the pride and vanity, and other evil qualities, of the human heart, and on the rapid and universal spread of a faith which tends to destroy these qualities, and to bring the heart into an entirely new condition, is to indulge in mere quixotism, and to manifest an impatience at variance with the calmness of the gospel. *Quixotic ideas of the spread of the gospel*

Thirty miles from Benares, on the southern bank of the Ganges, is the once flourishing commercial city of Mirzapore, which, before the opening of the East Indian Railway, was the chief place of trade between Calcutta and Lahore. It still receives many of the productions of the hilly regions to the south; but its great trade in cotton has been almost destroyed. Here, in the year 1838, a mission was established by the London Society. The Rev. Dr Robert Cotton Mather, its founder, is still at the head of the mission, and is able to indulge the supreme satisfaction of tracing its growth through a period of thirty-five years. During this time it has undergone many changes, yet all have conduced to its firm and steady progress. As a mission, it is one of the most compact and well-organised that I know. Several hundred persons have been baptized within it, many *Mirzapore. The London Mission. Rev. Dr Mather.*

of whom have died, and many more have left for other stations in these provinces, while it has still upwards of a hundred and thirty Christians connected with it. It possesses a flourishing institution, and several schools, a considerable orphanage, two Gothic churches, and an extensive press. Many books, principally of a Christian and educational character, the production chiefly of its learned founder, have been yearly printed. Dr Mather is well known for his highly important labours as a translator of the Bible into Hindustanee.

One hundred miles to the south of Mirzapore is a country full of hills and valleys, covered with dense jungle, and inhabited by aboriginal races, which long ages were driven by the Aryan invaders of the country into these inaccessible fastnesses. Ten years ago, the same society commenced a mission among the aborigines of this tract. The missionary, the Rev. William Jones, lived a simple and almost ascetic life among the people, to whose spiritual and material welfare he unsparingly surrendered himself. By his unwearied kindness, his liberality, his plans of usefulness, his integrity, his steadfast resistance of oppression, his genial sympathy, and his holy life and conversation, he won the confidence of the natives, who trusted him as they had never before trusted any human being. Full of earnestness and love, he sacrificed health and comfort in his privations and toils, and died in the midst of his usefulness, and in the maturity of his powers, singing in his delirium the old Welsh hymns which his mother had taught him in his childhood. Few men in modern times better deserve the name of an apostle.

Mission among the hills of Singowlee. Rev. W. Jones.

There are three important chains of missions in North-Western India, belonging to three distinct societies, and embracing a large number of stations. One is connected with the Church Society; the other two are in the hands of the American Presbyterians and American Episcopal Methodists. These three series of missions occupy most of the principal cities of the North-Western Provinces, Oudh, Rohilkhand, and the Punjab. The stations in each series are exceedingly well situated in regard to one another; for while sufficiently near to react upon each other, they are at the same time so far separated as to have an independent existence. They finely illustrate the principle which should always govern missionary societies in establishing new missions in India, namely, that of occupying a certain limited tract of country, and endeavouring to evangelise *that;* and not to seize on every eligible post, wherever it may lie, irrespective of its contiguity to, or distance from, other stations which they may possess in the country. This, I contend, is a fundamental principle of large and permanent success in the prosecution of mission work in India. And it will be found, I am persuaded, that one chief reason of the non-success of some missions is the neglect of this principle, and the occupation of immense regions, in which the stations are placed at enormous distances from one another, so as to be totally unable to exert the smallest moral influence one upon another.

I shall speak of each of these chains of missions separately; but as the work of the individual missions in each chain is of a very similar character, I shall endeavour to set forth each series as a whole, only referring to the mission stations so far as they exhibit any feature of missionary labour of peculiar and special interest.

The Church Society's missions in North-Western India.

The Church Society has central missions at Goruckpore, Azimgarh, Jaunpore, Benares, Chunar, Allahabad, Agra, Aligarh, Bulandshahr, Meerut, Dehra Doon, and Landour, in the North-Western Provinces; at Fyzabad and Lucknow, in Oudh; and at Bareilly, in Rohilkhand. Most of these places are cities of wealth and importance; and all are centres of great influence. Some of these missions are much larger than others, and some, like that in Benares, engage in a great variety of labour, all, directly or indirectly, promoting the main object in view. Yet some idea of the extent of their aggregate operations may be gathered from the following facts. They have a staff of forty-five native preachers; their scholastic institutions are seventy-one in number, eight of which are either colleges or high schools, in which, exclusive of Hindoo teachers, there are one hundred and thirteen native Christian teachers; and they have four thousand four hundred and seventy-seven pupils under instruction. Since 1850 the Christian community in these missions has more than trebled. In that year the number was a thousand and forty-six; but in 1871 it was three thousand four hundred and eighty-eight. During this period the society has lost an unusually large number of its missionaries in Northern India, who have either died or retired from the work. Nevertheless, true to its great enterprise, it fills up the gaps as they occur, so that its stations do not suffer. Would that all other societies were equally faithful and zealous!

The Goruckpore Mission displays in considerable perfection two features of missionary labour about which there has been much discussion of late years in India, raised for the most part by persons who indulge in theories about their utility, but who have themselves had no personal experience of their real value. These are the two systems of Christian villages and Christian orphanages. Respecting the practical working of both in Goruckpore, the Rev. H. Stern, who has resided in the mission for the last twenty years, gives the following interesting account. He says of the Christian village of Basharatpore, near Goruckpore, "This is wholly an agricultural establishment. It was first commenced by the late Rev. Mr Wilkinson, who, after obtaining from Government a jungle grant of twelve hundred acres, set to the work of clearing away the jungle by the hands of native Christian orphans. There is now there a Christian village consisting of about two hundred and fifty souls, all cultivating land paying rent to the mission. There is a church and school; and a Punchayet (or native council of five persons) manages all internal affairs. The whole is under the superintendence of the missionary, who, in the name of the society, is virtually the zemindar (or landholder). This village is inhabited only by native Christians; but there are heathen villages all around, and some on the mission-land. It is not exactly a model village, and I fear the native Christians are not always so zealous as they ought to be, and sometimes their influence is not for the best. But this is no fault of the village system, but of the Christians themselves, whom no human system can regenerate.

But, notwithstanding all our imperfections and shortcomings, I could wish that every mission would have a Christian village, and also a sufficiently large allotment of mission-land to build a Christian village upon, and to make it self-supporting. It gives stability to the mission; and the possession of land by native Christians entitles them to some respect and importance in the eyes of the other natives. By this means our scattered Christians obtain also a home, which they love and cherish as much as any other home-Christian. Here the Christian learns to look to the soil as the earthly source of his maintenance; and he will cling to it, though the mission may be abolished. With ordinarily favourable seasons, the native Christian cultivator lives, under God's blessing, a humble but contented life."*

Orphan boys as cultivators. On the subject of the employment of orphan boys, Mr Stern adds: "There is now connected with this village an orphanage for boys, whom we desire to train up from their very childhood to the hard and self-denying labours of the cultivator. We have found that it is useless to bring up orphans, and then put them to the plough. It is necessary to teach them to look to the soil for their daily bread from their very childhood. Our orphans have about thirty *beegahs* (twenty acres) of land to cultivate for themselves, and they thus produce, in a great measure, the grain for their own consumption. As soon as any orphan is sufficiently advanced, he receives a small portion of land for his own individual use; and when

---

* Report of the General Missionary Conference held at Allahabad 1872, 1873: Paper by Rev. H. Stern, on the Christian Village System, pp. 355, 356.

he has by his own labour succeeded in collecting a small sum of money, this sum being supplemented by a grant-in-aid from the common fund of the orphanage, he is allowed to marry, and is then drafted off to the Christian village, where he then commences to manage his own affairs, quite independent of the mission. We only start them in life; and then they, instead of being supported by the mission, become supporters of the mission. In this orphanage we have not only agriculture, but also various other trades, such as carpet-weaving; and a blanket-manufactory is in contemplation. So far, then, as we in Basharatpore are concerned, we have, under God's blessing, succeeded with the so-called village system."*

Prosperity of the mission. The Goruckpore Mission has added one hundred and fifty-nine to its numbers during the last ten years, and has now four hundred and fifty-eight native Christians. Its schools contain upwards of eight hundred pupils. Altogether, the mission is in a most flourishing condition, and is exerting a powerful influence upon the city and neighbourhood.

The Allahabad Mission. Allahabad, although comparatively a small city, yet, being the seat of Government in the North-Western Provinces, is invested with an importance which it would not otherwise have possessed. Formerly it had but one mission, which was established by the American Presbyterians in 1836; but of late years two others, in connection with the Church and Baptist Societies, have been established. But I shall

* Report of the General Missionary Conference held at Allahabad 1872, 1873 : Paper by Rev. H. Stern, on the Christian Village System, p. 356.

only speak at present of the last-mentioned, which, although only commenced in 1859, has four hundred and sixty native Christians, the Presbyterian Mission having one hundred and forty-one, and the Baptist Mission, begun in 1867, fifteen. The reason, however, of this great disparity in numbers is manifest. Most of the Christians of the Church Mission were connected with the Government press when the headquarters of the North-West Government were in Agra, and on their transference to Allahabad came with them there. It has a beautiful village for its Christians a short distance from the city, in which they live in comfortable and substantial buildings, the whole being under the supervision of the Rev. D. Mohan, their intelligent and laborious native pastor. The village is called Muirabad, from Sir William, the Lieutenant-Governor of the North-Western Provinces, who has taken great interest in the welfare of the native Christians.

The Agra Mission, St John's College.

Notwithstanding the removal of so many Christians from Agra, the numbers in the Church Mission there have not diminished; on the contrary, have considerably increased. In 1871 it had nine hundred and sixty Christians; but of these as many as four hundred and twenty were in the orphanage. Yet the mission has for many years had a large orphanage, and I am not aware that its numbers have been sensibly altered beyond what they formerly were. St John's College, in connection with the mission, has had the advantage of distinguished principals, through whose instrumentality it has flourished greatly, and has been brought to a high state of efficiency. Such men as the Rev. T. V. French and the Rev. H. W. Shackell, not only by their scholarship, but also, and chiefly, by their entire consecration to the holy work of doing spiritual good to the people of the city and neighbourhood, and others of the same elevated purpose, have left an influence behind them which will never be effaced. The Rev. E. Schneider, who has grown old in the service of the society, laboured for many years in Agra. The Baptist Society has had a station in this city for a long period, having been originally established, as already stated, in the year 1811, by the Rev. J. Chamberlain. It has passed through a series of vicissitudes; but has of late years acquired new life, and is vigorous and strong. The missionaries, as in many other of the Baptist missions, devote themselves exclusively to preaching. In the two stations of Agra and Mathura, about twenty-five miles distant, founded in 1843, there is but one school, and this contains only twenty pupils. The two missions together number one hundred and seven Christians, which is one more than they possessed twenty-one years ago.

The Baptist missions at Agra and Mathura.

The influence of the outbreak of 1857 on the inhabitants of the North-Western Provinces generally, in inducing them to pay greater deference to the Christian religion than formerly, is observable everywhere. In some instances a spirit of inquiry has been awakened, unknown before. This has been the case in Agra, Mathura, Meerut, and Delhi. "In the village of Malyâna, three miles from Meerut," writes Dr Mullens in 1862, "there was quite an excitement produced by some tracts and Scriptures left by a Christian during the disorders of the mutiny; and after due inquiry, the Rev. Mr Medland, the Church

Beneficial effects of the Indian mutiny of 1857.

missionary in Meerut, baptized several converts. The inquiry spread to Kunker Khera, and one or two other large villages, on the east of Meerut; and congregations have also been gathered there."* The good work then commenced has since made steady though not rapid progress. This single mission possesses five separate congregations of Christians living in six different villages, and has two ordained native pastors, besides fifteen native Christian teachers and unordained preachers. It is under the care of the venerable missionary, the Rev. C. T. Hoernle, whose long and efficient labours place him in the front rank of Indian missionaries.

Rev. C. T. Hoernle

The second chain of missions in North-Western India, and also the third, are the product of American benevolence and enterprise. In the judgment of the writer, acknowledgments have never been sufficiently made of the spontaneous and entirely disinterested zeal and liberality of our Western cousins, in planting missions at great expense in various parts of India, and in taking part with English missionaries, and, I may add, with the British Government likewise, in the generous endeavour to enlighten and elevate its ignorant and degraded races. Their missions are well organised, are conducted with great ability and spirit, and will favourably compare with some of the best English missions in India. Moreover, it is hard to say which American society surpasses the others in the skill displayed in the prosecution of mission work, inasmuch as all exhibit in this respect great judgment and tact. The last

The American Presbyterian missions in North-Western India.

---

* Ten Years' Missionary Labour in India, p. 53.

arrived, the Episcopal Methodists, in zeal and efficiency, seem not a whit behind the American Baptists and Congregationalists, who came first.

The missions of the American Presbyterians run in a continuous line from Allahabad, in the North-Western Provinces, to Rawal Pindi, in the Punjab. Leaving those in the latter country, the North-Western Provinces have missions of this society in Allahabad, Fathpore, Fathgarh, Mainpuri, Etawah, Muzaffarnagar, Saharunpore, Rurkee, and Dehra Doon. In them is a Christian community of eight hundred and ninety-three persons; and they possess the large number of seventy-two schools, containing two thousand nine hundred and seventeen male and female pupils. They have also a staff of ninety-nine native Christian preachers and teachers. *Their native Christians and schools.*

The mission in Allahabad has for many years been well sustained by the Home Society. Occasionally it has had no less than four or five missionaries engaged in various departments of mission work. The Rev. Dr Joseph Owen, one of the most learned missionaries the American societies have sent to India, was attached to this mission for a long period. He was also for a time connected with the Presbyterian Mission in Agra, which, however, is now abandoned. He wrote a new translation of the Book of Psalms in Hindustanee; and also several commentaries, besides other works, in the same language. A very important theological seminary or college has lately been established in the mission, the object of which is to train the native preachers belonging to the numerous stations of this society in the North-Western Provinces in various branches of theology, as well as *Presbyterian Mission in Allahabad. Rev. Dr Owen.*

Theological colleges.

to impart to them by systematic teaching such secular knowledge as shall thoroughly fit them for the very difficult duties of the posts they occupy. A similar work, though on a smaller scale, has been also undertaken by the missionaries of the Church Mission in Benares. At Lahore, in the Punjab, likewise, the Church Society has an institution of this nature, only far superior to either of these, under the superintendence of the Rev. T. V. French; but further reference will be made to it when I come to speak of the Punjab missions. The American Union Zenana Mission is engaged in a most extensive work among the native women of Allahabad. As many as five ladies devote their time to the toilsome and self-denying labour of visiting the zenanas, and in affording instruction to their inmates.

American Union Zenana Mission.

The mission at Fathgarh is perhaps the largest in the series. Here resided for years the Rev. Messrs Scott, Ullmann, and Walsh, men of true sympathy with the natives, and of great love for the Christian converts. For many years the Maharajah Dhuleep Singh has maintained ten village schools in connection with the mission. Altogether, the mission has charge of twenty-five schools, containing about eight hundred pupils—a large number for one mission to superintend. The native Christians manage a tent-manufactory, independently of the mission, from which they derive a very considerable income, sufficient for the comfortable support of all engaged in it. Great attention is also paid here to zenana-teaching. In the mutiny the mission was called to pass through a fiery ordeal. Its four missionaries, with their wives and two children, were all killed by order of the cruel Nana at

Mission at Fathgarh. Maharajah Dhuleep Singh.

Four missionaries of this mission, with their wives and two children, killed by the Nana of Cawnpore, in the mutiny.

Cawnpore. About thirty of the native Christians, including Dhokul Parshad, the head teacher of the city school, were killed on the parade-ground at Fathgarh. Yet no instance occurred, so far as is known, of any one of the Christians apostatising. On the re-establishment of the mission, the Rev. J. L. Scott remarked of the Christians who returned, "They are poor, but generally in good spirits, and their trials have, in my estimation, improved them, by giving them a more manly and independent spirit." And such, indeed, was for the most part the result of the mutiny in its influence upon the native Christian community throughout the whole of the large tract of country which revolted from its allegiance to the British Government. *Thirty native Christians also put to death.*

At Dehra Doon an interesting experiment is being tried, of giving to the daughters of native Christians the highest education which it is possible for the missionaries and their wives to impart. Perhaps no such ambitious project has been attempted by any other society or mission in India. Boarding schools and normal schools are undoubtedly numerous in the country, and a considerable amount of knowledge is given to the pupils instructed in them. But the Dehra Boarding School has aims much surpassing those of similar institutions elsewhere. It was commenced in 1858, and now numbers one hundred girls. The school is designed to be a home. "To make it such," says the excellent superintendent, the Rev. D. Herron, "we brought the children under the same roof with ourselves, received them into our own home, and took them to our hearts. We have tried to take the place of their parents, and to treat them as our own *The Dehra Doon Boarding School.* *Rev. D. Herron.*

children. They are required to do almost all the domestic work of the institution. Every large girl has charge of a small one, and is responsible for her cleanliness and neatness. One hour each day all the children are taught needlework, during which time they make and mend their own clothes. We require the children to sit at tables, and use spoons at their meals. Another design of the school is, to give the children committed to us the highest intellectual culture that they are capable of receiving. It is our plan that instruction be given only by missionaries, and those that have been educated in the school. The children are first taught to read and write the Roman Urdu; and during the whole course of their studies they have lessons in reading and writing both in the Hindee and Urdu, in the Nagaree and Persian characters. The English, however, is the medium of communicating knowledge and training the mind. The English becomes their language as much almost as their mother tongue; and they seem to be puffed up with the one no more than with the other. A third design of the school is, to bring the children to Christ, and to cultivate in them the Christian virtues. This is the principal design, and the one that justifies us in giving so much time and attention to the other parts of the work. In this respect God has especially blessed the labours of His servants. We have seen in our school very much more evidence of the Spirit's presence and work, in converting souls and beautifying Christian character, than in all the other operations of our mission. Another design of the school is, to lead the native Christians to value the education of their daughters by making them pay for their children's support, when they are able to do so."* After a trial of twelve years, the Dehra Boarding School must be pronounced to be a great success. Christian parents of all missions in the North-Western Provinces and the Punjab, who can afford it, wish to send their daughters to be educated in it, for it is well known that nowhere else can they obtain such a complete education as it bestows.

Indian missionaries of various Presbyterian societies, anxious for unity, have formed themselves into a Confederation, in order that, while retaining connection with their own distinctive denominations, they may act together in India as one undivided community. The importance of the organisation will be seen in the fact, that missionaries of the following societies are associated with it: the American Presbyterian Church, the Church of Scotland, the Free Church of Scotland, the United Presbyterian Church of Scotland, and the Reformed Church in America. The Confederation held its first conference in Allahabad in the month of November 1873. A similar conference is to be held every two years.

Confederation of Indian missionaries of various Presbyterian societies.

The third chain of missions in Northern India is in connection with the American Episcopal Methodists, and is of recent establishment. The Rev. Dr Butler, the pioneer of these missions, arrived in India a few months before the mutiny. After consultation with many persons, he decided on occupying the chief cities of Rohilkhand, a tract of country which hitherto had never received the benefit of missionary preaching

Missions of the American Episcopal Methodists. Rev. Dr Butler.

* Report of the General Missionary Conference at Allahabad: Paper on Female Education, by the Rev. D. Herron, of Dehra Doon, pp. 167-177.

and teaching, a portion of Oudh, which was also a new missionary field, and part of the provinces of Kumaon and Garhwal, in the hills. Bareilly was fixed upon as the headquarters of the missions to be established. Very soon after Dr Butler had entered on his work there, the mutiny broke out, and soon extended as far as Bareilly, which quickly fell into the hands of the rebels, and became a hotbed of strife and sedition. Twelve days before the insurrection in Bareilly, Dr Butler left for Nynce Tal, the first station in the hills, and so escaped the massacre which took place in that city. When peace was restored, he returned to Bareilly, and recommenced the mission there. In two or three years eighty-eight converts were received into the mission, who in 1871 had increased to four hundred and sixty-four, of whom two hundred and twenty-three were communicants.

Statistics of the missions. This society has fifteen principal stations, of which six are in Rohilkhand, situated in the cities of Bijnour, Amroha, Moradabad, Budaon, Bareilly, and Shahjehanpore; six are in Oudh, namely, in Sitapore, Bahraich, Lucknow, Barabankee, Roy Bareilly, and Gondah; two are on the hills, namely, at Nynee Tal, in the province of Kumaon, and Paori, in the province of Garhwal; and one is at Cawnpore, in the North-Western Provinces. There are twenty-one foreign missionaries, eighty-one native preachers, of whom six are ordained, and ninety-six native Christian teachers connected with all these missions. At the close of 1871 they possessed eighteen hundred and thirty-five converts, of whom one thousand and seventy-four were communicants, divided into thirty-seven congregations, and living in ninety-seven separate villages. They had also one hundred and forty-six schools, in which instruction was given to five thousand two hundred and six male and female pupils.

The American Methodist missionaries give great prominence to their Sunday-schools, which are conducted in a very systematic manner, and with great earnestness of spirit. They are both for Christian and heathen children. In Lucknow alone, in 1872, there were sixteen, with forty-seven teachers and nine hundred and sixty-seven scholars. Only one of the schools is frequented by Christian children. "While great credit is due," the missionaries say, " to all the faithful friends who have assisted in this work, it is but just that special mention be made of five or six native Christian girls, who have done a good work, and set a noble example, by collecting children and organising small Sunday-schools in or near their parents' houses. These girls have succeeded better than could have been expected; and their earnest efforts have furnished the most hopeful feature of the work among our native Christians during the past year. We are more than ever convinced of the great importance of this Sunday-school work. The children, both boys and girls, in all the schools, join in singing Christian hymns, commit verses from the Bible, learn the catechism, and, in short, shrink from nothing that is done in an ordinary Sunday-school, except kneeling during prayer. The parents of the children frequently visit these schools, and manifest a very encouraging interest in all they see and hear." *

Sunday-schools

* Report of the American Methodist Episcopal Missions in India for 1872, pp. 26, 27.

At Moradabad the Sunday-schools are attended by all the native Christians, and also by two hundred and fifty children, and take the place of one of the regular Sabbath services.

Theological School. A theological school has been established in Bareilly for training young men for the work of catechists and ministers. The course of instruction for the year 1872 was as follows : Biblical exegesis in the Old Testament, sacred geography, Biblical introduction, systematic theology, homiletics, and the Persian and Arabic languages. An endowment has been attached to the school, towards which one of the missionaries, the Rev. D. W. Thomas, has contributed the munificent sum of four thousand pounds.

Medical missionaries For several years a medical missionary, the excellent Dr Humphrey, was stationed at Nynee Tal, on the lower slopes of the Himalayas, where his benevolent labours were highly appreciated by the natives. There he trained a number of Christian women in the healing art, who subsequently laboured with success in the practice of their profession among their fellow-countrywomen. On the departure of Dr Humphrey to America, this medical class was abandoned. At Bareilly, Miss Swain — a doctor of medicine — not only treats patients in the mission dispensary, but also has an extensive practice among native ladies in the city.

Christian village of Panahpore. Ten miles from Shahjehanpore is the Christian village of Panahpore, or "city of refuge," situated upon nine hundred acres of jungle-land purchased from the Government in 1869. It now numbers one hundred and fifty individuals. It has "its church, and schools, and happy homes." "They, in their collective capacity," said its energetic founder, the Rev. Dr Johnson, in a short address delivered before the Allahabad Missionary Conference, " have become a missionary to other villages. Only a week ago I had the pleasure to baptize fifteen adult persons thus brought in; and not less than thirty have already received baptism in the neighbourhood, as the result of the presence of this village."

In the district of Moradabad is a considerable body of Mazhabi Sikhs, followers of Nanak Shah, who, it is reported, migrated from the Punjab two generations ago. They are regarded as an unclean race by the Hindoos among whom they live, and are not permitted to associate with them promiscuously in their villages, but have a certain quarter assigned for their residence, to which they are rigidly confined. Shortly after the mutiny, many of these Sikhs expressed a desire to receive Christian instruction, which was imparted to them by the Rev. Dr Humphrey and the Rev. J. Parsons. At first it is evident they were influenced more or less by a desire of improving their temporal condition; for on finding that their expectations in this respect would not be fulfilled, not a few fell back from the profession of Christianity, and returned to their former ways. Nevertheless, the work among them has been for fourteen years steadily advancing, until about three-fourths of all the Mazhabi Sikhs of the district have become converts to Christianity, and the remainder are so far affected by its truths as to bid fair to follow in their steps. The importance and extent of this movement in the direction of Christianity are manifest from the fact that these Sikhs are found residing in upwards of

The Mazhabi Sikhs of Moradabad.

Three-fourths have embraced Christianity.

one hundred villages. They are chiefly village watchmen, cloth-weavers, and small farmers. The mission has nothing to do with their temporal or financial condition, except to encourage industry and economy. Many of the Christian Sikhs are employed in various capacities as cooks, grooms, general servants, and the like, in the principal stations of the mission. It is an interesting circumstance that most of the Christians of the missions in Rohilkhand, excepting those in Budaon, the children of the orphanages, and the students of the theological school, are from this class of people. They have already supplied from their ranks two ordained native preachers, nearly a dozen teachers, and about twenty catechists and Bible-readers. The numerous stations in which the Christian Sikhs exist are under the charge of a young ordained native, with eight assistants, each of whom has the care of from twelve to fifteen villages.

Christians of the Sweeper caste in Budaon. A work of the same character, but more circumscribed in range, has been accomplished among the Mehtar or Sweeper caste of the Budaon district. Protracted Christian meetings have been held in their villages, frequently two or three services daily for as many as eight or ten days, the result being that more than three hundred persons, connected with twenty villages, have embraced the gospel, of whom two-thirds are communicants. The caste numbers ten thousand in the district, who are mostly engaged in agriculture. From the religious excitement evinced by them, the missionaries indulge the hope that gradually the entire caste will be gathered into the Church of Christ.

Such are some of the features of the noble work which the missionaries of the American Episcopal

Methodist Society have been able to achieve in the short space of fourteen years. Men of great piety, earnestness, and ability, and endued with the Spirit of God, they have come to India with the high purpose and determination of devoting themselves heartily and unsparingly to the single enterprise of making known the gospel to the inhabitants of this land, and of delivering them from the gross superstition and ignorance by which they are enslaved. And it must be conceded, even by the strongest opponents of missions, that they have not laboured in vain. The society has been exceedingly fortunate in the choice of its missionaries. Possessing very varied gifts, yet all animated with ardent love to Christ and to their fellow-men, they have laboured with remarkable pertinacity and zeal. Some, like Messrs Thoburn and Humphrey, have been men of lofty devotion; others, like Messrs Parker and Thomas, with their pioneer Dr Butler, have shown great practical skill; while others still, as Dr Waugh and Messrs Scott and Mansell, have exhibited considerable literary power; but it is almost invidious to take special notice of any, where all have done so well.

[margin: Great earnestness of the American Methodist missionaries.]

There are a few other mission stations connected with various societies, scattered over the extensive tract of country now under review, besides those which have been already described. The Society for the Propagation of the Gospel has two stations in the North-Western Provinces, one at Cawnpore, the other at Rurkee. The former made encouraging progress between the years 1861 and 1871, its converts having increased from seventy-two to two hundred and fifty-seven, while its schools, in the latter year, numbered

[margin: Missions of the Propagation Society at Cawnpore and Rurkee.]

And of the Baptist Society at Allahabad, Agra, and Mathura.

upwards of eight hundred pupils. The Baptist Society is doing a useful work in its three missions of Allahabad, Agra, and Mathura, although the Christian communities in them continue small.

The London Society's missions at Almorah and Ranee Khet. The Rev. J. H. Budden.

The London Society has two missions on the hills, one at Almorah, established in 1850; the other at Ranee Khet, commenced in 1868. These have eleven schools, containing between seven and eight hundred scholars. One very interesting feature of the Almorah Mission is its leper asylum, in which more than one hundred lepers are clothed and fed. A few years ago most of the lepers then in the asylum became Christians; and although some of the lepers are still heathen, yet a large proportion of those admitted from year to year eventually adopt the Christian faith. There is a handsome little church in the leper settlement, about two miles from Almorah, in which the lepers regularly assemble for Divine service. The mission has likewise a noble school, built of stone, the most imposing edifice in Almorah, perhaps in the whole province of Kumaon. It is under the superintendence of the Rev. J. H. Budden, the founder of the mission, whose enthusiasm and ability are conspicuous in its many important. institutions. Mr Budden is distinguished for his intimate acquaintance with the two languages spoken in the North-Western Provinces, Hindee and Urdu, in which he has written several works of utility and weight, displaying great idiomatic correctness, as well as much beauty of expression.

Rev. W. Ziemann.

The German Mission at Ghazepore, in which is the fine old missionary, Mr Zeimann, whose fame is in all the churches in these provinces, has, in the decade, made a leap from a community of seventy Christians to one of three hundred.

The following summary will represent the aggregate results of mission labour in North-Western India, excluding the Punjab, so far as they can be brought within the range of statistics:—

SUMMARY OF MISSIONARY LABOUR IN THE NORTH-WESTERN PROVINCES, OUDH, AND ROHILKHAND, FOR THE YEAR 1871.

Number of Native Christian Congregations,	96
Number of Protestant Native Christians,	8,039
Increase in Ten Years,	4,097
Number of Communicants,	3,031
Number of Towns and Villages containing Christians,	178
Number of Ordained Native Ministers,	19
Number of Unordained Native Preachers,	185
Number of Mission Colleges and Schools,	344
Number of Pupils, Male and Female,	17,265
Number of Christian Teachers, do.,	328

As in Bengal, the native Christian community, in this tract of country, has more than doubled in ten years.

CHAPTER VI.

MISSIONS IN THE PUNJAB.

Great administrators and missionaries in the Punjab

THE Punjab is the chief outpost of British rule in India. It is also the principal outwork of Christian missions in that land. There some of the truest and bravest of England's sons have fallen fighting with the valiant Sikhs; and there, too, some of the noblest men ever sent forth as missionaries have died waging severer conflicts with superstition and error. Under the administration of well-selected officers of commanding ability, the province has rapidly developed into its present flourishing condition. And under the superintendence, likewise, of devoted Christian missionaries of education and talent, of entire and unreserved consecration to their work, the Punjab has been brought under Christian influence and training; multitudes have been more or less enlightened by the truths of the gospel; and the foundations of a sound Christianity have been deeply laid in their midst. The list of great and honoured names of those who have thus laboured is too large for me to attempt to mention them. Yet before all others, certain names present themselves which it is impossible to pass by. The saintly Newton, the learned Pfander and Loewenthal, the generous Martin, the patient and loving Clark, the devout Morrison, the gifted Knott and French, and the earnest Janvier and Rudolph, awaken in the minds of those who know their labours the profound conviction that these, and many others like-minded, were precisely the kind of men needed for the great and difficult task of planting the gospel in the rugged and untamed soil of the Punjab. By the agency of largehearted, self-denying missionaries on the one hand, and able administrators on the other, this splendid province has within the space of twenty-five years been so transformed and improved, has so shot forth into intellectual life and activity, that it exhibits all the difference which exists between an unsubdued jungle and cultivated, fruit-yielding soil.

As Delhi has been transferred from the Government of the North-Western Provinces to that of the Punjab, it is now included within the latter province, although geographically it is far removed from it. In this city the Baptist and Propagation Societies have been labouring for many years, the former from 1818, and the latter from 1854. The Baptist Mission was founded by the Rev. J. T. Thompson, a man of fervid spirit, who laboured in the city and neighbourhood with great devotion for a long period. How many converts were the result of his ministry is unknown. As early as 1823, we find, however, that he baptized an elderly Brahman, a man of considerable reputation for his knowledge of Sanskrit literature; and that in the following year he baptized five other persons, of whom one was a Brahman. The congregations became numerous, although the number of Christians seems to have remained small. On the death of Mr Thompson, no successor was appointed for some years;

but his widow and two of his daughters continued in the mission, and in the year 1856 a new missionary, the Rev. J. Mackay, was sent from England to take charge of it. Meanwhile an eminent native Christian preacher, Wilayat Ali, was its principal working member, whose spirit and zeal were of a truly apostolic character. When the mutiny occurred in 1857, and the city revolted, all these persons, ladies included, were massacred. Wilayat Ali, on being captured, boldly declared his faith in Christ. "Yes, I am a Christian," he said to the Mahomedan troopers who had seized him, "and am resolved to live and die a Christian." His last words, before his execution were, "O Jesus, receive my soul!"

The pruning-knife saves the mission. After the siege of Delhi this mission made sudden and rapid, but not very steady, progress. Many persons became inquirers, and large numbers were baptized, not a few of whom either apostatised or proved worthless converts. In consequence of the strong measures afterwards adopted by wise and conscientious missionaries, the dead and useless branches were unsparingly cut away, with what vigour will be seen by the remarkable fact, that in 1861 the mission had six hundred Christians, while in 1871 it numbered only three hundred and ninety-five. The pruning-knife saved the mission, which is now healthy and strong.

Mission of the Propagation Society. The other mission, that of the Propagation Society, having been begun in 1854, was at the time of the outbreak still in its infancy. Nevertheless, by the commencement of 1857 it had made such satisfactory, not to say unusual progress, that the Bishop of Madras, who went to the Punjab at the beginning of that year, says of it in his Visitation Report, that it is "among the most hopeful and promising of our Indian mission-fields. The intelligent and well-informed converts, holding, as they do, high and important positions independent of the mission, the superior nature of the school with its one hundred and twenty boys—among the best I have visited in India—and the first-rate character for attainment and devotedness of the missionaries and schoolmasters, are making an impression which is moving the whole of that city of kings." Less than five months afterwards, the missionary, the Rev. A. R. Hubbard, and three assistant missionaries, Messrs Sandys, Cocks, and Koch, were put to death by the rebels, and the mission was broken up. But it was soon renewed, and is now more prosperous than ever. It has one hundred and ten Christians, one of whom is an ordained minister; and thirteen schools, giving instruction to six hundred and fifty pupils. The mission has had a succession of faithful and laborious agents; and the present head of the mission, the Rev. R. R. Winter, is a man imbued with the same spirit as his predecessors.

Massacre of all the missionaries

I must not omit to mention the important zenana work which is being carried on in Delhi through the agency of both the missions existing there. In 1872 the Propagation Society had seven ladies devoting their time to this most interesting branch of Christian labour. The zealous lady at their head, Mrs Winter, remarks, "There are five zenana missionaries (ladies) who manage the two normal schools for Hindoo, Mussulman, and Christian women; four day-schools for Mahomedan girls; one industrial school; and

Work in the zenanas. Mrs Winter.

classes in Bengalee, up-country Hindoo, and Mussulman zenanas. A sixth missionary gives her whole time to training English and Eurasian girls as teachers; a seventh is a female medical missionary, visits patients in zenanas, and has a dispensary and hospital for women only. There are also three branch zenana mission out-stations. The numbers under instruction have increased tenfold in ten years. Had we not been crippled at every turn by the want of funds, the increase might, without doubt, have been a hundredfold."*

The first mission established in Loodianah in 1834.

But, as already remarked, Delhi is only nominally in the Punjab. The first mission introduced into the country of the Five Rivers was established at Loodianah by the American Presbyterians in 1834. At that time a school was existing in this city, which had been opened by Sir Claude Wade, the political agent of the English Government, and which was attended by the sons and other relatives of Sikh Sardars or chiefs, of Afghan exiles, and of respectable natives of the city. The school was transferred to the mission, but its generous founder continued to support it so long as he remained in that part of the country; and it is still, I believe, under the superintendence of the mission. As early as 1837 a Christian Church was formed at Loodianah; and "two of its first three native members have since become valuable labourers in the missionary work, one as a minister of the gospel, and another as a teacher." The press in this mission has been a very effective auxiliary in the prosecution of its Christian

* Report of the General Missionary Conference at Allahabad: Paper on Missions to Women, by Mrs Winter, p. 169.

enterprise. It has issued the Sacred Scriptures and numerous books and tracts in Punjabee, Hindustanee, and various other languages.

Eight separate missionary societies have undertaken to plant the gospel in the Punjab, exclusive of two ladies' societies, whose labours are confined to the female portion of the native community, and the Christian Vernacular Education Society, whose special vocation is to issue useful books and tracts, and to promote vernacular education. Connected with these societies are thirty central missions, which with their numerous out-stations are scattered in all directions about the province, extending far into the Himalayas to the borders of Tibet, stretching beyond the Indus, and embracing Srinagar in Cashmere. The efforts of the missionaries are directed to all classes of the people—to the Sikhs, forming the major portion of the population; to the Hindustanees, who, as merchants, traders, and in other capacities, frequent the province; to the low-caste tribes found there as in all other parts of India; to the Mahomedans, especially, in some places, to those of them who are well read, and are consequently of the greatest weight and authority among their co-religionists; to the stalwart and majestic Afghans, also attached to the creed of Islam; to the hill races, so far as they are accessible; and to the Buddhist mountaineers on the Tibetan frontier. To all of these diverse tribes and classes the missionary is the pioneer of a true faith, and of an advanced civilisation; and with the one hand offers forgiveness of sin, peace to the conscience, and life and immortality, through the merits and sufferings of Christ; and with the other, social happiness,

Eight missionary societies have their missions in the Punjab.

secular knowledge, and whatever else can make a nation blessed and glorious, good as well as great.

Diversity of labour. By some missionaries much is done in the way of bazaar-preaching, that is, in public exhortations delivered regularly in the thoroughfares of cities and towns. By others, with whom this method has little favour, steady work among the villages is pursued. By others still, house-to-house visitation; and especially the cultivation of friendship and intercourse with respectable and educated natives, are preferred. Other missionaries, moreover, employ much of their time in schools and colleges, in imparting a complete education to the young in various branches of knowledge, and paying particular care to the moral and religious training of their pupils. While all, with few exceptions, engage more or less in literature, in writing, compiling, or translating suitable books for the use of the different classes of the community for which they are intended. Female education and the visiting of zenanas are also sedulously attended to. And the native Church is not forgotten, for great anxiety is shown towards its development and spiritual growth. In short, the Punjab presents a model of the various Christian labours which are for the most part carried on throughout India. Some differences will, doubtless, be found to exist, especially in regard to the peculiar village systems prevailing in Chota Nagpore, and in the missions of Southern India. Yet in the main, with a few important exceptions, the missionaries of the Punjab are following out the same diverse and multitudinous methods and plans of labour in their limited tract as are being prosecuted over the whole of the remaining country.

The Presbyterians of America commenced their missionary work in the Punjab in the year 1834, and selected Loodianah as the site of their first mission. They have now ten principal and six subordinate stations in that country, with four hundred and eleven converts, and a large number of schools, containing nearly five thousand pupils of both sexes. Their missions possess ninety-one native Christian preachers and teachers, of whom seven are ordained ministers. At the beginning of the year 1874 the brother of the reigning prince of the state of Kupurthala was baptized by the Rev. Golaknath, one of the native missionaries. This is an event of immense importance, not merely on account of the high rank of the convert, but also because of the great influence the event is likely to exert on the nobility of the Punjab and of other parts of India. In the mutiny the mission church in the city of Loodianah was destroyed by fire. "The school building shared a similar fate, and with its library, extensive and valuable philosophical apparatus, and depot of books for sale, became a desolate pile. The depository on the mission premises, with its contents of many thousand volumes of books for distribution, was reduced to ashes, its broken and blackened walls alone remaining. The bindery, with its large stock of printed sheets, binders' tools and materials, to the value of several thousand rupees, shared a similar fate. The paper-room, with a large supply of printing paper newly stocked, and the church on the mission premises (distinct from that in the city above alluded to), were set on fire; the former destroyed, the latter much injured. The dwelling-houses were rifled. On the arrival of the mutineers, the native Christians and orphan girls fled, and found shelter on the premises of one of the Cabul princes living in the neighbourhood. Thus the Lord was pleased to preserve the lives of all our company. Their houses were rifled, and some of them set on fire; but not one of themselves was permitted to be injured. Soon after this work of destruction was over, that of retribution commenced; for additional troops arrived, and the magistrate found it in his power to execute summary justice. Much of the stolen property was recovered, and, agreeably to an old law of the country, a tax was levied on the inhabitants, to make good the losses that the mission and other parties had sustained." *

Dr Janvier and Mr Loewenthal killed by natives.

Two distinguished missionaries of this society met with a cruel death at the hands of the natives. One was the Rev. Dr Janvier, of Sabathoo, who was killed by a fanatic in the month of October 1863; the other was the Rev. J. Loewenthal, of Peshawur, who was shot by his watchman on the 27th April 1864. The latter was a man of brilliant intellect. He spoke Persian and Pushtoo fluently, and had made considerable progress in colloquial Cashmiree. His translation of the New Testament into Pushtoo is still in circulation among the Afghans.

Divinity School at Lahore. Rev. T. V. French

In one department of labour, and in one mission only in the Punjab, an experiment is being tried, which, so far as I am aware, is not being attempted in the same way elsewhere. This is in the matter of training expressly for the ministry young native Christians of conspicuous piety and ability. The Rev. T. V. French, of the Church Society's Mission, for-

* Report of the Loodianah Mission for 1857, pp. 5, 6.

merly the Principal of St John's College, Agra, with the assistance of the Rev. J. W. Knott, originated a divinity school at Lahore, in which instruction is imparted in the Hebrew of the Old Testament and the Greek of the New, in ecclesiastical history, in theology in all its branches, and, in short, in all those subjects generally taught in the theological colleges of England and America. The aim is to make young ministerial students not only talented preachers, but also good scholars in all the subjects pertaining to the holy office to which they aspire. It should be added, that the method adopted by the excellent principal is not merely theoretical, but also eminently practical. By associating familiarly with them, taking them in his company when he preaches publicly to the natives or holds conversation with them, permitting only carefully-prepared addresses to be delivered by any of them, at his discretion, and the infusion into their minds of his own Christian spirit, and of his own earnestness and zeal, he endeavours to prepare the students for their future work. Very soon after the opening of the college, Mr French lost his gentle, saint-like colleague, Mr Knott, who, of all spiritually-minded men whom it has been our privilege to meet, seemed to be the most like Enoch, of whom it is said that "he walked with God."

The views of Mr French on the importance of close intercourse with his pupils are given in the following suggestive statement: "The very last thing which has been practised among us as missionaries was, what the greatest stress was laid and effort expended upon by Hindoo sect leaders, and by the early British and Anglo-Saxon missionaries, as well as by Mahomedan Moollahs everywhere; I mean, giving a few instruments the finest polish possible; imbuing a few select disciples with all that we ourselves have been taught of truth, and trying to train and build them up to the highest reach attainable to us. It is but seldom that this has been the relation of the missionary to the catechist—of the schoolmaster to the student—what the Soofie calls 'iktibâs,' lighting the scholar's lamp at the master's light. The perpetuation of truth (must we not add, of error also?) has, in every age, depended on this efficacious method of handing down teaching undiluted and unmutilated. To this we have become scarcely awake as yet. The learned missionary, or the deep, spiritually-taught missionary, is rather in his study and his books than reproducing his doctrine, spirit, and character in the minds and hearts of some chosen followers. It was such a method of working to which our Lord has encouraged and led us, not by His own example alone, but by those memorable words, 'The disciple is not above his master; but every one that is perfect shall be as his master.'"*

The number of students in the Divinity School at the end of 1872 was thirteen, drawn from missions of the Church Society in the North-Western Provinces as well as in the Punjab. Several of these have made considerable progress in their studies; and of nearly all of them Mr French indulges the sanguine hope, that from their piety, earnestness, application to study, and general ability, they will become able ministers of the New Testament. Five of these stu-

* Annual Letter of Rev. T. Valpy French on the Lahore Divinity School for 1872, p. 6.

dents were ordained to the ministry at the close of the year by the Bishop of Calcutta, two to deacon's orders, and three to priest's orders.

The missions of the American Presbyterian Society are occupied with a great variety of Christian labour. In addition to the extensive work which they carry on in the direct preaching of the gospel, they have numerous schools for the instruction of young people of both sexes. Moreover, the orphanage, the poorhouse, the leper asylum, and the dispensary are all in operation among them, and are valuable means of doing good both of a temporal and spiritual character. A large boarding school has been of late years established, in which many of the daughters of Christian parents, not merely residing in the Punjab but also in the North-Western Provinces, receive a superior education, similar to that imparted in the school at Dehra Doon of the same society. It is one of the most hopeful evidences of the growth of Christian civilisation in Northern India, that young educated native Christians are no longer willing to marry half-educated young women, but seek out wives for themselves from well-trained girls who have been brought up in superior mission schools. *Varied labours of the American Presbyterian missions.*

A very important movement in favour of Christianity manifested itself a few years ago among the Muzabee Sikhs, of which the Rev. Robert Clark, of Lahore, gives the following account. "The Khairabad Mission of the Church Missionary Society," he remarks, "a branch of the Peshawur Mission, was commenced in July 1860, in consequence of a movement in favour of Christianity which had sprung up spontaneously among the men of the late 24th Punjab Infantry, *The Muzabee Sikhs.*

P

now the 32d Native Infantry. The men of this regiment are Muzabee Sikhs, who were enlisted during the mutiny of 1857, in which they proved themselves brave and faithful soldiers. An outcast tribe, they no sooner found their position in society changed by their daring gallantry, and their sudden acquisition of wealth, than they evinced a desire to shake off their present religious bonds, which associate them with the very lowest class of Sikhs and Hindoos. Some of them, through the study of Christian books which they found at Delhi, and through the instruction which they received at various places from missionaries who visited their quarters, have in this regiment become Christians." By the end of the year 1862 as many as forty persons of the corps stationed at Khairabad and Attock had been baptized. The Government for a time threw an impediment in the way of their conversion and baptism, although it does not appear that it thought it worth while to interfere with the men of the regiment becoming Mahomedans, for it is a fact that more became Mahomedans than Christians. "About one hundred and ten boys," adds Mr Clark, "in two schools, with the two wings of the regiment, and twenty-three girls, are under daily instruction. They are receiving a thoroughly Christian education. The boys all come to church, and repeat the responses at the services. They have also been taught to sing, and form the choir at church. Many of their parents also attend the services; most of the native officers are present at least once on the Sunday. The elder boys have had gardens allotted to them, in which they work with their own hands, and for which they pay rent. The sum of three hundred and thirty rupees has been contributed by the natives alone during 1861, chiefly towards the expenses of the school. The congregations on Sundays and Wednesday evenings vary from forty to two hundred, and the attendance at daily prayers is about twenty."*

It is extremely interesting to learn that at the great military station of Peshawur, the frontier outpost of the British possessions in India, lying beyond the Indus, a successful Christian work is being carried on among the Afghan population. The mission was commenced in 1855, two years, therefore, before the mutiny. The first missionary to the Afghan race was the eccentric Joseph Wolff, a converted Jew and a clergyman of the Church of England, who in 1831 travelled from Armenia to Hindostan across the unknown regions of Central Asia. "Soon after the establishment of the Church Society's Mission," says the Rev. T. P. Hughes, "the Rev. J. Loewenthal, of the Presbyterian Mission, arrived and engaged in the translation of the New Testament into the Pushtu language, which was printed and published in 1863, not many months before its gifted translator was shot by his *chokedar* (watchman). The Peshawur Mission bears evident signs of the wisdom and forethought of its able founders. There are large and commodious mission houses and schools, and all the apparatus required for the operations of missionary work. There are now some seventy Christians on the mission roll, twenty-five of whom are communicants. The Afghans in days of yore came down from their mountain fastnesses and conquered India; and if ever, through God's grace,

Missions to the Afghans of Peshawur.

* Ten Years' Missionary Labour in India, pp. 60, 61.

a large Afghan Church should be gathered, it will make its influence felt over the widespread plains of Hindostan.

Afghan converts selected by the Government for important service.

"Amongst our Afghan converts there have been men who have done good service to Government. When Lord Mayo wished to send some trusted native on very confidential and very important service to Central Asia, it was an Afghan convert of our mission who was selected. Subadar Dilawari Khan, who had served the English well before the gates of Delhi, was sent on this secret mission to Central Asia, where he died in the snows, a victim to the treachery of the King of Chitral. Some three years ago, an officer employed on a special service of inquiry as to the doings of the Wahabees, wanted a trustworthy man to send to ascertain the number and condition of those fanatics who now reside at Palori, on the banks of the Indus. An Afghan convert was selected for this difficult and dangerous undertaking. In the Umbeyla war of 1863 it was necessary that Government should have a few faithful men who could be relied on for information. Amongst others selected for this work were two Afghan Christian converts of our mission.

Methods of labour among the Afghans.

"The schools of our mission contain five hundred pupils, one hundred of whom are Mahomedan females. The Afghans are strongly prejudiced against the study of English, and consequently there is some difficulty in inducing them to enter our schools. I attach great importance to itineracy amongst the villages, which are beyond the corrupting influences of a large city and a large military cantonment. The farther I go away from Peshawur, the more kindly am I received by the people. On these occasions I usually wear the Afghan dress, which, in my opinion, is more elegant and graceful than our Western costume; and I find it does not excite the curiosity of the villagers half as much as my ordinary English dress would. The Afghan villagers are a very sociable class of men. Hospitality is the bond of perfectness to the Afghan mind. A missionary to the Afghans should be careful to observe the apostolic rule, and be 'given to hospitality.' In order to do this, it has been the custom of the Peshawur missionaries to keep up guest-houses for the reception and entertainment of Afghan visitors."*

The mission at Srinagar in Cashmere has been lately deprived of its talented and devoted medical missionary, Dr Elmslie, who was cut off in the midst of his usefulness. Respecting the great difficulty of the work in this province, the Rev. T. Valpy French, Principal of the Divinity School, Lahore, makes some practical observations in his annual letter for 1871. "I must say a few words," he remarks, "about our visit" (meaning that of himself and of the Rev. Robert Clark) "to Lahore. Since I was among the Pathans on the frontier, this was the sharpest campaign I have yet been engaged in. Two new students, John Williams, the native Christian doctor from Tonk, and a young Afghan convert, with a former Cashmeric convert, accompanied us; and the two former made a start in the originals of the Bible. It was a great pleasure to be associated with this dear brother in the old field of his labours; for in Cashmere he was the first to raise the standard of the cross. Hearers we

Mission in Cashmere.

* Report of the General Missionary Conference: Paper by the Rev. T. P. Hughes, on the Afghans, pp. 74–78.

had in great numbers; and sometimes they seemed struck and thrilled through with the preaching of repentance, and the call to come out and yield themselves to God through Christ. But on not a few occasions they were with difficulty restrained from personal violence; and we were treated as the offscouring of all things. The bitter speeches and howls of derision with which the vices of some English tourists in Cashmere were dwelt upon, and held up to reproach, were shocking to a degree; and yet, it seems to me, it is well they should know that this is not Christianity, but the clean contrary. With all their demonstrations of violence, it is impossible not to feel attracted towards the Cashmeries."

Missions in the Himalaya Mountains

Step by step Christian missions have been spreading among the hills on the northern flank of the Punjab. The American Presbyterians were the first in the field on the hills as well as on the plains of this province, and as early as 1837 occupied Sabathoo, on the lower slopes of the Himalayas. The mission there, up to the present time, has made but few converts. In 1843 the Church Society commenced a mission at Kotgarh, farther north. "Schools were established at Kotgarh, and Simla, and in Kulu; the gospel was preached east and west of the Sutlej; and the *melas* (or fairs) at Rampore, where natives from all parts of the hills, and even from the Tibetan plateau, are met with in large numbers, were regularly attended. About three hundred pupils, of both sexes, have passed through the schools connected with the Kotgarh Mission. Not much could, or can even now be done, in the distribution of books in the hills, where not one per cent. can read. The living voice and personal intercourse of the missionary have been, and still are, the chief means of influencing the natives there."* A mission at Kangra, north-west of Kotgarh, was started by the same society in 1854. More northerly still, in the region of frost and snow, the Moravians established their mission at Kyelang, in British Lahoul, in 1855. Here, exposed to the intense cold of that region, far away from civilised life, the missionaries have laboured, in a lofty spirit of self-abnegation, from that time to the present. They have translated portions of the Bible, Barth's Bible Stories, and a Harmony of the Gospels; and have written a grammar, a geography, a short History of the World, and other books, together with several tracts, in the Tibetan language. Most of these works were printed by Mr Heyde with his own hands on a lithographic press. They now occupy two stations, and have had the honour and gratification of forming two Christian churches among the Mongolians. They have eight schools, attended by one hundred and eighty pupils, of whom forty are of the female sex. In addition to these missions among the hill tribes of the Himalayas, there is a flourishing one in the small independent state of Chumba, originated in 1863 by the Rev. W. Ferguson, formerly a chaplain of the Scotch Kirk in India. There are now ninety Christians connected with the mission, which was until lately under the charge of its spirited founder, who sustained it entirely by private resources placed at his command, but was made over in the year 1873 to the Established Church of Scotland. The mission

* Report of the Punjab Missionary Conference of 1862, 1863: Paper on the Hill Tribes, by the Rev. J. N. Merk, p. 259.

enjoys the assistance of the unusually large number of three ordained native ministers. Altogether, among these hill missions, there are nine separate congregations, with two hundred and four converts inhabiting fifteen villages. They have, moreover, twenty-seven schools, with five hundred and eighty-two scholars.

Ten new missions established in the Punjab since 1860.

It should be borne in mind that most of the missions in the Punjab are of comparatively recent date. Ten of them have been established since 1860. This shows the energy and enthusiasm with which the missionary enterprise is now being prosecuted in that province; yet it is only a fair example and illustration of the zeal and spirit observable in most other parts of India. Never was there exhibited a greater determination to persevere in the extension of Protestant missions in India than is displayed by missionaries now in the country. Some societies at home, made somewhat timid and unfaithful by the constant demand of their adversaries for large success, and by their own ignorance of the tremendous difficulties in the way of conversions among Hindoos proper, are showing symptoms of weariness and diminished zeal; but spite of this, the missionaries of these very societies, on reaching India, and labouring among the people, become animated with a spirit of unwavering trust in God, and with a growing consciousness of the absolute certainty of the downfall of heathenism, and the ultimate triumph of Christianity in India; and feel themselves burning with an enthusiasm which becomes stronger and stronger every year. Moreover, they see new missionary societies being continually established in England, Scotland, and America, which, with all the eagerness of youth, are sending forth labourers into the mission-field of India, to take part in the religious struggle there, now assuming gigantic dimensions. Thus it has come to pass, that in the Punjab, and elsewhere in India, the glorious work of conveying the gospel to the people of all races, ranks, and castes has attained to a vigour and a universality never before known.

Summing up the results of missions in the Punjab, we have the following statistics of their condition and achievements in the year 1871:—

STATISTICS OF MISSIONARY LABOUR IN THE PUNJAB FOR THE YEAR 1871.

Number of Native Christian Congregations,	47
Increase in Ten Years,	25
Number of Protestant Native Christians,	1,870
Number of Towns and Villages containing Christians,	73
Number of Ordained Native Ministers,	14
Number of Unordained Native Preachers,	66
Number of Mission Colleges and Schools,	181
Number of Pupils, Male and Female,	10,547
Increase in Ten Years,	6,939
Number of Christian Teachers, Male and Female,	105

CHAPTER VII.

MISSIONS IN CENTRAL INDIA, INCLUDING RAJPOOTANA, HOLKAR'S COUNTRY, THE CENTRAL PROVINCES, THE BERARS, AND THE NIZAM'S DOMINIONS.

THE missions collected together in this chapter stretch over an enormous extent of country, a tract the most destitute of Protestant missions of any in India. Until recently, with the exception of three cities, namely, Jubbulpore, Nagpore, and Secunderabad, it was entirely destitute of missionary labour. Since 1860, however, and including that year, nineteen other central stations have been established. This is a large number for a period of only twelve years, and augurs well for the future in regard to all this region. Considering its vastness, being equal to Britain, France, and Spain combined, the number of missions seems small, as it in reality is; and yet the increase within so short a term has been manifestly very great. The truth is, since the mutiny there has been a marvellous revival of missionary zeal all over India; and it is not too much to affirm that the number of missions in the land has nearly doubled since that catastrophe. It is singular, moreover, that although the spasmodic excitement awakened in England at that time, in favour of the conversion of the Hindoo races, does not appear to be sustained, yet that the spirit of earnestness among missionaries in India is

Nineteen new missions added since 1860

year by year being quickened; and displays itself in the origination of new missions, and in the prosecution of more extensive labours.

The six missions of the United Presbyterians of Scotland in Rajpootana were formed within the space of twelve years, commencing with 1860. That society, in beginning its work in this country, was wise enough, which all societies at first starting are not, to concentrate its operations on a limited tract, and to select a region altogether unoccupied by other missions. This society is the only one which has missions in the congeries of states known as Rajpootana, the land of the Rajpoot or princely tribes. Its talented and well-trained agents have already acquired an extensive influence over the districts which they occupy. Their leader and pioneer, the Rev. W. Shoolbred, a man of much tact, delighting in personal intercourse with the people, clear of intellect, and a forcible expounder of Christian doctrine, has made for himself, even in these few years, a very honourable position among Indian missionaries. The missions are situated at Jeypore, Ajmere, Nasirabad, Deoli, Beawr, and Todgarh, in which are found four hundred and ninety-four native Christian converts gathered into six congregations, and belonging to nine separate towns and villages. They have the large number of sixty-seven schools, containing two thousand three hundred and twenty-two male and female pupils. And they have twenty-two native Christian preachers and teachers. This measure of success, as the result of only twelve years' work, is most encouraging.

The Rajpootana missions have paid great attention

The Medical Mission Dr Valentine to the healing of the sick, and in this way have won the affection and esteem of the people. In ten years they have had the assistance of five medical missionaries, and two others have since joined, making seven, or one-half of the entire mission staff. Dr Valentine, the senior medical missionary, speaks thus of his labours in his twofold capacity of doctor and missionary. "My first station," he remarks, "was Beawr in Rajpootana. Close by was the city of Nya Nuggur, containing a population of between eight and nine thousand people, with numerous and pretty populous villages in the neighbourhood. My custom was to ride out to one of these villages each alternate morning, and to take along with me my medicine-box and surgical pocket-case. On these occasions oftentimes the whole village turned out, some to get relief, more attracted by the strangeness of the scene, women bringing along with them their children for vaccination. Medicines were dispensed, minor surgical operations were performed, and sometimes as many as a hundred children, brought by their mothers, were vaccinated in one morning. And then, do you think I would have been doing my duty as a medical missionary, had I considered my work finished, and dismissed these poor village men and women 'to seek and find elsewhere food for their spiritual sustenance'? I was then, and am more fully convinced now, that I would not have been doing my duty by acting thus, and therefore, as soon as I was able, I stood up beneath the burr-tree (*Ficus Indica*), in the centre of the village, and pointed them, there and then, to the great Physician of souls. In this way my brother Shoolbred and myself, several times, went all over

Mairwara, and visited villages where the face of a white man had never been seen, the practice of a European doctor never been known, and the name of Jesus never been heard."*

Throughout the whole of Scindia's and Holkar's Dominions there is but one mission, which has been lately established, and was for nearly two years under the charge of the Rev. N. Goreh, formerly a Pundit of Benares, and now a learned controversialist on the side of Christianity, and a devoted clergyman of the Church of England. He had two stations under his care situated at Mhow and Indore, forming one mission. The work in both places, while still in its infancy, was deprived of the services of Mr Goreh, who in the beginning of 1872 proceeded to Chanda, and commenced a mission there, an account of which is given farther on. [Mhow and Indore.]

In the Central Provinces, the capital of which is Nagpore, there are ten missions, all which, with two exceptions, date from the year 1862. Consequently, this great tract of country can hardly be said to have been yet brought under Christian influence. Five societies have undertaken its evangelisation, one, the Original Secession Synod of Scotland, as recently as 1872. The oldest mission in these provinces is that of the Free Church in Nagpore, which was commenced in 1844. Its founder was the Rev. T. Hislop, a man of science and literature, who originated the public museum in Nagpore, and promoted greatly the study of archæology and the early history of the province. He was, nevertheless, a missionary of the truest type; [Rev. T. Hislop.]

* Report of the General Missionary Conference: Paper on Medical Missions, by C. Valentine, Esq., M.D., pp. 195, 196.

but, in carrying out his great Christian purpose, he conceived very broad views of the duties and labours of a missionary, and held that whatever was of moment to the people was a proper subject for his investigation. He met with a premature death by drowning while in the height of his popularity. His loss was regarded at the time as a national calamity.

<small>Mission of the Free Church of Scotland at Nagpore.</small> The Nagpore Mission of the Free Church was established at the solicitation of Captain, now Major-General Sir William Hill, who gave a sum of upwards of two thousand six hundred pounds towards its foundation. The province has a population of nearly five millions, consisting partly of Hindoos, partly of Mahomedans, and partly of aboriginal races. An idea of the ignorance prevailing may be gathered from the fact, that in 1856 a colporteur travelled two hundred miles in the province, and although passing by a large number of villages, only met with two schools, and these possessed not more than forty pupils. "The inhabitants in the western or more cultivated part of the country speak Mahrathi; and in the east a corrupt dialect of Hindee; while in the south a few are found to use Telugu. In the jungly tracts various aboriginal dialects prevail, which, with the exception of that spoken by the Kurkis or Moasis, may all be classed as Gondee, and bear a close affinity to Tamil." On entering upon the work of the mission, Mr Hislop was assisted by two German missionaries, Messrs Bartels and Apler, the sole survivors of a band of six missionaries who on reaching India attempted to establish a mission among the aboriginal Gonds of Amar Kantak. In one week four of their number fell victims to disease, and the others fled, but only to die

at Nagpore, one six months after the foundation of the mission, the other in 1848.

Soon after the establishment of the mission a singular question arose in regard to the authority of the Rajah over his subjects, should they desire to embrace the Christian faith. A young man of good caste, wishing to be baptized, fled to the missionary's house in order to escape from the violence of his friends. The Rajah demanded his surrender, and appealed to the British Resident to enforce his demand, stating that, according to existing treaties, he was absolute over his subjects, and that such as were discontented should be given up. The Resident complied with the Rajah's request, and compelled Mr Hislop to send back the youth, who was at once placed in confinement by the Mahratta Government. The Governor-General in Council, on being appealed to, declined to interfere; but at length public opinion became strongly aroused throughout India in favour of the young man, so that after three months of captivity he was set at liberty. Had the tyrannical spirit of the Nagpore Government continued in force, it is clear that missionary operations in this and other semi-independent Indian states would have been impossible. *No personal liberty under native rule.*

The growth of the Nagpore Mission has been steady, and of late years rapid. In 1850 there were but twenty-four native Christians in connection with it. In 1861 they had increased to one hundred and thirty-eight; and by 1871 they amounted to two hundred and seventy-one, with ninety communicants, having thus nearly doubled in number within the space of ten years. It had also eight schools, with upwards of five hundred pupils. There is likewise a *Growth of the mission.*

mission of the Church of England in Nagpore, established a few years ago, and already numbering seventy-five converts, who, being added to those in the Free Church Mission, show a body of three hundred and forty-six native Christians now existing in that city.

Missions of the American Evangelical Society.

The American Evangelical Society has two stations in Central India, one at Bisrampore, established in 1868, the other at Raipore, commenced in 1871. The former is at the eastern extremity of the Nagpore province, and is situated among an outcast and semi-aboriginal race of Satnâmee Chamârs. The Chamârs are very numerous throughout Northern India, and amount to several millions of people, who are mostly engaged in agriculture. They are divided into seven great clans or tribes, which hold no social intercourse with each other. The word *satnâmee* means seven-named; and it is by no means improbable that representatives of all the seven Chamâr clans, having found their way to Bisrampore, have associated together and formed themselves into a homogeneous community, of which seventy-four persons were baptized in three years, of whom thirty-four were communicants.

The Satnâmee Chamâr Christians.

Mission among the Gonds of Chindwara.

A mission to the Gonds of Chindwara was originated in 1866, under the auspices of the Free Church. The missionary, Rev. J. Dawson, has lately published a grammar of the Gond language, and has translated the Book of Genesis and three Gospels, besides printing materials for a larger grammar, and also for a dictionary, in the same dialect. In addition, he has written a Gondi First Book, for the Christian Vernacular Society. Mr Dawson has gathered a small Christian community of Gonds, an earnest of the great harvest yet to be reaped. These aborigines occupy a vast extent of country in Central India, and are computed to be not less than five millions in number. It is a highly important feature in missionary labour in India, that throughout the country the aboriginal tribes and inferior races generally, from extensive experience acquired in a great many places far apart from one another, are found to be much more readily influenced by the truths of the Christian religion than the Hindoo races. The reason of this is doubtless a complicated one. They have much less to unlearn than Hindoos; have no sacred books, no arrogant priesthood, no imperious caste bonds; and consequently can approach the subject of Christianity with a spirit of less prejudice and greater fairness than if they were entangled in the intricate meshes of Hindooism.

The Church Missionary Society has two important missions in the Central Provinces, one at Jubbulpore, in the north, the other at Dumagudiem, in the south, on the frontier of the Nizam's Dominions. The former was established in 1854, the latter in 1862. The more recent mission has two hundred and forty-four converts; and the older, one hundred and five. The Christian work in the Jubbulpore Mission is of an elaborate and very interesting character. It has its native preachers ministering to the people in the streets of the city and surrounding villages. It has its orphanages for boys and girls. It has charge of as many as ten schools, in which about eight hundred children of both sexes are instructed. Some of its Christians are men of great local influence, while one of them is a writer on the Christian Mahomedan con-

The Church Mission at Jubbulpore.

troversy of considerable power. The mission has been for many years under the able management of the Rev. E. Champion; but it was established by the Rev. E. Stuart, the talented Secretary of the Calcutta Committee of the Church Missionary Society. It has an out-station among the Gonds inhabiting the Mundla district, of great interest and promise. The Christians connected with the Dumagudiem station are divided into four congregations, the members of which are scattered over twelve villages. In the year 1871 as many as thirty-five adults embraced Christianity, and received the rite of baptism on the profession of their faith. The Society of Friends has a small mission at Jubbulpore, at the head of which is a Quaker lady. She has charge of two girls' schools containing fifty-six pupils.

The Chanda Mission established in 1872.

As already stated, the Chanda Mission was founded by the Rev. N. Goreh early in 1872. His labours have been chiefly among an outcast race called Mhar, of whom he gives the following account: "There are a people called Dhers or Mhars in Chanda. They live in many parts of the town in groups of small houses. They are considered to be of a very low caste. Men of higher caste do not touch them, do not allow them to enter their houses, do not allow them to ascend their shops, or draw water from the same wells. These Mhars follow the profession of weavers, which trade, however, they tell me, does not bring them much profit, on account of the importation of English-made cloths; and they can hardly maintain themselves, they say, and their families by it. There is a group of these Mhars living just outside the town wall. The district is called Jutpoorah, which is both inside and outside the wall. In the outside Jutpoorah there is a mission chapel. I began to hold meetings in the evenings in this chapel, and these Mhars used to come in large numbers, and to hear attentively. I soon found out another group of Mhars in the inside Jutpoorah, in a part called Lumburee. There also I began to hold meetings in the evenings, and large numbers used to come and listen respectfully."* In a few months some ten or a dozen persons were baptized, and formed the nucleus of a Christian Church.

There are two small missions in the Berars, one lately established at Chikalda among the Gonds, and the other at Buldana, which was commenced in 1862. There is a good opening here, and also in Holkar's Country, and beyond as far as Rajpootana, for a large number of missions. These vast tracts have been scarcely touched by Christianity. The same likewise may be said of the Gond territory, and of the extensive country ruled over by the Nizam, which possesses only four missions, belonging to the Free Church, Scotch Kirk, Church, and Propagation Societies. Two of them are at Secunderabad, and all four are superintended by ordained native ministers, there being no foreign missionary at all in the province. The Propagation Society's Mission was established in 1844, the rest in 1860, and subsequently. All seem to be in a flourishing condition, and to have made great numerical progress, so far as converts are concerned, during the past ten years. In 1861 there were only three hundred and fourteen Protestant native Christians throughout the whole of the Nizam's Dominions; but by 1871 they had increased to eleven

* Report of the Chanda Church Mission, by Rev. N. Goreh, pp. 8, 9.

hundred and thirty-seven, living in nineteen villages, and forming fifteen congregations, which is a very encouraging rate of augmentation in so short a time. Of this number, four hundred and five are communicants. There are twenty-one schools, with nineteen hundred and sixty-seven scholars, connected with the four missions. It is manifest, therefore, that a very useful and successful work is being prosecuted by them. It is matter, however, for regret that the missions in the province are so few in number. Instead of four, there is ample room for fifty, at the least, in so wide a territory.

The Free Church Mission at Jalna, Rev. Narayan Sheshadri.

The Free Church Mission at Jalna, in the Nizam's Dominions, demands special attention. As early as the year 1855 Christian work was commenced among the natives there, but after a time, was, for various reasons, abandoned. In the winter of 1861 Dr Murray Mitchell visited the station, and was much interested at finding that, notwithstanding its relinquishment by his society, some fruit of the labours which had been put forth were still visible. From representations made by him, the society determined to re-establish the mission, and the Rev. Narayan Sheshadri was appointed to take charge of it. But this gentleman was already at the head of a new station at Judapore, in the Bombay Presidency, which was opened in 1862. Thus he had for a time the care of these two missions, which were separated by a wide tract of country. Twice only in the year Narayan Sheshadri visited Jalna; and yet in 1867, so wonderfully rapid had been its growth, that in three years after the recommencement of the mission, the native congregation numbered one hundred and sixteen members, with eighty-eight communicants. "As a large number of the converts," says Mr Hunter in his account of the Rural Mission at Jalna, "had no hereditary right in the villages in which they resided, Mr Narayan thought it would be expedient to found for their use a Christian village. The Nizam's prime minister, the enlightened Sir Salar Jung, was favourable to the project, and granted land to be rent free for twenty-five years. The site chosen was on a most elevated spot, visible from afar. The village was to be built on sanitary principles. Its name was to be Bethel; and pecuniary aid, it was stated, would be required to enable its founder to sink half-a-dozen wells, erect a good church, a manse, two schoolhouses, one for boys and the other for girls, an inn for strangers to dwell in, a market-shed, an industrial shed, and construct macadamised roads bordered with trees. It was proposed that the natives should build houses at their own expense."* This great project has already been to a considerable extent carried out. Of the grant of upwards of six hundred and fifty acres of land, more than two hundred and fifty have already been brought under cultivation. The houses are all built after a certain model, with gardens both in front and behind. As to the native Christians, they have so multiplied, that in 1871 they were three hundred and ninety-three in number, with one hundred and ninety-four communicants. The great success of this enterprise presents in striking colours the great mistake which missionary societies are apt to make, in closing their missions, or expressing discontent at their

* Mr Hunter's History of the Missions of the Free Church of Scotland, p. 287.

operations, because of the smallness of their results at the outset, or even after an existence of many years.

The increase observable in the Central India missions between the years 1861 and 1871 is proportionally very great, being nearly at the rate of four hundred per cent. on the numbers existing in 1861, which is ground for much encouragement and hope. The statistics of all the missions for 1871 are as follows :—

STATISTICS OF MISSIONARY LABOUR IN CENTRAL INDIA, INCLUDING RAJPOOTANA, HOLKAR'S COUNTRY, THE CENTRAL PROVINCES, THE BERARS, AND THE NIZAM'S DOMINIONS, FOR THE YEAR 1871.

Number of Native Christian Congregations,	37
Increase in Ten Years,	30
Number of Protestant Native Christians,	2509
Increase in Ten Years,	1983
Number of Towns and Villages containing Christians,	60
Number of Ordained Native Ministers,	6
Increase in Ten Years,	3
Number of Unordained Native Preachers,	41
Increase in Ten Years,	35
Number of Mission Colleges and Schools,	126
Increase in Ten Years,	103
Number of Pupils, Male and Female,	6130
Increase in Ten Years,	4984
Number of Christian Teachers, Male and Female,	66

CHAPTER VIII.

MISSIONS IN THE CITY AND PRESIDENCY OF BOMBAY.

THE island of Bombay was ceded to the British Government in 1662, and became the seat of a flourishing trade, from which not only the native inhabitants of the island and the mainland, but also, and especially, merchants in Great Britain derived great profit. Its maritime position in relation to the rest of India, and also to Western nations, has been exceedingly favourable to its prosperity; and now that commerce can pass so easily and so rapidly between the East and the West by the Suez Canal, there is every reason to believe that its wealth and importance will continue to increase. In the early years of British possession, little effort seems to have been made to foster religious feeling among the European residents. For fifty years they had neither chaplain nor church. Christian services were held for those who wished to attend them in one of the high rooms in the fort. On the arrival of the Rev. R. Cobbe, the first chaplain, he very soon made arrangements for the erection of a church, and collected upwards of five thousand pounds for the purpose. It was a spacious building, large enough for a cathedral, which, more than a hundred years after its erection, it became. A singular ceremony,

The English residents in Bombay without a church for fifty years.

Ceremony at the opening of the first church.

significant of the times, was performed at its opening. This is described by Mr Cobbe himself. "Sermon ended, the Governor, Council, and ladies repaired to the vestry, where, having drunk success to the new church in a glass of *sack*, the whole town returned to the Governor's lodgings, where was a splendid entertainment, wine and music, and abundance of good cheer. After dinner the Governor began Church and King, according to custom; but upon this occasion an additional compliment of twenty-one great guns from the fort were answered by European ships in the harbour. Thus was the ceremony of opening Bombay Church, with all possible demonstrations of joy, with that decency and good order which was suitable to the solemnity."*

Mission of the American Board commenced in 1812.

The first mission established in Bombay was that of the American Board of Commissioners for Foreign Missions. It will be remembered that in the year 1812 very stringent measures were adopted in Bengal to prevent the increase of missionaries in that Presidency, and to repress the zeal of those who remained. Just at this time six missionaries arrived in Calcutta, having been sent out by this Board, who were at once ordered to depart from the country. Much excitement was caused among these missionaries, as well as among those in Serampore, by the violence of the Government in carrying out their new regulations, in the midst of which two of the American missionaries escaped from Calcutta, and found their way to Bombay, where they arrived on February 11, 1813. They were discovered, however, and a peremptory command came from the Supreme Government

* Hough's Christianity in India, vol. iv. p. 483.

to Sir Evan Nepean, the Governor of Bombay, to send them to England forthwith. Fortunately for the missionaries, Sir Evan was a man of deep religious feeling, who set an example of Christian conduct to the European residents of the city by his scrupulous attention to religious duties and obligations; and therefore, instead of treating the missionaries harshly, showed them kindness and sympathy. He received a memorial from them requesting to be allowed to remain in Bombay, and permitted them to continue there, pending a reference which he made to the Governor-General in their behalf. The document which he wrote represented the motives and objects of the missionaries so forcibly that the Governor-General was convinced of their integrity and peaceableness, and would have suffered them to take up their residence permanently in Bombay; but at this juncture war broke out between Great Britain and the United States, and consequently a fresh order came to Sir Evan to deport them from the country. Before, however, it could be carried out, they fled secretly in a coasting vessel, intending to proceed to Ceylon, whither they had been invited by the Rev. Mr Newell, one of their former colleagues in Calcutta, and another missionary. On their way they touched at Cochin, where they dwelt for a month. Meanwhile, the English magistrate, who behaved towards them with much consideration, and gave them accommodation gratuitously, received orders from Bombay to send them back. And they returned to Bombay. Sir Evan, although vexed and displeased at their flight, yet showed them all kindness on their return, and provided them with apartments in the Admiralty

House. A new Governor-General, Lord Moira, arrived in India in October 1813, to whom the friends of the missionaries in Bengal applied for his sanction to their continuance in India. Sir Evan Nepean also brought the matter before his own Council, and was so zealous in it that he wrote home to the Court of Directors in their favour. The decision which they came to was promoted by Mr Charles Grant, the chairman of the Court, who found it difficult to overcome the opposition of some of the members. The Directors, in their despatch, expressed themselves satisfied with the object of the missionaries, and permitted them to remain in Bombay. The mission was at once established, and has continued to the present time.

The first missionaries. The missionaries were the Rev. S. Nott and the Rev. Gordon Hall. The first soon returned to America from ill-health; the latter was joined by the Rev. Mr Newell, from Ceylon. In the year following the settlement of their difficulties, that is, in 1815, they had made such proficiency in the study of the Mahratta language as to be able to preach in public to the people, and also to commence the translation of the Scriptures into that tongue. Shortly after this we find that they had translated a Harmony of the Gospels, and had written several tracts, copies of which were already in circulation among the Hindoos in the neighbourhood. They likewise commenced several schools, which in 1816 had three hundred pupils. One of them was especially for the children of the Jewish population of Bombay, who were in-*The Black Jews of Cochin.* structed both in Hebrew and Mahratta. These Jews were an offshoot of the Black Jews of Cochin, and had a synagogue for religious worship in the city. In the course of this year a new missionary arrived, and the labours and plans of the mission were consequently increased. A press was established, from which Christian works began immediately to be issued. By 1818 the mission possessed three stations, one at Bombay itself, a second at Mahim, six miles to the north, and a third at Tannah, the chief town of Salsette. It had also twenty-five schools, in which fourteen hundred children of both sexes were educated, of whom a hundred belonged to Jewish families.

The Bombay Bible Society was founded in 1813, and the Governor, Sir Evan Nepean, who had been a member of the British and Foreign Bible Society in England from its commencement, gave it his hearty support. The society soon became the medium of circulating the Sacred Scriptures in many languages, not in Bombay merely, but also in other cities and towns along the Malabar coast. The Church Missionary Society commenced its operations in Bombay in 1818, when a Corresponding Committee, as it was called, was formed in connection with that society for making such preliminary arrangements as were thought necessary for the mission about to be commenced. The first missionary, the Rev. R. Kenney, was sent out in 1820, in which year the Church Society's Mission may be said to have been inaugurated. This missionary emulated the zeal of the American brethren who had preceded him. He set himself to the study of the Mahratta vernacular, and in a few months made himself sufficiently master of it as to be able to converse with the people. He originated schools for native children, which in two years were six in

The Bombay Bible Society founded in 1813; the Church Mission in 1820.

number, with one hundred and fifty scholars. He wrote two books in Mahratta, and commenced a translation of the Liturgy of the Church of England, which he completed. He also undertook a journey into Northern Concan in the company of an American missionary, for the purpose of preaching the gospel to the inhabitants of that province. And thus he soon proved himself to be a diligent and efficient labourer in the mission-field.

Church of Scotland. The Church of Scotland sent out a chaplain to Bombay as early as 1815, and a church was erected by the Scotch Presbyterians in 1819. A second chaplain arrived in 1823.

School-Book and School Society; and Bombay Missionary Union. Various societies were from time to time established in Bombay, with the object of promoting the Christian enterprise which was now being earnestly prosecuted in that city. A "School-Book and School Society" was formed in 1825, which was specially directed to the work of education. Its intention was to provide suitable books for schools, as well as to increase the number of such institutions. About the same time also a "Bombay Missionary Union" was organised, an association of much importance, as it aimed at uniting all missionaries in that part of India by a tie of Christian brotherhood—a scheme which in England has never yet been practicable, yet is found to work for the most part harmoniously and successfully in all places in India in which missionaries of different societies are gathered together. One direct result of the Missionary Union formed in Bombay was, that in 1827 it founded another society, for the publication and distribution of tracts, and therefore called the "General Tract Society," "to aid Christians of all

Tract Society.

denominations in their efforts to benefit the people of the East."

Both Bishop Middleton and Bishop Heber visited Bombay, which at that time was included within the see of Calcutta. The latter, while in Bombay, in association with the Governor, the judges, the members of the Council, and others, formed a committee in connection with the Society for the Propagation of the Gospel in Foreign Parts; but no mission was established there by that society until many years afterwards. Committee of the Propagation Society.

The year 1828 was distinguished by the commencement of a third mission in Bombay, which was undertaken by the Scottish Missionary Society, in whose hands the mission remained till 1835, when it was transferred to the General Assembly. The first agent was the Rev. J. Stevenson, who removed to Poona in 1831. The Rev. Dr John Wilson was sent out by the society to Bombay, and began his labours there in 1829. Grown old in the glorious work of endeavouring to enlighten the native inhabitants of that great city, he still clings to it with all the ardour of his first love. With a keen and well-balanced intellect, amply furnished with knowledge of many kinds, eager to investigate not only the social and political problems of the native races, but also the many phases which their various religions assume, delighting in historical and scientific researches, and taking supreme interest in every subject bearing upon Hindoo life and character, this noble missionary during the last forty-four years has exerted an immense influence over the native and European population of the Presidency of Bombay. But his Mission of the Scotch Kirk. Rev. Dr Wilson.

mental vigour and varied learning have never led him astray from the singleness of that purpose which first led him to consecrate himself to missionary toil and labour. His numerous contributions to Christian literature, his zeal in acquiring several vernacular languages, and preaching in them with much effect, his steady prosecution of the work of education in the splendid institution or college which he founded, and which mainly through his unremitting attention has risen to the high position which it now occupies, and the various other missionary duties which he has performed, are sufficient testimony to his earnestness, faith, and love as a missionary of the cross of Christ.

Labours of the Rev. D. Mitchell.   As early as 1822 the Scottish Missionary Society had designed to establish a mission in the Bombay Presidency, and had actually sent out the Rev. D. Mitchell, formerly an officer of the Indian army, who reached Bombay in the month of January 1823. He immediately formed a Corresponding Committee in relation with the society; but instead of remaining in that city, with the sanction, and probably at the instigation of the committee, proceeded to Fort Victoria, called by the natives Bankoot, sixty miles to the south of Bombay, and commenced a mission there. He founded ten schools, with nearly five hundred pupils, in the course of a few months. But his labours were soon closed, for he died in November of the same year. Yet before the year closed, three more missionaries arrived; and in the following year, another; two of whom joined the mission at Fort Victoria, and the remaining two went thirteen miles farther south, to Harnee, near Severndroog, where they began their Christian labours among the people. In 1826 these united missions had forty-two schools, in which eighteen hundred and twenty-six scholars received religious and secular instruction. Much also was done by the missionaries in the way of direct preaching of the gospel to the natives of Bankoot and Harnee, and among the villages in their neighbourhood.

<small>Missions in Bankoot and Harnee.</small>

The three missions existing in Bombay carried on their work with steady perseverance, although it does not appear that many converts were made. Nevertheless, the constant daily exposition of the truths of Christianity in various parts of the city, the numerous schools which had been originated in all directions, the circulation of the Bible and Christian books and tracts in the vernacular languages, produced by degrees a powerful effect upon the public mind. The result of this was, that while many were led to admire and even approve of some of the fundamental principles of the Christian religion, a spirit of opposition was awakened in the minds of not a few, who plainly saw that Christianity and Hindooism could not coexist, but that one must destroy the other. Indeed, the religious history of Bombay at this period appears to have been precisely similar to that of Calcutta of about the same time already described. The growing excitement of the people culminated in the year 1839, on occasion of the baptism of two Parsee youths by the Rev. Dr Wilson. "They were supposed to be the first proselytes from the religion of Zoroaster in modern times. Their Parsee friends became much enraged, and would have laid violent hands on them, but they had taken refuge with the missionaries. A legal

<small>The first Parsee converts.</small>

process was instituted against the missionaries, but in vain. They then attempted to break up the schools by threats against the parents, and succeeded to some extent. They published a tract in defence of Hindooism, and petitioned the Government for protection against the influence of the missionaries, but all with very little effect, except to show that the progress of the gospel had begun to be such as to disturb the native conscience, and awaken their fears for the safety of their ancient system of idolatry." In a year after this, the excitement having subsided, the young converts could appear in public without molestation. One of these was .Dhanjibhai Nauroji, a young man of great promise, who afterwards visited Edinburgh, and finished his education at New College. He was subsequently ordained to the ministry, and has for many years been one of the most prominent native members of the mission.

Rev. Dhanjibhai Nauroji.

The struggle between Christianity and the religions of the country, instead of abating, became stronger from year to year. The efforts of the leaders of native opinion on this subject, although violent, were, unconsciously to themselves, controlled in a singular manner by the civilising influence which education and Christianity exerted upon them. "In 1843 the more wealthy Hindoos commenced printing by subscription a series of their most popular religious books in monthly numbers. None of these books had ever before been printed, and the manuscripts were scarce and costly, but in the printed form they were afforded at little cost. A Hindoo at Bombay expended nearly four hundred pounds in printing and circulating one of the sacred books of his religion. Thus a new and

Efforts of the natives to resist the spread of Christianity.

extraordinary effort to sustain idolatry showed that the presence and power of Christianity were beginning to be felt. This was still further felt a year later, when the periodical press was for the first time brought to the aid of Hindooism. Three weekly newspapers, and one monthly magazine, all in the Mahratta language, and bitterly opposed to Christianity, were published at Bombay. A paper was also issued at Poona, and a monthly journal and three weeklies in the Gujeratee language, spoken by seven or eight millions in the region north of Bombay, besides two papers printed in the Persian language. The Gujeratee papers especially attempted to refute Christianity by quotations from the writings of Paine and Voltaire, and other infidels. Thus ten papers and magazines in and around Bombay, armed not only with all that heathen learning could furnish, but with the most approved weapons of infidelity, were brought to bear against the religion taught by the missionaries. But meanwhile the Christian press in Bombay was never more efficient. It had the means of issuing periodicals, tracts, and portions of the Scriptures, in English, Sanskrit, Mahratta, Gujeratee, Hindostanee, Persian, and Arabic; and thus the issues of the idolatrous and infidel presses were met face to face, and their influence in great measure counteracted. It was with great joy and thankfulness that the missionaries at Bombay were able to say in 1845, 'Thirty-three years ago the doctrine of Christ crucified was unknown to the people of the Mahratta country. No portion of the Sacred Scriptures had been given to them in their own language. Not a single tract from which they could learn the way of salvation was in existence. Unbroken darkness covered the land. Now the sound of the gospel has gone out into all the land. The people of the most distant villages have heard, at least, that "there is none other name under heaven given among men whereby we can be saved, but the name of Jesus."'"*

Rev. Dr Murray Mitchell.

The Rev. Dr J. Murray Mitchell was for a long period connected with the Free Church missions in the Bombay Presidency. A man of refined taste and excellent scholarship, a "distinguished graduate of Marischal College, Aberdeen," it was to be expected that he would become popular in his intercourse with the natives, especially among the young men whom he instructed. His labours were chiefly, though by no means exclusively, of an educational character. He made himself well acquainted with Mahratta and other Indian languages, and preached in them to the people. He published various useful works in Sanskrit, Mahratta, English, and other tongues, intended to remove the doubts of intelligent natives on the truths of Christianity. One on the evidences of the Christian religion, containing also a discussion on Hindooism, Parseeism, and Zoroastrianism, has had a large circulation not only in the Bombay Presidency,

Rev R. Nesbit.

but also in Northern India. Another missionary of this society, the Rev. R. Nesbit, one of the earliest it sent to India, laboured with great zeal and enthusiasm, and has left a lasting impression behind him. The truth is, the missionaries of the Free Church in Bombay, as in Calcutta and Madras, have been a distinguished race, and have throughout been in the

* Cyclopedia of Missions, by the Rev. H. Newcomb, New York, p. 386.

foremost rank of educators and philanthropists. They have done also a good work as direct preachers of the gospel in the languages of India. Mr Nesbit was suddenly carried off by cholera in the year 1855. His funeral was attended by a large number of Europeans and a great crowd of natives. "To see the children and those of extreme age crying at the grave," says a spectator, "was a day never to be forgotten. Natives of all classes, Hindoos, Parsees, and Mahomedans, without distinction, all shed tears, nay, even cried loudly over the dust of their departed friend and wellwisher." "No wonder," says Mr Hunter; "for a more loving spirit than Robert Nesbit, especially in his later years, it would have been difficult anywhere to find. His conscientiousness, too, was very notable, as was his insight into the human heart. Hormasji Pestonji once took Mr Nesbit for a god, on account of what appeared the infallible rectitude of his judgments."*

It is rather remarkable, that although portions of the Bible in the Mahratta language had been in circulation for many years, yet that the translation of the Bible into that language was not completed till 1847. Twenty-one years before this, the New Testament had been completed and put in circulation; and a revised edition had been issued in 1830, the translation and revision having been accomplished by the missionaries of the American Board, and the work itself having been printed by the press of their mission. It would seem, however, that by the year 1847 the entire Bible had been translated not only

Translation of the Bible into Mahratta.

* History of the Missions of the Free Church of Scotland, by the Rev. R. Hunter, p. 239.

into Mahratta, but also into Gujeratee, the two principal languages on the western side of India.

<small>Act removing the disabilities of converts.</small>

One reason why the number of converts to Christianity in Bombay had been small was, that "there had been no special law for the protection of converts, who were tried by heathen laws and subjected to every indignity, with confiscation of goods." This was the condition of native Christians throughout Western and Southern India. But in 1849 the Government yielded to the representations which had been made on the subject, and passed an Act, by which the old harsh laws were repealed, and Hindoos, on becoming Christians, were protected against all civil disabilities and forfeiture of rights.

<small>Female education.</small>

Not until 1850 had the matter of female education engaged the attention of the Bombay Government. Incited by the labours and representations of the missionaries and their friends, the Government at last ventured to show its interest in so important a question, although fully aware of the strong prejudice of the natives against the education of their females. This prejudice while quickened in some places, on account of the discussion which had taken place upon it, had diminished in others; and for the most part, educated native gentlemen of Bombay, like their fellow-countrymen of Calcutta, were beginning to indulge the wish that their wives and daughters might be educated like themselves, and so be their companions in private life in a much higher sense than they had been. All Indian governments have been slow in promoting education, especially the education of Hindoo females; and therefore it is not to be wondered at that the Bombay Government

followed suit. They are now making amends for
years of sluggishness and timidity, for which the
natives owe a great debt of gratitude to the missionary
community throughout the country, by whom mainly
all changes for the better on this subject among the
various governments of India have been instigated
and brought about.

When the Disruption in the Church of Scotland occurred, the missionaries in connection with it in Bombay having separated themselves from its communion, a new mission was formed, and another large educational institution was soon established. Thus there are at the present time as many as three mission colleges in Bombay belonging to the Church of England, the Scotch Kirk, and the Free Church of Scotland. In these about a thousand students receive instruction. The American Board, although it originally devoted so much time and energy to schools, yet in 1871 had only charge of one small school in the city. The Propagation Society commenced a mission in Bombay in 1859; but it, too, devotes itself to a very small degree to the education of native youths. There are now in Bombay twenty-six mission colleges and schools belonging to all the missions, and in them two thousand two hundred and ninety-nine scholars of both sexes are being educated, of whom four hundred and seventy-nine are women and girls; but as many as three hundred and ninety-four of these belong to the Free Church Mission.

<small>Three mission colleges now in Bombay.</small>

There is a considerable population of Jews in Bombay, amounting to eight or ten thousand persons, "whose physiognomy seems to indicate a union of both Abrahamic and Arabic blood. About fifty years

<small>The Bombay Jews.</small>

ago they were found combining the worship of Jehovah with divination and idolatry. They have been settled in India for many centuries, whither they probably came from Arabia, with the Israelites of which country they have had much intercourse, and who are the most contiguous to India. They may be descendants of those who went into Egypt (Jeremiah xl. 43), and were overtaken by the judgments threatened, perhaps leaving Yemen in the sixth century of the Christian era, about which time also the Cochin Jews may have come to India."* Some members of this Jewish community in Bombay have been brought under Christian influences. The author, on visiting that city several years ago, was shown the girls' schools of the Free Church Mission by the Rev. Dr Wilson, and was much gratified to find them well attended by young intelligent Jewish children.

Comparative statistics. As already remarked, the Christian community of Bombay has increased but slowly. Yet of late it has multiplied with much greater rapidity than formerly. This is manifest by comparing one period with another. In 1861, according to the mission census then taken, there were only three hundred and forty-one native Christians in the city of Bombay; but in 1871 this number had more than doubled, for we find that there were seven hundred and twenty-six, separated into eight congregations.

Native Christians of various parts of India have been for some time yearning after a united Indian

* *The Indian Evangelical Review* for July 1873: Paper on Early Glimmerings of Divine Truth in India, by the Rev. S. Mateer, of Trevandrum, p. 60.

Church. In several places they have formed themselves into associations with this special object in view. Although outwardly belonging to different sections of the Christian Church, yet they are anxious as far as possible to fuse into one body, and eventually to become actually one. The purpose they have placed before them is undoubtedly good, as it seems altogether unnatural and improper for the multitudinous phases of Christianity existing in the West to be introduced into the newly-born Church of India. Still, practical difficulties are in the way which it were folly to overlook. Early in 1871 some of the principal members of the native Christian communities of Bombay formed themselves into an eclectic society known as the "Western India Native Christian Alliance." It started well, but its first enthusiasm has been much put to the test. "By means of this alliance some of the Christians are making the endeavour to manage their own affairs, to undertake and conduct, on their own responsibility, evangelistic labour, and to do for themselves what, to a great extent, has hitherto been done for them by the missionaries. Theirs is an effort to secure some degree of self-support and independence on the part of the Native Church."* The Calcutta native Christians have taken a step in advance of their Bombay brethren. Their proposition is, that there shall be a National Christian Church of Bengal, with an organisation more in accordance with Oriental habits and tastes than the ecclesiastical systems of England, America, and Germany will permit. The association which has been formed has its branches not only in

Marginal notes: Endeavours of native Christians of different Churches to unite themselves into one community.

* *The Indian Evangelical Review* for July 1873, p. 122.

Bengal, but also in the North-Western Provinces. "A bishop was to be elected for life, but with the same powers as are possessed by a Presbyterian moderator; and the congregations were to be free to manage their own affairs. In order to make the scheme as comprehensive as possible, it was also proposed that, 'as a rule,' baptism by immersion should be the mode of observing this ordinance."* For the present, it is impossible to form a sound judgment either of the utility or feasibility of these schemes.

<small>Missions in Poona</small>
At the large military station of Poona, a hundred miles to the south-east of Bombay, are three missions of the Church, Propagation, and Free Church Societies, and, in addition, a Ladies' Association connected with the Church of Scotland. The oldest and most important of these missions is that of the Free Church, which was originated in the year 1831. It has several fine schools, in which between five and six hundred young people are instructed. The Ladies' Association has two girls' schools, a considerable number of zenanas, and a female orphanage under its charge. The Christians in Poona have multiplied more than threefold in ten years, and now number between three and four hundred persons.

<small>Mission of the American Board at Ahmednagar.</small>
Numerically considered, the most successful and prosperous missions in the Bombay Presidency are those situated in the district and city of Ahmednagar. The American Board formed a mission in that city at the end of 1831, and the first missionaries appointed to the station were the Rev. Messrs Read and Boggs. These, and their successors, were men of earnestness

* *The Indian Evangelical Review* for July 1873, p. 134.

and diligence. The methods and plans they adopted at the outset were similar to those in operation elsewhere, and therefore do not require special notice. Like most missions which have achieved eminent success, this one at Ahmednagar was blessed with many zealous workers, some of whom were conspicuous for lofty enthusiasm, and seemed to tower above their fellows, like tall trees of the forest rising majestically above all the rest. The marvellous influence which individual piety and talent can exert has been nowhere more forcibly seen than in the labours of missionaries in India. And so in looking over the list of those who have spent many years of their lives in Ahmednagar, and have left indelible marks behind them of what the grace of God can effect through the instrumentality of human love and fervour, the names of Read, and Burgess, and Ballantyne, and Fairbank, and others of the same noble cast, rise up before us. At the end of twenty years, three hundred converts had been gathered into the mission, which possessed also nineteen schools containing nearly eight hundred children. The mission was now, however, to undergo a fundamental change. A deputation to the society's Indian missions having been sent from America, on arriving in Ahmednagar and becoming acquainted with the nature of the work carried on there, it suggested to the missionaries, as it had done to those of other parts of India under the superintendence of the Board, the advisability of relinquishing to a large extent the education of the young, to which they had hitherto devoted much time and attention, and of employing themselves in direct evangelistic labours. The deputation also recommended, that instead of

Change of method.

only one or two separate congregations or churches, several new ones should at once be established in the villages and towns of the neighbourhood, in which the number of native Christians was sufficient to warrant such a step; and that native pastors should be placed over them, so far as was prudent and practicable. The missionaries gave heed to this counsel, and forthwith endeavoured to act in accordance with it. They closed their principal schools, and organised a number of separate Christian churches or communities. Earnest, faithful men, qualified to be set apart as pastors, were found among the Christians, and one by one were ordained to this important office.

Results. Great increase of converts and churches.

And what, it may be asked, have been the results of these changes? One result is, that in the twenty years or so which have elapsed since they were introduced, the number of schools has fallen to twenty, and the number of scholars to three hundred and thirty-five, most of whom, I believe, are the children of Christians. But this is more than counterbalanced by the great increase which has taken place in converts, Christian churches, and native preachers, and by the expansion of the mission in many other ways. This will be plain by the following statistics representing its condition at the end of 1871. In place of one congregation, it had eighteen. Its converts had multiplied to eleven hundred and four, scattered over one hundred and four villages, of whom five hundred and eleven were communicants. Instead of two native preachers, as in 1850, it had fifty, ten of whom were ordained ministers of the gospel and pastors of native churches. The success of the enterprise, therefore, in a missionary point of view, has been most satisfactory. What has been done in Ahmednagar no doubt might be done elsewhere. It needs, however, great caution and skill to make the experiment in other missions. Nor is the principle of discarding schools for the heathen to be, as a general rule, admired or advocated. Other missions have, at the call of a deputation, abolished their schools, and have been almost ruined in consequence. Not only is the same class of intensely earnest men, like those in the Ahmednagar Mission, required to carry the experiment into execution, but also the same or nearly the same conditions are necessary as existed in that mission and among the native population surrounding it. Like causes will produce like results; yet much care is demanded lest the causes should be the same in appearance, and not in reality.

An interesting experiment has been tried in Ahmednagar, in regard to the employment of native Christian Bible-women. The plan adopted has been, in some important respects, different from that pursued in London and New York, as will be at once perceived by persons acquainted with the operations carried on in those two cities. Mrs Fairbank, wife of one of the missionaries, has superintended the labours of eight such women. In her report of them for 1872 she says: "For the last two months of the year, four of these Bible-women hired a cart, and went on a preaching tour among villages fifteen, twenty, and thirty miles away from where they reside. One of the colporteurs of the Bombay Tract Society joined them, to be a sort of protector for the company.

Native Christian Bible-women.

They have had great success in interesting the women. Women of high caste even have invited them to their houses by night, to tell them of Jesus, and especially to sing to them of Jesus. These Hindoos are very fond of songs and singing, and will listen quietly to singing when they will not to any talk you can make them. This tour has been an experiment; and I wait to see what the results will be. The women seem to have enjoyed it highly, and give glowing accounts of the interest manifested on the part of their listeners. They will now return to their homes, and continue their regular routine of work. The average number that these Bible-women have addressed in the course of a month has been two hundred in seventeen visits. In the tour that those four women made, they visited thirty-two villages in one month, and their audiences numbered twelve hundred and forty-three persons. Sometimes they visited three villages a day; and sometimes they were persuaded to remain three days in one place. At one village the women declared they should have no dishes to use, for they were not going to be defiled with persons who were in the habit of eating with the lowest castes. After a while, one woman helped them a little, and the rest began to scold her; but just then an old woman came along, and told them they were crazy, that they ought to help these women, for they were God's people. They listened to her, and soon became much interested in hearing the gospel. When evening came they brought oil for a light, so that the Bible-women might read to them. They begged them to stay the next day; and would hardly let them go after they had remained three days."* I have given this extract for the reason that it is important to know all the phases which missionary labour assumes in the country. Whether the plan of employing native Christian women to preach the gospel should be practised generally in India is very questionable. Nevertheless, there is doubtless a great work for Bible-women to accomplish, in visiting their own sex from house to house.

At Nasik, to the north of Ahmednagar, is a very prosperous mission of the Church Missionary Society, commenced in 1832. For many years it made but slow progress, so that in 1850, eighteen years after its establishment, it numbered only fifty-seven converts, who were by no means in a satisfactory condition, being entirely dependent on the mission, in one way or another, for their support. The Christians of that period are described by the Rev. Mr Price, through whose instrumentality chiefly the mission has so greatly developed of late years, as consisting of two classes, preachers and paupers. Under the powerful conviction that this was a very unsatisfactory state of things, Mr Price started an industrial school, in which the Christians were to be taught various trades, and so be fitted to earn a living for themselves. Much difficulty was found at the outset in persuading heathen artisans to teach the Christians, although they were promised good pay for doing so; the consequence of which was, that Mr Price had personally to devote a considerable portion of his time to the enterprise. Here, it will be said by those

The Church Society's Mission at Nasik. Rev. Mr Price.

Success of the Industrial School.

---

* Report of the American Mission among the Mahrathas for 1872, pp. 23, 24.

whose views of missionary labour are circumscribed to the mere preaching of the gospel, that Mr Price went beyond his duty in taking this step. He thought otherwise—and many other missionaries, placed in similar circumstances, also think otherwise—and the event proves triumphantly the excellence of his judgment, and the wisdom of the experiment. By the year 1861 the Christians had increased to two hundred and forty-eight, were in a position of respectability, and were regarded by the heathen with admiration as hard-working people. The mission continued to prosper, and year by year numbers of Hindoos abandoned their religion and became Christians; and in another ten years, that is, in 1871, the Christian community consisted of upwards of five hundred persons, with one hundred and seventy-five communicants. For a long time Mr Price perceived it necessary for him to continue his oversight of the institution; but he determined that as soon as possible his connection with it should cease, and the Christians be left to themselves. And now his purpose has been accomplished, and he has separated himself entirely from it. The Christians manage the Industrial School by their own energy and skill. The question often put by a Hindoo when wishing to become a Christian, "How am I to be supported?" is now answered, for he is immediately introduced into the school, where he is taught a trade, and earns his own livelihood. The rule of the Christian village is, if any man will not work, neither shall he eat. So that there is no temptation to improper characters to come for support. Not only is the institution self-supporting, but the native Christians employed in it contribute a considerable amount annually towards the expenses of the mission.

Thus it is apparent that two important missions exist in the same district of country, both flourishing and successful, and yet conducted upon totally different principles. Let none despise the means employed, provided they be in themselves good and honest.

There are five missions in Gujerat, situated at Surat, Borsud, Rajkote, Gogo, and Ahmedabad, all which are under the charge of the Irish Presbyterian Society. At one time the Propagation Society had a station at Ahmedabad, but as it did not prosper, it was given up. The oldest of these five missions is that in Surat, which was commenced by the London Society as long ago as 1815. Even in 1795, when this society was first established, we find from the minutes of its proceedings for that year, that Surat was one of the places in which it desired to found a mission. Two missionaries were actually sent out in 1804 to establish the mission, but one was detained at Madras, and the other, a medical missionary, never reached the station ; but having remained for a time in Bengal, and then in Bombay, finally accepted an appointment from the Government. After many disappointments, extending over twenty years, the London Society eventually accomplished its purpose, and two other missionaries, the Rev. J. Skinner and the Rev. W. Fyvie, were appointed in 1815, and entered upon their work in Surat at the close of that year. They at once commenced the study of the language, and established two schools, one for Europeans and East Indians, the other for natives. The

Irish Presbyterian missions in Gujerat.

Transfer of the London Society's missions.

mission which was thus formed, was made over to the Irish Presbyterian Society in 1846. All the remaining stations of the former society in Gujerat were transferred to the latter in 1859. By the second transfer the valuable mission premises at Borsud, and those at Divan and Jambusir, and with them one hundred and forty-five native Christians, were brought under the charge of the Irish Mission. The reason for taking this step was, that the London Society felt that its Gujerat missions were isolated from all its other Indian missions, and could not be practically associated with them in any way. And therefore, although they had been fairly prosperous, and were acknowledged to be of great interest and importance, yet it most wisely retired from them, and surrendered them to another society which had other missions in the neighbourhood, and whose missionaries were men of earnestness and ability. The London Society even made the first overtures on the subject; and the arrangements were carried out with great goodwill on both sides. Were the same work done in regard to many other isolated missions in India, the benefit accruing would be enormous. There are numerous small missions scattered about in all directions, which are weak because they are alone; but which, if associated with other missions, would soon become effective and strong.

Colony of Christians came from Borsud and settled in Ahmedabad.

The Irish Presbyterian Society occupied Rajkote in Katiyawar in 1841, and is now the only society labouring in Gujerat. Under the guidance of experienced men it has multiplied its stations in the province, and has produced a powerful effect upon the people. It possesses between five and six hundred

Christians, nineteen schools with twelve hundred pupils, a large orphanage, a training school, and a printing press. An interesting experiment of colonising one part of the country by Christians brought from another part was attempted in 1862. "In the beginning of the rainy season," says the Rev. R. Montgomery, one of the able veterans of these missions, "thirteen families, consisting of fifty-six persons, migrated from Borsud, and settled on a tract of land within about four miles of Ahmedabad. They borrowed, on their own personal security, three thousand rupees, and contributed from their own resources in stock and implements nearly an equal amount. The whole risk was undertaken by themselves, and none by the mission. The colonists, after enduring many trials from the want of suitable dwellings, the unkindly nature of the soil, deficient rain in some seasons, and in one a most destructive visitation of locusts, hold on their way, and continue to increase both from within and without." *

An important movement in the direction of Christianity has lately manifested itself among the Dheds, a low-caste tribe in Gujerat, which has been occasioned chiefly through the instrumentality of an old convert who has lived among this people for several years. They are anxious to have their children educated; and if only a few influential persons of their community led the way, no doubt the entire race would speedily embrace the Christian faith. Nearly sixty members of this caste were baptized in one month in the beginning of 1873.

<small>The Dhed tribe.</small>

* Report of the General Missionary Conference of 1871-72: Paper on Missions in Gujerat, by the Rev. R. Montgomery, pp. 501, 502.

Missions at Karachee and Hyderabad, in Scinde.

The province of Scinde has only two missions, both which are connected with the Church Society. These are at Karachee and Hyderabad, the former having been established in 1850, and the latter in 1857. They unitedly contain eighty-five converts, which, however, is nearly double the number they possessed ten years ago. They have likewise seven schools with five hundred scholars. There is scope in this large province for many more missions; and I earnestly trust that means may soon be adopted by some society—anxious to open a large number of new stations in India within a short distance of one another—of spreading a network of effective missions over this splendid province.

Missions in the South Mahratta country. Twenty-one congregations.

In the Southern Mahratta country are twelve missions in association with six societies. The Basle Evangelical Missionary Society has the care of five of these stations, which will be more fully described in the next chapter. But the London Society's Mission at Belgaum is the oldest and largest of all. It was established in 1820, and has now about two hundred Christians, of whom nine are preachers of the gospel, two of them being ordained ministers and pastors. The mission does an important work by its schools, of which there are eight, with more than five hundred scholars. The Rev. W. Beynon has spent nearly fifty years in the mission, having been appointed to it in the year 1825. The American Board has missions at Sholapore, Satara, and Bhuinj. The American Presbyterians and the Propagation Society have each a station at Kolapore, the converts of which, as of the three previously mentioned, are few in number. The

Rev. R. G. Wilder, American missionary at Kolapore, has visited and preached in two thousand four hundred towns and villages since his mission was established in 1861; and in two thousand and ninety-six of them he discovered no traces of any missionary having visited them before. Altogether, the South Mahratta missions have twenty-one congregations and seven hundred and seventy-eight Christians, fifty-four native Christian preachers and teachers, thirty-three schools, and twelve hundred and sixty-nine scholars. In this spacious region the number of missions and schools should be multiplied tenfold.

The Basle missions, and the London Society's Mission at Belgaum, properly belong to the Canara country, inasmuch as Canarese is the language of the people among whom they are situated. The last-mentioned mission was established in 1820. One of the existing staff of missionaries, the Rev. W. Beynon, was appointed to the station in 1828, having already spent three years at Bellary, a station of the same society. For many years he was associated in his labours with the Rev. Joseph Taylor, who died in 1852, after having devoted forty-four years to missionary work in India. It is singular, that although the population is chiefly Canarese, yet that the greater portion of the converts baptized in the mission have been Tamil people, with a few Mahomedans, who were connected with the army in various capacities. "For some years after the mission was commenced," says Mr Beynon, "we met with the most liberal support from Christian friends, many of them the fruits of our own labours. We were not only able to support the institutions in connection with our own station, but in a short time remitted as much as three thousand five hundred rupees to the general funds of our society. With my present experience, I am sorry we did not lay out the money for the permanent advantage of the mission. Our three chapels, and all our schoolrooms, as well as the poorhouse, were all built through the liberality of Christian friends. The books also prepared by Mr Taylor and myself, were also printed, in the first instance, in this manner. At the request of a friend, Mr Cathcart, a Madras civilian, I translated the 'Pilgrim's Progress,' which he requested me to divide among the Canarese missions then existing." * He then states that the first editions of some tracts were printed by friends; and adds, that the same spirit of liberality among Christian people which he then witnessed, he does not see in India at the present day. Missionaries of the prolonged service and vast experience of Mr Beynon impart a stability to the mission with which they are connected, which men of small experience, though of equal zeal, fail to exert.

Although the number of native Christians in the Bombay Presidency is still very small, yet during the last ten years, as compared with the commencement of this period, its increase has been considerable, amounting indeed to sixty-four per cent. The condition of the missions in this Presidency in 1871 will be seen from the following statistics :—

* Report of the General Missionary Conference of 1871-72 : Paper by Rev. W. Beynon, on the Belgaum Mission, pp. 109, 110.

STATISTICS OF MISSIONARY LABOUR IN THE BOMBAY PRESIDENCY
FOR THE YEAR 1871.

Number of Native Christian Congregations,	64
Increase in Ten Years,	20
Number of Protestant Native Christians,	4177
Increase in Ten Years,	1646
Number of Towns or Villages containing Christians,	175
Number of Ordained Native Ministers,	20
Increase in Ten Years,	8
Number of Unordained Native Preachers,	113
Increase in Ten Years,	46
Number of Mission Colleges and Schools,	132
Increase in Ten Years,	15
Number of Pupils, Male and Female,	7184
Number of Christian Teachers, Male and Female,	107

CHAPTER IX.

MISSIONS OF THE BASLE EVANGELICAL SOCIETY IN THE SOUTHERN MAHRATTA COUNTRY, CANARA, AND MALABAR.

The Basle Evangelical Society.

THE Basle Evangelical Society has not only sent its missionaries all over India in connection with other societies, but has also maintained and superintended a large number of missions which it has established on the western coast. These are situated in the Southern Mahratta, Canara, and Malabar. From the first they have been carried on with great vigour and with distinguished success. The German character is peculiarly fitted for the missionary enterprise. The German mind has a wonderful facility for acquiring and assimilating Indian languages. The German heart has a depth of sympathy and an intensity of feeling; the value and importance of which are immense in any attempt to enlighten and Christianise the races of India. The German missionaries in that country, therefore, are not surpassed by any in those qualifications which distinguish the noblest and most effective missionaries.

Its labours in heathen countries.

Since the commencement of the Basle Mission in 1834, about eighty German missionaries have been sent out to its various stations, most of whom came from the small kingdom of Wurtemburg. Indeed it was calculated a few years ago, that of the Protestant missionaries then living, scattered over heathen nations, about one-tenth of the whole were from this small kingdom.

The first station occupied by the Basle missionaries in India was Mangalore, to which in 1834 three missionaries were appointed. In 1837 they entered the Southern Mahratta country, and began a mission at Dharwar. In 1839 they extended their labours southwards to Malabar. In 1846 the Neilgherries was added to their mission-field. And in 1853 they entered the small principality of Coorg. The mission has five central stations in the South Mahratta country, which although thus designated, and in the Presidency of Bombay, properly belong to Canara, inasmuch as the language spoken in the whole of them is Canarese. Next to these come three stations in South Canara, and two in Coorg, in all which Canarese is the vernacular language of the people. To the south are the Malabar stations, six in number, among which Malayalim is the common tongue.

Canarese is the literary language of Canara, yet other languages are prevalent in various parts of the province. "Not to speak of the sixteen or more languages," says the Rev. W. Hoch, "occasionally heard at Mangalore, the missionary ought to know, at least, Tulu, Canarese, Konkani, and Hindustani, in order to converse freely with all classes of natives. Tulu is no doubt the prevailing language of South Canara, which, in consequence, is frequently called the Tulu country. It is the language of the bigoted Tulu Brahmans, as well as of the farmers, toddy-drawers, fishermen, and of most of the lower classes in these parts. Though it has some old remains of literature, and its characters are nearly the same as those of the Malayalim, it is no longer written; and, with the exception of a few Christian books in use among our converts, and printed with Canarese characters, Tulu books are altogether unknown. The Tulu people live scattered all over the country, every family on its own farm. They are given to the worship of demons, and are on the whole very illiterate, uncommonly stubborn, and wedded to their old customs. Konkani is the language of the most intelligent and wealthy classes of Brahmans. It is a dialect of the Mahrathi, without any literature whatever. The books they make use of are almost exclusively written in Canarese. If anywhere, a systematic plan of itinerancy seems to be necessary in the Tulu country, where the bulk of the population cannot be brought under the influence of the gospel, except by being followed to their farms and houses. Street-preaching, however, is not neglected wherever opportunities offer. At Mangalore especially it is regularly attended to, where from a schoolroom, in a central position of the town, the gospel is preached to the passers-by on fixed days and hours of the week, so that the people may always know the time beforehand. They are invited to hear by means of a hymn sung with some catechista. After a short prayer, suitable passages are read from the Word of God, either in Canarese or Tulu, according to circumstances, and pressed as much as possible upon the hearer's memory, if not upon his heart. The whole is concluded with a hymn and prayer."*

* Proceedings of the South India Missionary Conference, held at Ootacamund in 1858: Paper on the Missions of the Basle Society in Canara and Malabar, by the Rev. W. Hoch, pp. 78, 70.

At the commencement, the work of conversion made slow progress. A few persons were baptized in Mangalore in 1837; but in 1840 the Christian community only numbered nineteen individuals. Yet in five years from that time there were three hundred and twenty-four baptized Tulu Christians in the mission. The old proverb, "All is not gold that glitters," was, to the chagrin and disappointment of the missionaries, singularly verified in Hubli, one of the stations in the South Mahratta country. The circumstances are very interesting and instructive. "It was in the year 1840," says the Rev. G. Kies, "that a number of men from several villages and towns to the east of Hubli came to the missionaries there, declaring that they were deputies of several thousands of the members of a sect who called themselves 'Kalagnanis,' because they adhered to the prophecies of some old Shastra, according to which Gurus (or religious guides) would come from the West, teaching the people heavenly truth, and introducing new laws and new usages into the country. These prophecies they now believed to be fulfilling by the arrival of the teachers of the Christian religion. To the new missionaries such an invitation was of course only too welcome. From want of experience, they could not share the doubts and misgivings of their elder and more cautious brethren at Belgaum, to whom these people had previously applied. When our missionaries first visited their villages and towns, hundreds and thousands declared themselves ready to become Christians, if they could only dwell together in places of their own. They therefore asked the missionaries to take from Government, for this purpose, some

Deceptive practised on the missionaries.

towns and villages as zemindars (landowners). Of course the missionaries neither would nor could go as far as this; but in order to give an opportunity to the sincere, and to facilitate their coming forward, they determined upon the establishment of a settlement at Malasamudra for the cultivators, and of another at Bettigherri for the weavers. This was the origin of these two stations in 1841. But, alas! no sooner had the missionaries settled at these two places than they had the great mortification of finding out that the whole of the Kalagnana movement was nothing more than a deep-laid fraudulent plan of a few cunning Hindoo rogues, who in 'this way tried to take advantage of the inexperience of the missionaries; for as soon as they found out that they could not obtain their real objects, they, together with all their followers, at once broke off all connection with the missionaries, and left the latter alone in their newly-built houses. After this heart-rending disappointment, our brethren tried to make themselves useful amongst the heathen by preaching, and establishing schools, in the usual way. In addition to these regular efforts, the missionary at Bettigherri thought it desirable to trouble himself very much with the family and social affairs of the people, in the way of a justice of the peace, with the view of thus making them more inclined to receive the gospel. But instead of seeing the fond hopes of his well-meaning heart realised, all he accomplished by ten years' toil was, that when leaving his station on account of failing health, he reaped a rich harvest of praise from all the inhabitants; but not one Christian had been made by all these efforts. Since then the station has been recruited by fresh strength; and during the past few years a little congregation has been gathered, principally from the weavers, with which an orphan school for girls is connected. At Malasamudra, after its first destination as a mission colony for the cultivators from the Kalagnanis had been frustrated, the missionaries carried on a little farm together with a sugar-manufactory on a small scale. But they saw little visible fruit of their labours until about three years ago (1855), when, in consequence of the drought and scarcity of food to the cast of us, several crowds of poor people took refuge in the mission colony for a time, of whom afterwards a number was baptized."* The two missions of Hubli (with which I suppose the station at Malasamudra is connected) and Bettigherri contained unitedly in 1871 two hundred and twenty-five Christians.

The history of the Basle missions is rich in experience of a very diverse character, and in various points is worthy of close study. Under the pressure of expostulations from earnest but often short-sighted Christian friends at home, of sanguine temperament, eager for tangible and numerical results, missionaries in India become sometimes too anxious to increase their Christian communities, and are apt occasionally to admit persons of doubtful principle from among the heathen into their fellowship. An instance of this kind occurred at Mangalore, where the founder of several Tulu congregations, not being himself a sincere believer, led many astray, and did infinite

Evils resulting from excessive enthusiasm.

* Report of the South India Missionary Conference: Paper on the Basle Mission in the South Mahratta Country, by the Rev. G. Kies, pp. 89, 90.

mischief to the Christian communities he had established. "Caring more for numbers than for spiritual life, he admitted many to baptism who ought never to have been baptized; and church discipline grew necessarily lax in his hands, though he was able to hide the real state of things from his fellow-labourers. Since then," say the missionaries, "it has been our arduous task to rouse many of our Christians from a state of spiritual lethargy into which they had sunk by degrees, and to maintain church discipline with greater strictness than ever. In consequence, many forsook us, and others who had shown a desire to join us kept aloof." Such experience, though dearly bought, was of priceless value. Indeed, most missions, first or last, have to pass through an ordeal of this nature, arising from the imprudence, or idiosyncrasies, or excessive enthusiasm of missionaries, whose isolation and independence of action are sometimes fruitful causes of waywardness and folly.

Boarding school commenced in 1837; abolished in 1848.

A boarding school was commenced in Mangalore in 1837, with the object of training young men to become preachers and schoolmasters, and continued for eleven years; but in 1848 it was broken up. Most probably it was found in Mangalore, as in some other missions, that this hothouse system of providing labourers for mission work was unnatural, and liable to gross abuse. "The most advanced lads were formed into a catechist class; others were apprenticed to different trades; and the younger pupils were received into a newly-established orphan school." The great difficulty of providing suitable labour for the converts, whereby they might obtain the means of subsistence, was powerfully felt in the

Mangalore Mission, as in other Indian missions. The missionaries first attempted to make sugar from the juice of cocoanut-trees, but unsuccessfully, on account of the great expense of fuel. They then established what is termed an industrial department, of a very elaborate character. "A first effort was made in 1840, when a large piece of ground close to Mangalore, with some public buildings, destroyed by the Coorg insurgents in 1837, was purchased by a friend, and presented to our mission. At first a coffee-plantation was tried, but soon given up as a failure. The ruined buildings, however, were repaired and enlarged, and are at present inhabited by the brethren in charge of our industrial undertakings, and occupied by our workshops. In the compound, to which another piece of ground was added, a Christian village sprung up in the course of time, containing at present twenty-one houses and one hundred and ninety-eight inhabitants. The first workshop established on these premises was that of a lithographic press in 1841, to which two typographic presses have been since added. It employs twenty-one workmen, chiefly Christians. In 1845 a bookbinder's shop was combined with it. This branch is now carried on at Mangalore by one of our converts on his own account, while some of our former apprentices have set up similar shops at other stations. In 1850 two lay brethren arrived to teach our converts some new trades. Watch and clock making was commenced. A carpenter's and smith's shop was set up. In 1852, however, the latter was abandoned, its superintendent leaving our mission. In 1854 watch and clock making also was given up, being found not suited to the capacities and requirements of our people. Much more satisfactory results were attained by a workshop for weavers. In 1847 a first trial was made with a European loom. In 1851 a lay brother arrived to introduce European improvements, when tablecloths, napkins, handkerchiefs, turbans, native dresses, and so forth, were manufactured, and began to command a brisk sale. Thirty European looms are now (1858) at work at Mangalore, and forty-eight Christians have thus the means provided of maintaining themselves by the labour of their hands. A successful trial of growing silk has been lately made, and promises fair to open a new resource to our boarding schools and women. A widow and orphan fund for our catechists has of late been set up, every catechist being bound to contribute to it two and a half per cent. of his annual income. These funds are generally laid out in cocoa-nut-gardens and paddy-fields; and as long as we have Christians practised in farming, they have the preference. In all these concerns our lay brethren prove of intrinsic value, as they relieve us more and more of all secular affairs in connection with our congregations. But we had to learn that our object cannot be obtained so long as ordained missionaries, as such, are placed above the lay brethren; for if so, the latter will not only fail to command the necessary respect on the part of the natives, but the former also will be continually forced by appeals of the converts to take notice of their secular affairs. Only when ordained and unordained brethren are placed on the same footing, and a Christian spirit of co-operation exists among them, every one attending to that work to which he has been specially called, and thinking it a grace to serve the Lord in his part, can the full benefit of such a division of labour be secured. Such, at least, has been the experience in our mission."*

Near the mission station of Udapi in South Canara some religious excitement has been lately manifest among the toddy-drawers, who in numbers are embracing the Christian faith. The motives which influence them are various. "In many cases it was the conviction that what the missionaries had been preaching for so many years was true. This conviction was aided by the feeling that their own religion was vain, and their manner of life corrupt. They saw and appreciated the difference which separated them from the native Christians with whom they were familiar. In addition to this, may be mentioned as a motive having some weight, the desire to escape from the bondage of their former demon-worship. Worldly motives may also have been present, at least in the first instance."†

The area of Malabar consists of six thousand two hundred and fifty-eight square miles. The language of its population is Malayalim; and the lower classes are much more intelligent than the Tulu tribes of Canara. The capital of the province is Calicut. In this city is a beggar caste called Nayadi. Some of the Nayadi families of this city and of the southern part of Malabar became Christians. But in 1850 a singular defection occurred among the Christian Nayadis of Kodakal, where a colony of them had been located on land bought for the purpose, who were enticed away by Mahomedans,

Religious excitement among the toddy-drawers

Defection of Nayadi Christians to Mahomedanism.

* Report of the South India Missionary Conference: Paper on the Canarese Missions, by the Rev. W. Hoch, pp. 62–84.
† *The Indian Evangelical Review* for January 1874, p. 361.

and were adopted into the faith of Islam by the rite of circumcision. Fireworks and processions announced the triumph of Mahomedanism, and these Nayadis were lost to Christianity for ever. Another Christian colony, but not of Nayadis, subsequently occupied the spot.

Occupations of the Malabar Christians.
Various means were adopted to give employment to the Christians of the Malayalim congregations. Weaving establishments were set up at Cannanore, Tellicherry, and Calicut. A lithographic press was introduced into the Tellicherry Mission, and has not only given support to some of the Christian families, but has also provided them with many useful books of a Christian and secular character. Some of these are a translation of the Bible, Bible Stories, a Harmony of the Gospels, a Church History, a General History, a Grammar, a Hymn-book. At Chombala the Christians have a fishery; and at Calicut some are carpenters. The Malabar district has been fruitful as a mission-field. "Several Christian colonies have sprung up, and mission stations and out-stations compass the whole length of the province."

Sect of the Guru Nudis in the South Mahratta country.
In the Southern Mahratta country is a curious sect, calling themselves followers of the "Guru Nudi" or "Word of the Teacher." The founder of the sect lived at Kodekall, on the banks of the Krishna, three hundred years ago. He was a Lingaite or worshipper of Shiva; but he travelled about the country preaching the unity of God. The religious books written by him contain the pantheism of the Vedanta, intermingled with doctrines derived from Mahomedanism, and with others of a Christian origin. They bring prominently forward the reappearance of Chanaba-

sava, one of the founders of Lingaitism, whose advent is to take place, strange to say, twelve hundred and sixty years after the rise of the Mahomedan power. He is to come on a white elephant, "in order to punish and annihilate his enemies, and to gather his faithful ones into a paradise on earth. For this purpose he will raise the dead, and transform the carnal bodies of the living into spiritual bodies, by the power of his Guru Mantra." The members of this sect were much astonished at finding that some of their principal doctrines were identical with those taught by the missionaries; and a number of them have, on this account, been led to embrace Christianity.

The Rev. G. Kies, in his essay already quoted, makes several profound observations on the comparative influence of the systems of agriculture adopted in India, and of the support which they do or do not receive from Government, in leading the inhabitants of rural districts to approve or disapprove of Christianity as a means of advancing their temporal welfare. And he adds a statement of his views on the effect of English manufactures on native industry. The passage is as follows: "The dead but weighty ballast which, in some of the southern missions, appears to have been materially assisting in driving many a soul and community into the mission harbour, does either not exist in our province (the Southern Mahratta country), or is on the wrong side of the vessel. For, under the ryotwary system of cultivation, especially now since the introduction of the revenue survey, by which the rate of Government rent has been considerably reduced and most justly equalised, and with the improved roads for export to the western coast,

[side note: Material influences promoting or retarding the progress of Christianity]

the cultivators of our extensive plains of fertile black cotton-ground are comparatively well off, and consequently cannot see of what possible use the missionary might be to them. Very different from this, however, are the prospects of the weavers, who dwell in numerous towns and villages scattered over the country, and whose manufactures become cheaper and cheaper in consequence of the rapidly-increasing influx of English cloths, whilst cotton and country yarn are rising in price every year through the increased facility for the export of raw materials."*

<small>Aboriginal tribes of the Neilgherries.</small> The Neilgherries, or Blue Mountains, are of great reputed sanctity among the Hindoos of Southern India. They are in the form of a trapezoid, or square of unequal sides, are fifty miles in length, and vary from fifteen to twenty in breadth. The plateau above is inhabited by the Todas, Kotas, and Badagas, three different tribes, with three separate languages. The Todas are considered to be the aborigines of these hills. They only number a few hundred persons, are gradually decreasing, and will die out shortly, unless placed under more favourable conditions than at present, which is hardly likely. The Kotas are a somewhat larger community, but even they only inhabit seven villages. The Bodagas are more numerous than either, and have a population of as many thousands as the Kotas have hundreds. Those in the north are supposed to be Canarese peasants, who from various reasons have sought refuge on the hills. The slopes of the Neilgherries are inhabited by the Iruler and Kurumber tribes.

As pure Canarese is not understood by the Badagás,

* Report of the South India Missionary Conference, p. 92.

among whom the missionaries sought to establish themselves, it was necessary that they should acquire the language of the tribe. Schools were commenced, but the people were at first altogether unconcerned about their children learning to read in their own tongue. At length, however, through the instrumentality of an eminent Christian gentleman, Mr Casamajor, who carried out his benevolent scheme with his own resources, a school of one hundred boys was formed among the Badagas. This gentleman began the study of Canarese and Badaga at the age of fifty-five. He translated the greater portion of the Gospel of St Luke into the Badaga dialect, which was afterwards finished and published by the missionaries. During four years he devoted himself especially to improve the Badaga tribe. He was a man of much prayer, and prayed for this race unweariedly. And his prayers, the missionaries say, were answered. He died in 1849. "His last will, if any other proof had been wanted, bore testimony to his unreserved devotion to the cause of the gospel on the Neilgherries. With the exception of a few legacies, he bequeathed all that he had to the Neilgherry Mission. Besides the rent of two houses at Coonoor, twenty-six thousand rupees have been realised and invested in Government paper, and the interest goes to the exclusive support of the Neilgherry branch of our mission. Among the whole population he was held in the highest veneration. The Badagas do not hesitate to declare that he was like an angel of God among them; and therefore his name is remembered on these hills as no other European name."*

Labours of Mr Casama- jor among the Badagas

* Report of the South India Missionary Conference: Paper on the Mission on the Neilgherries, by the Rev. C. Moerike, p. 95.

I will now give a statistical summary of the present condition and progress of the Basle missions on the western coast, which have been thus briefly reviewed :—

STATISTICS OF MISSIONARY LABOUR AMONG THE BASLE MISSIONS OF THE SOUTHERN MAHRATTA COUNTRY, CANARA, AND MALABAR, FOR THE YEAR 1871.

Number of Native Christian Congregations,	48
Number of Protestant Native Christians,	4612
Increase in Ten Years,	1615
Number of Communicants in 1871,	2272
Number of Towns and Villages containing Christians,	84
Number of Ordained Native Ministers,	6
Number of Unordained Native Preachers,	57
Number of Mission Colleges and Schools,	64
Number of Pupils, Male and Female,	2217
Number of Christian Teachers, Male and Female,	69

CHAPTER X.

MISSIONS IN BELLARY AND THE MYSORE.

THESE missions are situated, for the most part, among a Canarese-speaking population. That at Bellary was established in 1810, by the London Society, through the Rev. John Hands, and is one of the oldest in that part of India. Mr Hands had previously endeavoured to commence a mission at Seringapatam, but without success, and therefore, by permission of the Government, which, as already seen in former chapters, was in those days very jealous of all Christian movements in the country, he removed to Bellary. By 1812 he had, with wonderful diligence, translated the first three Gospels into Canarese, and had commenced a grammar and dictionary of the language, which at that time was destitute of such facilities for its acquisition. Gradually schools were organised, a Christian church of Europeans and East Indians was formed, and a Tract Society was founded. Yet the Government hesitated to give its sanction to a printing-press for the publication of books and tracts, and therefore, though much needed, it was kept in abeyance. Of what use the Tract Society was without a press to print its works is hardly apparent. But its members doubtless hoped for better days, and prepared themselves for the time when all restrictions on knowledge and education would be removed. In

1818 a Bible Society was established in Bellary. The next year Mr Hands proceeded to Madras, in order to superintend the publication of the Canarese Scriptures, whereby it is evident that up to this period the mission at Bellary had not the means for printing it there.

The missionaries labour, and wait for success.

Nine years passed away before a single convert was made. Then a Brahman was baptized; and the year following, two Rajpoots, who had been in the service of Hyder Ali and Tippoo Sahib. But the work of conversion proceeded slowly. Yet the ardour of the missionaries was not diminished in consequence. They continued their preaching, their schools, of which they had a large number, and their publications of Christian and secular books. They could do what many persons, ignorant of the practical opposition to Christianity in India, cannot do—wait for success.

Not till about the year 1826 was a press, though the great need of the mission, and eagerly desired by every one connected with it, obtained; and when it was brought into operation, there was much rejoicing throughout Canara and the Mysore, and the event was held to be of historical importance. A man of great originality and power of untiring zeal, and of high-toned spirituality, a man of very superior gifts, intellectual and moral—a kind of apostle in his way—had a few years previously been brought among the native Christians of Bangalore, and was in 1827 transferred to Bellary, where he laboured for twenty years with marked fidelity and success. The Rev. J. Sewell, formerly of the Bangalore Mission of the London Society, gives the following interesting account of this extraordinary man: "During the first year of the mission (in Bangalore) an individual was

Samuel Flavel, a convert of great gifts, natural and spiritual.

received by the missionaries whose subsequent career proved him to have been specially prepared by God for great usefulness as a native preacher of the gospel. This was the devoted and excellent Samuel Flavel. The circumstances leading to his conversion were remarkable; and his sincerity and the native energy of his character were strikingly evinced by his immediately beginning, almost without aid or countenance, to preach to his countrymen the new faith he had embraced. He was led to commence his labours at Mysore; and the success of these first efforts was such as to attract the attention of the Bangalore missionaries. He was invited by Mr Laidler to Bangalore, and was soon appointed to a sphere of labour in the mission. He was first employed as a schoolmaster, and then as an evangelist; and at length, in 1822, he was ordained pastor over the native church and congregation, which was entirely the fruit of his faithful labours. Being richly endowed with natural gifts, and singularly devoted to the spread of the gospel, his labours were remarkably blessed. There are several instances recorded in the life of this eminent native preacher, in which heathen men were converted by the very first sermon they heard from his lips, the same being preached in the open air. The writer once had the pleasure of seeing him, and was much struck with the combined dignity and gentleness of his spirit, and the attractiveness of his ordinary conversation in English. He could not only converse freely and correctly in that language, but would frequently be listened to by a whole company of English gentlemen and ladies in preference to any other person in the company.

His conversation was marked by sincerity and humility, and abounded in anecdote. In 1824, about three years after he joined the Bangalore Mission, and only two years after his ordination, he had baptized, besides children, seventy-eight adults, and had then thirty members in the church under his pastoral care. After Mr Laidler returned to England in 1827, Mr Flavel was appointed to the pastoral charge of the Tamil church and congregation at our older station of Bellary, where he continued his faithful, talented, and successful labours to the day of his death, which took place in 1847, when he was suddenly removed by cholera. Several of his converts became native catechists and preachers."* Would that the native Church in India had more men of the genius and fervour of Samuel Flavel! The instrumentality for converting India must be mainly that of her own sons and daughters, on whom, rather than on foreign agencies, rests the responsibility of interpreting the country's future.

After eighteen years of service, during which the Rev. Mr Hands had been the guiding spirit of the Bellary Mission, he retired to England to recruit his health. He had acquired a thorough knowledge of the Canarese without the helps now possessed, had translated nearly the whole Bible into that language, had written or translated various books and tracts, had founded a Christian church, &c., had been the means of the conversion of many, and of fostering love and zeal in many more. The mission, however, continued to develop. Some of the schools were

* Report of the South India Missionary Conference. Paper on the Bangalore Mission, by the Rev. J. Sewell, pp. 97, 98.

raised to a higher grade, though, strange to say, not without opposition from the natives themselves, especially the Brahmans. Missionaries of intense earnestness, like the Rev. Messrs Shrieves, Wardlaw, and Coles, and many others, from time to time joined the mission, and carried on the good work with vigour and success. In 1861 there were three hundred and fifty-one Christians in the mission. It is remarkable, that during the next ten years the number of converts, instead of increasing, diminished by sixty-one, so that in 1871 there were only two hundred and ninety. The reason of this decrease I have been unable to learn. The mission sustains eight schools, with nearly five hundred scholars. It has also a staff of eight native preachers. There is a much smaller Christian community in Bellary, lately organised in connection with the Church of England. It has no missionary, but possesses two native preachers, and one hundred and fifty Christians. This is a large number for a young congregation. There are therefore four hundred and forty native Christians in all now belonging to the Bellary missions; and although the London Mission has fewer members than formerly, yet the two missions together show the satisfactory increase of eighty-nine for the preceding ten years.

Mission of the Church of England in Bellary

The London Society has another Canarese mission, namely, that situated at Bangalore. This was founded in 1820 by the Rev. S. Laidler and the Rev. A. Forbes. At its commencement, the native Government of Mysore seems to have shown a spirit of antagonism to the missionaries; and consequently for some time the Canarese population was not fully accessible to the preachers of Christianity, who de-

The London Society's Mission at Bangalore

voted much of their attention therefore to the Tamil people connected with the native army. I have already described the important work accomplished by the native minister, Samuel Flavel, in the early days of this mission, which soon, however, was deprived of his very efficient labours by his removal to Bellary. Great skill and much common sense are needed in the management of a mission, especially in its infancy; and its future prosperity is often dependent on the possession of these qualities by its first missionaries. But it is very clear that some of the early missionaries of this society at Bangalore were singularly deficient in both. A grand project was started by two of them in 1824, of establishing an English college in Bangalore, for which "professors in almost every department of science, literature, and theology were to be obtained from Europe, and the most learned Pundits to be found in India were to be associated with them. Students, it was anticipated, would be attracted from all parts of India. The project was warmly espoused by many Europeans, and by a good number of wealthy natives." It met, however, with no favour from the London Society's other missionaries in India, and did not receive the sanction of its directors. The promoters of the scheme, in their zeal, visited England to collect the necessary funds for carrying it out, but failing in this, and not being warmly received, they abandoned the enterprise, and the mission likewise, and remained at home. In these days, the scheme does not appear so quixotic as it did in those. Indeed many such schemes, perhaps not quite so imposing, have been subsequently worked in not a few missions in India with signal success.

Project of a college.

Much depends upon the men. Clearly, the two missionary literati of Bangalore, though clever enough to conceive, were not practical, or zealous, or wise enough, to execute their brilliant project. Had they possessed more of these qualities, they might perhaps have accomplished their design, and astonished India and the world.

The year 1824 was an unfortunate year for Bangalore in one other respect still. A new missionary arrived, kept aloof from the grand project just alluded to, and devised one of his own. "He confined his labours almost exclusively to the Canarese people, and after a few years gathered a church and congregation around him (whom he formed into a Christian village), a boarding-school, and a vernacular seminary for the training of native teachers. He was opposed to the employment of English as a medium of instructing the natives of India, and especially as an instrument for the training of native teachers." After many years, when the missionary had left for England, "it was discovered that nearly all the converts and teachers had continued to retain their caste, and that many of them were very unworthy characters." In two years more, the Canarese church was dissolved, as it was found to be radically corrupt. *A Christian church on a wrong foundation.*

One of the missionaries of this earlier period was the Rev. W. Reeve, a man of great learning and ability, who having spent many years at Bellary, returned to England, and on coming back to India in 1827, was appointed to Bangalore. Between this year and 1834, when he finally retired to his native land, he completed his great work, the Canarese and English Dictionary, "which will ever be a monument of his extensive knowledge of the language, and of his persevering industry." *Rev. W. Reeve. His Canarese Dictionary.*

With a change of missionaries and plans, the mission

commenced a new career, and soon became very prosperous, which it has continued to be for many years. One important element in its efficiency has been, that it has retained several of its most devoted missionaries for a considerable number of years. Two of its present agents, the Rev. Colin Campbell and the Rev. B. Rice, joined the mission, one in 1835, the other in 1837. The Rev. James Sewell was connected with it for twenty-five years.* The ardour and ability which have been displayed for so many years have imparted great strength to the mission. Their plans for its improvement have always been sound and practical. The peculiar system of what is technically termed boarding-schools, though in some missions open to great objection, has been under them eminently successful. "A very considerable proportion of those who have remained in these schools, both male and female, have, sooner or later, become the true disciples of Christ, and not a few of them valuable helpers in mission work." It is interesting to observe, that while public preaching in the streets of Bangalore, and in the towns and villages of the province, has always formed a prominent feature in the operations of the mission, yet that little direct fruit has been the result. Yet it is thought that much good has been done in this way by spreading a knowledge of Christianity among the people. A small theological college

Rev. Colin Campbell; Rev. B. Rice; Rev. James Sewell.

Little direct results from street and village preaching.

* The Indian Civil Service in Northern India is notoriously ruining its influence among the natives by its members being perpetually shifted from one place to another. Just as a magistrate is getting known in any place, and becoming popular, he is suddenly removed to another station. And so with every official from the highest to the lowest. The system produces great dissatisfaction among the people, and is fatal to the efficiency of the Government in its most important departments.

for the training of native Christian young men to become preachers and teachers of the gospel, was established in 1849. Its method is somewhat peculiar. All instruction is conveyed in the English language, but examinations of the students are conducted in the vernaculars; and not only the amount of knowledge which they have received and understood is thus ascertained, but also how far they are able to represent such knowledge in the languages of the country. It is thought, with some reason, that by this method the principal advantages of both the English and the vernacular systems of training are secured. The mission now numbers three hundred and ninety-one converts, of whom one hundred and thirty-four are communicants. It has no less than fourteen schools, with more than a thousand pupils. One-half of the schools are for native girls, of whom more than five hundred are educated in them.

The Wesleyan Society has also an extensive mission in Bangalore, and four others scattered over the Mysore territory. Fifty years have elapsed since its first station was commenced by the Rev. Messrs Hoole and Mowat. It has now five hundred and sixty Christians, three hundred of whom belong to Bangalore. "Wesleyan missions," says the Rev. J. Hutcheon, in an historical sketch of the Mysore missions of this society, "are strictly itinerant in their character; and consequently the preaching of the gospel to the adult population in the native languages has always occupied the largest share of the labours of its missionaries. Still, so far from despising other agencies, it has constantly and systematically employed every means best calculated to reach all the different classes of society. Hence, from the very commencement of the mission, the educational department has received a considerable amount of attention, and some of its missionaries have been specially devoted to this work. These include the Anglo-vernacular institution, vernacular village schools, and girls' day and boarding schools."*

Method adopted in preaching to the people.

In regard to missionary labour among the villages, the system adopted is an excellent one for securing the contemplated end. A plan is drawn up for about three months' work at a time, according to which the missionaries and their catechists proceed, two together, every day to certain parts of the city and to the outlying villages, so that these places receive their ministrations with the greatest regularity and precision. The schools also are visited and examined under the same system. And thus it comes to pass, that instead of the gospel being preached to indiscriminate crowds, it is brought before the same persons in the same places periodically.

Petition in nine languages from the natives of Mysore to the Wesleyan Conference in England, praying them to establish a High School in that city.

This society has a mission at Mysore, the chief seat of idolatry in the province of this name. Formerly the London Society had a station there likewise, but it has been abandoned. In 1853, a few years before the famous despatch of Sir Charles Wood, giving a new bent and impetus to education in India, was promulgated, a large number of respectable natives of this city, both Hindoos and Mahomedans, drew up a petition in nine languages, which was presented to the General Conference of the Wesleyan Society in England, praying the society to establish a first-class

* Report of the South India Missionary Conference: Paper on the Wesleyan Missions in Mysore, by the Rev. J. Hutcheon, p. 112.

English school in Mysore. The document "occupied many folios of India paper of a large size, neatly backed with blue ribbon," and bore the signatures of three thousand three hundred and forty persons. Doubtless, the instigators of this remarkable paper were the Wesleyan missionaries at Mysore; but this is conjecture only. Be this as it may, the circumstance is very significant of the desire for an English education, which, so long ago as nearly thirty years, had been awakened in the minds of the native inhabitants of this city. It is, moreover, an index of a similar desire existing in many other cities of India at that time. But since then it has increased in all directions with wonderful rapidity, until it has become, in the estimation of most natives of position and influence, a necessity of the most vital character, indissolubly associated with the honour of their families, that their sons should acquire a knowledge of English, and of Western learning through its instrumentality. The document was read before the Conference, which that year met at Bradford, and was listened to with the deepest interest and attention. Its prayer was, that the Conference should establish a High School of the kind asked for, should send out a qualified teacher to superintend it, and should bear half the expenses of its maintenance, the petitioners promising on their part to defray the other half. The Conference granted their request; the money for the object was soon subscribed, valuable apparatus was provided and sent to India, and the school was established, and is still in existence. During the last ten years twenty students from this institution have passed the matriculation examination of the Madras University, and six the first examination in arts, which, in a literary point of view, affords a fair criterion of its prosperity and success.

The Mysore missions of this society have derived great assistance from the extensive press which they possess at Bangalore, from which is issued every year an immense number of books of a Christian and educational character. They have had the assistance of men of learning, such as the Rev. Joseph Roberts, who died after thirty years' missionary labour; the Rev. E. J. Hardey, a man of singular clearness of intellect and of much force of character; the Rev. W. Arthur, subsequently one of the secretaries of the Wesleyan Missionary Society, and president of the Wesleyan Conference; and J. Garrett, Esq., the erudite Director of Public Instruction for Mysore and Coorg, but formerly a missionary of this society, and many others. In devotion and enthusiasm their missionaries yield to none. And it may be remarked that without these qualities it is useless, not to say intensely absurd, for any missionary to come to India. Yet missionaries destitute of them, or possessing them in an inferior degree, or not beyond many perfunctory ministers to be found at home, do occasionally come to India to perform the official duties they have undertaken. It would have been far better had they remained in their native land. There they might have had some scope, and been appreciated. Here they are a dead weight, and worse than useless.

The oldest mission in the Mysore is that of the Propagation Society, whose headquarters in that state are at Bangalore. Here it has been established

[margin: Rev. Joseph Roberts; Rev E J. Hardey.]

ever since the year 1817. It has now a Christian community of four hundred and thirty-six persons, which is nearly double the number it had ten years ago. These reside in the city and in thirteen adjacent villages, and are divided into fourteen congregations. Although the number of Christians is so considerable, and although they are so scattered about, yet one pastor suffices for the whole, and he is a native minister. In 1871 there was no European agent in the mission. This state of things is eminently satisfactory, and is that towards which all missions in the country should aim. It is the first instance of self-government, on so large a scale, among the native churches of India, which the writer has yet had occasion to notice. Other instances much more striking are to be found in the churches of Travancore and Tinnevelly, and will presently occupy our attention. This one is of peculiar interest because of the circumstance that it occurs in a large city in which are two other missions; in one of which (the Wesleyan Mission) there are five European missionaries and two ordained ministers; and in the other (the London Mission) there are three of the former and two of the latter. These missions have an elaborate system of schools and colleges, in addition to their direct evangelistic work, in which are employed fifteen native preachers, and also four ordained native ministers; while the Propagation Society's Mission has only three schools with a hundred pupils, and one native preacher besides the ordained native. Yet the result, in regard to the admission of converts, in the three missions, is exceedingly remarkable. The following table will show the matter clearly:—

The Propagation Society's Mission, the oldest in the Mysore.

BANGALORE MISSIONS.

Name of Society.	Native Christians in 1861	Native Christians in 1871.	Communicants in 1861.	Communicants in 1871.
Propagation Society....	220	436	45	132
London Society	229	391	59	134
Wesleyan Society.......	210	300	140	150

Comparison of the results of the three missions. From these statistics it is clear that the single native pastor with his single native preacher has been the means of accomplishing greater direct results in the ten years than either of the two other missions with their elaborate European and native machinery. This surely speaks volumes in favour of the simple method pursued by the solitary native pastor alluded to—in favour also of natives being placed in charge of native Christian communities wherever practicable—and in favour likewise of natives being left to their own independent action, and to the peculiar methods which please them, and probably please the Hindoo population to whom they minister. But if the result be taken as an indication of the uselessness of the various modes of labour pursued by the two other missions, over and above the simple preaching of the gospel—the only plan of procedure, apparently, in which all three are agreed—this will be a very narrow and unintelligible opinion to pass upon them. The truth is, that, rightly understood, the London and Wesleyan missions have alone made it possible for the third to exist at all. Without the Sacred Scriptures, Christian books and tracts, as well as important secular books, which their missionaries publish in the vernacular languages; without their numerous schools which educate the masses in the great principles of Christianity; without the extensive street and village preaching which they and their agents carry on from day to day throughout the year, the one native clergyman, with his single unordained native preacher of the third mission, would be unable to make any progress whatever, and would find himself trying to reap where no one had ploughed, and no seed had been sown. There must be knowledge before faith. To imagine that there can be genuine faith without adequate knowledge, and that a veritable change will be produced in the heart of an idolater who knows little or nothing of the great truths lying at the foundations of Christian faith and conduct, is to indulge in a hallucination altogether foreign to the Divine method of conversion represented in the Word of God.

I shall conclude this sketch of the Bellary and Mysore missions by a tabular statement of their recent progress and present condition.

STATISTICS OF MISSIONARY LABOUR IN BELLARY AND THE MYSORE FOR THE YEAR 1871.

Number of Native Christian Congregations,	30
Number of Protestant Native Christians,	1827
Increase in Ten Years,	680
Number of Communicants,	641
Number of Towns and Villages containing Christians,	35
Number of Ordained Native Ministers,	5
Number of Unordained Native Preachers,	36
Number of Mission Colleges and Schools,	60
Number of Pupils, Male and Female,	3952
Increase in Ten Years,	1106
Number of Christian Teachers, Male and Female,	55

CHAPTER XI.

MISSIONS OF THE CHURCH MISSIONARY SOCIETY IN NORTH TRAVANCORE AND COCHIN.

The Syrian Christians of Malabar.

THE historical associations of the Christian Church in Travancore carry us back to remote ages of antiquity. When it was discovered that a body of Syrian Christians had existed there and in Malabar from the earliest periods of Christianity, the phenomenon was regarded with profoundest interest. On Vasco de Gama reaching India, in the beginning of the sixteenth century, he found that these Christians were not subject to any Hindoo potentate, but had a sovereign of their own, whose dominions were in Malayâla, the name designating the countries now known as Malabar and Travancore, in which the language spoken was the Malayâlim. The Portuguese, on extending their power and authority along the western coast, endeavoured to force the Syrian Christians into subjection to their Church. Aided by the terrors of the Inquisition, the persecutions at Goa, and the sacrifice of some of the heretics, as they were termed, they accomplished their purpose in respect of the Syrian communities near the coast, which were thenceforward termed Syro-Roman churches, a name which they bear to the present day. A concession was made to them on a point on which they were peculiarly sensitive, and for which they were appar-

Their persecution by the Portuguese.

ently ready to risk their property and lives, and everything dear to them. This was the retention of their own language in their prayers and liturgy. The churches inland continued independent; and as they could not be so easily reached by Romish inquisitors, were at length left to themselves. These continue the observance of their rites as of old. The Rev. Claudius Buchanan, who visited the Syrian Christians in 1806, thus speaks of the picturesque appearance of their churches, and of his visits to them:—

"The first view of the Christian churches in this sequestered region of Hindostan, connected with the idea of their tranquil duration for so many ages, cannot fail to excite pleasing emotions in the mind of the beholder. The form of the oldest buildings is not unlike that of some of the old parish churches in England; the style of building in both being of Saracenic origin (*sic*). They have sloping roofs, pointed arched windows, and buttresses supporting the walls. The beams of the roofs being exposed to view are ornamental, and the ceiling of the choir and altar is circular and fretted. In the cathedral churches the shrines of the deceased bishops are placed on each side of the altar. Most of the churches are built of a reddish stone, squared and polished at the quarry, and are of durable construction. The bells of the churches are cast in the foundries of the country; some of them are of large dimensions, and have inscriptions in Syriac and Malayâlim. In approaching a town in the evening, I once heard the sound of the bells among the hills, a circumstance which made me forget for a moment that I was in Hindostan, and reminded me of another

[margin: Description of their churches, priests, and religious service, by Rev. Claudius Buchanan.]

country. When we were approaching the church of Chinganoor, we met one of the Cassanars, or Syrian clergy. He was dressed in a white loose vestment, with a cap of red silk hanging down behind. Being informed who he was, I said to him in the Syriac language, 'Peace be unto you.' He was surprised at the salutation, but immediately answered, 'The God of peace be with you.' I was received at the door of the church by three Kasheeshas, that is, presbyters or priests, who were habited in like manner, in white vestments. Their names were Jesu, Zecharias, and Urias. There were also present two Shamshanas, or deacons. The sight of the women assured me that I was in a Christian country. In every countenance now before me I thought I could discover the intelligence of Christianity. But, at the same time, I perceived all around symptoms of poverty and political depression. I then produced a printed copy of the Syriac New Testament. There was not one of them who had ever seen a printed copy before. They admired it much; and every priest, as it came into his hands, began to read a portion, which he did fluently, while the women came round to hear. I attended Divine service on the Sunday. Their liturgy is that which was formerly used in the churches of the Patriarch of Antioch. During the prayers, there were intervals of silence; the priests praying in a low voice, and every man praying for himself. These silent intervals add much to the solemnity and appearance of devotion. They use incense in the churches. At the conclusion of the service, a ceremony takes place, which pleased me much. The priest (or bishop, if he be present) comes forward, and all the people pass by him as they go out, receiving his benediction individually. If any man has been guilty of any immorality, he does not receive the blessing; and this, in their primitive and patriarchal state, is accounted a severe punishment." *

Again, Dr Buchanan says, "In every church, and in many of the private houses, there are manuscripts in the Syriac language. It appears that the Syrian Christians have latterly been denominated Jacobitæ, or Jacobites, so called, according to their books, from (Jacobus) James the Apostle. The Jacobites are also called Eutychians, as following the opinions of Eutychus; and are sometimes styled Monophysites, or those who hold that Christ had but *one* nature. This opinion is the distinguishing doctrine of the Eutychians. When the author visited the Syrian Christians, he found a few of the priests who held this tenet; but they seemed to explain it away in words, for they spoke of Christ's human nature like Protestants. The nation in general are called St Thome Christians. This is their name in all parts of India, and it imports an antiquity that reaches far beyond the Eutychians or Nestorians, or any other sect. In process of time certain Nestorian bishops obtained supremacy among them; and after them, Eutychian. In the acts of the Council of Nice it is recorded that Johannes, Bishop of India, signed his name at that Council in A.D. 325. The Syriac version of the Scriptures was brought to India, according to the popular belief, before the year 325. Some of their present copies are certainly of ancient date." † One of the Syrian bishops presented Dr Buchanan with

Connection with the Nestorians.

* Buchanan's Christian Researches, pp. 111-119.
† Ibid., pp. 124-137.

a very valuable ancient manuscript of the Syriac Bible, which, it was conjectured, had been in the possession of the Syrian Church in India for nearly a thousand years.

Such was the commencement of the intercourse between members of the English Church and the Syrian Christians in this country. A few years later, Colonel Munro, the Resident at Travancore, applied to certain members of the English Church for clergymen to be sent out to India, with the object of imparting instruction to the Christians of the Syrian faith. The application being forwarded to the Church Missionary Society, was received by that body with the greatest cordiality. The society selected three clergymen for the purpose, the Rev. Messrs Bailey, Baker, and Fenn, who started on their interesting errand in 1816. The intention of the society was, if possible, so far to associate the Syrian Church with the Church of England, that although it should continue independent, and should practise as heretofore its own ancient rites and ceremonies, yet that an ecclesiastical union should be established between the two Churches. Mr Bailey resided at Cottayam, where was a Christian college, erected by a rich Syrian noble, and endowed by a member of the reigning family of Travancore, in which the Metran or Syrian bishop resided. Presently the three missionaries and the Metran formed themselves into a committee, or what was in fact a legislative and judicial council, which took upon itself the secular and ecclesiastical management and control of all the Syrian churches in Travancore and Cochin, from which appeals, in civil matters only, could be presented to another court, consisting of the Resident and the Dewan of Travancore. It speaks well for the moderation and judgment of these courts on the one hand, and the goodwill of the Syrian churches on the other, that this arrangement should have been so successful, and should have lasted so long.

The missionaries, who seem to have been admirably chosen, set themselves at once to their great task of improving the Syrian Christians, by originating various useful enterprises for their welfare. Mr Fenn was the principal of the educational department. Mr Bailey commenced a translation of the Scriptures into Malayâlim. With the assistance of other persons, the Bible, the Book of Common Prayer, and other books were translated into that language, and two elaborate dictionaries, the sole work of Mr Bailey, were written and printed. Mr Baker was a Visitor in charge of seventy-two Syrian churches. "There were vernacular schools at each of these churches, which the children of all Syrians were required to attend, the Church Missionary Society furnishing books and the salaries of the teachers. There was also a superior grammar-school preparatory to the instructions at the college, under Mr Baker's care. In all the schools a strictly Scriptural education was given in the Malayâlim; but in the grammar-school situate at Cottayam, English was also taught. Some of the pupils in the college were Syrian deacons, whom Mr Fenn instructed in Latin, Greek, the elements of mathematics, and the general course of an English education. Syriac was taught by a Malpan, or literary doctor, and Sanskrit by Moonshees."* Such was the organisation intro-

* Report of the South India Missionary Conference: Paper by the Rev. H. Baker, junior, on the Missions of the Church Society in Travancore and Cochin, p. 67.

duced among these Syrians by the able and learned missionaries of this society. The scheme worked excellently. The Metrans, or bishops, only ordained persons to the ministerial office who could produce testimonials not merely from the committee, but also from the principal of the college. These happy relations between the Church Missionary Society and the Syrian Church subsisted from 1816 to 1838, when a radical change was effected.

Changes introduced. The new Syrian bishop opposed to the missionaries and their proceedings.

There were reasons for this change on both sides. Mr Baker has given them in few words. "The Metran Dionysius, who had been a friend to the missionaries, and who desired in some measure to reform his Church, was now dead. Colonel Munro also had left the country. Consequently the English clergy had lost a portion of their influence, and hence were not regarded in the same favourable light by the body of the people. The new bishop was an extremely avaricious man. He at once began to ordain *children* and ignorant youths, on the receipt of sums of money; and also let out the college lands on excessive rents, appropriating the surplus to his own purposes. The combined ruling committee he utterly neglected; and soon discouraged the college and parochial schools, and forbade the habitual preaching of the gospel by the missionaries in the several churches. Mr Fenn had been succeeded by others; and Messrs Bailey and Baker had visited England for their health, which had been much impaired. Some of these old missionaries had pleaded for a change of system, and were desirous of commencing an independent mission. They argued, that though they had been the means of diffusing some light, yet that while the Syrians used the Syriac language (understood by very few, even of the priests) in their church services, and as long as all the errors of the Greek Church were cherished and adopted by them, the co-operation of the Church missionaries with them, as with a Church regularly constituted, tended rather to strengthen the rule and system of that Church than to reform it. Hence there would appear to be no prospect of permanent good effected for the Syrian body. About this time, Bishop Wilson, of Calcutta, visited Travancore, and at once saw that much labour had produced very little results. He accordingly made a proposition, that the Syrian Church should reform itself of all errors that had been acquired by their connection with the Nestorians, and in later times with Menezes and the Portuguese; in short, that they should restore their own ancient canons, which were extant, thus returning to the periods nearest to the apostolic times. A synod was consequently held, in which the Syrian bishop, by bribes and intimidation, succeeded in preventing the reforming party from being heard; and then, by means of a majority of his followers, dissolved all connection with the Church Mission, their Church, and objects. The engagements made between the Syrians and the Church Mission by Colonel Munro, were thus broken *by the Syrians*. I would particularly notice that *we* did not leave the Syrians to their own blindness, nor did Bishop Wilson wish to force them to adopt our creed or forms; but, on the contrary, *they refused our help*, and determined not to return to their own rules, tenets, and doctrines of centuries gone by. On this the Travancore Government appointed an arbitration, by which the endowment of the Syrian

The union dissolved

college was fairly divided. Half was given to the Metran, to be employed in education; and the other half was intrusted to the Church Missionary Society, for educating native Christians. With the latter portion a new college and chapel were erected at Cottayam. The Syrian half of the endowment fund is claimed by various Metrans and their adherents, each through jealousy preventing the other from using it. One of the present Syrian bishops is a man who has had a good English education in our institution; but was dismissed by us as unfit for the ministry, although he had been one of the Syrian deacons who had adhered to the missionaries at the time of the separation. On finally leaving us, he went to Merdin in Mesopotamia, was there made a bishop, and is the one now recognised by the Governments of Travancore and Cochin." *

The missionaries form another mission in 1838.

The Syrian Church having thus voluntarily severed its connection with the Church of England missionaries, they felt at liberty, with the sanction of their society, to commence a new and independent mission, which was founded in 1838, the year of the separation. Some of the Syrian clergy and laity continued with the missionaries; and the number of the Syrian laity with them in the year 1858 was about eighteen hundred. Several mission stations were at once established. One was at Cottayam, in charge of Mr Bailey; another was in the neighbouring villages, and was superintended by Mr Baker; a third was at the large town of Mavelikara, twenty miles to the south, in the hands of Mr Peet; and a fourth was at Trichoor

* Report of the South India Missionary Conference: Mr Baker's Paper, pp. 67, 68.

in Cochin, which, however, was not begun till 1841. Gradually other stations were formed, both in Travancore and in Cochin, including the capital itself of the latter state.

The proximity of the Church missions, and the indirect influence which they have continued to exert on the Syrian churches, have prevented the latter from sinking into that condition of utter stagnation which characterised them formerly. And now we hear of a revival of spiritual life among them. "The demand for copies of the Holy Scriptures has increased wonderfully; meetings for prayer are held where such things were previously unknown; the Catharas, or priests, are bestirring themselves for the instruction and reviving of their own people, and doing something, it is said, in some cases, for the enlightenment of the heathen around them."* These are certainly signs of religious life and earnestness of a most interesting and hopeful nature. *Revival of spiritual life among the Syrian churches*

The Church missions established in these two principalities have, it must be acknowledged, been very successful. The converts have come partly from the Syrian community; partly from the Nairs and Velläla Chetties, Brahmans, and Chogans; and partly from the slave Paläries, and aborigines in the hill regions, who are devil-worshippers. The numerical growth of these missions from 1850 to 1871 has been steady yet rapid. This will be seen from the following table:—

CHURCH MISSIONS IN TRAVANCORE AND COCHIN.

Number of Native Christians in 1850,		. . .	3,809
Do.	do.	1861, . . .	7,919
Do.	do.	1871, . . .	14,306

* *The Indian Evangelical Review* for January 1874, p. 364.

In the period between 1850 and 1861 the increase was at the rate of upwards of a hundred per cent.; and from 1861 to 1871 at the rate of eighty per cent.

A large number of native Christians employed in the missions.

One of the most interesting features of these missions —of which there are now eleven central stations, nine being situated in Travancore and two in Cochin—is that most of the Christian work is performed by the natives themselves; the missionaries being chiefly needed for the purpose of superintendence and giving advice. In all the missions there are only ten European missionaries, while there are twelve ordained native ministers and seventy-six unordained native preachers. Then, again, in regard to education, in the one hundred and twenty-four schools in connection with the missions, there are not less than one hundred and eighteen native Christian teachers. Indeed, all the teachers employed, with the exception of four, are Christians. These are most healthy signs, and are elements of vitality and progress of a very satisfactory nature.

Discipline practised on converts.

To those engaged in the practical working of Indian missions, it will be useful as well as important to know what are the various disciplinary steps necessary to be taken by converts in these missions preparatory to initiation into the rites of the Christian Church. They must remove their *kúdumi*, or top-knot of hair, and all other caste marks, and must eat with Christians, no matter what their original caste may have been. Although they have received Christian instruction before, yet it is continued, and becomes more regular and definite. "When the candidates are able to tell what Christianity is, and have proved by their moral conduct that they are fit to be numbered among those baptized, that rite is conferred on them at their earnest request. A further period is generally passed before they are admitted to the communion; but to this rule there may be exceptions, arising from the known Christian character of the converts, or other sufficient reason." It is a matter of no small significance, as a mark of the genuineness of the Christianity which influences the Christians of these missions, that in the year 1871 they contributed for religious purposes the sum of three thousand four hundred and thirty-nine rupees, or upwards of three hundred and forty-three pounds.

The leading statistics of these missions are as follows:—

STATISTICS OF MISSIONARY LABOUR OF THE CHURCH SOCIETY'S MISSIONS IN TRAVANCORE AND COCHIN FOR THE YEAR 1871.

Number of Native Christian Congregations,	86
Number of Protestant Native Christians,	14,306
Increase in Ten Years,	6,387
Number of Communicants,	3,317
Number of Towns or Villages containing Christians,	109
Number of Ordained Native Ministers,	12
Increase in Ten Years,	5
Number of Unordained Native Preachers,	76
Increase in Ten Years,	26
Number of Mission Colleges and Schools,	124
Number of Pupils, Male and Female,	3,458
Number of Christian Teachers, do.,	118

CHAPTER XII.

MISSIONS OF THE LONDON MISSIONARY SOCIETY IN SOUTH TRAVANCORE.

WE now come to the great Tamil missions, conspicuous for their numerous converts and elaborate organisation. The first geographically, next in order to the missions described in the last chapter, are those of the London Missionary Society. Two of these, however, one at Quilon, the other in Trevandrum, are in that part of Travancore in which Malayâlim is the spoken language. But they are close upon the border-land separating the two languages in this state, and, for the sake of unity, will be associated with the other missions of this society in Travancore. These missions lie in a nest, being situated in a very limited tract, of not more than one hundred miles in length and from thirty to forty in breadth, at the very extremity of the Indian Peninsula.

The heathen population of Travancore is about equally divided between the Nairs and other Sudra castes, and the Shânârs, Elavers, Pariahs, and other inferior and outcast tribes. There are some Brahmans also, who, of course, as the privileged twice-born race, hold their heads very high. The Mahomedans are few in number. They are principally traders, and live in the towns. Christianity has been embraced

Christianity spreads chiefly among the lower castes and tribes.

chiefly by the Shânârs, the Elavers, and some of the slave tribes; but only to a small extent by the Sudras, and other castes above them.

Missionary work among this people was commenced in the year 1806 by the Rev. Mr Ringletaube. He had formerly, as stated in a previous chapter, been connected with the Society for the Promotion of Christian Knowledge, and had been sent to Calcutta; but suddenly, without any adequate reason, had resigned his office, and returned to England. He was subsequently employed by the London Missionary Society, and came to India with two other missionaries in 1804. These latter proceeded to the Northern Circars, but Mr Ringletaube preferred to follow his own course, and travelled southwards to the extremity of India. He laboured to some extent in Tinnevelly, and preached the gospel along the coast from Tuticorin to Cape Comorin. There was already a scattered community of Protestant Christians in Tinnevelly before his arrival, who had been brought into the Christian fold through the instrumentality of catechists sent among them by Schwartz in the preceding century. But the history of the introduction of Christianity into this province will be discussed in the next chapter. At the time of which we are speaking, the Christians were very ignorant, and were guilty of various abuses inconsistent with their Christian profession. Ringletaube earnestly and zealously set himself to correct their abuses, and to impart to them sound religious instruction. He is reputed to have been a man of great eccentricity, uncertain, and spasmodic; but it is unquestionable that his spirit was consumed with enthusiasm, that he endured much privation and personal discomfort, and that the work which he accomplished was a genuine work of usefulness both among Christians and heathen. Before undertaking his journey to Travancore, and settling there, Ringletaube spent a whole year in Madras, engaged in the study of Tamil, the language of the country to which he was going. So great was his ardour, that at the end of this period he had not only acquired a knowledge of the language, so as to be able to write it, but had also compiled a small dictionary in English and Tamil. Early in 1806 he sailed from Tranquebar to Tuticorin, and on arriving there at once began to preach in Tamil to a congregation of fifty Christians whom he found there. He travelled more than a thousand miles, preaching everywhere, and baptizing many, both adults and children. In his estimation, there were five thousand Protestant Christians, and thirty native teachers, in the districts of that part of Southern India. He went also to Trichinopoly, where he baptized thirty-six adults.

His labours and successes.

Through the kind offices of Colonel Macaulay, the British Resident at the Court of Travancore, Ringletaube received permission from the Rajah to reside at Malâdi, to the south of the Ghauts, contiguous to the province of Tinnevelly, and to erect a church there. This was the first station of the London Society in the province. The missionary lived in the most primitive fashion. He occupied a small native hut, in which the sole articles of furniture were a rude table, two stools, and a cot. Here he trained two young men of piety and talent for the ministry. The labours of Ringletaube were suspended for a season on account of an attack on the British troops stationed in Travancore, during which time he retired to Tinnevelly; but on the restoration of peace he returned to his post. Soon other stations were formed; and we find that in 1810 there were six in connection with the mission. In this year he administered the rite of baptism to more than two hundred persons, and stated that there were many more anxious to receive the rite. The year following he baptized four hundred, and was only restrained from baptizing many more from the fear that the applicants were influenced by mercenary motives.

A question often arises in the mind of the missionary in India on the subject of baptism. He sees persons coming to him professedly desiring to become Christians, but he has perhaps good reason for judging that they are influenced rather by selfish and worldly motives than by the honest purpose of embracing Christianity. Now, in various parts of the country, especially in the south, such persons are not rejected, much less denounced as hypocrites. On the contrary, they are received into the Christian community, provided they discard all their heathen habits, and outwardly conform to Christian usages; but they are not baptized. They and their children are placed under regular instruction, are present at the public religious services, and thus soon acquire a considerable amount of Christian knowledge. Those of them who by their penitence for sin, seriousness of demeanour, and humility, seem to possess faith in Christ, are afterwards admitted to the rite of baptism: the rest remain mere nominal or unbaptized Christians. In some missions in Northern India a practice very different from this prevails. There no man is welcomed who

<small>Different methods of procedure in the reception of inquirers.</small> has not an apparent genuine desire to seek after salvation, in the full import of the Bible signification of that term. All other persons are shown the cold shoulder, because of their mixed motives, or of the supposed predominance of worldly motives. No allowance is made for their expressed desire to receive Christian instruction, or for any small amount of interest which they profess to exhibit in the great truths of our religion, or for the inherent weakness of their moral character, or for the necessarily imperfect and very inadequate notion which, at the best, they may have formed of that radical spiritual change which is involved in becoming a disciple of Christ. The result is, that few additions are made to such missions from year to year; and they continue feeble from one decade to another, because of the paucity of native Christians which they possess. Moreover, these very Christians, although received with extreme caution, are found to be by no means perfect. Though previously to baptism they may have been for many months in close intercourse with the missionary, until he has become thoroughly persuaded of their sincerity, yet not long after the performance of the ceremony, all fear of not being accepted by the missionary having consequently passed away, in how many instances does the new Christian not show that he was all along under the influence of purely selfish motives, and had never experienced that regeneration for which the missionary hoped and prayed? Indeed, so numerous are the cases of this description, that it is questionable whether the one system does not produce as many nominal Christians proportionately as the other. If this be so, or nearly so, the advantage of the South

Indian system over the North Indian is manifest. There the mission is filled with Christians more or less sincere, or more or less insincere, as you choose to view them; yet all, with their families, having abandoned Hindooism in every form, and having voluntarily placed themselves under regular Christian training. But among the missions of Northern India which I am describing, there are comparatively only diminutive Christian communities to deal with, and there is little prospect of Christian growth, or of numerical expansion, either from inward development or from accretions from without. So that the conclusion to which the writer has arrived is, that all persons who present themselves for admission into the Christian community of any mission should be received and cordially welcomed, no matter their motives, provided that they abandon all heathenish rites together with caste, that they associate and eat food with the Christians, that they adopt Christian usages, attend Divine service, and, in short, submit themselves and their children to that new religious instruction which the missionary and his coadjutors desire to impart to them. It is hardly needful to add, that for baptism they should wait until fit for it.

All applicants should be cordially received, no matter their motives.

To resume, Ringletaube continued his labours with unwearied devotion. By the end of the year 1812 there were six hundred and seventy-seven communicants in all the stations of his mission. It was his custom to visit each congregation twice every month, and in this way he stimulated the feeble, corrected the erring, and gave suitable advice wherever it was needed. His habits were of the simplest character. "Scarcely an article of his dress," says the Rev. J.

677 communicants in 1812

Hough, "was of European manufacture. He seldom had a coat to his back except when furnished with one by a friend in his occasional visits to Palamcottah. Expending his stipend upon his poor people, his personal wants seem never to have entered into his thoughts. But simply and heartily as this singular man appeared to be given to the instruction of the poor people while he remained among them, in the year 1815, in the full tide of his useful labours, he suddenly left them, no one seemed to know why, only that something appeared to have come into his strange head of other more hopeful work somewhere to the eastward. While at Mádras, whither he went to embark for that place, he called on the Rev. Marmaduke Thompson, with whom he spent an evening, in a very ordinary costume, for he had no coat even then, though about to undertake a voyage to sea. The only covering for his head was something like a straw hat of native manufacture; yet, wild as was his appearance, Mr Thompson was greatly interested in his conversation. No one ever knew whither he went, nor was he heard of again."* In a similarly mysterious manner disappeared many years later the Rev. Mr Schatch, one of the founders of the Chota Nagpore Mission, and its chief guiding spirit during all the years of its early history.

Disappearance of Ringletaubs in the height of his usefulness.

The mission had been left in the charge of a catechist; and it was not until the beginning of 1818 that a missionary arrived from England to undertake its control. This was the Rev. Charles Mead, who was joined in September of that year by the Rev. Richard Knill, who had formerly laboured in

Rev. Charles Mead; Rev. Richard Knill.

* Hough's History of Christianity in India, vol. iv. pp. 284, 285.

the Madras Mission, but had been obliged to leave it from ill-health. These missionaries took up their residence at Nagercoil, in a house provided by the Ranee of Travancore, at the instigation of Colonel Munro, the Resident. This native lady also presented them with five thousand rupees, to be laid out on the purchase of rice-fields in behalf of the mission. The important theological college established in 1819 has been from that time to the present mainly sustained by the produce of these fields. It is plain that the preaching of the noble-hearted Ringletaube had powerfully influenced the people, and had prepared the way for the rich harvest that was about to be reaped; for we find that multitudes now embraced the gospel, and that as many as three thousand professed themselves believers in Christ, and became connected with the mission. The number of Christians, when Ringletaube left it, was at least nine hundred. Thenceforward the mission continued yearly to increase. In 1822 there were nine congregations; the next year there were twenty-nine; while in 1824 there were forty-eight. A valuable missionary, the Rev. C. Mault, entered the mission in 1819, and spent a long lifetime in it.

In a few years the converts had so far multiplied that the mission was separated into two divisions. Neyoor, four miles from Travancore, was made the headquarters of the western division, under Mr Mead; and Nagercoil, of the eastern, under Mr Mault. The Christians were now exposed to considerable persecution on account of their growing influence and importance, and several of their chapels were burnt. Nevertheless, they increased, and instead of being injured, were greatly improved by their troubles. Their congregations were one hundred and ten in number in 1830, and the Christians themselves exceeded four thousand persons. Moreover, the missions at the end of this year possessed ninety-seven schools, containing three thousand one hundred scholars. Boarding-schools had been in existence for several years, in which a thorough Christian training was given to many young men and women. The girls' boarding-school at Nagercoil was long under the care of Mrs Mault, and was a most useful institution, not only in imparting habits of industry to the girls, but also in the spiritual influence which it exerted over them, whereby many became zealous Christian women. The manufacture of lace having been introduced into the school, brought a considerable income to the establishment, which was largely supported by the profits which were made. As this school proved in every way so successful, similar schools were commenced in Neyoor, Parachaley, and Sandhapuram, and were crowned with similar satisfactory results. Both at Nagercoil and Neyoor printing-presses were set up, and were sustained for many years; but they were eventually merged into one, which has every year sent forth a very large number of books and tracts.

The various stations of the mission were from time to time reinforced by missionaries sent from England, some of whom greatly distinguished themselves by their zeal and ability. The Rev. John Abbs and the Rev. James Russell, who joined the mission in 1838; the Rev. J. O. Whitehouse, who took charge of the important theological seminary at Nagercoil; and the

PROTESTANT MISSIONS IN INDIA.

Rev. E. Lewis, the Tamil scholar, were of this stamp, by the aid of whom, and of others of the same spirit, the mission, humanly speaking, was prevented from becoming stagnant and feeble. In later years they have had their successors in men endued with the like earnestness. By 1840 the Christians in the two districts had increased to the large number of fifteen thousand, while the schools in them had seven thousand five hundred and forty children, of whom a thousand were girls.

15,000 converts in 1840.

The admission of one of the missionaries, the Rev. F. Baylis, respecting the purely worldly motives which have influenced most of the converts who have become connected with the mission, is of much importance in elucidation of the observations on the introduction of nominal Christians into Indian missions at the commencement of the present chapter. "Of those who have joined the mission at various times," he says, "it is probable that few came from having first experienced a change of heart, or even from having an earnest desire to learn the truth." And yet he shows that, through the instrumentality of a Christian training, many of these unpromising persons have become genuine disciples of Christ. "But by the preaching of the gospel," he adds, "the inculcation of Christian truth by means of catechisms, the teaching imparted to the young in schools, especially in boarding-schools, and other means used, many, we believe, have been brought to Christ, some of whom are doubtless now rejoicing in His presence, and others still, with weak and faltering steps it may be, but humbly and sincerely, walking as His dis-

Important statement of the Rev. F. Baylis on the worldly motives of many of the converts.

ciples here below. We cannot know what is in the heart, and in most cases can only rejoice with trembling; still we have reason to hope that most of those received as Church members are true Christians; and a good number too of those who have not yet been received into the Church, appear, though often very ignorant, to be building on the true foundation." He states, moreover, that "strong efforts have of late been made, especially in some districts, to exercise a stricter discipline, and not only to remove all unworthy and inefficient agents, but to purge the mission of all those who do not at least desire to know the truth by a regular attendance on the means of grace, and by walking in accordance with Christian rules." *

Prejudice of the native Government against the Christians. The strong prejudice against the native Christians of Travancore cherished by the native Government, is strikingly manifest from the following statement of the Rev. S. Mateer, missionary at Trevandrum. "The district Government schools," he says, "should certainly be opened, as in British India, to all decently-clothed and cleanly members of the community who present themselves. The exclusion of our native Christians from most of these schools, is a crying shame and a serious blot upon the administration. On this subject, I would even venture to add, that surely the time must be near when Christians of various denominations, who form no less than one-fourth or one-fifth of the population of Travancore, should be allowed, as in British India, some share in

* Report of the South India Missionary Conference: Paper by the Rev. F. Baylis, on the Travancore Tamil Mission, p. 9.

the revenue and magisterial departments of the public service."* It is high time that in every state in India, whether under native or foreign rule, the same political privileges which are enjoyed by Hindoos and Mahomedans should be extended to native Christians. In many places, in all three Presidencies, they are still subjected to various restrictions and disabilities, and are objects of contempt to not a few Europeans as well as to high-caste natives, who, though of different creeds and nationalities, unite in their desire to humiliate native Christians, and to prevent their rising in the social scale.

The Malayâlim stations of this mission extend from the northern limit of the Tamil stations at the Nayattankerra river northwards to Quilon. Here the Rev. J. Cox laboured with much patience and perseverance for many years. In 1822 out-stations from Nagercoil were formed both at Trevandrum and Quilon. It is remarkable, as indicating the eagerness to have presses in operation in the earlier periods of mission work in India, that one was established in Quilon, making three in connection with the Travancore missions of the London Society. But this also has been given up. For some time the Travancore Government refused to grant permission to the missionaries to open a station at the capital city, Trevandrum. But in 1838, through the influence of General Fraser, the Resident, this opposition was withdrawn, and Mr Cox commenced the mission. Moreover, the Rajah generously gave a piece of ground for the purpose, on which buildings were at once erected. Mr Cox

* Report of the Travancore Missions of the London Missionary Society: Trevandrum Station, pp. 10, 11.

found forty Christians already on the spot, one of whom was a relative of the Rajah himself, and had been baptized by Ringletaube many years before. By the end of the year they had increased to one hundred and seven. Schools were formed for boys and girls, which were seventeen in number in 1846; while in that year also there were between six and seven hundred natives regularly attending Divine service in the mission chapels. The converts at first were mostly from the Shânâr tribe; but in 1844, and subsequently, they came from the Elaver and higher castes as well. It was found difficult to eradicate the evils of caste altogether from the infant Church, which, together with other heathenish customs, would occasionally manifest themselves among its members. The absence of marriage among some of the Malayâlim tribes was also a barrier to the progress of the Christian religion in their midst. It is interesting to learn that in a large English school established in Trevandrum, entirely under the patronage of the Rajah, and at his expense, the Bible was introduced and taught. The Rajah expended twenty-five pounds on the purchase of a stock of Bibles for the use of his school. In 1861 there were fifteen hundred and seventy Christians in Trevandrum, while ten years afterwards there were two thousand nine hundred and forty-two—that is, they had nearly doubled in the interval. There is also a small mission in that city in connection with the Church of England, numbering about one hundred persons.

The missions in Southern Travancore, which have been thus reviewed, have added nearly ten thousand to the number of their Christians during the last ten years, and are advancing with such rapidity that they bid fair, before many years have passed away, to evangelise the entire tract of country in which they are situated. The statistics they show are of the most interesting and encouraging character. The following is a summary of them:—

STATISTICS OF THE LONDON SOCIETY'S MISSIONS IN SOUTH TRAVANCORE FOR THE YEAR 1871.

Number of Native Christian Congregations,	251
Number of Protestant Native Christians,	32,122
Increase in Ten Years,	9,434
Number of Communicants,	2,599
Number of Towns and Villages containing Christians,	250
Number of Ordained Native Ministers,	11
Increase in Ten Years,	11
Number of Unordained Native Preachers,	198
Number of Mission Colleges and Schools,	138
Number of Pupils, Male and Female,	4,513
Number of Christian Teachers, do.,	139

CHAPTER XIII.

MISSIONS OF THE CHURCH MISSIONARY SOCIETY, AND OF THE SOCIETY FOR THE PROPAGATION OF THE GOSPEL IN FOREIGN PARTS, IN THE PROVINCE OF TINNEVELLY.

Rapid growth of the Christian community.

THE Christian work carried on in the province of Tinnevelly exhibits features of peculiar interest. Foremost among them is the large number of converts found there. If the same proportion of Protestant Christians which this province possesses existed throughout India, there would be in the country not less than twelve millions and a half. Rapid as has been the growth of the Christian community in Tinnevelly, and bright as is the hope which it inspires of the speedy extension of Christianity over the whole land, yet it by no means furnishes the most striking instance of direct progress in the conversion of the people from Hindooism to the religion of Christ, which Protestant missions can produce in India. The Chota Nagpore missions, already described, have multiplied with far greater quickness; and the records of the last ten years, showing how a Christian population of two thousand four hundred persons has increased to upwards of twenty thousand, dazzle the mind with their brilliancy. Other instances, on a smaller scale, even more remarkable, have yet to be noticed.

PROTESTANT MISSIONS IN INDIA. 335

The province is at the southern extremity of India, and is separated from Travancore by the Ghauts, a mountain-chain running from north to south, on the east of which is Tinnevelly, and on the west Travancore. Palamcottah, the capital, is fifty-seven miles from Cape Comorin. Three miles to the east of it is the town of Tinnevelly, and between the two flows the Tambrapoorny river, at the source of which are the famous falls of Papanasum. The country is covered with cotton and rice fields. Betel and palmyra plantations, especially the latter, abound. The people live on rice, fish, and the produce of the palmyra-tree.

Physical conditions of Tinnevelly.

During the latter half of the last century Tinnevelly was a kind of out-station of the Danish missions at Tranquebar, from which native ministers and catechists were occasionally sent to afford Christian instruction to the natives of the province; but no one of them took up his permanent residence there until 1771. In this year, Schavrimutu, a Christian of the Trichinopoly branch of these missions, went to Palamcottah, where he continued for a number of years, expounding the gospel to the people. He was followed after a time by the great missionary Schwartz, who seems to have taken peculiar interest in the evangelisation of the province. When the congregation amounted to a hundred converts, he sent a catechist to administer to them the rite of confirmation, according to the custom of the Lutheran Church. In 1785 he visited Palamcottah again, and found that the Christians had increased to one hundred and sixty. He administered the sacrament to eighty persons. "Many of the members of this congregation,"

An out-station of the Danish Mission at Tranquebar.

Schwartz visits Palamcottah twice.

he reported, "behaved as real Christians ought to do, and gave him great comfort; while others, he frankly acknowledged, were the occasion of sorrow, remarking that this is no more than what is usually seen, wheat and chaff united together; but he entertained hopes of seeing them really reformed. He left with them two catechists and a schoolmaster. One of the catechists, Satiyanâdan, had for many years sustained the character of a sincere Christian and an able teacher. A portion of the English Liturgy, translated into Tamil, was regularly used in the church, and proved a valuable aid to this little flock. While without a stated pastor they were visited annually by one of the country priests from Tranquebar, for the administration of the sacraments."*

The Palamcottah Mission, therefore, may fairly date from the year 1785, if not earlier. Satiyanâdan seems to have laboured zealously and steadily, and the work made progress from year to year. In 1788 the Christian Knowledge Society, which considered itself the patron of the Tinnevelly Mission, sent to Tranquebar the Rev. J. D. Jœnické from Halle. He was a scholarly man, and soon acquired a practical knowledge of Tamil. At first he was employed in the mission school at Tanjore, but as he was anxious to be engaged in more active and direct missionary work, and as it was deemed desirable that the Tinnevelly missions should receive the aid of a European missionary, he was appointed to Palamcottah, to which place he proceeded in the autumn of 1791. At the end of the previous year, however, Satiyanâdan had received Lutheran orders at the hands of the Tran-

* Hough's Christianity in India, vol. iii. p. 663.

quebar missionaries. Schwartz speaks in the highest terms of this excellent man. "Really, as to my own feelings," he says, "I cannot but esteem this native teacher higher than myself. He has a peculiar talent in conversing with his countrymen. His whole deportment evinces clearly the integrity of his heart. His humble, disinterested, and believing walk has been made so evident to me and others, that I may say with truth I never met with his equal among the natives of this country. His love to Christ, and his desire to be useful to his countrymen, are quite apparent. His gifts in preaching afford universal satisfaction. His love to the poor is extraordinary; and it is often inconceivable to me how he can manage to subsist on his scanty stipend, and yet do so much good. His management of children is excellent; and he understands how to set a good example in his own house."* The sermon which Satiyanádan preached on occasion of his ordination was one of unusual power. It was translated from the Tamil into English, and a copy sent home to the society; and was considered so remarkable that it was printed in the society's report, together with the prayers which Satiyanádan delivered at the commencement and conclusion of his discourse.

Following in the steps of Schwartz, Jœnieké devoted himself to the great work of preaching the gospel. In those times, it must be confessed, this was the chief means used in converting the people to Christianity. It was apparently the acknowledged custom to itinerate over large tracts of country, and to form Christian communities wherever the missionary went.

Preaching the gospel, the chief method pursued in those days.

* Hough's Christianity in India, vol. iii. p. 665.

Chapels were erected, at Schwartz's expense, in various parts of the province; and it was in the country districts in which the Christians were mostly found. The people assembled in hundreds to hear; and many were so excited by the Christian message, that they led the way to the villages to which Jœnické and Satiyanâdan were going. At the end of the first year Jœnické baptized seventy-three persons, while in the previous year one hundred were admitted to the rite. Under the faithful ministrations of these two men, great additions were now made to the Tinnevelly Church. At Palameottah, Ramnadpuram, and Manapur, the Christians were continually increasing; but the largest congregation, numbering more than two hundred persons, was at the place last mentioned, where a catechist and an assistant resided. The system adopted by St Paul when he travelled from place to place confirming the churches, was that which, at this early stage, was introduced among the Christian communities of this province, and which is still carried out not only there, but also in the neighbouring province of Travancore, with incalculable advantage to the native churches. Jœnické, Satiyanâdan, and even some of the catechists or unordained preachers, were employed in this important enterprise; so that by frequent visitations to them the condition of all the congregations, together with their outstations, was well known. For several years, however, the missionary suffered from hill or jungle fever, and was often laid aside. Nevertheless, his ardour did not abate. At length he was obliged to retire to Tanjore from exhaustion, leaving his work to the care of Satiyanâdan. In consequence of this, Gerické, the

Gerické visits Tinnevelly.

missionary at Madras, determined to pay a short visit to Tinnevelly, and although Jœnické was still labouring under his disease at Tanjore, yet he roused himself to accompany Gerické on his tour to the south, and the two missionaries travelled together to Ramnad, and thence to Tuticorin and Manapur, Palamcottah, and other places; and finally leaving the province, they reached Madura, where they spent a short time in preaching to the people and in other Christian duties, and then parted.

But the faithful Jœnické's work was done. For few years only had he laboured, but he had laboured with intense earnestness, and with much inward joy. His disease seems never to have left him since its first attack in March 1792. Yet for eight long years, while struggling to rid himself of it, he nevertheless continued at his post with undiminished zeal, except during those intervals when the intensity of his fever compelled his retirement. On the 10th May 1800 he breathed his last. The announcement of his death was received with much sorrow by the Christian Knowledge Society, which, in the record that it made respecting this valued missionary, spoke of "the great endowments of his mind, the excellent dispositions of his heart, and his zeal for the glory of God and the good of souls."

Death of Jœnické

In consequence of an outbreak among the Polygars of Tinnevelly, the Christians of the province were exposed to much persecution. This arose from their being identified with their British rulers. The poor people were robbed of their property, and their persons were tortured and subjected to great ignominy. They therefore abandoned their villages, and fled into the jungles, leaving their houses and chapels to be destroyed by the rebels. Thereupon, Gerické undertook another journey into the province, for the purpose of gathering together again the scattered Christians, and of cheering and comforting them by his presence. He arrived at Palamcottah in the year 1802, to the great joy of the native congregation. In travelling through the villages he perceived that many persons were wishing to abandon their heathen practices, and to place themselves under Christian instruction. Moreover, as he observed a considerable number of catechumens in all directions, he purchased a piece of ground, and formed them into a Christian village. In this he showed much practical sense, which might be, in these later days, profitably imitated elsewhere. From the want of some such plan, whereby converts may be brought together, and also may possess a settled means of livelihood, I believe that in many parts of India Christian work is retarded, converts, instead of being numerous, are few, and even Christians themselves are discontented and unsatisfactory.

Gerické purchases ground for a Christian village.

Multitudes of people were ripe for baptism, the fruit of the earnest, loving, and hallowed labours of Jœnické and his native helpers. Although staying but a short season in the province, yet Gerické administered the rite to thirteen hundred persons. When he left, eighteen new congregations were formed, and the native brethren, carrying on the work which he had commenced, baptized the large number of two thousand seven hundred, thus making in all an increase of four thousand converts. "The conduct of Gerické upon this interesting occasion," says the

He baptises 1300 souls

Rev. J. Hough, in his able account of those times, "has been severely blamed; some persons assuming that he permitted this body of people to be baptized without sufficient evidence of their sincere conversion to the Christian faith. But the assumption is perfectly gratuitous; no good reason is given for it; and it appears to have been founded on the unusual number of candidates for admission into the Christian Church. We shall cease, however, to be surprised at this, if we bear in mind the various means which had so long been in active operation in the southern districts, the labour bestowed upon the people by Schwartz and his coadjutors, Jœnické and Satiyanâdan, and, above all, the fervent prayers which these diligent men had offered for the Divine blessing to descend upon the vineyard which they had cultivated with so much care."*

After this, much persecution was practised against the Christians by their heathen neighbours, which, if not sanctioned, was at least winked at by the British authorities in the province, who, strange to say, declined to interfere in behalf of the poor Christians. But redress was obtained from home. The Board of the Christian Knowledge Society laid the matter before the Court of Directors, who sent out orders of a most satisfactory character for the suppression of the persecution. It is important to observe that, during this time of heavy trial, not one convert apostatised from the Christian faith.

On account of the diminished number of missionaries sustained by the Danish and Christian Knowledge Societies, we find that in 1807 the Tanjore, Trichi-

* Hough's Christianity in India, vol. iii. p. 676.

nopoly, and Tinnevelly missions were under the charge of three missionaries, the Rev. Messrs Kohlhoff, Horst, and Pohle. It was found exceedingly difficult for so few persons to superintend missions so widely separated. The two first missionaries devoted themselves, for the most part, to Tanjore; and the last, Mr Pohle, to Trichinopoly, while Tinnevelly, with its yearly increasing body of Christians, was virtually left to itself. Satiyanâdan was getting old, and, to supply his place, a catechist, Wedanayagam, was ordained to the ministry, and sent to Palamcottah, to assist him in his labours. But it is painful, as showing the neglected state of this promising field, to learn that, during the ten years from 1806 to 1816, there is reason to believe not one visit was paid to it by missionaries either from Tanjore or Trichinopoly. The mission had, in this period, from the lack of proper supervision and of judicious counsel, become considerably weakened, and although there was still a large Christian community, yet its zeal had sensibly diminished. Providentially, the Rev. J. Hough, the talented author of the work so frequently quoted in this book, was appointed chaplain at Palameottah to the English residents stationed there. He at once inquired into the condition of the Christians, and so long as he remained in Tinnevelly, that is, from 1816 to 1821, was indefatigable in his labours among them, and became the means not only of reviving their religious fervour, but also of the introduction into the mission of missionaries from England, and of its transfer in 1817 to the Church Missionary Society.

The narrative of Mr Hough respecting the state of the mission on his arrival in 1816, is given in few words, and is of great interest. "He found," he says, *He describes the condition of the mission in 1816.* "Pastor Abraham diligently employed, and the Christians living together in peace. They consisted of three thousand one hundred souls, scattered in no less than sixty-three places, their numbers in each town or village varying from two individuals to between four and five hundred. Some of these Christians were respectable inhabitants, such as farmers, and others of that class; but the majority were mechanics and Shânârs, cultivators of the palm-tree: there were but few of the lowest castes among them. The increase during the last three years amounted to four hundred and seventy-eight. The establishment was possessed of little property in the district. Besides the chapel at Palamcottah, together with the mission-house adjoining, there was a substantial church at Mothelloor. The remaining places of worship were composed of mud walls, thatched with the palmyra-leaf. There were a few schools, which, being without one regular teacher, were conducted by the catechists, who had little time to attend to them. There were very few books either for the schools or the congregations. A Tamil Testament was preserved here and there in the chapel; but very rarely was such a treasure found in possession of an individual. The scholars were taught to read out of such *cadjan* writings, or native compositions written on the palmyra-leaf, as they were able to procure, the general subject of which was little calculated to improve their minds."*

To supply the manifest pressing wants of the *His labours in its behalf.* numerous stations of the mission was Mr Hough's first

* Hough's Christianity in India, vol. iv. pp. 251, 252.

care. He procured copies of the Sacred Scriptures and of the Liturgy of the English Church, and other important books, which he distributed among them. He established schools in various places, with the view of removing the ignorance which existed in many of the Christian families. He next set himself to learn the Tamil language, and having done so, composed a number of Christian books, in diglot—Tamil and English—of a practical and very useful character, which for several years were the only works of the kind in use among the people. The labours voluntarily undertaken by this excellent man were the highest recognised by the Church of Christ. He was not merely an evangelist and teacher, but he undertook the care of all the churches in Tinnevelly. He superintended all their ecclesiastical affairs, helped them in their differences, gave them the aid of his sound judgment, and, in short, was their bishop without the name. And the memory of his great influence, of his unfailing kindness, and of his large-heartedness, continues to the present day; and even in remote districts his name is still known and revered.

Mr Hough purchased a piece of land in Palamcottah adjoining that on which his own house stood, and on it erected two buildings, one for an English school, the other for a Tamil school. Afterwards the entire property came into the possession of the Church Missionary Society, and is now the headquarters of the society's Tinnevelly missions. At this time the missions in this province were supposed to be connected with the Christian Knowledge Society, though, as the society could send no missionaries to their help, and was able to render them only a very limited

Its connection with the Church Missionary Society.

assistance in other ways, the connection was more nominal than real. Strictly speaking, the missions were independent, as is evident from the circumstance that they were left so many years to themselves without the smallest ecclesiastical supervision on the part of the society and its recognised agents. As the Christian Knowledge Society was unable to supply the increasing wants of the missions, and especially as it could not send out any European missionary to their aid, Mr Hough applied to the Church Missionary Society, and laid before its members his plans for the more effective prosecution of his Christian labours in the province. The Church Society cordially responded to his application, and forthwith helped him with funds. This was in 1817, which may be regarded as the date of this society's connection with Tinnevelly. Several years elapsed, however, before it entered formally on the work there; and it was not until 1820 that its first missionaries arrived.

From 1816 to 1820 three hundred converts were received into the Christian community, and ten new schools were established. At the beginning of this period there were scarcely a dozen copies of the Tamil New Testament in all the stations in Tinnevelly, although the Christians consisted of twenty-five congregations; but so great had been the diligence shown by Mr Hough in procuring copies of the Scriptures, that hundreds were in circulation before he left the district, and during the last nine months he distributed no less than sixteen hundred Bibles and tracts. At the time of his departure there were two English and eleven Tamil schools, with four hundred and ninety-seven scholars, in all the stations.

Rhenius joins the mission in 1820.

We now approach a very important epoch in the history of the Tinnevelly missions, namely, the appointment to them of the Rev. C. P. E. Rhenius and the Rev. B. Schmid. The former reached Palameottah in July 1820, and the latter in October of the same year. Mr Schmid took charge of the schools, but Rhenius devoted himself to preaching. His perfect acquaintance with the language, and his charming manner, peculiarly fitted him for this department. He possessed the wonderful talent of swaying large bodies of men, and his influence over them was of the most attractive and winning character, and may be compared to that of a mother over her young children. Mr Hough had already established a seminary for the training of catechists and teachers, to which special attention was paid by the newly-arrived missionaries.

Theological seminary closed because of caste prejudice.

Some difficulty arose, however, in regard to its management, as the young men of the Sudra caste, thinking themselves superior to those of the other castes, refused to eat with them, and consequently the seminary had to be closed for a time. It should be remembered that caste was permitted among the Christians at this period, and indeed for long afterwards. But the missionaries, with great judgment, refused to yield to the prejudices of the Sudras, and rather than submit to them, preferred to have no such institution at all. It was shortly after reopened under better auspices, and with more definite rules. On the 30th October 1822 a Religious Tract Society was originated, a Bible Society having been formed by Mr Hough several years before.

Soon multitudes of persons expressed their desire to abandon Hindooism. In 1823 as many as one hundred and thirty-six families, belonging to seventeen villages, placed themselves under Christian instruction. "Small prayer-houses of the simplest construction were built, and native catechists appointed to live among them and instruct them." The next year two hundred and ninety-three families, connected with eighteen villages, followed their example. In 1825 five hundred and fourteen families, dwelling in eighty-nine villages, attached themselves to the mission. And thus, five years after Rhenius and Schmid had entered upon their work in Tinnevelly, the Christian community had been increased by four thousand three hundred persons, who were separated into thirteen circles, with a catechist appointed to each. Not that all these were baptized; but they were all properly ranked under the general designation of Christians, as they abandoned their idolatrous practices, and submitted themselves to the new teaching.

<small>Increase of 4300 converts in five years</small>

The method pursued was of a simple character. "From the first," says the Rev. E. Sargent, "a system of adult instruction was arranged, by which every person capable of being taught was instructed in the great truths of the gospel. For this purpose a summary of Scriptural doctrines and duties was composed, and in every congregation committed to memory by old and young. Examinations in such lessons formed no small portion of the missionary's labour for the day, as he passed from congregation to congregation. Great caution was used not to let the people suppose that conversion to Christianity meant only a change of profession, a passage from heathenism to a visible standing in the Church of Christ; and therefore baptism was not so readily administered as some

<small>Method pursued.</small>

would perhaps think desirable. It was not till nearly two years after his arrival at Palamcottah that Rhenius baptized any of the converts; and then it was only two adults with their children. He was willing to teach any who came to him, whatever their motives might be; but he never baptized them till he saw that they understood all that is needful of the gospel scheme of salvation, that they submitted to Christian discipline, were well reported of by the teacher and people around, and expressed on their part a sincere desire for the ordinance."*

Method pursued.

The reasons influencing the minds of these people, and of those large numbers who in subsequent years entered the outer fence of Christianity, are admirably given, and with excellent precision of language, by Mr Sargent. The following statement, though lengthy, will bear close, thoughtful, and repeated perusal. Speaking of the multitudes who every year flocked to the Christian standard, he remarks, "Doubtless a mixture of motives operated in bringing about this result. Here was a people degraded by idolatry and social position; but not slaves of the soil, like others of the lower orders; nor addicted to the debasing vice of drunkenness, as is the practice among many other classes. These were redeeming features in their otherwise deplorable condition. But they had no one who cared for their good, either temporally or spiritually. A European missionary appears among them, speaks kindly and persuasively to them; they all feel and acknowledge their demon-worship to be useless;

* Report of the South India Missionary Conference: Paper on the South Tinnevelly Mission of the Church Missionary Society, by the Rev. Edward Sargent, p. 13.

and a few perceive the excellency of the Christian doctrine, and the high destiny to which it professes to call and raise them. These are forward to learn more of what has been told them. They ask to have a schoolmaster or teacher placed among them; and a commencement is thus made of a class of men under Christian instruction. When others saw the outward advantages which arose from association with European influence, and from having an educated man of their own class living among them as a teacher, and offering their children an education which otherwise was beyond their reach, the number materially increased of those who professed to forsake their idolatry, and learn what the gospel teaches. And among the multitude there was many a poor illiterate man who drank in with avidity what he was told of sin and of a Saviour, and who gradually showed that the gospel is now, as ever, 'the power of God unto salvation.' The character of the people, too, was such as is very powerfully acted on by the sympathy of numbers — few venturing to come alone, but almost invariably persuading others to come with them, from no other motive perhaps at the time than companionship. 'How can I learn alone? If ten men join, we might learn together.' This was, in a sense, the weak part of the work; and had they been left with but little instruction, and Christianity taught to consist in just a change of outward worship, it would have resulted in total disgrace, perhaps, to the cause of Christ. But Rhenius's principle was this — 'The majority of these inquirers have no proper motive for desiring instruction; but how in their present state can they know what right motives are? By God's help I will not let the opportunity which now offers itself, by their wishing to have a teacher among them, pass by. The good seed of the Word shall be sown as widely as possible, and God will bless it where it pleases Him.' But in every case there was the outward renouncing of idolatry.

<small>Method pursued.</small>

"Then trials and persecutions would arise. Some from among themselves would oppose, because of the restrictions which Christianity placed on their proceedings in public and private life; some from the illwill borne against the party from other personal causes. Some, and these among the higher classes, from their dislike of Europeans getting a standing in their village, and because of the influence they would lose by people understanding their own rights, and being put in the way of obtaining redress for their grievances, and by forming a common and closer bond of union with each other. These trials would serve to sift the unimprovable, and in many cases to confirm others in their profession. In the meanwhile, the preaching of the gospel was vigorously applied; and whatever might have been the first motive, yet here was a door of opportunity opened for declaring and teaching the truth without restriction. This opportunity was, with God's blessing, assiduously improved; and in almost every place, while many showed they were but wayside hearers, or stony-ground hearers, or hearers in whose heart the cares and pleasures of the world, like thorns, choked the good seed, yet there were not wanting those whose hearts were prepared by the Spirit of God; and the good fruits were manifest to all." *

* Report of the South India Missionary Conference: Mr Sargent's Paper, pp. 12, 13.

During the next five years the converts continued to multiply in the same proportion as they had done in the previous years, and we find that in 1830 there were seven thousand five hundred Christians, belonging to two thousand families, and living in two hundred and forty-four villages. There were also sixty-two schools, in which thirteen hundred children were instructed. Rhenius gives his own opinion respecting the religious character of these professed converts. He asks himself the question, "Are all these two thousand families true Christians? To this," he says, "we do not hesitate to answer, No, not at all. They are a mixture, as our Saviour foretold that His Church would be. 'The kingdom of heaven is like unto a net that was cast into the sea, and gathered of every kind.' But all have renounced idolatry and the service of devils, and put themselves and families under Christian instruction, to learn to worship God in spirit and in truth. And is not this a great blessing to them?" *

Were they all true Christians? Rhenius's answer.

Ten missionary districts were now formed in the province, over each of which an Inspecting Catechist, as he was termed, was placed. Once every month all the native agents of the missions in all departments were assembled at Palamcottah, for the purpose of rendering a report of their labours, and of receiving instructions for the future.

Ten missionary districts formed.

Meanwhile, the mission in Tinnevelly, which had been for many years subsidised by the Christian Knowledge Society, continued separate from the new missions formed by the Church Missionary Society through the instrumentality of Mr Hough.

* Report of the South India Missionary Conference : Mr Sargent's Paper, p. 13.

Rhenius and Schmid had taken charge of them, and had managed them in conjunction with their own. Indeed, a close union subsisted between the two, and the catechists of both met together at the same time to receive from the missionaries Christian instruction and advice. During all this time the Christian Knowledge Society had sent out no missionary to its Tinnevelly Mission; and had these missionaries not superintended its affairs, there is little doubt that it would have become weak and inefficient, and in many ways would have suffered severely. But in 1829 this condition of dependence was happily terminated. The society transferred its authority over the mission, such as it was—for it was apparently based on nothing more than on the pecuniary assistance which it rendered to it yearly—to the Society for the Propagation of the Gospel in Foreign Parts, which appointed in that year the Rev. D. Rosen to its management. From this period dates the commencement of the noble work which has been performed in Tinnevelly through the agency of the missionaries of this society. The province, in fact, has been divided between the two Church of England societies, the Propagation Society occupying chiefly the country to the east, bordering on the sea, and the Church Missionary Society the country to the north and west. The missionaries of these societies have laboured together with much brotherly love and goodwill, and have been animated by a spirit of Christian emulation in their efforts to spread the knowledge of Christ among the people. Both have been singularly successful; and possess at the present time a very large number of converts, as will be shown in the statistical table at the end of this chapter. Belonging to the same ecclesiastical system, it was only natural that the plans and methods which they adopted in their work should be very similar. Indeed, it may be considered a fortunate circumstance that this province has not, like many other parts of India, been troubled with several distinct ecclesiastical organisations, but has had, in reality, only one introduced into its midst.

The next five years were distinguished by the wonderful expansion of the Palamcottah Mission and its out-stations. The Christian community had increased with extraordinary rapidity, and in 1835 consisted of eleven thousand one hundred and eighty-six persons, belonging to three thousand two hundred and twenty-five families, and dispersed over two hundred and sixty-one villages. There were one hundred and two catechists in the mission, and one hundred and seven schools, with two thousand eight hundred and eighty-two children.

The prosperity of the mission had hitherto been uninterrupted and great. But it was now to be subjected to the ordeal of a bitter and painful controversy, extending over several years, and ending disastrously. Hitherto the mission had been in the hands of Lutheran clergymen, who so far conformed to the rites and ceremonies of the Church of England that they adopted its Liturgy, but were unwilling to follow the method of ordination prescribed by that Church. They were placed in a difficulty by the very success which had followed their labours. Anxious that some of the superior catechists should receive ordination, they proposed to ordain six of them, and an East Indian, according to the usages of the Lutheran

Church, giving the precedent of Satiyanâdan, who had been thus ordained. In reply to this request it was urged, that when Satiyanâdan was ordained there was no bishop of the English Church in India to perform the ceremony; but that now such a bishop was in India, who was, moreover, quite prepared to ordain the candidates. Rhenius and the other missionaries, however, were zealous Lutherans, and were not willing to surrender the point, by doing which they would appear to hold loosely to their own orders. The Church Missionary Society declined to comply with Rhenius's request, but at the same time did not require that the candidates should be ordained by the Bishop of Calcutta. Rhenius was not satisfied with this decision, and soon showed that he could not continue an agent of the society unless he was permitted to carry out his own views. The consequence was, that in May 1835 the society dissolved its connection with Rhenius, who left the mission together with the other German missionaries.

Rhenius separates from the Church Missionary Society.

It is not hard to understand that, in this sad controversy, both sides were in the right. Rhenius was right in not betraying the ecclesiastical system in which he had been brought up. The Church Missionary Society was also right in not permitting in its missions any other ecclesiastical system but its own. It was wrong, however, in obtaining the services of Lutheran missionaries unless it intended to maintain their independence as such. For many years in Tinnevelly, as in some other parts of India, the Church Missionary Society was unable to send out clergymen of the Church of England, for the simple reason, that they would not come to India in the humble capacity

Difficulty of the question in dispute.

of missionaries. In its necessity, it secured the assistance of Lutheran clergymen, who in those days were ready to exercise the self-denial which clergymen of the Church of England were by no means inclined to do. The case stands thus: Either the Church Society must send out men of the Lutheran Church, like Rhenius and others, or none at all, leaving its Tinnevelly and other Indian Christian communities to languish, perhaps to perish. These missionaries were doing the work of the Church Society with wonderful self-denial, intrepidity, and skill; and they were successful to a surprising degree. The position was doubtless paradoxical. I cannot see how the society could have acted otherwise than it did; and yet Rhenius was wronged, and was justly aggrieved. The society has its own principles of action, and it is natural that it should insist on the ecclesiastical rites of its Church being observed. For my part, it is manifest that a society without definite principles of action in regard to the organisation of its missions, is a society which ignores some of its highest functions. But the anomaly in this case was, that the actual work of the society was performed not by Churchmen, but by Lutherans, who thought as much of their own orders as Churchmen did of theirs.

On the retirement of Rhenius and his brother missionaries, the mission was placed in the hands of English missionaries ordained according to the ritual of the Church of England. But many of the catechists complied very unwillingly with the new system; and for several years much dissatisfaction prevailed; separations occurred, which were finally adjusted with the greatest difficulty; and the mission was a prey to

Rhenius commences a new mission.

discord and heart-burning. Returning to Palamcottah, Rhenius and his brethren formed a new society, which they designated "The German Evangelical Mission," and attached to themselves sixty-seven of the old congregations, leaving, however, nearly three times that number with the Church Society. While the feud was at its height, Bishop Corrie visited Palamcottah, and with all the winning persuasiveness which he possessed, attempted to heal it. But the attempt utterly failed. He had many conversations with Rhenius, who in various respects was a man of a like spirit to that of the good bishop. For nearly three years the disunion lasted, when it was terminated by the death of Rhenius. The event caused great sorrow to all parties, for he was universally regarded as a man of great holiness of character, and of ardent love and zeal in the service of his Divine Master. The Rev. G. Pettitt, of the Church Mission, who with his colleagues had acted with much judgment and wisdom during the sad period of strife and trouble, thus speaks of him: "In the month of May (1838) a change became perceptible in Mr Rhenius's health. That constant cheerfulness and buoyancy of spirits, for which he had always been so remarkable, had subsided; and it was observed by his family that he had to make an effort to arouse himself from a growing dulness and lethargy altogether foreign to his nature. It soon became evident that his bodily system was oppressed by a tendency to apoplexy. Though confined to his room, he still corresponded with his friends, continued to manage the business of the mission, and to labour at that which was his great delight, translating the Scriptures into the native

Death of Rhenius.

language. I knew, indeed, that so long as he lived, there was little hope of union, because of the difficulties of the case. Yet, since I regarded him truly as a Christian brother, a faithful missionary, eminent for personal piety, and greatly honoured of God, I rejoiced in his labours for Christ. On the 5th June he suddenly became worse, and in the evening of the same day departed so gently from the scene of his long and indefatigable labours, that for some time it was uncertain whether he had ceased to live. The same day I reported the event to our committee at Madras, and suggested the propriety of at once proposing to his afflicted family to regard them as they would have done had Mr Rhenius died in connection with the society. The committee immediately adopted this suggestion, which was also confirmed by the parent committee in England. On the second morning I had the only relief left to me, of following, with his friends and all the gentlemen present in Palamcottah, in the funeral procession, and of hearing our beautiful service read over his remains by his fellow-labourer in the mission, the Rev. P. P. Schaffter, while a crowd of native catechists and Christians wept around. Every native Christian's heart in Tinnevelly was sad that day; for not only his own catechists and people, but ours also, entertained for him the highest affection and esteem." *

In the beginning of the following September, one-half of the separated congregations, with Mr Schaffter at their head, reunited themselves with the Church Mission, and the remainder, under Mr Müller, in 1840. Notwithstanding all the troubles which had occurred,

Reunion of the congregations.

* The Tinnevelly Mission, by the Rev. G. Pettitt, pp. 157-160.

both sections of the missions during their separation were singularly prosperous in receiving accessions from the heathen; and at the end of 1840, when it was again an undivided mission, we find that it had increased by more than six thousand converts, and possessed the large number of nearly seventeen thousand five hundred Christians connected with three hundred and fifty-four villages, and also one hundred and eighty-seven schools, with five thousand five hundred and thirty-four children.

Prosperity of the Propagation Society's missions.

Nothing specially noteworthy occurred in the Propagation Society's Tinnevelly missions until the year 1839, when, with the advice of Bishop Spencer, they were "divided into small districts, to each of which a resident missionary was appointed, to carry out, as far as possible, the parochial system, much as it exists in the missions of the Church Missionary Society." The success of this system was soon manifest. Great general movements of the natives towards Christianity occasionally took place. One was at Sawyerpuram in 1844, when "many villages expressed their desire to receive Christian instruction, and many hundred natives were at once admitted as catechumens." Another was at Christianagram, in which, and at the same time, a similar result to that which had been seen at Sawyerpuram was exhibited.

In 1849 there were at this station fifteen hundred and seventy-nine persons under Christian instruction. So, likewise, at Edeyenkoody and Nazareth, multitudes embraced the gospel, for we find that by 1850 the former had two thousand Christians, and the latter nearly four thousand.

Both branches of the Church of England's missions

in Tinnevelly have been favoured with earnest and conscientious workers. Some of the most prominent of them are, the Rev. Dr Caldwell, the learned author of "A Comparative Grammar of the Dravidian Languages," who was formerly connected with the London Society, but has been for many years one of the leading spirits in the Propagation Society's Mission; the Rev. E. Sargent, the Rev. T. Spratt—men of indefatigable zeal—the saintly Ragland, and the devoted David Fenn, of the Church Society's missions.

<small>Rev. Dr Caldwell and others.</small>

The plan adopted in the Church Society's missions is one which brings all that part of the province in which they are situated under Christian teaching and influence. The province is divided into a number of districts, presided over by a resident missionary; attached to which are smaller circles under the charge of ordained native pastors. "The brethren meet together every quarter in conference, when matters of general interest are discussed, and friendly intercourse and exchange of mind promoted, with the view of carrying on the work with efficiency, harmony, and economy. The catechists and masters (teachers) meet at their respective missionary stations at least once a month; in some places twice; and in others, where there is not much ground to travel over, four times a month. Where this system is more or less sustained, the order and efficiency of the agents are proportionably manifest. The people of the several congregations in a district have the opportunity of meeting at their respective missionary stations once or twice in the year, for the anniversaries of their local societies; and a general meeting is held twice in the year at Palamcottah, as the more central station, for the gen-

<small>System of labour adopted.</small>

eral business of the several societies, and the examination of the several educational establishments."*

Plan of prosecuting the work among the villages.

The method of itinerating pursued by the Rev. T. G. Ragland, the latter years of whose valuable life were entirely spent in this work, and by other missionaries, was of the most systematic character. In his highly instructive essay on Vernacular Preaching, Mr Ragland gives a clear and detailed account of the course adopted. "Our usual plan of prosecuting our work," he says, "is the following. Each of the European missionaries has his tent, which he pitches in some convenient *tope* (or clump of trees), generally for about a week at a time. A longer stay would oblige us, except our numbers were greatly increased, to leave many parts of our district unvisited for a considerable length of time. A more frequent change, as we very early discovered, would soon wear out our servants, if not ourselves; and as we are engaged in itinerating for nearly eleven months in the year, our plans require to be such as admit of being permanently acted upon. During the week each is able, with the assistance of the catechist who may be with him, to visit every village within a radius of three or four miles; and when, as is very often the case, there are two catechists, the principal and nearer villages receive two or three visits at each encampment. The superior native catechists, or at least two of them, have also each his tent; and sometimes, though not as often as we wish and intend, each has the assistance of one of the catechists sent from the south. The time occupied

* Report of the South India Missionary Conference: Paper on the South Tinnevelly Mission of the Church Missionary Society, by the Rev. E. Sargent, pp. 14, 15.

by the European missionary in actual preaching, in a morning or evening visit, varies from about half an hour to an hour. Our native brethren, who have no fear of the sun, stay out longer in the morning, and sometimes start a little earlier in the afternoon. Sometimes the European missionary visits a village in company with one of the native brethren; and if there be two of them, they sometimes go out together; but our visits are for the most part paid singly. As we and our object are well known, and as we are with our catechists during the day, there is not much advantage in two preaching at once in the same place. The occasions on which we do so are, 1*st*, when one of the party is for some reason less equal to the exertion of preaching than usual; or 2*d*, when the catechist is young, and has just joined us; or 3*d*, when there is reason for expecting peculiar opposition on the part of the heathen.

"At our tents there is seldom a day when we have not visitors, often many, and on some occasions crowds. To them we speak, and read, and distribute Scripture portions and tracts, as in the villages. On the day of moving our tents, if there be no body of inquirers whom we find it convenient to visit, or if there be no other tent sufficiently near, the day is generally spent in a Sâvadi, or small native resthouse, sometimes in a Chattram. Here we have excellent opportunities of speaking to the heathen. We make a point of visiting every village throughout our district at least once in each half year. The whole is well mapped out; and we have, besides, a register of villages, in which our visits are noted down; so that it is scarcely possible for one to escape.

The same.

Many, however, are visited two, or three, or four times in the half year, and even more frequently still. We should be very glad if our numbers allowed of our making much more frequent visits. To engage in, or at least to commence, a system of itinerating preaching, it seems to us essential that the missionary should be entirely released from work of every other description. The charge of catechists, schoolmasters, and congregations is quite incompatible with that freedom and vigour of mind which the duty in question requires. There is nothing at all, we think, to be apprehended from a tent life on the score of health. We are all of us very careful to keep out of the sun, and our work does not require exposure to it. We encamp usually, and in fact nearly always, apart from one another; and sometimes our tents are forty or fifty miles distant, though we try as far as possible to prevent this. Generally we contrive to meet once a fortnight. Once, too, in the year, that is, for five or six weeks in October and November, during the rains, we retire to a bungalow; and twice in the year we pay short visits to the south. By these means, and by visits we sometimes receive from our brethren in the south of Tinnevelly, we have been kept from any feeling of loneliness. It is well for the itinerator to keep the number of his servants as low as possible, and worth very much labour to have them, or at least the principal ones, Christians. Each of us has a lascar, a cook, and water-boy, a horse-keeper and grass-cutter; no more are required." *

To show the progress which these missions had

* Report of the South India Missionary Conference: Paper on Vernacular Preaching, by the Rev. T. G. Ragland, B.D., pp. 145-148.

PROTESTANT MISSIONS IN INDIA. 363

made since their establishment to the year 1850, I will give the numerical statistics of the converts for that year, and farther on will show how they have increased subsequently.

STATISTICS OF THE TINNEVELLY MISSIONS IN 1850.

Name of Society.	Number of Native Christians.	Number of Native Churches or Congregations.	Number of Native Preachers.	Number of Schools.	Number of Pupils, Male and Female.
Church Missionary Society...............	24,613	73	81	257	6,752
Propagation Society	10,295	6	8	86	2,381
Total.............	34,908	79	89	343	9,133

It is perhaps remarkable, that in the progress of Christianity in India, so few actual schisms should have taken place. In the districts of Benares and Mirzapore, in Northern India, is a sect of schismatic Christians, originally the followers of a devotee, called Ramáyá Bábá, who was baptized in the Church Mission, Benares. This man exercised enormous influence over large numbers of Hindoos; and it was hoped that when he became a Christian he would induce many of his disciples to follow his example. Though wild and erratic in some of his ways, he seemed a sincere believer in the Lord Jesus Christ as the Saviour of the world. It was soon found, however, that his old habits were too strong for his new religion. In intercourse with his former friends he blended the worship of our blessed Lord with the worship of Rám. His poetical effusions, which were very numerous, were all of this mixed faith, presenting a kind of Hindooised Christianity, which excited

Heretical Christian sects.

Followers of Ramāyā Bābā in Northern India. powerfully the imaginations of his sect. The members of the fraternity regarded themselves as Christians, and received baptism at the hands of their leader. Ramāyā Bābā died not long since, but the sect continues as before. It holds no communion with other Christians, yet is quite willing to receive instruction from missionaries and native preachers.

The Nāttār schismatics of Tinnevelly. A schism of another character occurred in the Tinnevelly missions. "It commenced," says Dr Caldwell, "in a large Christian village in the district of Nazareth, and involved a contiguous part of the Church Missionary Society's district of Megnanapuram. It owed its origin to a personal dispute between the missionary then at Nazareth and a portion of his flock; but as soon as the leaders of the schism had formed their plans, and declared themselves, they took advantage of the strong caste feeling which prevailed among the Shānār Christians of that neighbourhood, and placed their cause on a caste basis. The adherents of the schism number, it is said, more than two thousand souls,* and were without exception Shānārs. They used many endeavours at first to induce the Shānārs generally throughout Tinnevelly to join their ranks, but without success. They call themselves in their documents 'The Hindoo Church of the Lord Jesus;' but amongst their neighbours they call themselves, and are generally called, the Nāttār, or 'National party.' In their zeal for caste and Hindoo nationality, they have rejected from their system everything which appeared to them to savour of a European origin. Hence they have abandoned infant baptism and an ordained ministry. Instead of wine,

* This was more than five years after the schism had commenced.

they use the unfermented juice of grapes in an ordinance which they regard as the Lord's Supper; and observe Saturday instead of Sunday as their Sabbath. It is not greatly to be wondered at that a schism like this should have taken place during the progress of the native Church towards maturity."* It is satisfactory to find that occasionally some of the seceding families return to the true faith. The Rev. M. Yesudian, native minister at Nazareth, in his last report, states that fourteen such families had, in the course of the year, reunited themselves with the mission.

An interesting circumstance, as illustrating the oneness of feeling existing among the missionaries of various religious communities in Southern India, occurred in 1865. The London Society had many years previously established six important stations in the south-western portion of Tinnevelly, which were connected with its missions in Travancore. As the Propagation Society advanced in Tinnevelly, and multiplied its congregations there, the London Society's stations became eventually intermingled geographically with those of the Propagation Society. "An amicable arrangement," remarks Dr Caldwell, "was entered into by the two societies in 1865, in virtue of which the operations of the London Missionary Society were for the future to be restricted to Travancore, and those of the Propagation Society to Tinnevelly. In consequence of this arrangement, the six congregations referred to were made over, in the most generous manner, by the London Missionary Society to the Propagation Society; and the field was now made clear

The London Society surrenders six congregations to the Propagation Society.

* Ten Years' Missionary Labour in India, between 1852 and 1861, by Rev. Dr Mullens, pp. 51, 52.

for the formation of the whole of this tract of country into a new S.P.G. district." *

Dr Caldwell on the spiritual condition of the native converts.

In his review of his own personal work in Tinnevelly during the last ten years, Dr Caldwell makes some exceedingly important observations of a general character, which refer not merely to that portion of the province of which he had charge, but which are doubtless more or less true of the province at large. On the subject of the spiritual condition and growth of the Christian community, he says, "Judging from what I know of my own district and people, I am sorry I cannot say that the growth of the native Christian community in spiritual religion appears to me to keep pace with improvements in organisation, and the growth of the principle of self-help. External work is ever far easier than inward and spiritual work. The spiritual and moral condition of the native Christian congregations does not certainly seem to me to be anything like so satisfactory as their progress in order and liberality would lead us to expect. I can only hope that better times are in store for us, 'times of refreshing from the presence of the Lord.' I do not wish it to be supposed, however, that because there is only a small handful of people in proportion to the mass, in whose consistent piety we can place perfect confidence, therefore the mass of the native Christians are no better, or little better, than the heathen. This would be too harsh a judgment. The mass of the baptized people will bear a comparison, perhaps a favourable comparison, with the mass of nominal Christians of the same position

* Review of Ten Years' Missionary Labour, by the Rev. Dr Caldwell, p. 2.

in society in older Christian countries. They are subject to moral restraints and checks, of which heathens know nothing. High Christian ideas of sin, and redemption, and a new life, and grace, of living their lives in a Divine presence, and dying deaths to be followed by a judgment, cannot prevail in a community without producing an elevating effect. They furnish in all cases something to appeal to—something to hope from. There is always in such a community a power of reformation, a capacity for moral and religious revival, a seed of righteousness wanting only to be developed, which makes it differ widely from the heathen communities by which it is surrounded." *

On the work of proselytism among the heathen, Dr Caldwell gives the following opinions: "There are two particulars affecting the progress of the mission in the future, about which I confess I feel anxious. First, Christianity is still confined too much within the limits of the Shânâr caste. Fair progress is being made, in this district, at least, amongst the Pariars and similar castes; but there has been very little progress amongst the so-called higher and middle castes, the members of which form certainly the most influential portion of the people. Much has been done amongst the Shânârs. The problem of the future is, how a work similar to what has gone on amongst the Shânârs, is to be commenced and carried on amongst the so-called higher castes. The second point is, the cessation even amongst the Shânârs

His opinion on future labours among the heathen.

---
* Review of Ten Years' Missionary Labour, by the Rev. Dr Caldwell, pp. 6, 7.

themselves of accessions to Christianity on anything like a considerable scale. Accessions do still take place; but they are generally few and far between; and what I especially note with regret is, that they are fewer and further between in old districts than in new. It is to be borne in mind also that the majority of the wealthier sort of Shânârs—those who call themselves by a name signifying 'lords of the soil'—are not Christians, show no intention, generally speaking, of becoming Christians, and are, in some instances, as much opposed to the idea of actually joining the Christian Church as any class of people in the country. In many places, therefore, in the older districts, the Christian Church has now become more or less stationary; and people on both sides are now beginning to be tempted to regard the present condition of things, and the mode in which the people are at present divided, as likely to become permanent. The heathen are beginning to reconcile themselves to the Christianity of their Christian neighbours, as a transmitted, inherited form of religion peculiar to a certain circle of families, and as such entitled to the profound respect of conservative-minded Hindoos; and the Christians, if left to their own ideas, are beginning to accept the retention of heathenism by their heathen neighbours as an accomplished fact, which may be regretted, but which cannot be helped. This is a danger which seems now to be taking form and shape in many villages where congregations have long been established; but we are aware of the danger ourselves, the better class of our Christian people are also well aware of it, and regret it; and we hope to work against it with all our vigour as time goes on."*

These are bold statements, and most candidly expressed. He who makes them is evidently fully alive to the dangers from within and from without, with which the Tinnevelly missions are now assailed. But it is not the language of a faltering faith; on the contrary, is the language of one who is not downcast at the difficulties to be contended with, but who looks at those difficulties in every possible aspect, conscious that his strength lies in thoroughly understanding them. Moreover, in respect to some features of these circumstances, Dr Caldwell himself observes, that "though they may cause us anxiety, though they may constrain us often to 'look to heaven and sigh,' they seem to me to suggest no reason why we should despair, but many reasons why we should feel hopeful, and take courage."

I shall now give a summary of the statistics of the missions in Tinnevelly, in connection both with the Church Missionary and Propagation Societies.

STATISTICS OF THE TINNEVELLY MISSIONS OF THE CHURCH AND PROPAGATION SOCIETIES FOR THE YEAR 1871.

Number of Native Christian Congregations,	580
Number of Protestant Native Christians—Church Society, 39,005; Propagation Society, 19,836,	58,841
Increase since 1861—Church Society, 5314; Propagation Society, 3563,	8,877
Number of Communicants,	9,151
Increase since 1861,	2,949
Number of Towns and Villages containing Christians,	1,116

* Review of Ten Years' Missionary Labour, by the Rev. Dr Caldwell, pp. 7-9.

Number of Ordained Native Ministers—Church Society, 33; Propagation Society, 13,	46
Increase since 1861,	32
Number of Unordained Native Preachers—Church Society, 221; Propagation Society, 79,	300
Number of Mission Colleges and Schools—of these, Girls' Schools are 100 in number,	603
Increase in Ten Years,	125
Number of Pupils, Male and Female—of these, Female Pupils are 4620 in number,	19,242
Increase in Ten Years,	7,198
Number of Christian Teachers, Male and Female,	539

CHAPTER XIV.

MISSIONS IN THE PROVINCE OF MADURA, OF THE AMERICAN BOARD OF COMMISSIONERS FOR FOREIGN MISSIONS, AND OF THE SOCIETY FOR THE PROPAGATION OF THE GOSPEL IN FOREIGN PARTS.

THE Danish missionaries who, in the last century, raised up their flourishing missions in Tranquebar and Tanjore, were anxious to extend the Christian religion to the neighbouring provinces. Stations were occupied in Trichinopoly, and native preachers were occasionally sent to the province of Madura, in the south, where gradually a small Christian community was formed, whose scattered members were found from the capital itself as far as Ramnad. These were taken under the special charge of the missionaries at Trichinopoly. In this way, therefore, they may be said to have become connected with the Christian Knowledge Society, which long rendered essential aid to the Danish missions. We find that in the beginning of the present century, the Rev. Mr Pohle, of the Trichinopoly Mission, sent two catechists to Dindigul and Madura, "to visit and instruct the Christians in those parts, and preach to the heathen. He also supplied them with suitable books for distribution. Satiyanâdan, the senior catechist, baptized several converts at Dindigul, where the congregation

Christian work commenced in Madura by the Danish missionaries.

was now increased to seventy souls. After an absence of two months they returned, and gave a satisfactory report of their proceedings. Mr Pohle was himself too infirm to undertake so long a journey to inspect their work; but in the same year Gerické visited those places for him, and quite confirmed the catechist's report. He found the church at Dindigul augmented to seventy-five, of whom twenty-nine received the sacrament of the Lord's Supper at his hands."*

The missions transferred to the Propagation Society. These Madura Christians, like those in Tinnevelly, although nominally under the charge of the Christian Knowledge Society, seem to have been for many years greatly neglected, owing, doubtless, to the total inability of the society to render them the aid they required. It was therefore an important epoch in their history when they were all transferred to the Propagation Society, which has endeavoured with great zeal and success to build up the Church of Christ in Southern India. The labours of this society in Madura are now confined to Ramnad and its immediate neighbourhood. There it has a flourishing mission of between four and five hundred converts under the charge of an ordained native pastor. The Christians are divided into six congregations, the members of which are spread abroad among as many as twenty-two villages.

Missions of the American Board commenced in 1834. But by far the most important and extensive missions in this province are those of the American Board, which commenced its operations there in 1834, and has since covered the entire province with a network of stations. The work was begun by mis-

* Hough's Christianity in India, vol. iii. pp. 543, 544.

sionaries of this society from the northern districts of Ceylon. As in both places Tamil is the spoken language, they were able at once to preach to the people; and in doing so brought to their aid all the practical experience they had acquired previously. Two arrived at first from Jaffna, namely, the Rev. Messrs Hoisington and Todd. These were soon joined by reinforcements from America; so that by 1837 as many as eleven missionaries were already in this new field. The great object at the outset, and for many years, was to make the ancient and renowned city of Madura, the capital of the province of that name, the central mission, round which all other stations which might be formed were to cluster like grapes around the central stalk. However beautiful in conception such a system might appear, as possessing the double advantage of centralisation and mutual dependence, yet after many years the plan was abandoned as practically a failure, and gave place to that which now exists, in which all the stations—which have been greatly increased in number—are on an equality, centralisation having given place to individuality, although the stations themselves are still united together by a bond of the closest character. Indeed, a scheme like this is the only one adapted for India. All others are weak, and more or less inoperative. But missions of the same society, existing in the same tract of country, are only strong when possessed of independent authority in regard to all the details of their inner movements and life, combined with intimate union of purpose and action in relation to all matters of mutual interest. A central mission is apt to be autocratic, harsh and imperious in its treatment of subordinate stations; while missions altogether separate from one another, and only connected by their visible relation to one and the same society, often lack spirit and energy, and display self-satisfaction, ignorance, and sloth.

Heathen schools closed in 1853.

For several years the missionaries devoted themselves zealously, not only to preaching, but also to the work of education. Two years after the formation of the mission they had thirty-five schools, with twelve hundred children; and in 1840 they had three thousand three hundred and sixteen scholars under instruction. And the number after this increased still more; but from 1845 diminished interest seems to have been cherished towards this branch of missionary labour, and in 1853 the heathen schools were closed. This must have been in consequence of a new order from the Board, issued about that year to all its Indian missions, to pursue a different system of Christian work, to abolish schools except for Christian families, and to pay special attention to the multiplication of Christian congregations, an account of which has already been given in the chapter on the Ahmednagar missions in the Bombay Presidency. Respecting this complete abandonment of heathen schools in the Madura missions, the missionaries make the following singular observations, showing that their former enthusiasm in this species of labour had entirely passed away. "We can have but little to do hereafter," they say, "with the general desire of the heathen to have their children receive from us an English and Tamil education. The Lord in His providence has given us a people to educate for Him."

The peculiar institution of boarding-schools, which

has at times been so prevalent in Southern India, but has been almost unknown in Northern India, was introduced into these missions at four different stations, those for young men and boys having two hundred and sixteen pupils in 1845. These were reduced to one in 1855, and in 1857 this too was closed. Two female boarding-schools were also early established, and were afterwards blended into one. A seminary, as it is technically styled, but which in reality was a theological and training college, for raising up a properly-qualified native agency, was opened in 1842, and has been the means of imparting great strength to the missions through the instrumentality of the catechists and teachers who have been educated and fitted for their work in it. *Boarding-schools closed in 1857. Theological college.*

Like most missions, those in Madura had to pass through a season of fiery trial. This occurred in 1847, and arose from the prevalence of caste among the native Christians. Most of the missions in Southern India had received the infection of this pernicious evil from the Danish missions of Tranquebar, which permitted it from the first among their Christians, and perpetuated it for many long years. Every mission which had thus sanctioned the enormity at the outset of its history, found immense difficulty in emancipating itself from its iron grasp. Not that the missionaries of Madura gave it the slightest approval; nevertheless, their vigilance was not sufficient to prevent it creeping into the Christian congregation, and working terrible mischief there. The Rev. W. Tracy, in his account of the matter, says, "Caste distinctions had never been countenanced by the mission; no separate seats in church were *Entire abolition of caste by the mission.*

allowed; and all communicants partook of the sacred emblems of the Lord's death from the same cup, as well as from the same bread; and all distinctions of castes among native Christians in their social intercourse with each other were discountenanced. Still it was evident that caste was cherished, and some flagrant instances of this having occurred, the mission, in July 1847, passed the following resolutions: 'That the mission regards caste as an essential part of heathenism; and its full and practical renunciation, after proper instruction, as essential to satisfactory evidence of piety: and that renunciation of caste implies at least a readiness to eat, under proper circumstances, with any Christians of any caste. That we will not hereafter receive into our service as a catechist any one who does not give satisfactory evidence of having renounced caste.' In consequence of these resolutions, and the subsequent action upon them, many of our catechists, some of them, in many respects, very valuable men, left the service of the mission; and the seminary was almost entirely disbanded."* Indeed, so violent was the agitation caused by the decisive measures taken by the missionaries, and so strong was the influence of caste upon the Christians, that as many as seventy-two persons were suspended from church fellowship, and were for a time prohibited from participating in the sacrament of the Lord's Supper.†

Seventy-two Christians suspended from church fellowship.

The effect, however, was salutary. "The storm," says Mr Tracy, "though violent at first, rapidly passed

The result salutary.

---

* Report of the South India Missionary Conference: Paper on the American Madura Mission, by the Rev. W. Tracy, p. 20.
† Newcomb's Cyclopædia of Missions: Article Hindostan, p. 393.

away, leaving a purer atmosphere behind it. Some of those who had left, returned, and complied with the requisitions of the mission; and from that period to the present, the renunciation of caste, in every form and place, in social life as well as in public, is a *sine quâ non* of admittance to the Church." The promptness, determination, and thoroughness which the missionaries displayed in the excision of this destructive gangrenous evil from their Christian community, cannot be too highly praised. It is only right to state, that the Madura missions, like those of the same society at Ahmednagar, in the Bombay Presidency, have been managed with conspicuous skill and energy. For zeal, efficiency, and success, American missionaries everywhere in India take high rank in the noble calling in which they are engaged; and those of the American Board are among the most distinguished of their countrymen for scholarship and ability, and for all those varied gifts which combine to form a practical and talented missionary.

<small>High qualifications of American missionaries.</small>

The records of these missions show from what small beginnings, in the most unpromising tracts of country, extensive results sometimes follow. In a remote quarter of the Madura province, a few persons in 1842 expressed a desire to receive Christian instruction, which desire was of course readily complied with. They simply entered into an engagement "to renounce heathenism, and to submit themselves, so far as their knowledge extended, to the requirements of the gospel." "Others," says Mr Tracy, "in different parts of the district, followed the same course; and though some drew back when they learned the strict requirements of the Word of God,

<small>Great results from small beginnings.</small>

others have remained firm, often in the face of much persecution. Of the motives which have induced them to renounce heathenism, it is impossible to speak with much certainty. No hopes of worldly advantages have ever been held out by the missionaries, though doubtless such hopes have sometimes been indulged. Whatever variety of motives may have influenced them, not a few have given the best evidence of their sincerity by the patient endurance of those innumerable annoyances which the heathen know so well how to practise."* Such is the simple tale which many missions can tell in India. The good seed sometimes falls on soil of apparently the most unproductive character, but which presently proves to be rich and fertile. "The wind bloweth where it listeth, and thou hearest the sound thereof, but canst not tell whence it cometh, and whither it goeth : so is every one that is born of the Spirit."

Growth of the Christian community.

The Madura missions of the American Board now consist of eleven central stations, and one hundred and thirty-eight separate congregations. There are only nine resident missionaries to superintend these Christian communities, but they have the assistance of eight ordained native pastors, of more than one hundred unordained native preachers, and of nearly the same number of Christian teachers. It is clear, therefore, that the chief work of these missions is performed by native converts, and that the missionaries, as overseers of the churches, are much like bishops elsewhere. During the last twenty years the Christians have more than doubled in number. The

* Report of the South India Missionary Conference : Paper on the American Madura Mission, by the Rev. W. Tracy, pp. 20, 21.

statistics of these most interesting and flourishing missions are as follows:—

STATISTICS OF THE MISSIONS OF THE AMERICAN BOARD, AND OF THE PROPAGATION SOCIETY, IN THE PROVINCE OF MADURA, FOR THE YEAR 1871.

Number of Native Christian Congregations,	145
Number of Protestant Native Christians,	7341
Increase in Twenty-one Years,	4154
Number of Communicants,	1597
Number of Towns and Villages containing Christians,	275
Number of Ordained Native Ministers,	9
Number of Unordained Native Preachers,	107
Number of Mission Schools, including Theological and Training Seminaries,	118
Number of Pupils, Male and Female,	2852
Number of Christian Teachers, do.,	125
Amount contributed by the Christians exclusively, during the Year,	£374

CHAPTER XV.

MISSIONS IN TANJORE, TRICHINOPOLY, POODOOCOTTAH, COIMBATOOR, AND THE NEILGHERRIES.

Geographical relations of the missions described. THIS dissertation on the Protestant missions of India commenced with the establishment of the Danish Mission at Tranquebar in the year 1706, under the learned and saintly Ziegenbalg. Having given a brief historical sketch of the gradual development of this mission, and its extension to Tanjore, Trichinopoly, and other provinces, during the last century, and having presented a bird's-eye view of the progress of Protestant missions in Bengal, beginning with Calcutta, Northern and North-Western India, Rajpootana, Central India, Bombay, the South Mahratta country, Malabar, Travancore, Tinnevelly, and Madura, we come again geographically to the place from which we started, leaving the states and provinces to the north of Tanjore, as far as the borders of Orissa, to be described in subsequent chapters.

Pecuniary difficulties of the Danish missions. The difficulty which the Danish missionaries had felt in maintaining efficiently all the missions which they had successively established, had been somewhat removed by the liberality of the Christian Knowledge Society; but at the time of the death of Schwartz, in the beginning of 1798, it began to wear a very serious aspect. In consequence of the war in Europe they could not communicate directly with Denmark, and the money sent to them from that country was first despatched to Bengal, and reached them after long intervals, and at great expense. Indeed, had not this noble society watched over them with special care, and supplied their necessities at this period, the Tranquebar Mission at least, if not several others likewise, must have been closed. The trials of the missionaries reached their height in 1801, when Tranquebar was captured by British troops, which event occurred on the 13th May of that year. In this emergency the British commanding officer showed great kindness to the mission, and wrote a report upon it to the Madras Government, which sent back instructions "to protect the missionaries in the full possession of their former privileges, and even to grant them what further immunities they might require for their peaceful work." Thus their anxiety was turned to joy and gratitude. During the whole time of the British occupation of Tranquebar they were treated with consideration. In 1802 peace was restored, and Tranquebar became once more Danish property. But soon the mission began to languish again from want of funds; and as war had broken out afresh in Europe, and Denmark was involved in the tremendous struggle that was shaking all the Western nations, the Tranquebar Mission was temporarily abandoned by the Danish Government, and must have been ruined but for the intervention of the Christian Knowledge Society. But the aid thus generously and opportunely given, was not sufficient to meet the full wants of the missionaries; and therefore they applied to the Madras Government for assistance,

Generosity of the Christian Knowledge Society.

which granted them two hundred pagodas (seventy-five pounds) monthly, on the stipulation that the money was to be returned on the termination of the war. Meanwhile the colony had again come under British authority, much to the relief of the mission, which received help from the garrison, and was treated by the commandant and other officers with attention and respect.

<small>Depressed condition of the mission. Evil of caste usages.</small>

It was painfully manifest, however, that this pioneer mission, once so prosperous and widespreading, was on the decline. Scanty and uncertain funds, a reduced missionary staff, a deficient supply of books, want of sympathy on the part of many of the Danish residents in the settlement, and other causes, had a depressing and wasting effect upon the entire mission. Moreover, as a natural result of this enfeebled condition, errors began to creep among the native Christians, and more than once the mission was placed in great jeopardy by the feuds which arose. The subject of caste occasionally gave the missionaries much trouble and vexation. It was not merely permitted among the Christians in their social life; but also presumed to intrude into one of the sacred ceremonies of the Christian Church. The venerable Dr John, though old and blind, set himself with great sternness against this heathenish association of caste with the holiest rites of Christianity. "The Christians," says Mr Hough, "contended for distinct places at church, and even for two cups at the Lord's Supper, for the higher and lower castes. The latter, however respectable for wealth, or moral and Christian character, were compelled to sit apart from the rest, and to have their separate cup. At last, Dr John resolved to endure this antichristian custom no longer, and gave notice, that if they would not, of their own accord, put an end to these odious distinctions, especially at the Lord's table, he would himself abolish them. His admonitions being obstinately resisted, he executed his threat, with regard to the sacrament at least, by melting the two cups into one. This effectually settled the matter. The men of caste made a great outcry at first, and left the Church; but finding that they could not intimidate their faithful pastor into a compliance with their wishes, they gradually returned, and henceforth drank out of one and the same cup with the Pariah."*

One of the last acts of this devoted man was to establish in the districts of Tranquebar, and also in some of the villages of Tanjore, a number of what he termed "free reading-schools," of which there were twenty in 1812, with nearly six hundred scholars. These schools soon became somewhat famous, for we find persons in Bengal contributing to their support, and the agents of the Church Missionary Society in Calcutta generously granting them the sum of one hundred rupees, or ten pounds, a month, from funds placed at their disposal by the home society, a grant which, as the schools multiplied, was afterwards increased to fifteen pounds monthly. This society, which has ever displayed the broadest Christian sympathies in its labours in India, was not content with rendering this substantial aid, but, with the consent and cordial approval of the College at Copenhagen, sent out two missionaries to Tranquebar, the Rev. Messrs Schnarré and Rhenius, the latter of whom

Free reading-schools. Rev. Dr John.

* Hough's History of Christianity in India, vol. iv. p. 203.

arrived in India with the mantle of Schwartz upon his shoulders, and was destined to become one of the most zealous and successful missionaries who ever laboured in the country. Their stay in Tranquebar was short, for as the society had determined to establish a mission of its own, and as Madras "was deemed a more eligible station for the commencement of the society's operations in South India," they left the Danish settlement, and proceeded thither in January 1815. The languishing state of the mission after their departure, led Dr Caemmerer to request the Church Missionary Society's committee at Madras to send back Mr Schnarrè, which was accordingly done. Various efforts were from time to time made by Christian people and societies to save the mission from ruin. The Bishop of Calcutta, on visiting Tranquebar, caused a grant of two hundred pounds to be made to it by the Christian Knowledge Society, in addition to the help it yearly afforded. At length it was found necessary to remove some of the congregations from the charge of the Tranquebar Mission, and unite them with the Tanjore Mission. The mission was thus relieved of the burden of eleven congregations, comprising thirteen hundred Christians.

Division of the Tranquebar Mission.

At this juncture the King of Denmark sent to Tranquebar, through the Royal Mission College at Copenhagen, the munificent sum of eighteen hundred pounds, accompanied by a cordial letter from the College, which, however, enjoined upon the missionaries the exercise of rigid economy. Even with this sum, so great were their straits, they were barely able to maintain their Tamil and Portuguese congrega-

Decay of the mission. Dr Caemmerer.

tions, and a school for each, while they "could not venture to resume the charge of the country congregations and schools, which had been transferred to the Christian Knowledge and Church Missionary Societies." The Danish Mission, stripped of its country churches, reduced to one missionary, and with small means of support, never revived. For several years, Dr Caemmerer, its sole remaining missionary, endeavoured to carry on the work in Tranquebar, and to minister to the diminishing congregations; but the mission had lost its early vigour, and sank into weakness.

The mission at Tanjore, over which Schwartz presided for so many years, being more immediately under the charge of the Christian Knowledge Society, did not suffer from those political and other causes which, as we have seen, had such a disastrous effect upon the Danish Mission at Tranquebar. On the death of that eminent missionary, the burden of the mission fell almost entirely upon his young colleague, Kohlhoff, who continued for many years to conduct its affairs with great energy and wisdom. From time to time he was joined by other labourers, and under their united care the churches and schools prospered. The Rajah of Tanjore, out of love and respect for his late friend and adviser, rendered important aid in various ways. With the permission of the society, four of the superior catechists were ordained to the ministry in Lutheran orders in 1811, one of whom was sent to Palamcottah in Tinnevelly. In the year 1818 three more were ordained. Kohlhoff had been for several years alone in the mission when he received help for a few months from the Rev. H. Baker, of the

Prosperity of the Tanjore Mission Kohlhoff.

Church Missionary Society, who afterwards proceeded to that society's mission in Travancore. The next year the Christian Knowledge Society sent a German missionary to Kohlhoff's assistance, and these two, with their native brethren, were able, with God's blessing upon their labours, to keep the mission in a condition of considerable prosperity. And although, as remarked above, a large number of the Tranquebar congregations, together with their schools, was made over to the Tanjore Mission, yet the missionaries did not hesitate to take the oversight of them, and also to burden themselves with their additional expense.

The Trichinopoly Mission. Pohle.

The Christian Knowledge Society sustained for many years also the Trichinopoly Mission, and gave liberal support to the distant stations, which were more or less closely connected with it. Indeed, but for the strenuous efforts made by that society, there can be no doubt that these older missions, established during the preceding century, would have all been brought into the most abject condition. In 1816 there were five hundred Christians in the Trichinopoly Mission, of whom upwards of three hundred were communicants. There were also small congregations at Madura and Dindigul. The head of the mission was the aged Pohle, a man of the lofty spirit and untiring zeal which are such distinguishing and prominent features of that glorious band of Danish and German missionaries who, throughout the last century, successively came forward to plant the gospel in India. He died in 1818, his mind filled with anxiety for his mission, which had no one to take his place, and was left like sheep without a shepherd. But the English chaplain of Trichinopoly, the Rev.

H. C. Banks, in the exercise of a genuine Christian spirit, took it under his charge until a missionary arrived in January 1820.

It was greatly to the interest of the Christian Knowledge Society's missions in Southern India that they passed into the hands of the Society for the Propagation of the Gospel, which was much more fitted to undertake their management and to provide for their necessities. The missions began a new career under a new organisation, and were eventually delivered from the impoverishment and despondency which had previously so frequently visited some of them. All the old Danish stations seem thus to have been occupied by the Propagation Society, although it is hardly to be supposed that the Christians everywhere approved of the change. Yet it was undoubtedly the best under the circumstances that could possibly have happened to them.

Improvement of the missions on their transfer to the Propagation Society.

Some years afterwards, that is, in 1841, the Lutheran Mission of Leipzic despatched missionaries to Tranquebar for the purpose of reviving the old Lutheran missions established by the Danish missionaries. Had this been done twenty years before, it is not improbable that all these missions would have continued as they were. But after the ecclesiastical system of the English Church had been introduced among them, and had been now in existence so many years, the presence of the Leipzic Lutheran missionaries threw them into consternation and difficulty. And the fact that, while all the younger Christians had been trained on the new system, all the elder Christians had been brought up on the old, and still, perhaps in many cases, remembered it with

The Leipzic Lutheran Society.

sincere attachment, was an additional source of trouble and anxiety.

Rapid progress of its missions. The Leipzic missions, for a reason I shall presently explain, have been popular with Hindoos, and have spread extensively about the country in the provinces of Tanjore and Trichinopoly, into the district of Coimbatoor to the west, of Arcot to the north, as far as Madras and its neighbourhood. Their missions are large as well as numerous. They have at present eighty-seven congregations, which is an increase of fifty-three in ten years. Their Christian community consists of nine thousand two hundred and sixty-five persons, which is an advance of four thousand and seventy-three since 1861. These are scattered over four hundred and nine towns and villages throughout the tract of country already referred to. They have seventy-six native lay preachers and four ordained native ministers. It is clear, therefore, that during the thirty years which have elapsed since these missions were formed, they have made very rapid progress; and, moreover, judging from the increasing ratio of progress from 1861 to 1871, they are destined in future years greatly to multiply and extend.

Its permission of caste. Yet it is necessary to state—and it is with much pain and unwillingness that I do so, for I have in this dissertation on Indian Missions carefully avoided subjects of a purely denominational or ecclesiastical character, and have striven to regard all sections of the Protestant Church as perfectly equal in their relations to one another in India—that the Leipzic missionaries, in prosecuting their missionary work, have adopted two principles of action which are directly opposed to the principles observed by missionaries of all the other Protestant societies in the country. One of these pertains to the subject of caste, which is permitted by the Leipzic missionaries just as it was by Ziegenbalg, Schwartz, and others of an earlier period. Although for a time it was found difficult not to permit caste in some form in the South Indian missions, yet gradually they have emancipated themselves from it; and now the consentient voice of all Protestant missionaries in India, with the exception of the Leipzic missionaries, is not to suffer caste in any shape whatever among their native Christians on pain of excommunication. It is not necessary in this place to defend the position taken by the great body of Indian missionaries in thus frowning upon and shrinking from all contact with caste, which is regarded by them as a monstrous evil of the same grade as idolatry itself—an evil pernicious in its influences, and destructive in its consequences. To uphold this mischievous Hindoo custom, and especially to introduce it into Christian congregations, they consider to be a serious and fundamental error in any Protestant missionary society which so acts. The Leipzic missionaries have unquestionably commended their Christianity to the Hindoos by the adoption of caste, and multiplied their Christians in consequence; but it is not too much to affirm, that in doing so, they have dishonoured our common holy religion, and have gathered to themselves a Christian community, which, from the differences of caste in its members, is not, as it should be, a Christian brotherhood.

The next point wherein the Leipzic missionaries differ from those of other Protestant societies is, that

It proselytises converts from other missions.

they make it a part of their system of action to proselytise Christians from other missions in their neighbourhood. In this way they have swelled their numbers considerably, much to the annoyance and vexation of those missionaries who have lost their converts. Now, it is quite true that, in many places in India, Christians of feeble principle are to be found who, from various causes, are too ready to leave their own missions for others; and it is equally true that some missionaries—but their number, I am satisfied, is small—occasionally receive converts from other missions too easily, and without sufficient inquiry concerning them. But no one except the Leipzic missionaries does this systematically, and as a recognised part of his missionary duty. Perhaps, indeed, they feel themselves necessitated to do this because of the condition of alienation from all other missions, by reason of their adherence to caste, in which they are unfortunately placed. If this be so, the sooner they release themselves from this social estrangement, and from their Hindoo bondage, and with clean hands enter the fraternity of Protestant missionaries in India, the better.

Protest of the missionaries of Southern India addressed to the Leipzic Missionary Society.

In the year 1858, when the missionaries of Southern India were gathered together in conference at Ootacamund, a protest was drawn up by the secretaries, in their name, respecting the course pursued by the Leipzic missionaries, and was addressed to the committee and supporters of the Leipzic Missionary Society. In it the following important statements were made: "We, the representatives of nearly two hundred missionaries belonging to nearly all the Protestant evangelical societies now engaged in the work of propagating the gospel in South India and Ceylon, address you with much grief of heart, in the hope that you may be inclined to take steps to remove what is a serious hindrance to the progress of our common work. That hindrance is found in the way in which the missionaries of your society, connected with the Tranquebar Conference, conduct their operations, in open disregard of some of those laws by which the missionaries of different societies are generally guided in their relations to one another. Your missionaries appear to consider it their duty to receive any one from our native congregations who professes to prefer their views on doctrinal subjects, without any searching inquiry into the probable motives by which such person may have been influenced; and it is believed that encouragement is thus given to the discontented and disorderly, in many of our congregations, to seek admission to those under the care of your missionaries, with the view of escaping wholesome and godly discipline, which is attended with the further evil of unsettling the minds of the better class who remain. These brethren also act in regard to that terrible evil, caste, in a way so different from all other Protestant missionaries, that, by that means alone, it is not difficult for them to draw away people from other communions, where that false and wicked institution is entirely discountenanced in all its forms. We wish not to dictate to others on matters of ecclesiastical polity, so far as the internal arrangements of their own communion are concerned; but when the proceedings of one body of missionaries directly interfere with the internal management of another community of native converts, we feel bound earnestly to protest against such conduct, as a departure from one of the first principles of our common Christianity."* It is matter for much regret that this representation has not been practically attended to, and that the Leipzic missionaries continue to the present time their observance of caste, and their old bad habit of proselytising Christian converts of other missions. Moreover, these converts conform as much as possible to Hindoo usages. Like them, they look out for "lucky days" for performing the marriage ceremony; and at funerals eschew the coffin, and carry the corpse exposed on a bier.

The Propagation Society's missions.

The Propagation Society has nine central missions in the provinces of Tanjore and Trichinopoly, besides numerous out-stations. To these missions four thousand six hundred and thirty native Christians are attached, who live in one hundred and thirty villages, are separated into one hundred and eighteen congregations, and are under the care of five native pastors and ninety-nine native preachers and teachers. The missionaries superintend sixty schools, with two thousand six hundred scholars. These statistics show that the labours of this society in this part of India are of great importance. The mission at Combaconum in the interior includes the stations of Porciar and Naugoor, and the old mission of Tranquebar. It is presided over by the Rev. F. J. Leeper, presbyter-in-chief, who is assisted by three native pastors. Respecting the Christians of Nangoor, a few miles to the north of Tranquebar, the Rev. M. Gnanakun, native pastor, gives the following interesting information: "Nearly all the Christians of this district are Valan-

* Report of the South India Missionary Conference, p. 338.

gamattars (a respectable name for Pariahs), a poor class of people, labouring under heathen Marasidars for their daily sustenance. Their indigent circumstances, as well as their want of civilisation, are a great obstacle in the way of their 'coming forward.' But it is my desire to 'bring them forward,' both in their temporal and spiritual welfare. I have every reason to believe that we already have the desired fruit of our labour in several of them, though not in all. No doubt there are several nominal Christians, who are like tares among the wheat, and chaff among the grain. The good and pious Christians are shining like the bright light, and a city set on a hill. They attend Divine service and prayer-meetings regularly. They listen well to the Word of God, when it is read and explained. They approach the Lord's table with due consideration and thought. They have prayer-meetings in their houses by turns." *

Respecting the social and spiritual condition of the Combaconum Christians, the native pastor, the Rev. D. Gnanapragasem, says: "All the congregations of my district, with a few exceptions, are of a low caste. They are slaves to Marasidars, and consequently in a very deplorable state, which prevents them from keeping the Christian rules, and properly observing the Lord's day. I regret to state that, after my arrival at this district not long ago, I met one of my low-caste communicants, and urged him to attend the service more regularly on Sundays. I gained the man, but the Marasidar, the heathen employer of the communicant, put him out of his business for five

* Report of the Madras Diocesan Committee of the Propagation Society for 1871-72, p. 107.

months, for the sole reason of his having attended the service on the Sunday previously. However, the man continued to be a regular attendant on the Sunday service, and became more strict than he had been before. The Marasidar, on seeing that it was difficult to turn the man from his religious duties, took him back to his former work, and allowed him to perform his devotions on Sundays."

<small>Wesleyan missions.</small>

The earliest missions established in the tract of country now under consideration, coming, indeed, next after those originated by the Danish missionaries, and subsequently taken in hand by the Christian Knowledge Society, were commenced under the auspices of the Wesleyan Missionary Society. The first was formed at Trichinopoly in 1818. Three others were begun in 1821, at Negapatam, Manaargudi, and Melnattam. Two more were afterwards added; and all

<small>Smallness of results. The matter worthy of inquiry.</small>

exist to the present day. But the number of Christians they contain is exceedingly small. In 1871 there were but one hundred and thirty-six native Christians in the six missions. After fifty years of labour in four of them, and ten in the two remaining, this meagre result is, to say the least, startling. Is it that the Methodist system is not suited to the people? Then why is the system so successful in Oudh, Rohilkhand, and elsewhere, where the native races are just as unpromising? Is it because proper men have not been placed in charge of these missions? This would be a very hard statement to make, especially as Wesleyan missionaries, as a rule, are always found to be zealous, able, and efficient labourers in the mission-field. Is it because the parent society has neglected this branch of its Indian-missions?

This, too, is equally difficult of belief. But whatever may be the cause of this most unsatisfactory issue of so much prolonged missionary toil—and cause there must be—it is a subject not unworthy of the serious consideration of the Wesleyan Missionary Society, and a careful inquiry into the matter might not unlikely be productive of important results.

The staff of agents in these Wesleyan missions is considerable. It consists of six European missionaries, four European lay agents, one ordained native pastor, twelve native preachers, and sixteen Christian teachers. The missionaries superintend twenty-three schools, with twelve hundred and eighty-five pupils. Of the teachers employed in their schools, I observe that fifty-four, out of the entire number of seventy, are non-Christian, that is to say, Hindoo and Mahomedan teachers.

The London Mission at Coimbatoor dates from the year 1830. It has now four hundred and thirty-five Christians, having added the large number of two hundred and two converts to its native community during the last ten years. Formerly, a large number of schools, with upwards of seven hundred scholars, belonged to the mission; but these have been reduced of late years to five, with a little more than two hundred pupils; so that the mission at the present time is chiefly engaged in the direct preaching of the gospel, for which purpose it possesses two native pastors and nine native preachers. *The London Mission at Coimbatoor.*

On the Neilgherry Hills are four missions of three separate societies. Two of these missions belong to the Basle Missionary Society, and have been already alluded to in the chapter on the Basle missions of *Four missions on the Neilgherry Hills.*

Malabar and Canara. The other two are in association with the Church Missionary Society, and the American Reformed Presbyterian Church, whose headquarters in India are in Arcot. The latter mission has two hundred and seven Christians, and is increasing rapidly. It was only established in the year 1855. The Church Society's Mission is at Ootacamund, and numbers two hundred and twenty-seven native members. Both these flourishing missions are under the management of two ordained native ministers, and have no Europeans connected with them.

The following summary will show the present condition statistically of the Protestant missions in the provinces and districts which form the subject of this chapter :—

STATISTICS OF THE MISSIONS IN THE TANJORE, TRICHINOPOLY, POODOOCOTTAH, COIMBATOOR, AND THE NEILGHERRIES, FOR THE YEAR 1871.

Number of Native Christian Congregations,	211
Number of Protestant Native Christians,	12,675
Increase since 1861,	3,540
Number of Communicants,	5,978
Number of Towns and Villages containing Christians,	421
Number of Ordained Native Ministers,	17
Increase since 1861,	8
Number of Unordained Native Preachers,	139
Number of Mission Colleges and Schools,	174
Number of Pupils, Male and Female,	5,843
Increase since 1861,	965
Number of Christian Teachers, Male and Female,	161

CHAPTER XVI.

MISSIONS IN THE PROVINCES OF ARCOT AND SALEM.

The province of Arcot was early chosen as a sphere of missionary enterprise. In the first chapter an account is given of the formation of a mission at Cuddalore, a town in Arcot situated on the sea-coast, as early as 1737. It was originated by the Christian Knowledge Society, at the instigation of Sartorius, who visited the town in 1734, after the establishment of a mission at Madras, under the auspices of the same distinguished society. This, however, was not the first effort to introduce Christianity into Cuddalore, for twenty years before, that is, in 1717, Ziegenbalg commenced a school there in connection with the Danish Mission at Tranquebar, and in it the first ordained native minister, Aaron, was educated. The Cuddalore Mission enjoyed for a time much prosperity; but the unsettled state of the country for many years in the middle of the last century, the frequent wars which occurred, and the numerous sieges and captures to which Cuddalore itself was subjected, had a disastrous effect upon the mission there. Had it not been for the presence of intrepid, self-denying, and earnest men like Kiernander, Hutteman, and Garické, the mission must have been ruined. But in times of greatest peril they remained at their post, and obtained consideration for the native Christians from the English and French governors who successively exercised authority over the town. Nevertheless, in spite of their exertions, the mission gradually decayed, and indeed never recovered its former condition. On the contrary, at the close of the century, its destruction seemed almost complete. Gerické, the last of the missionaries, had been compelled to retire to Negapatam, where, as he could not prevail on the French to repair the mischief they had done to the mission church and premises at Cuddalore, he thought it his duty to remain. Unfortunately, the missionary who at last was placed in charge of the Cuddalore Christians fell into bad habits, and was eventually suspended by the society. "The effects on the mission were lamentable in the extreme. The congregations and the schools dwindled to nothing, and scarcely a vestige of its institutions remained." The missionary, on mending his ways, was afterwards permitted to return, but was unable to do much active work. The mission, therefore, continued to linger on for several years. In 1817 an English chaplain took great interest in its affairs, and under his care the mission revived.

Its revival The prospects of this station, as of many others in Southern India which were transferred to the Propagation Society, were thereby greatly improved. It came then under an efficient and vigorous management, which gradually bore fruit in various ways. The mission became once more consolidated, and its schools were placed in a better condition. In 1850 it possessed three hundred and twenty-five Christians. But during the next ten years the numbers diminished considerably, by reason of the entrance into Cuddalore of the Leipzic Lutheran missionaries, which occurred in 1856. In five years the new mission already had two hundred and thirty Christians, while at the end of the same period the Christian community of the Propagation Society had fallen to one hundred and ninety-four members. Nor during the subsequent ten years has it been able to recover itself. On the contrary, it has suffered a further reduction, while the Leipzic Mission has gone on multiplying from year to year. In 1871 there were only one hundred and seventy-eight Christians of the Propagation Society, while of the Leipzic Society there were four hundred; the two together having nearly six hundred Christians, or almost double the number that existed in 1850.

The Leipzic Lutheran Mission.

But a far greater and more extensive work of evangelisation has been prosecuted in the province of Arcot within the last twenty years, by that active section of the Presbyterian body of America known under the designation of the American Reformed Protestant Dutch Church, than has been attempted by either of the above-mentioned societies. The history of the commencement of this important and successful enterprise, by which all the district has been covered with a network of mission stations, is given in the following brief and simple language: "In 1850 the Rev. Henry M. Scudder, M.D., after having laboured in connection with the American Madras Mission for several years, asked and gained permission to take a tour through Southern India, with the view of establishing an out-station. The Rev. Mr Dulles accompanied him on this journey. After having explored a large tract of country, they turned their attention

Missions of the American Dutch Reformed Church. Dr Henry Scudder.

more particularly to the district of North Arcot. Its million and a half of inhabitants, destitute of a single European missionary, and the willingness of the people to hear the Word of God in the streets, led these two brethren to urge the immediate occupancy of this immense district. The American Madras Mission at once adopted their report, and sent the Rev. H. M. Scudder and his wife to occupy Arcot as an out-station. By the express wish and sanction of the Board at home, and of the Madras Mission, the purely vernacular system was adopted as the foundation of this newly-organised station."* Another missionary was soon sent to co-operate with Dr Scudder, but the pithy remark is made, that "as his views were entirely in sympathy with the educational method, he was in a very short time removed to Madras."

The Scudders—a family of missionaries. Gradually new stations were opened, and one member after another of the great Scudder family was introduced; so that it has come to pass that, as a fact, nearly all the missionary work that has been accomplished in the district by this society, has been effected through the agency of devoted labourers bearing the honoured name of Scudder. There were seven missionaries there of this appellation in 1861, and five in 1871. This peculiar family characteristic of the mission has, I believe, secured for it an unusual amount of unity and harmony.

The Propagation Society transfers two missions to the Reformed Church. In 1855 the Propagation Society, not having been able to place a missionary over its two missions of Chittore and Vellore, retired from these places, and

---

* Report of the South India Missionary Conference : Paper on the North Arcot Mission of the Reformed Protestant Dutch Church of America, by the Rev. Joseph Scudder, M.A., p. 27.

committed their congregations to the care of the missionaries of the Reformed Church. It is very pleasing to find that "the transference was made with great cordiality."

The conversions to Christianity effected through the instrumentality of the Arcot missions have been chiefly, if not entirely, gained by the direct preaching of the gospel to the people. But then this work, simple as it seems, has been carried on with great method and skill. This will be apparent from the following statements, taken from the excellent paper of the Rev. Dr E. C. Scudder, on the "Mode of Gathering Native Congregations," read before the Allahabad Conference in December 1872. "Our chief and almost exclusive method has been," he observes, "to carry the gospel into the villages, and proclaim it again and again at the very doors of the people; in other words, to pursue among them a system, if it may be so expressed, of concentrated itinerancy. Experience has taught us that this is the most effectual mode of securing the desired result; in fact, that the only hope of making any decided and permanent impression upon the minds of the people, is by frequent, systematic, and persistent effort among them. Line upon line tells here with great force; and the most unpromising and almost hopeless material not unfrequently becomes impressed, and yields to persistent and pressing solicitation. I feel persuaded that this method is preferable to, and possesses many advantages over, the system of more extended, or rather more dispersive itinerancy. There is such a thing as spreading a plaster so thin as to destroy its efficacy. It may adhere for a moment; but, on the slightest tension, it loosens its hold and becomes inert. If, therefore, the object be to gather Christian communities, our efforts must be concentrated on those communities. We must make it our business to work away at them till they yield; not by our own strength, but by the Holy Ghost using us as His instruments. We have tested both these methods in our mission. Extensive tours over large tracts of country have been repeatedly made, and the gospel message proclaimed far and wide; but it was not until we restricted our limits, and maintained within them a steady succession of effort, that we began to gather fruit in the shape of village congregations. We found it better to sow one field thoroughly than to scatter a seed here and there in many. The fear which prevails in the outset is soon disarmed. Confidence is secured. The Word preached becomes effectual. Explained and illustrated as it is again and again, it finds a lodgment in the heart; and the desire to hear more, and know more, soon finds its expression in a personal application for further instruction. The result is, a congregation is born, or at least a nucleus is formed, which may in time, and frequently does, become a large and flourishing church.

The formation of native congregations.
"Let us look at some of the circumstances and conditions connected with the formation of native congregations. First, as to numbers. Our rule is, that at least three families must be ready to present themselves before any proposals for reception can be entertained. A smaller number would hardly warrant the time, expense, and energy that would be required to look specially after and supply them with the necessary apparatus for instruction, as we must do

when they subscribe to our conditions, and crave that instruction. Three families, too, are sufficiently strong in number to afford each other the mutual sympathy and support required to meet the reproach and opposition that inevitably follow the adoption of the new faith. Hence, upon the fulfilment of this condition, a catechist, if possible, is provided; Sabbath services are commenced; a school is opened; nightly lessons and prayers are instituted; and all, both old and young, are brought under the influences of Christian regulations and Christian instruction. Though three families have been made the minimum for reception, in most cases a larger number present themselves. Secondly, as to the mode of coming. This is usually effected by means of a deputation from the village requesting admission. Having made themselves previously acquainted with our principles, and the requisitions to which they must subscribe, they draw up and present to us a pledge, duly signed by all interested, in which the following points are emphatically designated: 1. We promise most faithfully to abandon idolatry, and worship the true God; 2. We promise to observe the Sabbath, abstaining from all secular work; 3. We promise to abstain from the use of flesh that has died of itself. Besides these specific requisitions, the paper contains a more general promise to walk according to the rites and usages of the Christian religion, and to submit to the discipline of the Christian Church, whenever a necessity for its application may arise."* The new converts,

* Report of the Allahabad Missionary Conference: Paper on the Mode of Gathering Native Congregations, by the Rev. Dr E. C. Scudder, pp. 228-230.

also, are required to abandon caste, to abstain from the use of intoxicating drinks, and to remove the *kudumi*, or tuft of hair upon the crown of the head. The *kudumi* is regarded, says Dr Scudder, as "one of the strongest links in the chain of religious superstition and caste feeling," and its excision by the converts as "one of the outward marks of their new faith."

<small>Mixed motives of applicants—measure ideas about Christianity.</small>

On the subject of the motives actuating many of the applicants, which has ever been a serious difficulty with Indian missionaries, Dr Scudder makes the following exceedingly important remarks: "Few, if any, of the people, when they first come to us and present themselves for Christian instruction, are fitted to receive the rite of baptism. They possess neither the knowledge nor the spirit requisite; in fact, their ideas upon the whole subject of Christianity, and the value of the atonement, are both meagre and indefinite. It is a mongrel mixture of faith and hope that influences many of them—faith that Christianity is, in all points, superior to the religions about them, and hope that it will bring them into a condition of prosperity and influence above that of their heathen neighbours. Whatever their motives for coming—and it is the universal acknowledgment of the missionaries in Southern India, that there is always more or less of a mixture, if not a predominance, of the secular—the very fact that they are ready to take the first step is encouraging, and sufficiently so to warrant their reception. It is certainly an important point gained when a man openly acknowledges Christianity; withdraws himself in a manner from heathen influence; places himself under instruction; and thus brings himself into a position for improvement. Hence, whatever the motive—provided it is not, as Dr Caldwell expressed himself to me, 'sordid and disgraceful,' and to be used as a cloak for the accomplishment of wicked ends; whether it be to free themselves from oppression, or improve their condition generally, and rise to a position of respectability in the land, we believe it to be both advisable and obligatory to receive them. Under the name of catechumens, or adherents, or nominal Christians, they are first taught, among other things, to repeat the Lord's Prayer, the Ten Commandments, the Apostolic Creed, and a Catechism containing the truths of the Word in a simple and comprehensive form. If, at the expiration of a year, in connection with the knowledge thus gained, any of them afford satisfactory evidences of newness of life, and so desire it, to them the rite of baptism is administered. We never baptize any one, be his proficiency in knowledge ever so great, unless we have reason to believe that he is the subject of regeneration, and fit to enter the Church."*

At a time when various methods of missionary labour are being discussed throughout India with great earnestness, the above extracts are of no little moment, inasmuch as they present with clearness and precision the plan which has been pursued in one of the most recently-formed missions in India, and which has been attended with distinguished success. At the expiration of less than twenty years since the mission was commenced, we find that it has yielded the following results. It has seven central stations possess-

* Report of the Allahabad Missionary Conference: Paper on the Mode of Gathering Native Congregations, by the Rev. Dr E. C. Scudder, pp. 236, 237.

ing two thousand two hundred and seventy-one native Christians, separated into forty-two congregations, and living in forty-five villages. The mission employs sixty-three native preachers; and two ordained native pastors are set over some of the congregations. It has upwards of forty schools for the instruction of Christian children, and about the same number of Christian teachers in charge of them. These results are sufficiently striking to prove the success of the simple preaching of the gospel, in the gathering together of Christian communities, and their gradual extension over a considerable tract of country, provided that the several methods adopted be of a practical character, and adapted to the attainment of the end designed.

Twenty villages sought Christian instruction in 1872.
In the year 1872 the inhabitants of about twenty villages and hamlets in the vicinity of Madnapilli, a station of this mission, though in reality not in Arcot but in the district of Cuddapah, expressed their desire to be placed under Christian instruction, with the view of adopting the Christian faith. They were for the most part cultivators and weavers of the Mala caste. It was natural that an extensive movement of this nature should excite much interest among the surrounding Hindoo population, and should be met with opposition and even persecution. But the movement has not been hindered thereby; on the contrary, has been quickened and deepened. By the middle of 1873 as many as twenty-four villages had formally embraced Christianity.

The Danish and Scotch missions.
The Danish Lutheran Society of Copenhagen commenced a mission in this province in 1861, which has now two branches, one at Puttambankam, the other

at Trikalore. There are four congregations of native Christians, who are about two hundred and fifty in number. The mission has four small schools; but the pupils in them consist entirely of orphans. The labours of the missionaries and of their native helpers are almost exclusively directed to the evangelisation of the people. The Church of Scotland has a station at Vellore, with a few Christians, established in 1861.

The large district of Salem, to the west of the province of Arcot, is chiefly occupied by the London Missionary Society, which has fourteen Christian congregations scattered about it. The chief of these are at Salem and Tripatore. They are all superintended by a single missionary, who is assisted by one native pastor and nineteen catechists or preachers. The mission was founded in the year 1827 by the Rev. Henry Crisp, who, however, did not live long to reap the fruit of his labours. At first the plan was tried of establishing schools in various parts of the district, taught by heathen teachers. In 1843 there were twenty-three of these schools, with eight hundred pupils. The teachers refusing to teach the Christian lessons which were selected, and determining to impart instruction from Hindoo books, the schools were at length closed as utterly useless in a Christian point of view. The mission has now fourteen schools; but these are mainly, I imagine, for the instruction of the children of Christian parents. As in Arcot, the principal mode of influencing the natives, and of bringing the gospel to them, is that of preaching, although the solitary missionary is hardly able to devote much time to this important work. It is satisfactory, as indicating the great utility of this species of labour,

The London Society's Mission at Salem. Its chief method, that of preaching the gospel.

to learn that during the last ten years the number of converts has more than doubled. The Propagation Society has also a small mission at Oosur in this district, in charge of a native pastor.

The following detailed summary will show the present condition of the Arcot and Salem missions:—

STATISTICS OF THE MISSIONS IN THE PROVINCES OF ARCOT AND SALEM FOR THE YEAR 1871.

Number of Native Christian Congregations,	75
Number of Protestant Native Christians,	4536
Increase since 1861,	3158
Number of Communicants,	1465
Increase since 1861,	1001
Number of Towns and Villages containing Christians,	142
Number of Ordained Native Ministers,	7
Increase since 1861,	4
Number of Unordained Native Preachers,	100
Number of Mission Colleges and Schools,	77
Number of Pupils, Male and Female,	1972
Number of Christian Teachers, do.,	80

We gather from the above statistics, that in these provinces the native Christian community, during the ten years intervening between 1861 and 1871, multiplied more than threefold, and that the number of communicants increased at the same rate.

CHAPTER XVII.

MISSIONS IN THE CITY OF MADRAS AND ITS VICINITY, INCLUDING THE PROVINCE OF CHINGLEPAT.

THE prospects of the Madras Mission at the opening of the nineteenth century were far from bright. Founded in 1726 by Schultze, by means of aid afforded chiefly by the Christian Knowledge Society, which undertook its especial charge, the mission soon became strong and flourishing, and hundreds and even thousands of converts were gathered into the Christian Church. But times of trouble arose, when the city was exposed to incessant danger, and the country was rife with war and tumult. Under the pressure of long-continued political disturbances, the Christian community, although for years increasing in numbers, began to lose health and vigour, a spirit of unrest crept over it, which gradually, and for a time almost imperceptibly, gave place to disorganisation and decay. Moreover, at the end of the last century, and for several years into the present, when the mission required a master-hand to guide it, and so, if possible, bring it back to its former prosperity, it was unfortunately under the care of a litigious missionary, prone to contention, and ever ready to send his recalcitrant Christians, whom his provocations had

Feeble condition of the mission at the beginning of the present century.

made a numerous body, to the courts of law, to the great scandal of the Europeans of the settlement.

Condition of European society in Madras at that time. Not only the native Christians, but also the English residents of Madras, were at this period, both religiously and morally, in an enfeebled condition. "The Lord's day was so disregarded that few persons ever thought of attending church. It was a rare occurrence at that time, and for several years afterwards, for more than one lady or two to be seen there, or any gentleman whose official position did not require his presence. The only exceptions were at Christmas and on Easter days, when it was customary for most persons to go to church; and on these occasions the natives used to crowd into the fort to see the unusual sight. They looked upon these festivals as the gentlemen's Poojahs, somewhat like their own annual feasts; and this thronging to the church created quite a sensation throughout the settlement. Every other Sabbath in the year was set apart as the great day of general amusement and dissipation. European society of India generally, high and low, was like the nation of Israel when without a king, 'every man did that which was right in his own eyes.'"* Men of great spirituality and earnestness, like the Rev. Dr Kerr and the Rev. Marmaduke Thompson, were fortunately successively appointed as chaplains at this time; and although it does not appear that much reformation was produced, yet their influence was extensively felt, and by degrees accomplished important results.

We have already seen how that the mutiny of the sepoys at Vellore in 1806 was attributed by many

* Hough's History of Christianity in India, vol. iv. pp. 136, 137.

persons, both in England and in India, to the spread of Christianity among the natives, and that this baseless suspicion was productive of great mischief in Calcutta, in leading members of the Government to frown upon the missionaries there, and also upon their labours. The same result, likewise, was manifest at Madras, though not to the same extent. Nevertheless, when an effort was made to establish a Bible society in that city, the Governor, on receiving information of the matter, became so excited, not to say alarmed, that he "peremptorily prohibited the formation of a Bible association, or committee, or even the general circulation of a subscription paper." Efforts to establish a Bible society frustrated by the Governor.

The London Missionary Society was the first to establish a mission in Madras, next after that which was connected with the Christian Knowledge Society, and which had been already in existence, as we have seen, for so many years. In 1805 the Rev. W. C. Loveless and Dr Taylor arrived from England, having been appointed to Surat, on the opposite side of the country. They found two missionaries of this society, the Rev. Messrs Cran and Des Granges, already in Madras, who were learning the language preparatory to commencing a mission at Vizagapatam, whither they shortly after proceeded. Dr Taylor entered the Government service at Bombay, but Mr Loveless was persuaded to remain in Madras. Several years elapsed before he could do anything in behalf of the natives themselves. He became Master of the Male Asylum, which position he held until 1812. In addition, he preached to the English and East Indian residents, among whom he laboured with great earnestness and success, and was very zealous in the formation of the The London Society's Mission established in 1805. Rev. W. C. Loveless

Bible and Tract Societies of Madras. In those days there were many obstacles to direct missionary work which happily do not exist now. The opposition of the Government was persistent and unrelenting. It is not surprising, therefore, that during those earlier years Mr Loveless found himself unable to fulfil his original intentions among the heathen population in a manner most agreeable to his tastes and wishes. An instance of the pertinacity with which the Government carried out the orders from home in hunting up and deporting new missionaries occurred in 1812, when the Rev. Mr Thompson arrived from England, on his way to Bellary, a mission lately founded by the London Society, having touched at the Isle of France on his voyage out. This gentleman received the following communication from the superintendent of police :—

"MADRAS POLICE-OFFICE, *May* 22, 1812.

Order for the deportation of the Rev. Mr Thompson.
"REV. SIR,—I am directed to acquaint you that the Honourable the Governor in Council is precluded, by the orders of the Supreme Government, from permitting you to reside in any place under this Presidency. You will therefore return to the Isle of France, or to Europe, by the first opportunity.—I am, Rev. Sir, your obedient Servant, J. H. SYMNS,
Superintendent of Police." *

His death. Rev. Richard Knill arrives.
Before this order could be carried out, Mr Thompson was suddenly taken ill with disease of the liver, and died. On the removal of restrictions from missionaries, the Rev. Richard Knill was first sent, and soon two others, to Madras, for the purpose of assisting Mr Loveless in commencing active operations there. From that time to the present a great work has been prosecuted by the missionaries of this society, both

* Report of the London Missionary Society for 1813, p. 460.

in the constant preaching of the gospel in the streets, bazaars, and surrounding villages, and in imparting instruction in the numerous schools which have been connected with the mission. Several hundred persons have been baptized, although no published record exists of the exact number. A Christian church was early formed, of which the pastor was the Rev. W. Taylor. This numbered in 1831 thirty-eight native communicants. Five years later, the Rev. W. H. Drew, a man of earnestness, piety, and learning, was appointed to the office of pastor, which he held for a period of twenty years, during which time two hundred and eighty communicants were added to the fellowship of the church, which is at the rate of fifteen for each year. These were chiefly gathered from the lower castes of Hindoos.

Rev. W. H. Drew.

In 1827 the mission had six hundred native youths under instruction in its various schools. For the next twenty-four years the average attendance was five hundred and fifty. This number has of late years greatly increased; and at the present time there are twelve schools, with ten hundred and ninety-six scholars, of whom four hundred and fifty-seven are young women and girls. A large institution or college was originated in 1852, which is affiliated with the Madras University, and imparts a high-class education to its pupils. The Rev. George Hall has been for many years its laborious and efficient principal. Some of the young men trained in the institution have embraced the gospel; and most of these have been of good family and caste. In three years as many as nine students were baptized. The boarding-school for native girls has been a successful de-

Rev. George Hall. Progress of the mission.

partment of missionary labour. It was for a few years managed by Mrs Drew, and after her death, until 1856, by Mrs Porter. "Many trained in the boarding-school," says the Rev. G. Hall, "have become members of the church, and have for years maintained a consistent Christian character. Some have died rejoicing in the Lord, while numbers are now mothers of families, exerting such an influence for good in one of the most important relationships of life as is generally needed, but is little known in India. It is also worthy of notice that several who have been trained in this boarding-school are now engaged in teaching children of their own sex in different parts of the country."* The mission has important out-stations in the country. One of these is at Pulicat, and another at Tripassore.

Several chaplains of the English Episcopal Church stationed in Madras had long desired that a mission might be established in that city in association with their own Church, and had personally taken practical interest in the evangelisation of the native population; but not until the East India Company had altered their rules in regard to the admission of missionaries into the country were their wishes gratified. In expectation, however, that the Church Missionary Society would soon send missionaries to this city, a corresponding committee was formed in 1814, through the instrumentality of the Rev. Mr Thompson, chaplain of St George's Church. Shortly after, the Rev. Messrs Rhenius and Schnarré arrived, having

Rev. Mr Thompson. Mission of the Church Society.

---

* Report of the South India Missionary Conference: Paper on the Madras Mission of the London Missionary Society, by the Rev. G. Hall, B.A., p. 36.

PROTESTANT MISSIONS IN INDIA.   415

stayed for a brief period at Tranquebar, and the mission was started in the following year. At first they rendered help to the mission of the Christian Knowledge Society, but soon became independent of it, and endeavoured to form a separate station. They laboured among the neighbouring villages and in the outskirts of the city. While engaged in this useful work, Schnarrè was sent back to the Danish Mission at Tranquebar, which greatly needed the presence and aid of another missionary. Several out-stations were commenced by Rhenius and his successors in various parts of the surrounding country, such as Pulicat, Tripassore, Conjeveram, and Chinglepat. This system Rhenius afterwards worked so successfully in Tinnevelly, on his transference to that province. Strange to say, the system, though so useful elsewhere, seems not to have been adapted to the circumstances of the country around Madras at the time it was introduced. Whether Rhenius, with his peculiar skill, and with the wonderful influence he exerted in swaying the minds of men, had he remained longer in Madras, could have completed the work which he commenced, and filled the district round the capital with small congregations of native Christians, is a question difficult to answer. Some men can accomplish what others cannot. Rhenius was removed to Tinnevelly in 1820, and the out-stations were one by one abandoned because of the "impossibility of giving them proper supervision," but most, if not all of them, were subsequently taken up by other societies. _{Rhenius removed to Tinnevelly.}

A mission church was erected at Black Town—a quarter of Madras—at the expense of the Government, in the year 1819. A theological school for the _{Mission church erected by the Government in 1819.}

training of teachers, catechists, and ministers was early established, and in it a number of very able men were educated, some of whom were sent to other missions of the Church Society in Southern India. The school was closed in 1846, as other institutions of the same character were opened both in Tinnevelly and Travancore. The missionaries from the commencement have paid great attention to the work of education. In 1825 their schools possessed six hundred and sixty-one pupils, nearly all of whom were taught in the vernaculars. In 1861 the mission had seventeen schools, with seven hundred and fifty-eight scholars. But during the last ten years the number under instruction has greatly increased. At the end of 1871 the missionaries had charge of twenty-six schools, in which thirteen hundred and nineteen pupils were receiving Christian instruction.

The Central Female School. Zenanas.

Much labour has been expended by this mission on female education. "Several of the earlier schools were merged into the 'Central Female School,' which, under successive teachers, has done incalculable good." As far back as 1827 there were two hundred and fifty native girls being instructed by the mission. In 1871 there were five schools, containing four hundred and twenty-seven young women and girls. A very important work was also in progress among the zenanas of respectable families of the city. In that year ninety-one zenanas were open to the religious and secular instruction imparted by the European ladies and their native Christian female fellow-workers of this mission.

Caste difficulties.

As in many other missions in India, caste showed its cloven foot in the Church Society's stations in Madras.

"In 1826," remarks the Rev. J. Gritton, "the mission was shaken by the pretensions of the caste-observing members. They were checked then, as well as subsequently, whenever they have made any movement. The chief struggles took place in 1847 and 1854. At present, although the leaven exists, and is at times detected, there is little that is tangible or open to censure. Caste observance is considered antichristian, and every effort is made to uproot and destroy it."* "Wisdom and love in the missionary were, by God's blessing, crowned with success," in the great caste struggle of 1854.

A very interesting event occurred in 1844, affording much gratification to the missionaries, and inspiring great hopes for the future prosperity of the mission. This was the ordination to the ministry of two Christian students of the institution by the Bishop of Madras. Others have been subsequently ordained; and there are at present two native ministers attached to the mission, one at each of its two principal divisions. *Ordination of two students.*

Strenuous efforts were made to bring the gospel before the attention of all classes of Hindoos. The lowest castes were made the objects of special consideration. In the prosecution of this apostolic work the missionaries kindled into enthusiasm, the glow of which animated their native coadjutors likewise. Bilderbeck, Fenn, Ragland, Meadows, Taylor, and others, formed a noble band of earnest, conscientious missionaries at this period. The peculiar nature of *Labours of Rev Mr Bilderbeck and others.*

* Report of the South India Missionary Conference: Paper on the Madras Mission of the Church Missionary Society, by the Rev. J. Gritton, p 50.

2 D

the self-denying work some of them had undertaken may be seen from the following statement: "Preaching to the heathen has been carried on in almost every thoroughfare of this great city with scarce any intermission, execpt that caused by bodily weakness or the intervention of other duties. Regular weekly meetings were held at the three great stables in Mount Road. Efforts to reach the boatmen of the north and south beaches were commenced, and plans laid for a regular mission to the city seavengers. The work at the stables has prospered. As many as eighty or ninety horsekeepers, week by week, listen to the gospel; and some few have been gathered into the fold. The Messrs T. & W. have opened schools in their extensive yards, the support of which they provide, while the mission has their management. The work on the north beach is scarcely maintained; but on the south beach the work has gone on till it occupies a reader and two schoolmasters. The effort for the scavengers has been organised, and now engages two readers. Almost every place of public resort has been visited by the agents, in order to communicate the knowledge of Christ and Him crucified. From one end of Madras to the other, north and south, as far as practicable, the living voice, as well as tracts and books distributed, have told of the love of the Saviour. Boatmen, scavengers, horsekeepers, cartmen, coolies, private servants, and Hindoos from the highest to the lowest walks of life, have all been addressed in their turn. Catechists Daniel and Waldegrave go with this view to cart-depôts, sheep-markets, jails, hospitals, the House of Industry, and dwellings of private families, and also assist the missionaries at other regular preaching stations. There have been pleasing and hopeful instances of conviction and awakening. Some have made an open profession of the faith in connection with this mission, while others have been directed to other quarters where they received the first elements of truths."*

In 1855 a separate mission was commenced in Madras by the Church Society in behalf of the Mahomedan community, and a school, called the "Harris School," was opened for the instruction of Moslem children. This is a handsome building erected partly from a legacy of the late Lady Sybella Harris, and partly by the Government. The school had in 1871 one hundred and twenty-four pupils. It had also seven native teachers, not one of whom was a Christian. Perhaps Mahomedan prejudice was too strong in Madras for the introduction of a Christian native teacher to be ventured on. No converts hitherto have been gathered in, although the mission has been in existence for sixteen years.

Special labours among the Mahomedans. The Harris School.

The progress of the Church Mission in Madras, since its establishment in 1815, has been steady and solid. In 1823, eight years after its commencement, it had one hundred and nine Christians. By 1850 the number had increased to four hundred and forty-five, of whom one hundred and eighty were communicants. In 1861 there were six hundred and forty converts, and three hundred and eighteen communicants. Ten years later, that is, in 1871, the former numbered thirteen hundred and twenty-five,

Results.

Report of the South India Missionary Conference: Paper on the Madras Mission of the Church Missionary Society, by the Rev. J. Gritton, p. 53.

and the latter four hundred and forty-five. Two hundred of these converts have been formed into Christian congregations rather by members of the Church of England than by missionaries of the Church Society. One of these is found at Pulicat, and the other at St Thomas' Mount. Moreover, a considerable body of converts, amounting to nearly four hundred, is the fruit of direct preaching among the villages of Chinglepat, carried on by missionaries and catechists specially devoted to this important work. Five congregations of these Christians reside in as many villages, in various parts of the district or province of this name, in which Madras itself is also situated.

The Wesleyan Mission. The Wesleyan Mission in Madras was commenced by the Rev. Mr Lynch at the close of the year 1816. Being joined by another missionary in 1818, they both found ample scope for their labours. They preached to the people in and out of the city, established schools in suitable places, and ministered to congregations of Europeans and East Indians. In 1826 the mission had four chapels in Madras and the surrounding country, and sixteen schools, with five hundred and forty-two scholars. Great attention has always been paid by the missionaries to the important work of English preaching; and perhaps it is not too much to affirm, that distinctive missionary work among the heathen has suffered in consequence. In 1858 there were three English congregations in Madras which were ministered to by four Wesleyan missionaries, who, in addition to their labours among their own countrymen, had the charge of an extensive range of Christian and educational operations in behalf of the Hindoo and native Christian population. In 1851 an institution or collegiate school was organised, which still exists. The missionaries "are convinced," says the Rev. E. E. Jenkins, chairman and general superintendent of the district, "that a school is the best field on which to contend with the great enemy of caste. It soon appears to the boys to be most reasonable that the highest rank should be awarded to superior intelligence, industry, and good conduct. During several years one of the missionaries on the station has devoted his main strength to this institution. Although the success of actual conversion has been small, and we have sometimes found it hard to suffer a long delay of visible or tangible prosperity, we teach with increasing confidence in the instrument of education. As far as our judgment can act on a question of spiritual success, we are assured that God's blessing has wrought considerable good in connection with the labours of our teachers; and every year discloses new proofs of it. Young men, whom we could never reach under other circumstances, listen daily to the glad tidings of salvation, and not seldom evidence the deepest interest in what they hear."*

This mission has been very successful with its boarding-school. The girls are entirely from low castes. Many of them have been "converted from idolatry and baptized, most of whom, when received into the Church, were not young children incapable of other motives than those of authority and kindness; but girls who yielded to instruction and conviction, and whose sincerity was tested by hindrance

* Report of the South India Missionary Conference: Paper on Wesleyan Missions, by the Rev. E. E. Jenkins, Madras, Appendix, p. xviii.

and persecution. The peculiar temptations to which this class of converts is exposed, would make instances of backsliding a matter of little surprise; but, with the exception of one or two cases of serious misconduct, when the girls had left the school, or were removed by their parents, the conduct of those who have taken upon them the profession of Christ, has been consistent, and awakens gratitude to God." *

Mission of the Christian Knowledge Society—its decline and renovation.

At the commencement of this chapter it was remarked, that at the beginning of the present century the mission of the Christian Knowledge Society at Madras was in a state of disorder, owing partly to the bad management of its missionary, between whom and the native Christian community a chronic feud existed. This deplorable state of things continued until 1816, when Bishop Middleton visited the city. He had been for years a member of this society, and therefore, before leaving England, was requested by its committee to investigate the condition of all their missions in Southern India, and his especial attention was directed to the society's mission in Madras. Mr Hough gives the following account of the mission at that time, and of the steps taken for its reformation. "The missionary and people," he says, "were still at variance with each other. The schools and the church were without order or discipline. The press, formerly so valuable and effective, had not been worked for a long time. And the society's books were found accumulated as mere lumber in the storeroom. Of these, the bishop ordered the English books to be delivered over to the

* Report of the South India Missionary Conference: Paper on Wesleyan Missions, by the Rev. E. E. Jenkins, Madras, Appendix, p. xix.

district committee of the society, for general use—directed an estimate to be made of the cost of setting the press to work again—and having strongly admonished both missionary and people, he commended the mission to the friendly care and supervision of some friends of the committee. The missionary did not long survive. Some time before, there had happily been an entire reconciliation with his former much-injured colleague, Dr Rottler; and at his death the mission was placed in charge of this excellent man, under whom it immediately began to revive, and went on successfully in an uninterrupted course of improvement to the end of his days." *

The large quantity of dictionaries, grammars, and other works in Tamil and English, accumulated in the mission, were as soon as possible put in circulation. The press was reopened, and in a few years an edition of the entire Bible in Tamil was reprinted under the superintendence of the missionaries. Dr Rottler published his Tamil translation of the Book of Common Prayer. The schools increased, and in 1819 had one hundred and fifty scholars; in 1821, nearly three hundred; and several years after, four hundred, most of whom were the children of Christians. In December 1823 the foundation-stone of a spacious church was laid. It was completed in 1825, and was a very handsome Gothic building capable of accommodating one thousand persons. The year following, Bishop Heber visited the mission, and passed upon it a very high encomium. "He had at that time," he said, "though he had visited several native congregations in the north of India and Ceylon,

marginalia: Rev. Dr Rottler. Church for 1000 persons erected in 1825.

* Hough's Christianity in India, vol. v. p. 16.

seen nothing that gave him so much pleasure, or that appeared to him so full of hope."

The mission transferred to the Propagation Society.

The mission was in this flourishing condition when the Christian Knowledge Society placed it in charge of the Society for the Propagation of the Gospel in Foreign Parts. Although it was henceforward carefully watched, and was kept free from those pecuniary embarrassments with which it had so frequently been afflicted, yet several years elapsed before the society was able to render it that additional aid which it required. Indeed, this society, in its praiseworthy zeal, was attempting more in Southern India, at this period, than it could immediately achieve. It multiplied missions without the capability of adequately supporting them. Yet it was hardly blameworthy in this, for, being conscious of its inherent strength, it looked forward confidently to the time when it should be in a position to exert it, and when it should not merely vigorously sustain its existing missions, but also greatly increase them. And that time eventually came. It is when a society plants its missions in many places throughout the country, and grasps at important positions of prominency and influence, without sufficient latent ability ever to nourish and maintain them properly, keeping back other societies which would have occupied such sites energetically and well, that it lays itself open to serious reproach, and also to the charge of folly and pride. And such societies there are; but it would be invidious to name them.

In 1825 the Propagation Society possessed nine missions in Southern India, which were managed by seven German missionaries. Ten years later, it had only nine missionaries; but in 1836 the number was increased to thirteen, and in the year following to sixteen. It is thought that the singular mortality among the Indian bishops had a very prejudicial effect upon this society's missions. Bishop Middleton died in 1822, Bishop Heber in 1826, Bishop James in 1829, and Bishop Turner in 1831. All these dignitaries manifested peculiar interest in the Propagation Society's missions; which, on their successive removal, were left without that superintendence-in-chief which had so much contributed to their confirmation and growth. Madras was favoured with a separate bishopric in the year 1835, since which time it is unquestionable that its bishops have in many ways afforded great assistance to the missions, both of the Propagation Society and of the Church Society, in Southern India, but especially of the former. Indeed, it is due to the bishops of the three Presidencies to observe, that they and their predecessors have, with some exceptions, though few, wrought a vast missionary work in their several dioceses, in the holy zeal and love for souls which they have exhibited; the influence of which has not merely been felt by missionaries of the two Church of England societies, but also by those of all other denominations who have been stimulated to increased earnestness and activity thereby.

Mortality among Indian bishops.

Good influence of Indian bishops.

The mission of this society in Madras numbered, in 1850, nine hundred and twenty-eight converts, including a congregation of one hundred and sixty-seven still retained by the Christian Knowledge Society, but which has since been given up. In 1861 the native Christian community consisted of nearly thirteen hundred members. The mission was stripped

Prosperity of the Propagation Society's Mission.

of many of its adherents through the caste system of
the Leipzic missionaries, who readily yielded those
questions of caste for which all other missionaries had
so pertinaciously contended. Nevertheless, the mission
continued to grow, and at the close of another decade,
rejoiced in the large number of fifteen hundred and
forty-four Christians, of whom six hundred and forty-
three were communicants.

The American Board relinquishes its Madras Mission.
The American Board of Commissioners for Foreign
Missions formed two stations in Madras in the year
1836, through the agency of the Rev. Dr John
Scudder and the Rev. M. Winslow; but after occupying them for upwards of twenty-five years, retired
from this part of the mission-field, in order that by
so doing they might be better able to consolidate
and develop their other missions. The judgment and
common sense evinced in this proceeding cannot be
too highly praised; and it would be well if many
other missions in India followed this excellent example, and concentrated their labours on certain
limited tracts of country, instead of striving to spread
them over the whole land, to the great detriment of
themselves and of many of their neighbours.

The Leipzic Lutheran Mission.
The Leipzic Lutherans entered Madras in 1848,
where, from their maintenance of caste, and their
unfortunate eagerness to receive proselytes from other
missions, they have not inspired that friendliness
of feeling which should always exist between the
missionaries of Protestant societies. The number of
their Christians in Madras is considerable; but, inasmuch as they have blended together their returns for
Madras and for other places, it is impossible to say
how many they possess in the city itself. These

mixed returns show, that two years after commencing their labours in Madras, and in other places associated with it, they had gathered together a community of five hundred Christians; which in 1861 had increased to seven hundred and forty-one, and in 1871 had further swelled to twelve hundred and forty-seven, of whom nearly one-half were communicants. These were divided into five separate congregations, and were scattered among twenty-five towns and villages.

I have reserved till now the delineation of the two great educational missions of Madras, namely, those of the Free Church of Scotland and the Scotch Kirk. These were commenced in 1837, before the two Churches had been divided. The mission then established owes its origin, it is said, to the impassioned eloquence of Dr Duff, who, "during his first visit to his native land, had stirred up such an interest in his educational system of operations in the East, that an ardent desire arose for the establishment of 'institutions' on the model of the Calcutta one at the other Presidency seats."* The Rev. John Anderson was the first missionary appointed, and became the principal of the institution which he founded in Madras, and which was destined, under his able management, to rise to the same position, and to exert the same influence, in that city, which Dr Duff's institution rose to and exerted in Calcutta. The object of the mission was to impart the highest forms of education, combined with Christian knowledge, to the better classes of native society in Madras. The instructions given to Mr Anderson by the General Assembly's

* History of the Missions of the Free Church of Scotland in India and Africa, by the Rev. Robert Hunter, M.A., p. 149.

Committee for Foreign Missions were "to the effect that he should mainly devote his energies to the respectable youths of Madras; confer on them the blessings of a sound, comprehensive, Bible education; and from the converts whom it might please the Lord to give him as seals of his ministry, to raise up thoroughly trained and pious teachers and preachers, who might go forth and evangelise the masses of their countrymen. It was deemed desirable to adopt this plan, in order to reach the higher classes of Hindoo society in Madras, which up to that time had been nearly inaccessible to the message of mercy proclaimed in the gospel."* The Rev. A. B. Campbell, the writer of the above extract, in a few words gives us an insight into the condition of the native population of Madras at this period, in relation to the superior education alluded to. "I shall be understood," he remarks, "as referring more particularly to the higher classes and castes of the heathen youth of Madras. At the commencement of 1837 there were, so far as I know, only three schools in existence which were specially designed for this class of the community. There was a school established by the Government, at which there was an attendance of somewhere about a hundred youths. There was another, called the Native Education Society's Institution, at which there was a similar attendance. And finally, there was a school in connection with the Church of Scotland's chaplains; and this latter formed the nucleus of the institution which Mr Anderson

* Report of the South India Missionary Conference: Paper on the Madras Mission of the Free Church of Scotland, by the Rev. A. B. Campbell, p. 37.

formed, and wrought with so much self-consuming zeal and success." *

The institution was opened, under the presidency of Mr Anderson, on the 3d April 1837, with fifty-nine scholars, who before the end of the following year had increased to two hundred and seventy-seven. But then it was suddenly almost broken up by the agency of that hydra-headed monster, Caste. Two Pariah boys had been admitted into the institution. "They came," says Mr Campbell, "spontaneously seeking instruction; and Mr Anderson felt that, at whatever sacrifice, the principles which he had laid down for his guidance, one of which was the perfect equality of all in the school, must be unswervingly maintained. The despised Pariahs were accordingly admitted to a full and equal share of all the advantages of the institution. The result was that immediately the school was broken up, and the missionary was left to empty walls and a sorrowful heart. Petitions and deputations from the parents of the late scholars followed. They besought Mr Anderson to dismiss the hated Pariahs; or at least to place them on separate benches, so that their sons might not be polluted. But all was vain. The missionary had taken a stand; he planted himself on the firm rock of principle; and whatever might be the issue, he was not to be moved. And, as might have been anticipated, he gained the victory. By-and-by the youths returned. The institution flourished more than ever; and Pariah and Brahman might be seen sitting together on the same bench, learning the same lessons, and struggling together for the mastery.

The institution almost destroyed by caste prejudice.

* Report of the South India Missionary Conference: Paper on the Madras Mission of the Free Church of Scotland, by the Rev. A. B. Campbell, p. 37.

To all who were acquainted with the condition of the people of Madras at that period, to all who know how bigoted and strong their attachment to caste was, this victory which was gained by the missionary will appear no light and trivial matter. Indeed, this was a blow given to caste, the effects of which were then felt throughout Southern India, and are so felt to the present day."*

<small>Baptism of three students. Excitement in the city</small> The first converts from the institution were baptized in 1841. These were three of its ablest and best students, young men of good social rank and of great intelligence. The effect upon the native community was as though it had been shaken by an earthquake. The whole city was in excitement, and rigid Hindoos everywhere were filled with indignation. It was felt that idolatry and caste had received a deadly blow. The institution lost four hundred scholars, and only thirty or forty remained. Gradually some of the pupils gained confidence and returned, and at the annual public examination in the beginning of the following year, two hundred and seventy-eight were present. The youths then baptized subsequently became licensed preachers, and occupied a very important <small>Rev. Rajahgopaul.</small> and honourable position in the Christian Church. One of them, the Rev. P. Rajahgopaul, visited Scotland with Mr Anderson in 1849, and addressed the General Assembly in the following year. "One of the most remarkable speeches which has been made in the Assembly," says an eyewitness, "was that by the young Indian convert and minister, Rajahgopaul."†

---

* Paper by the Rev. A. B. Campbell, on the Madras Mission of the Free Church of Scotland, pp. 37, 38.

† History of the Missions of the Free Church of Scotland, by the Rev. R. Hunter, p. 29.

In the year 1842 two other baptisms occurred, but they produced much less agitation than those of the previous year, as is evident from the increase of the pupils in the institution to upwards of five hundred. In 1846 eight students were baptized. By the year 1858 ninety-three adults had received the rite of baptism; "and the conversion of these persons was to be traced, under God, mainly to the teaching and preaching of the truth in the institution." Nearly all of these belonged to respectable classes and castes of native society. The number of members constituting the native Christian community of the Free Church Mission in Madras in 1871 was two hundred and thirty-five. It should be remembered that most of them have received a good education, and therefore exert an influence of a much more potent character than Christians of inferior education, or of no education at all. Moreover, the institution has produced hundreds of well-trained teachers, who are "engaged in mission and other schools over the length and breadth of the Presidency, and others are in various departments of the public service."

This institution, which has been so productive of converts, has from its establishment to the present time been conducted with great talent and skill. The missionaries attached to it have been men of high education, indefatigable zeal, and considerable force of individual character. Anderson, Johnston, and Braidwood, in its early days, were men of kindred spirit, though of diverse gifts. In later years we see the same distinguished excellences in Mr Campbell, Mr Macallum, and others, and also in Mr Miller, the scholarly and clear-headed principal now at the head

Rev W. Miller.

of the institution. It is a striking feature in relation to Indian missions, that the three Presidency cities should have possessed for so many years educational establishments, organised and sustained by two comparatively small Scotch societies with very limited incomes, which have unitedly accomplished greater results in educating the people in these cities than any other missionary society; and that they have done more in them to promote that higher education which has produced an enlightened and well-trained class of natives in India, not only than other societies, but also, when rightly understood, than the Government itself.

Success of the boarding-school.
The mission has had great success among native women of good caste in Madras. In 1843, schools for the instruction of Hindoo and Mahomedan girls were commenced in two quarters of the city, namely, in Black Town and Triplicane. In 1847 a boarding-school was established, which owed its origin, says Mr Campbell, to the following circumstance. "The senior class of girls in the Madras day-school began to be in deep anxiety regarding their souls. The Word of God laid hold of their consciences; the eyes of their understandings were opened to see the sin of idolatry in which they were then living; the love of Christ began sweetly to constrain them; and under these deep convictions they resolved to leave father, mother, and home, and follow Christ. What could the missionaries do but welcome such of them as carried out this resolution, and afford them a shelter and home in place of that which, for the gospel's sake, they had abandoned for ever? This was accordingly done; and thus was laid the foundation of

our female boarding-school, over which Mrs Anderson presided with so much Christian fidelity and affection. This school was designed to receive girls who in the day-schools had been convinced of the sin of idolatry, and desired to cleave to the Lord Jesus Christ. Any one thoroughly acquainted with the present state of the Hindoo community may know that these girls could not follow the dictates of their consciences in their own homes."*

On occasion of five of the adult girls seeking baptism, the native population was once more violently aroused. A writ of *habeas corpus*, in the case of one of them, was served on Mr Anderson, and the matter was tried in the Supreme Court. As the girl was of age, and remarkably intelligent, she was left to follow her own judgment, and in the course of time she and the rest were baptized. Many other young native women were afterwards received into the Christian Church; and Mr Campbell, in 1858, states, that "of the thirty-three females who have been baptized, almost all are from the caste girls' schools which were begun by the mission in 1843."

These girls' schools have formed a most important branch of the Free Church Mission's operations in Madras. In 1851 there were eighteen hundred scholars, male and female, in the institution and schools of the mission, of whom four hundred and thirty-nine were caste girls, most of whom were very poor.† In 1861, in Madras and Chinglepat, the mission had two thousand

---
Paper by the Rev. A. B. Campbell on the Madras Mission of the Free Church of Scotland, pp. 40, 41.

† History of the Missions of the Free Church of Scotland, by the Rev. R. Hunter, p. 175.

one hundred and forty-five pupils under instruction. Of these, six hundred and sixty-eight were girls attending nine schools. Ten years afterwards, that is, in 1871, the entire number of scholars was two thousand two hundred and thirty-three, and of them as many as eight hundred and eighteen were young women and girls. It is very gratifying to find that the girls had paid the sum of one hundred and fourteen pounds as fees during that year. Moreover, "sixteen girls, all native Christians, had passed the Government examination for female teachers' certificates, and the name of one of these appeared in the highest grade." * Mrs Anderson continued her useful labours in connection with the boarding-school until the beginning of 1872, when she resigned from ill-health.

Church of Scotland and Free Church missions. The Church of Scotland and the Free Church missions in Madras are, properly speaking, two branches of the same primitive mission, the separation having occurred in the year of the Disruption, 1843. Yet, strictly, the Church of Scotland's Mission, as a new mission, was commenced in 1844. But evidently the same class of hard-thinking, hard-working, and faithful men have guided its affairs as those who have made themselves so eminent in the sister mission of the Free Church. In the year 1850 it had four hundred and twenty youths in its institution, while its two female schools were attended by two hundred and nine girls. In 1861 all the schools of the mission possessed a thousand and ninety pupils; but of these, seven hundred and twenty-one were of the gentler sex. It had at that time also a native Christian com-

* History of the Missions of the Free Church of Scotland, by the Rev. R. Hunter, p. 199.

munity, consisting of two hundred and forty persons. At the close of the next decade, or in 1871, the mission imparted instruction to eleven hundred and twenty-one scholars. Of these, there were four hundred and fifteen girls and women, which was a falling off of upwards of three hundred. Putting together the operations of these two Scotch missions in the three Presidencies, it is clear that the Disruption has proved a great blessing to India at least.

One of the very few Baptist missions in the Madras Presidency is that of the Strict Baptists at Poonamallee and St Thomas' Mount, which was established in the year 1866, and is under the superintendence of a native minister. The Christian community is at present exceedingly small. The mission has five schools, two of which are for girls.

The Baptist missions.

That most useful and catholic institution, the Christian Vernacular Education Society for India, owes its origin to the intense interest excited in England on Indian subjects by the mutiny and rebellion of 1857. Its objects are threefold, namely, the training of vernacular teachers, the publication of school-books, and the support of vernacular day-schools. Its chief station is in Madras, where its indefatigable secretary, Dr Murdoch, resides, except when on his annual tour through India and Ceylon, which occupies his time during eight or nine months of every year. The society has three training institutions, situated at Amritsur, in the Punjab; at Ahmednagar, in the Bombay Presidency; and at Dindigul, in the Madras Presidency. It has two hundred native teachers in the same number of vernacular schools, in which seven thousand eight hundred children receive instruction,

The Christian Vernacular Education Society. Dr Murdoch.

exclusive of five thousand more who are educated by this society in schools of various missionary societies. The society has issued since its establishment upwards of four million books and tracts in fifteen languages. It has twenty-seven depots of its own for the sale of books, and gives employment to sixty colporteurs. Altogether, the society accomplishes a great work, not only by its schools, but also, and chiefly, by its numerous publications. One of its prominent virtues lies in its unsectarianism. Its catholicity is admirably represented by its zealous Indian secretary, who has been known to the writer for many years, who, however, is utterly unconscious of the denomination of Christians to which Dr Murdoch belongs.

Christian work in zenanas. A work of a special character, for the enlightenment of native ladies, who from the stringency of caste and prejudice are confined to the seclusion of their zenanas, has been in progress for several years in Madras, as in Calcutta and in many other cities of India; and has been there, as everywhere else, so remarkably successful, as to inspire the hope that it will eventually effect both an intellectual and social revolution, not only in Madras, but also throughout the land. In that city, in addition to the labours of the missionaries' wives and daughters, there are two ladies' societies in active operation, namely, the Society for Promoting Female Education in the East, and the Female Normal School Society.

The accompanying statistics will show the present numerical condition of the various missions in Madras and its neighbourhood, throughout the province of Chinglepat. They also embrace the separate stations of the Leipzic Mission, in connection with its central station at Madras.

STATISTICS OF THE MISSIONS IN MADRAS AND CHINGLEPAT
FOR THE YEAR 1871.

Number of Native Christian Congregations,	34
Number of Protestant Native Christians,	5085
Increase since 1861,	1488
Number of Communicants,	2200
Increase since 1861,	414
Number of Towns and Villages containing Christians,	49
Number of Ordained Native Ministers,	11
Increase since 1861,	1
Number of Unordained Native Preachers,	48
Number of Mission Colleges and Schools,	112
Of these, 34 are Girls' Schools.	
Increase since 1861,	19
Number of Pupils, Male and Female,	8252
Of these, 2795 are Female Pupils.	
Increase since 1861,	1613
Number of Christian Teachers, Male and Female,	151

CHAPTER XVIII.

MISSIONS IN THE PROVINCES OF CUDDAPAH, KARNOOL, AND NELLORE.

<small>Rapid progress of these missions.</small>

NEXT to the missions in Chota Nagpore, in Northern India, those in the provinces of Cuddapah, Karnool, and Nellore have made the greatest comparative numerical progress of any missions in India during the ten years intervening between 1861 and 1871. The Christian community has increased in them with wonderful rapidity. Twenty-one years ago, that is, in 1850, the three provinces only contained one hundred and twenty Protestant Christians. But in 1861 there were three thousand three hundred and thirty-five; and ten years later they had multiplied to the very large number of thirteen thousand seven hundred and ninety-eight. This augmentation in so short a space of time is very marvellous; and affords ground for the prophecy, which we hear occasionally, of a sudden and speedy conversion of some of the Hindoo races to Christianity. Yet it is important to state that most of these converts have come from low-caste tribes, and not from Hindoos proper. Indeed, while in several districts of India, widely separated from each other, the aboriginal and out-caste races have of late years exhibited strong excitement under the magnetic influence of the gospel, nowhere throughout the country has any extensive caste or clan of Hindoos proper displayed a similar agitation These Hindoos embrace our religion by individuals, or at most by families; but whole villages of the despised and inferior tribes spontaneously adopt the Christian faith.

The Propagation Society has had some connection with the province of Cuddapah ever since the year 1817, but little fruit was obtained until many years afterwards. The same may be said likewise of the London Mission, which commenced its labours in the capital city in 1822; and yet, twenty-seven years afterwards, its converts were only one hundred and ten in number. But suddenly both societies had to rejoice in a plenteous harvest. In ten years, that is, in 1861, the Propagation Society's stations had eighteen hundred and five native Christians; and those of the London Society fourteen hundred and eighty-six. Let not missionaries, therefore, in other parts of India, who have laboured in their Master's service with unwearied zeal and earnestness for many long years, and reaped but scanty results of all their toil, give way to despondency, but, taking courage and comfort from the example of the missions in Cuddapah, continue "steadfast, unmovable, always abounding in the work of the Lord," believing that "their labour shall not be in vain in the Lord."

The London Mission was established through the instrumentality of the Rev. J. Handa. Schools were opened, and a few converts were baptized, who numbered in 1828 twenty-five persons. These had increased by the year 1833 to one hundred and fourteen, which in five years was encouraging progress. But from this time forward, for a period of eighteen years, the Christian community continued nearly stationary. Yet the work was steadily carried on. The schools were maintained with vigour. The villages in the southern part of the province were constantly visited. The gospel was preached with zeal and earnestness both by the missionaries and their native helpers. Occasionally a convert was gained. But the influence of Christianity upon the people was hitherto mainly of an indirect character; yet it was manifest that the minds of many had been impressed with the truth, and had begun to lose faith in their own creeds and religious customs. In the province is a tribe of very low-caste Hindoos known by the designation of Mala. They are a degraded race, and worship chiefly rude stone images. In 1851 several villages of these Malas to the north and north-west of Cuddapah became strongly impelled to renounce idol-worship and caste, and to embrace Christianity. After instruction and due preparation, many families were baptized. The spirit of inquiry gradually spread to other villages, and in 1853 extended to the Malas in the neighbouring province of Karnool. As an instance of their eagerness and sincerity, some of them inhabiting the villages of Poloor and Jotoor, eighty miles north of Cuddapah, came to that city seeking Christian instruction. "They brought with them their idol, Narku Simhum, an incarnation of Vishnoo," says the Rev. E. Porter, "with an umbrella and other paraphernalia of its worship, and surrendered it into the hands of the missionary, saying that they needed instruction in a better way.

The Malas, a low-caste tribe.

Many embrace Christianity.

Rev. E. Porter.

Two of the headmen, after being instructed in the main doctrines of the Christian faith, were, at their earnest request, baptized in the presence of a large congregation. They returned to their village, and through their influence upwards of one hundred Malas, in the same and neighbouring villages, came forward, and placed themselves under Christian instruction." * The year closed with an addition of two hundred and seventy-four persons to the Christian congregations of the mission, most of whom belonged to villages in the country. All these were baptized after a twelvemonth's training; while there were many more remaining as catechumens. In three years eight hundred persons received the rite of baptism.

The two villages of Poloor and Jotoor, referred to above, being situated near the large and important town of Nundial, in the Kurnool province, it was determined to make this place the centre of a new mission. Accordingly the London Missionary Society directed the Rev. R. Johnston of Chicacole to proceed thither in the year 1855. The result has been satisfactory in the highest degree. At the end of 1861 this mission possessed two hundred and thirty-six converts; and in ten years more, nine hundred and thirty-nine. But the year 1872 has been the most encouraging of all. During that year there was an accession of six hundred and fifty-one Christians; † raising the entire number in the mission to fifteen

_{Nundial a separate mission.}

* Report of the South India Missionary Conference: Paper on the Cuddapah Mission of the London Missionary Society, by the Rev. E. Porter, pp. 119, 120.
† *Monthly Chronicle of the London Missionary Society* for September 1873, p. 101.

hundred and ninety. Thus, at the present time, the two missions of this society at Cuddapah and Nundial have a community of between four and five thousand native converts, and are yearly receiving augmentations on a scale which bids fair speedily to alter the religious aspect of considerable tracts of country.

Nearly 5000 converts in the two missions

Success of a similar nature is visible in the missions of the Propagation Society in the same region. In 1871 they had upwards of three thousand Christians, and in 1872 they received a further increase of one hundred and sixty-three. It is interesting to observe the method adopted in imparting Christian knowledge to those desirous of receiving it. "Dasarapatte," remarks the Rev. J. Clay, "is a hamlet about twelve miles south-east of Mutyalupad (the mission station). Eleven families in this village placed themselves under Christian instruction early this year. The headmen of the village came to me in December last, and after inquiring into their motives and circumstances, I agreed to send them a teacher, provided they erected, at their own expense, a small building, where they could all assemble for daily prayers, and the children be taught their lessons. Early in February they had everything ready. There was no one in the boarding-school advanced enough to be sent out as a teacher; but I was able to engage the services of a young man who had been trained in our boarding-school, and had left us about four years ago, to return to his own village. When I last visited Dasarapatte, I was much pleased with the quiet and orderly conduct of the people, and with the lessons they repeated; which showed that they were regular in their attendance at prayers, and that the master

Missions of the Propagation Society.

was diligent in instructing them. The eleven families there were brought over by an old woman of that village, who renounced heathenism two years ago, and used to go every Sunday a distance of six miles, for worship, and to be instructed in Christianity. The instruction she received, she used to communicate, as well as she could, to the people of her village, and gradually brought them round to adopt her views."*

Commenting on the above, the Rev. J. Clay observes, " I have made it a rule not to give a teacher to a village seeking Christian instruction, till the people themselves, in the first place, get up a building of some sort, where they can all assemble and worship God quietly, orderly, and reverently. Our former practice, of beginning by assembling them in the open air, or in one of their own houses, till we could raise the funds for building a school-chapel, I look upon as very objectionable. After an experience of many years, I have learned that unless our catechumens are from the very outset trained to habits of reverential devotion, a coldness and weariness generally pervades their public worship. Besides, a demand of this kind becomes a good test of the earnestness and sincerity of those who come seeking Christian instruction."†

Method pursued.

Unquestionably, the recent progress of the missions which have thus been briefly reviewed, is most exhilarating to all interested in the evangelisation of the Hindoo race. Yet what shall we say of the religious movement now in operation in the province of

* Report of the Madras Diocesan Committee of the Propagation Society for 1871-72: Report of Mutyalapad, by the Rev. J. Clay, pp. 120, 121.
† Ibid.

Nellore, on the sea-coast, to the east of Karnool and Cuddapah? A Christian community of more than six thousand six hundred persons has suddenly sprung into existence. In 1861 there were only forty-six Christians in the province; but in ten years they have increased to the number just stated. Most of them belong to the missions of the American Baptist Missionary Union, which opened a station in Nellore in the year 1840. At the end of ten years only ten converts had been gained, and at the end of twenty-one only twenty-three; but at the end of the next decade, that is, in 1871, this society possessed upwards of six thousand four hundred Christians. The seed sown took long to germinate and spring up—but how abundant the fruit! The converts are, as usual, from the lower castes; and it is gratifying to find that as many as two thousand one hundred and seventy-five are communicants, showing a most healthy condition of the native Church. They are separated into twenty congregations, and are scattered among two hundred and seventy-eight towns and villages; from which it is manifest that the rural population is principally affected. In the year 1871 alone as many as eight hundred and seventy-five persons were admitted into the Christian brotherhood; and the good work is still going on. The schools for the children of the Christians are very few, being only seventeen in all. But the mission has six theological and training schools, a circumstance sufficiently significant, as indicating that the great and pressing want of the missionaries now is properly-trained Christian natives, who shall be able to take charge of congregations, and minister to the religious necessities of both converts and catechumens. They have already prepared a staff of sixty-four Christian preachers and teachers, and one ordained native pastor, which speaks well of their labours in this direction, in as quickly as possible preparing from among the Christians themselves qualified men for the various departments of Christian work which have so recently been formed. But as this work increases, other catechists and teachers will be needed, as well also a strong body of ordained native ministers.

The Free Church of Scotland has also a station in Nellore, established in 1840, the same year in which, as we have seen, the American Baptist Union entered the province. But its labours have been almost entirely confined to imparting instruction in the excellent institution which it sustains. Although its converts have been very few in number, yet it has accomplished a vast amount of good, in imparting a sound Christian education to many native youths, who have grown up under the influence of Christian ideas, and with their Hindoo prejudices shaken, if not destroyed. Thus the Free Church Mission has supplemented the American Baptist Mission, and has been its invaluable auxiliary. *The Free Church Mission at Nellore.*

The institution was founded by the Rev. Mr Anderson, principal of the large institution of the Free Church in Madras. It was established on two important principles, "the inculcation of the Word of God upon the mind of every scholar, and equal freedom of admission to all castes, be they what they may, to all the privileges of the school." The effect of this method of procedure upon the minds of the students was soon apparent. "From the first," says *The institution.*

the Rev. J. M. Mackintosh, "the study and exposition of the Bible was carried on in a way not a little startling to those who had been unaccustomed to such direct, solemn, and powerful appeals to their hearts and consciences. This led to the retirement of a few of the scholars, who left the school in fright; but the greater part remained, and manifested great interest in the instruction communicated, and the devoted man who laboured among them. A few Brahman boys also left the school, in consequence of the practice having been discontinued by which the Pariah boys had been obliged to occupy a separate bench. But their removal was not felt; and within six months the attendance was doubled."*

Remarks of the Rev. J. M. Mackintosh on the great importance of education as an evangelistic agency.

Mr Mackintosh makes some very pertinent observations on the smallness of the direct results from the institution, which will apply to all other similar branches of missionary labour throughout India: "The mission colleges and schools, although yielding little fruit in the way of conversions, are nevertheless of the highest importance in diffusing, in a systematic form, a thorough knowledge of the Word of God. Close them, and you inflict an irreparable wound on the missionary enterprise in India. So far as direct conversion is an evidence of missionary success, it must be allowed that little claim can be laid to it, although we have not been left without encouragement in the past, and see much that is hopeful for the future. We are by no means inclined, however, to measure our success by this standard only. We are confident that

---

* Report of the South India Missionary Conference: Paper on the Nellore Mission of the Free Church of Scotland, by the Rev. J. M. Mackintosh, p. 123.

a great work has been done in spreading among the community more correct views of the truth. Many a prejudice which rendered the message of salvation to a great extent a dead letter has been assailed, and, we believe, greatly shaken. Many errors and false views which but too frequently impeded the progress of the gospel have been exposed, weakened, and in some cases wellnigh destroyed. We are confident, also, that whoever lives to reap the harvest, there will one day be a plentiful return gathered from the field that is now under cultivation, and the seed we are now sowing, when many who sit in our schools and hear the Word of God shall have taken the places of those who for the present so stoutly resist the truth." * These words should be seriously pondered by all opponents of mission schools, who should bear in mind that the Christian religion is taught to the heathen population of India, in a methodical and complete manner, almost exclusively in such schools, and to a very small extent, in the same degree and on the same elaborate plan, by other agencies.

In addition to the above missions, the Hermannsburg Lutheran Society, of Hanover, has stations in Nellore. These are to the south of the province, and are six in number, all which have been established since 1865. They have eight German missionaries connected with them; and although the work has been so recently commenced, they already, in 1871, numbered more than two hundred converts. But it has proved exceedingly difficult to obtain any infor-

The Hermannsburg Lutheran missions.

* Report of the South India Missionary Conference: Paper on the Nellore Mission of the Free Church of Scotland, by the Rev. J. M. Mackintosh, p. 125.

mation of the labours of these brethren, for the reason that they are peculiarly reticent about them. Their scruples on this subject, however, will, it is hoped, give way as their prosperity increases.

Summing up the numerical results of missionary labour in these three provinces, we find them to be as follows :—

STATISTICS OF THE MISSIONS IN THE PROVINCES OF CUDDAPAH, KARNOOL, AND NELLORE, FOR THE YEAR 1871.

Number of Native Christian Congregations,	122
Number of Protestant Native Christians,	13,798
Increase since 1861,	10,463
Number of Communicants,	2,828
Increase since 1861,	2,662
Number of Towns and Villages containing Christians,	393
Number of Ordained Native Ministers,	3
Number of Unordained Native Preachers,	92
Number of Mission Colleges and Schools,	89
Of these, 9 are Theological and Training Schools.	
Number of Pupils, Male and Female,	2,062
Number of Christian Teachers, do.,	36

CHAPTER XIX.

MISSIONS IN THE KISTNA AND GODAVERY DISTRICTS, AND IN VIZAGAPATAM AND GANJAM.

THE Kistna district, immediately to the north of Nellore, was occupied by a German Lutheran Society of America in the year 1842. This society owed its origin to the unfortunate misunderstanding which arose between the devoted Rhenius, of the Tinnevelly Mission, and the Church Missionary Society, of which an account has already been given in the chapter on that mission. The object of the society, in the first instance, was to afford aid to Rhenius in the Lutheran missions which he was establishing in Tinnevelly. On the death of that eminent man, these stations gradually returned to the bosom of the Church Society, and perfect concord was at length fully restored, which has continued unbroken to the present time. The Lutheran Society of America, however, happily did not retire from India, but with much wisdom, and no little charity, sought for itself a sphere of labour in some other part of the country. The tract selected was the Kistna district, to the south of the river Kistna, the Church Society having the year before, that is, in 1841, commenced a mission at Masulipatam, in the same district, but to the north of the river.

American Lutheran Society establishes missions to the south of the Kistna river.

The Lutheran Synod of Pennsylvania appointed the Rev. Mr Heyer as its first missionary, who on reaching the district, at the urgent request of the magistrate-collector, settled down at Guntoor. For several years Mr Heyer, and a colleague who was sent to his assistance, laboured diligently among the villages of the district, in imparting to the people a knowledge of the distinguishing truths of the gospel. Seventy miles west of Guntoor is Palnâd, which had been visited occasionally by missionaries of the North German and Baptist Societies, through whose instrumentality an inquiry had sprung up among the people on the important subjects which had been brought before them. Under these favourable circumstances the Lutheran missionaries established their second mission in the district. The same year they administered the rite of baptism to thirty-nine persons in Palnâd. In 1850 there were one hundred and sixty-four Christians at both stations. By 1861 they had increased to three hundred and thirty-eight. But now came a rapid augmentation. After twenty years of persistent and faithful labour, sowing the seed by the side of all waters, hoping and praying for an ample blessing, and gathering in occasionally a little fruit as an earnest of the coming plenty, at last the longing expectations of the missionaries were gratified. A movement of the people towards Christianity began, like that which happened in Cuddapah, Karnool, and Nellore, described in the preceding chapter. And at the end of 1871 the result was as follows. The Christian community had increased to two thousand one hundred and fifty, of whom six hundred and thirty-eight were communicants. Their congregations

Increase of nearly 2000 converts in twenty-one years.

were thirty-two in number, and were connected with fifty-two villages.

The Church Society's missions to the north of the Kistna have a similar history to record. Begun in 1841, as already stated, the various labours connected with them have been carried on with the greatest enthusiasm. Men of intense earnestness, like Noble, Fox, Sharkey, and others, have devoted their talents and lives to the Christian enterprise of teaching the adherents of a degrading system of idolatry the worship of the one living and true God. At the end of nine years they had gathered together one hundred and eleven converts. In 1854 two other stations were opened, and in 1859 a third; making, with Masulipatam, four separate missions. In 1861 the Christian community had advanced to two hundred and fifty-nine. After this a wonderful change was manifest among the people. They seemed to be possessed with a new spirit, and began in considerable numbers to abandon their idolatrous and superstitious practices, and to turn to the Lord their God. In the course of the next ten years as many as sixteen hundred and twenty-three persons embraced the Christian religion, and laid aside all their heathenish customs. The work of the missionaries is twofold. They expend much time and toil in preaching the gospel to the village population, but they also labour diligently in the numerous schools which they have established. These are sixty-one in number, two of them being collegiate institutions, and contain between sixteen and seventeen hundred male and female scholars. Thus these missions keep true to the principle which the Church Missionary Society pursues in its operations in India, in maintaining in vigorous action the two chief departments of missionary labour among both Hindoos and Mahomedans, namely, preaching and education. The Christians inhabit sixty-two villages, and are separated into twenty-six congregations. Three of their number are ordained pastors, and seventy-eight are employed either as catechists or teachers.

Stretching away to the north-east is the Godavery district, cut in two by the Godavery river. In the year 1838 some German missionaries established a mission on the sea-coast, where they have remained, endeavouring to evangelise a very limited tract, to the present time. Connected with no home society, but living on their own resources, and those which they are able to accumulate, like the German and Norwegian missionaries of the Indian Home Mission in the Santal country, they have formed themselves into an association, which bears the appellation of the Godavery Delta Mission. Enthusiastic, self-denying, and persevering, they have carried on their benevolent enterprise in a manner so quiet and unobtrusive that the very existence of the mission was little known even in India. That painstaking and cautious compiler of the statistical tables of missions in India, Ceylon, and Burmah, for the year 1861, the Rev. Dr Mullens, does not give them a place in his tables, but altogether passes them over, although the mission at that time possessed three hundred and fifty converts. Since then the number has increased to a thousand, with three hundred communicants, composing eight congregations. The Rev. W. Bowden, one of the founders of this interesting mission, is still connected

The Godavery Delta Mission. Possesses 1000 Christians.

with it. To have been the means, in conjunction with his colleagues, of one thousand persons entering into the outward and visible Church of Christ, must be to him and them a source of exquisite satisfaction and joy, with which no earthly gratification can be for one moment compared.

At Rajamandry and its neighbourhood, in the same district, the American Evangelical Lutherans, who have been, as shown above, so successful at Guntoor and Palnâd, in the Kistna district, have several flourishing stations. In 1861, after fifteen years' labour, they had a community of only twenty-nine Christians; but since then the progress has been strikingly rapid. At the close of the next ten years of labour, the mission could rejoice in three hundred and twenty converts and ninety-three communicants. In 1871 alone thirty-six adults were baptized, representing, with the children connected with them, an addition of nearly one hundred persons. The Strict Baptists commenced a mission at Cocoanada during this year, which is superintended by an ordained native minister. A Christian church seems to have sprung up spontaneously; for already there are ninety-seven converts, of whom nearly one-half are communicants; and the congregations are five in number. Such the fruit of one year's toil!

The mission of the London Society at Vizagapatam is of much older date than any of those hitherto described in this chapter. It was commenced in 1805, a perilous period for Indian missions, in which, as we have seen, the Government of the country, instigated and impelled by the East India Company, set its face determinately against them, and forbade

their establishment in the Company's dominions.
Nevertheless, two earnest men, not easily frightened,
the Rev. George Cran and the Rev. Augustus Des
Granges, proceeded in that year to the Northern
Circars, and founded a mission in the capital city,
which exists to the present time. They were soon
invited to perform Divine service in the fort, for the
benefit of the soldiers and other British residents,
for which duty, strange to say, an allowance was
made to them by the Governor of Madras. These
services were held not merely on the Sunday, but also
on several days in the week, and it is evident that
for a considerable time they devoted to them much
time and attention. They also opened a school for
the instruction of the natives; and as soon as they
gained a sufficient knowledge of Telugu, began to
translate the Liturgy and Articles of the Church of
England into that language. They also composed
several tracts, consisting chiefly of extracts from the
Sacred Scriptures. This was a prelude to the translation of the Scriptures themselves. In this important work they soon received the assistance of
a converted Brahman from Tranquebar, who, from
his learning and ability, was able to render them
essential aid. Both missionaries died early, Mr Cran
in 1809, and his colleague in 1810, in the midst of
their usefulness and of the plans they were forming
for the prosecution of their great undertaking.
Before these events happened, however, other missionaries had arrived.

It is not without instruction that we learn the
methods the missionaries at this time adopted in
carrying on their work. "They went by rotation

thrice a week into the populous villages, and read to the inhabitants a portion of the Scriptures in their own language, conversing with them on the subject read, and distributing copies of the New Testament to those who could read and were willing to accept them. They stated with much concern, that in several villages few persons beside the Brahmans were able to read, or willing to learn. In their Telugu school they had forty scholars, and in the English twenty. 'At first,' they observed, 'with all our solicitude to exclude everything heathen, we were careful not to be too rigid, lest we should defeat our own object; but we have gradually prevailed, so that it is now altogether a Christian seminary. Instead of a prayer which the scholars were accustomed to present to a female deity, whom they suppose to preside over letters, and whom they in some way identify with their books, and even with the sand in which they inscribe the characters, Anandarayer (the Brahman convert) composed for them a suitable address to the true God. Before they are dismissed from school, one boy repeats the prayer, and is followed by the others sentence by sentence."* Clearly the methods of procedure among Indian missionaries have radically improved since those days; and the scruples of the natives also have marvellously diminished.

Throughout the entire history of this mission, from its commencement down to the present day, its missionaries have ever been occupied more or less with the translation or revision of the Telugu Scriptures, and in writing works in the same tongue.

* Hough's History of Christianity in India, vol. iv. pp. 267, 268.

When the natives once possessed copies of the New Testament in their own language, they exhibited much interest in the sacred truths they contain. In 1827 there were twelve schools at this station, with five hundred and twenty-five scholars. The missionaries daily preached to the native population. Yet with all the labour and anxiety which had been expended by successive missionaries, thirty years passed away before a single convert seems to have been gained.* This is hard to account for. No one can question the fidelity, earnestness, and piety of the Christian men and women who had thus for so many long years toiled in their Master's service without fruit. To the writer one thing appears very clear. Their labours were too miscellaneous, and were not sufficiently aimed at the conversion of the heathen. They had undertaken too much English preaching, were engaged too much in the work of translation, were possibly too much occupied with their schools, and consequently were too little employed in direct and prolonged intercourse with the persons whose hearts they wished to reach, and whose salvation they wished to secure, to enlist their affections, and to exert over them any great or weighty influence. The natives of India are an impressible people, much affected by kindness and personal attention, and ready to place confidence in those Europeans who associate freely and generously with them. It is not sufficient for a missionary to have his heart *in the work;* he must also have his

* Report of the South India Missionary Conference: Paper on the Visagapatam Mission of the London Missionary Society, by the Rev. J. S. Wardlaw, M.A., p. 134.

heart *in the people*—must "spend and be spent" *among them*. One undoubted cause of the wonderful success of missions in Burmah, Chota Nagpore, Tinnevelly, Travancore, and in the provinces and districts described in the last chapter, and in the former part of this, is to be attributed to the steady, persistent, loving labours of missionaries living in personal and constant contact with the people, who have thus learned to regard them as friends whom they can thoroughly trust, and to whose counsel and guidance at length they have committed their eternal interests. I believe that the want of this perpetual personal intercourse with the natives is the chief reason why so many small missions in the country continue small, and why so many languid missions continue feeble.

The first regular public services in the native language were commenced by the Rev. J. H. Gordon, who entered the mission in 1835. Hitherto the "native work had been confined to short addresses to the people in different parts of the town, and in conversations with them. He had the pleasure shortly after of baptizing two or three native women. He also commenced meetings with the schoolmasters for Christian instruction and prayer." Two boarding-schools for native girls were also opened. One of them was very large, and contained at one time upwards of eighty girls, who had been rescued from the severe famine which desolated the province. In 1837 a collegiate institution was founded, which continues to the present day; and in 1840 a printing-press was established. The town of Chicacole, to the north, was taken up as a branch mission station in

Rev. J. H. Gordon.

458   PROTESTANT MISSIONS IN INDIA.

Missions at Chicacole and Vizianagram. 1844 ; and the Rev. W. Dawson was placed in charge of it. In 1850 the two missions had a Christian community of one hundred and forty-four persons. Two years afterwards a third central station was added. This was Vizianagram, a place of some importance, from which the generous Maharajah, who has extensive estates in this tract of country, takes his title. In 1871 the three missions had nearly three hundred converts.

Mission of the General Baptist Society at Ganjam. In the province of Ganjam, between Vizagapatam and Orissa, is a flourishing mission of the General Baptist Society, which has existed there since the year 1837. Its headquarters are in the town of Berhampore. There are two congregations of Christians in the mission, containing two hundred and seventy converts, of whom one hundred and six are communicants. In the same place is a native Christian church of ninety-seven members, in connection with the Church of England.

The numerical condition of the various missions reviewed in this chapter is as follows:—

STATISTICS OF THE MISSIONS IN THE KISTNA AND GODAVERY DISTRICTS, AND IN VIZAGAPATAM AND GANJAM, FOR THE YEAR 1871.

Number of Native Christian Congregations,	81
Number of Protestant Native Christians,	6107
Increase since 1861,	4646
Number of Communicants,	1449
Increase since 1861,	1100
Number of Towns and Villages containing Christians,	166
Number of Ordained Native Ministers,	6
Number of Unordained Native Preachers,	38
Number of Mission Colleges and Schools,	123
Number of Pupils, Male and Female	2891
Number of Christian Teachers, do.,	114

CHAPTER XX.

REVIEW OF THE PREVIOUS CHAPTERS—CONCLUSIONS DRAWN FROM THEM.

SUCH are some of the prominent results of Protestant missions in India. They are results which may be tested by any one, for they are tangible and visible. They are scattered over a wide extent of country, among the cities, towns, and villages of India, each of which has felt, and to some extent yielded to, those elevating and enlightening influences which Christianity, in one or other of its numerous phases, has exerted upon them. The missions exist to make converts; and converts they have made. Every mission has its converts, who are increasing numerically from year to year. Most missions have their schools and colleges; and these, too, are multiplying continually. The Christian community consists of converts of varied character, undoubtedly; yet in morality and truthfulness they are far superior to the heathen, and their influence, as a whole, upon their fellow-countrymen is highly beneficial. Almost all schemes of usefulness, having for their object the intellectual, religious, or temporal welfare of the people, have either been originated by the missionaries, or have received their countenance and support. The native Christians are a power in the country; and

Results of missions in India: Direct.

united with the missions with which they are connected, constitute an ethical agency superior to all other such agencies in the good which they are accomplishing, and are destined to accomplish. The land is spread over with a network of Christian congregations, which, like the stars in the sky, are so many small luminaries shedding light upon the surrounding darkness.

Indirect. But great and wonderful as are the direct results of Indian missions, their indirect results are greater and more wonderful still. As they were the pioneers in the work of national education, so they continue to the present day in the front rank of this important enterprise. They have striven everywhere to civilise the people, and to make them happier in their social relations, more honest one to another, wiser, holier, and better. They have soothed the harshness of foreign rule, and drawn the natives closer to their alien governors. They have been a living exemplification of the benevolent intentions of the British Government towards its Indian subjects. They have awakened the sympathy and secured the confidence of a large portion of the various Hindoo races scattered over the peninsula, in a manner and degree surpassing all other humanising agencies existing in the country. To them mainly is to be attributed the zeal now exhibited on many sides in the cause of female education and elevation. It is their agents especially who enter zenanas, teach native ladies, and superintend girls' schools; and who are almost the only persons who are intimately acquainted with the domestic life of native women, and hold familiar intercourse with them. These missions have loosened

the bonds of caste, have made it easier for the lower
castes to bear the yoke of the upper, and have resisted
strenuously the authority of this inveterate enemy of
human society wherever they have been able. They
have led many Hindoos to abandon idolatry, though
they may not have embraced Christianity. They
have, in some places, effected a revolution in the indigenous religions, and caused multitudes to desire a
purer faith. By the reflection of the higher spiritual
sentiments which they teach on the minds of the
people, new religions, moulded more or less by Christian truths, have sprung into existence, leading not a
few away from superstition to clearer, though it may
be not to perfect, views of God and their relations to
Him. They have brought all India to reverence the
Christian religion, and to recognise its lofty, if not its
Divine, character. They have given essential aid in
the abolition of gigantic national evils which filled
the earth with horror, such as the burning of widows
on the funeral pile of their husbands, female infanti-
cide, drowning the aged in the Ganges, swinging
festivals, and many inhuman practices at Jagannath
and elsewhere; and in the introduction of enlightened
usages from the West, such as the remarriage of
Hindoo widows, and the education and more con-
siderate treatment of women. They have fostered
the growth of public spirit and manliness among all
classes of natives, who from long centuries of oppression had lost the sense of independence. Their
Christian labourers have scattered knowledge of every
kind, both secular and religious, over the land with
marvellous prodigality, have written books, edited
newspapers and other journals, and have toiled with

unwearied perseverance in the production of an extensive literature in at least twenty spoken languages and dialects.

India no longer unprogressive. The spread of education.

India of the present day differs from India of fifty years ago, as England of modern times differs from England of the reign of Queen Anne and the Revolution. It is fast losing its ancient landmarks. Its former condition of unprogressiveness and stagnation is rapidly disappearing under the renovating and life-giving influences of education, civilisation, and Christianity. The Hindoo race is awakening from the sleep of centuries, and is determined to make up for lost time by the celerity with which it adapts and assimilates the knowledge and discoveries of more advanced nations. Yearly, thousands of native youths proceed to the examinations for degrees and honours instituted by the universities which have been established in the three Presidencies. Colleges and schools in all directions are full to overflowing. The Hindoo mind is naturally inquisitive, yet its powers of application and retention have fairly astonished foreign teachers, who, ripe in knowledge and cultured in intellect, have come to the country to impart to the people such instruction as they have themselves acquired. In mathematics, medicine, and general literature, Hindoo students attain marvellous proficiency with comparatively small effort or strain. Hitherto they have exhibited little originality, owing doubtless to the degeneracy of the past still operating upon them. Every considerable town has its coterie of learned men trained on European models in all the principal branches of human learning, who look with supreme contempt on the childish ways of their forefathers and the empty folly of the great multitude around them. Yet the mental reaction is manifest everywhere, even among the strictest Pharisees of Hindooism; and signs of improvement fill the land. Now, while many of these healthy changes in native society are due, in no small degree, to the excellent Administration which governs the country, to the intellectual vigour of Europeans in India acting upon the native mind, and to the numerous scientific projects and schemes which they have set on foot, it is beyond dispute that the most prominent, earnest, and indefatigable agencies in producing these results have been Protestant missions, which have operated like a regenerating power upon all classes of the community.

<small>Signs of improvement visible everywhere.</small>

The testimony of every one acquainted with the subject amply confirms this statement. The several Indian Governments, though officially neutral on the matter of religion, have again and again expressed the deepest obligations to Indian missions, under which they have considered themselves to lie, for the untiring zeal their missionaries have displayed in promoting the welfare of the people. And such sentiments have been uttered in times even when opposition has been shown to the missions themselves. I shall, however, only quote the opinions of the Supreme Government as given in the "Statement exhibiting the Moral and Material Progress and Condition of India during the Year 1871-72," drawn up by Clements R. Markham, Esq., Assistant-Secretary to the India Office, and ordered by the House of Commons to be printed, 28th April 1873. I shall furnish rather lengthy extracts from this important

<small>Testimony of Mr Markham on the results of Protestant missions in India.</small>

paper, both on account of the valuable information afforded by so unbiassed an authority, and because of the spontaneous and emphatic acknowledgment it renders to the extraordinary labours and eminently useful results of Protestant missions in India.

<small>Distribution of missions.</small> "The Protestant missions of India, Burmah, and Ceylon are carried on by thirty-five missionary societies, in addition to local agencies, and now employ the services of six hundred and six foreign missionaries, of whom five hundred and fifty-one are ordained. They are widely and rather evenly distributed over the different Presidencies; and they occupy at the present time five hundred and twenty-two principal stations, and two thousand five hundred subordinate stations. The entire Presidency of Bengal, from Calcutta to Peshawur, is well supplied with missionaries, and they are numerous in the southern portion of the Madras Presidency. The various missions in Calcutta, Bombay, and Madras are strong in labourers; and almost all the principal towns of the empire have at least one missionary. A great impulse was given to the efforts of these societies by the changes in public policy inaugurated by the charter of 1833, and since that period the number of missionaries, and the outlay on their missions, have continued steadily to increase. In 1852 there were four hundred and fifty-nine missionaries in India at three hundred and twenty stations; and in 1872 the number of missionaries was increased to six hundred and six, and of stations to five hundred and twenty-two.

<small>Union among missionaries.</small> "This large body of European and American missionaries settled in India, bring their various moral influences to bear upon the country with the greater force, because they act together with a compactness which is but little understood. Though belonging to various denominations of Christians, yet from the nature of their work, their isolated position, and their long experience, they have been led to think rather of the numerous questions on which they agree, than of those on which they differ; and they heartily cooperate together. Localities are divided among them by friendly arrangements; and with few exceptions it is a fixed rule among them, that they will not interfere with each other's converts and each other's spheres of duty. School-books, translations of the Scriptures, and religious works, prepared by various missions, are used in common; and helps and improvements secured by one

mission, are freely placed at the command of all. The large body of missionaries resident in each of the Presidency towns form missionary conferences, hold periodic meetings, and act together on public matters. They have frequently addressed the Indian Government on important social questions involving the welfare of the native community, and have suggested valuable improvements in existing laws. During the past twenty years, on five occasions, general conferences have been held for mutual consultation respecting their missionary work; and in January last, at the latest of these gatherings, at Allahabad, one hundred and twenty-one missionaries met together, belonging to twenty different societies, and including several men of long experience who have been forty years in India. The railway system rendered such a gathering easy, and brought the members of the conference from all parts of the empire.

Five general missionary conferences held during the last twenty years.

"The labours of the foreign missionaries in India assume many forms. Apart from their special duty as public preachers and pastors, they constitute a valuable body of educators; they contribute greatly to the cultivation of the native languages and literature; and all who are resident in rural districts are appealed to for medical help to the sick.

Labours of missionaries.

"No body of men pays greater attention to the study of the native languages than the Indian missionaries. With several missionary societies, as with the Indian Government, it is a rule that the younger missionaries shall pass a series of examinations in the vernacular of the district in which they reside; and the general practice has been, that all who have to deal with natives who do not know English, shall seek a high proficiency in these vernaculars. The result is too remarkable to be overlooked. The missionaries, as a body, know the natives of India well: they have prepared hundreds of works, suited both for schools and for general circulation, in the fifteen most prominent languages of India, and in several other dialects. They are the compilers of several dictionaries and grammars; they have written important works on the native classics and the system of philosophy; and they have largely stimulated the great increase of the native literature prepared in recent years by educated native gentlemen.

The same.

"The mission presses in India are twenty-five in number. During the ten years between 1852 and 1862 they issued 1,634,940 copies of the Scriptures, chiefly single books; and 8,604,033 tracts, school-books, and books for general circulation.

Mission presses. Rev. Dr Wenger.

During the ten years between 1862 and 1872 they issued 3410 new works in thirty languages; and circulated 1,315,503 copies of books of Scripture; 2,375,040 school-books; and 8,750,129 Christian books and tracts. Last year two valuable works were brought to completion, the revision of the Bengali Bible, and the first publication of the entire Bible in Sanskrit. Both were the work of the Rev. Dr Wenger, of the Baptist Mission in Calcutta.

Mission schools and colleges.

"The missionary schools in India are chiefly of two kinds, purely vernacular and Anglo-vernacular schools. The former are maintained chiefly, but not exclusively, in country districts and small towns; the education given in them is confined pretty much to reading, writing, geography, arithmetic, and instruction in simple religious works, such as the 'Peep of Day.' In the Anglo-vernacular schools a much higher education is given, not only in those subjects which are taught in English, but in those in which the vernacular is employed; a higher knowledge even of the vernacular languages is imparted in these schools than is usually given in purely native schools. These schools are most in demand in country towns, in the Presidency cities, and in the districts immediately around them. Bengal has long been celebrated for its English schools; and the missionary institutions of Calcutta still hold a conspicuous place in the system and means of education generally available to the young Hindoos of the city. All the principal missionary institutions teach up to the standard of the entrance examination in the three universities of India; and many among them have a college department, in which students can be led on through the two examinations for B.A., even up to the M.A. degree.

Training colleges. Zenana schools.

"In addition to the work of these schools, it should be noted that several missions maintain training colleges for their native ministers and clergy, and training institutions for teachers. These colleges and institutions are 85 in number, and contain 1618 students. The training institutions for girls are 28 in number, with 567 students. An important addition to the efforts made on behalf of female education is seen in the zenana schools and classes, which are maintained and instructed in the houses of Hindoo gentlemen. These schools have been established during the last sixteen years, and now number 1300 classes, with 1997 scholars, most of whom are adults. Of these, 938 classes, with 1523 scholars, are in Bengal and the North-West Provinces. The effort has not yet much affected the other provinces of India.

"The great progress made in these missionary schools, and the area which they occupy, will be seen from the following fact. They now contain 60,000 scholars more than they did twenty years ago. The figures are as follows: In 1852 the scholars numbered 81,850; and in 1872 the number was 142,952.

"The high character of the general education given in the college department of these institutions may be gathered from the following facts. Between 1862 and 1872, 1621 students passed the entrance examination in one or other of the three Indian universities; 513 passed the first examination in Arts; 154 took the degree of B.A.; 18 took the degree of M.A., and 6 that of B.L. A considerable proportion of the amount expended upon education by the missionaries in India, is provided by school-fees, which in recent years have been much increased. In the higher education it is believed that little expenditure falls upon the missionary societies beyond the salaries of the superintending missionaries.

<small>Number of graduates and undergraduates from mission institutions.</small>

"The statistical returns * state very clearly and completely the number of the converts who have been gathered in the various Indian missions, and the localities in which they may be found. They show also that a great increase has taken place in the numbers of these converts during the last twenty years; as might be expected from the lapse of time, the effects of earlier instruction, and the increased number of missionaries employed. In 1852 the entire number of Protestant native converts in India, Burmah, and Ceylon amounted to 22,400 communicants, in a community of 128,000 native Christians of all ages. In 1862 the communicants were 49,688, and the native Christians were 213,182. In 1872 the communicants were 78,494, and the converts, young and old, numbered 318,363.

<small>Increase of converts in twenty years.</small>

"But the missionaries in India hold the opinion that the winning of these converts, whether in the cities or in the open country, is but a small portion of the beneficial results which have sprung from their labours. No statistics can give a fair view of all that they have done. They consider that their distinctive teaching, now applied to the country for many years, has powerfully affected the entire population. The moral tone of their preaching is recognised and highly approved by multitudes who do not follow them as converts. The various lessons which they inculcate have given to the people at large new ideas, not only on purely religious questions,

<small>General influence of the teaching of the missionaries.</small>

* Statistical Tables of Protestant Missions in India, Ceylon, and Burmah, for 1871.

but on the nature of evil, the obligations of law, and the motives by which human conduct should be regulated. Insensibly a higher standard of moral conduct is becoming familiar to the people, especially to the young, which has been set before them not merely by public teaching, but by the millions of printed books and tracts which are scattered widely through the country. On this account they express no wonder that the ancient systems are no longer defended as they once were; many doubts are felt about the rules of caste; the great festivals are not attended by the vast crowds of former years; and several Theistic schools have been growing up among the more educated classes, especially in the Presidency cities, who profess to have no faith in the idol-gods of their fathers. They consider that the influences of their religious teaching are assisted and increased by the example of the better portions of the English community, by the spread of English literature and English education, by the freedom given to the press, by the high standard, tone, and purpose of Indian legislation, and by the spirit of freedom, benevolence, and justice which pervades the English rule. And they augur well of the future moral progress of the native population of India from these signs of solid advance already exhibited on every hand, and gained within the brief period of two generations. This view of the general influence of their teaching, and of the greatness of the revolution which it is silently producing, is not taken by missionaries only. It has been accepted by many distinguished residents in India and experienced officers of the Government; and has been emphatically endorsed by the high authority of Sir Bartle Frere. Without pronouncing an opinion upon the matter, the Government of India cannot but acknowledge the great obligation under which it is laid by the benevolent exertions made by these 600 missionaries, whose blameless example and self-denying labours are infusing new vigour into the stereotyped life of the great populations placed under English rule, and are preparing them to be in every way better men and better citizens of the great empire in which they dwell." *

The Government expresses its great obligations to them.

Opponents of Indian missions.

The opponents of Indian missions are numerous. They are, however, resolvable into two classes, those who are ignorant of their labours and successes, and

* Statement exhibiting the Moral and Material Progress and Condition of India during the year 1871-72: ordered by the House of Commons to be printed, 28th April 1873, pp. 124-20.

those who expect too much from them, in forgetfulness of their very limited resources, and the enormous population which they endeavour to influence. Moreover, most persons who object to missions, do so, as they imagine, on principle. That is to say, they hold that missions are quixotic in purpose and aim; and that it would, all things considered, be better to leave the idolater to his idols than to attempt to convert him to Christianity, a religion which many of this class conceive to be merely one out of a multitude of possible religions, all being more or less good. They look upon a missionary in a humorous light; account him a fair object for jest and ridicule; and experience the keenest relish and enjoyment at the very thought that he should strive to reclaim a people worshipping many-armed, goggle-eyed, grinning deities, thinking indeed more of the strangeness and oddness of his humility than of the abjectness of their condition.

In India, the number of foreign residents outside the missionary circle, taking practical interest in the progress of Christian missions in the land, is exceedingly small. Few contribute towards their funds; fewer still know what is being done by missionaries and their native coadjutors in their own immediate neighbourhood; most persons display a grotesque ignorance of the methods of procedure which they adopt; and from the beginning of the year to the end, the entire foreign community, as a class—with here and there bright exceptions, whose very singularity, however, constitutes them "peculiar people" in the opinion of the rest—agrees to ignore missions,

Apathy of European residents.

so far as most of its members are personally concerned. Though missionaries mix with them in society, yet the conversion of the natives is, as a subject, studiously avoided. Questions upon it are rarely put; and when they are, they are evidently the result of mere casual curiosity. As to visiting the mission stations, with the object of becoming acquainted with their various branches of labour, and of evincing real anxiety in the spiritual enlightenment of the natives, and in the elevation and expansion of the native Christian Church, and so showing the missionaries the genuine sympathy felt in the great work in which they are engaged, this is practised in a most minute degree even in large cities where the number of European residents is considerable. The moral support which such residents could give, if they chose, Indian missions do not obtain. Instead of being a help to them, they often, on account of their intense apathy, or of the flagrant immorality of some of them, are a direct obstacle to their advancement and success.

Their report of mission-work, therefore, often founded on ignorance.

As it is impossible for persons so little acquainted with missions in India to give accurate information about them on their return home, many do not hesitate to conceal their dense ignorance by making disparaging remarks against the missionaries and their labours to the friends who put to them awkward interrogatories about the missions in whose vicinity they have been living; while some will boldly assert that nothing is being accomplished, and that the heathen are just as far away from Christ as they ever were. Thus, instead of honestly confessing their ignorance, they prefer to cast a stigma on the missionaries, and to bring an evil report upon their doings.

A few of the public journals of India, notably the *Friend of India*, started by Mr John Marshman, and edited for many years by him, and latterly by Dr George Smith, are in favour of missions. Speaking generally, however, the Indian press is unfriendly to them, and manifests little or no concern in their prosperity. Though compelled occasionally to pay tribute to their usefulness in promoting the enlightenment of the people, yet it does so with ill-concealed unwillingness. It is fault-finding and cynical, and is never wearied at reciting the threadbare tale of the failure of missions. Some influential journals have taken in hand to praise various forms of Hindooism, especially caste, and to disparage Christianity. Some adopt by turns a spirit of Deism, Positivism, and Eclecticism. Others express a languid faith in Christian truth, and are quite content to leave the world in error. And others still, while ready to ignore religion in all its phases, exhibit a prurient love for indelicate writing, which in England would be a scandal to a paper of any sort of respectability. One reason of the opposition to missions on the part of some of these journals is, that their editors are amateur writers drawn from England; and being young, inexperienced, and without settled principles or convictions on any subject, but possessed of an aptitude for penning short, spirited, mirth-provoking articles, fall readily into the snare of writing merely for amusement and stage effect.

The various Governments of the country under

The British Indian Governments friendly to missions.

British rulers, are certainly not antagonistic to missions, while many of their individual members are their earnest friends and supporters. Indeed, the higher you go in the social scale among the foreign residents in India, the greater proportionate amount of sympathy in the missionary enterprise do you find. Still, it sometimes happens that a man in high position will set himself against missions; and it is astonishing how much mischief, directly and indirectly, he may do them. But such instances, it must be confessed, are exceptional. On the contrary, great officials, well knowing the value of missions in promoting the welfare of the people, and in securing the loyalty of all those natives who embrace the Christian faith, speak warmly in their favour, and sustain them with their money. The Indian Governments, however, in their very proper anxiety to maintain a neutral position in the matter of religion, do not exert that healthy repressive influence in regard to licentious rites and preposterous usages prevalent among the people, which they might easily do without their neutrality being called in question. They have always pursued a timid policy. A little more boldness in the defence of morality and purity, and in resisting and frowning upon the vicious habits of the natives, would be beneficial to them in every way.

Of late years education has made rapid strides in India. Its rulers have prosecuted the good work with praiseworthy zeal, and have been vigorously seconded by the missionaries. In 1871, as already stated, there were upwards of one hundred and twenty-two thousand male and female pupils under instruction in mission schools and colleges in India alone. The work, therefore, which Christian missions are accomplishing, even in this direction merely, is extensive and important. Many of the mission educational establishments are partly supported by grants-in-aid from the Government, in accordance with the terms of Sir Charles Wood's Educational Despatch of 1854. Yet very often frivolous difficulties have been placed in the way of their reception, to suit the whim of Lieutenant-Governors or of Directors of Public Instruction. Rules, too, for granting aid, quite proper in their way, have, nevertheless, from the commencement to the present time, been so constantly changed, that they have never been more than tentative, have ever been liable to fundamental alteration, and have not been framed in any one governorship according to fixed and certain principles. Moreover, missionaries have occasionally had ground of complaint on account of the utter absence of consideration shown to them and their interests by the heads of administration. An instance of this is the following. In the North-Western Provinces the amount of grant given to a school for the instruction of boys is made dependent on the sum raised for their tuition apart from the grant. It is manifest, therefore, that whatever reduces this sum jeopardises the grant in proportion. In the month of August 1873 the Government of the North-Western Provinces issued an order, and published it in its *Gazette*, that the fees of all the Government colleges and schools throughout the provinces should be diminished according to a certain scale. The rate of diminution may be judged from the fact that, in the Benares Government College, the students who paid six shillings previously, were called upon to pay in future only one shilling. The youths were well able to give the full fee, and many of them were the sons of wealthy parents. The order was issued suddenly, without the statement of any reason for the step, except the pleasure of the Lieutenant-Governor, and without the smallest consultation with the principals and head-masters of non-Government institutions, who had, however, to follow suit immediately, or witness the loss of most of their pupils. Their funds, in consequence, fell off at once, thereby greatly lessening their ability to continue the staff of teachers they had hitherto possessed, endangering the grant-in-aid they had enjoyed, and imperilling the efficiency of the institutions themselves. This course of proceeding, to say the least, was arbitrary and ungracious. Moreover, it was positively mischievous, as, instead of leading the natives on to the desirable goal of paying fully for their education, it tended to produce in them a pauper feeling of subjection, and to make them more than ever dependent on the State.

Grants of the Government to female schools.

The same uncertainty and caprice displays itself in the management of female schools by the Indian Governments. At one time, mission schools for the female sex are liberally helped; at others, the most vexatious obstacles assail them, until the missionaries and their wives would be only too glad, if they could possibly afford it, to be delivered from the grievous burden of the Government grant, connected as it is with so many petty annoyances, and with the patient endurance of so much bald advice and needless reproach on the part of Government officials.

Every reflective person reading this narrative will

PROTESTANT MISSIONS IN INDIA. 475

have been struck with the numerous methods of labour adopted in the prosecution of the missionary enterprise in India. In some missions, great attention is paid to preaching the gospel to the heathen, and little to their education. In others, the chief work pursued is education. In others still, both are blended. Some missions are mainly engaged in village work; others are entirely devoted to the cities. In some places, large orphanages and boarding-schools exist; while in others they are entirely discarded. Some missions have maintained a system of extreme simplicity; and others have carried on their operations with considerable outside pomp and show.

Diverse methods of missionary labour.

The test of all these methods, provided they are in themselves unobjectionable, is their success. It should be, moreover, borne in mind that plans suited to one locality, and to one class of natives, might not be adapted to other localities and to other classes of people. It is indisputable that some of the most useful and best equipped converts gained to the Indian Church, have been young men trained in the great mission colleges, where they have received an elaborate education, which has fitted them to take a prominent and often distinguished part in the evangelisation of their fellow-countrymen. The Scotch institutions in the three Presidency cities, and elsewhere, have been singularly successful in this department of missionary labour. Indeed, education is almost the only means of making known Christian truth to the upper ranks of Hindoo society; and were it not for this instrumentality, they would remain profoundly ignorant of the gospel. Bazaar and village preaching, as a rule, only reaches the

Great importance of education

Bazaar and village preaching only reaches the lower grades.

lower grades of the people. Persons of any pretensions to respectability will not stop on the wayside to listen even to a European. Consequently, it will be found that few natives of position become Christians after this manner.

Direct preaching fitted to rude and uncultured tribes.

On the other hand, the direct method of preaching is peculiarly fitted to rude and uncultured tribes, and in some districts is attended with marked success. Practically, the simpler the system employed among such communities, the greater the chance of influencing them. The introduction of any elaborate machinery to compass their conversion, would not only be absurd in itself, but would be unproductive of result. The error which many missionaries, in love with their own pet schemes, make, is that they imagine such schemes, while eminently useful for certain classes of natives, are equally good under all circumstances and for all kinds of people. There are some who consider, for instance, that preaching is the only legitimate means to be employed throughout the length and breadth of India in Christianising its inhabitants; and that those persons who adopt any other are deviating from the primitive rules laid down in the New Testament, and courting the Divine displeasure. The writer has heard a missionary of considerable intelligence utter the sentiment, that so long as preaching the gospel was so much neglected, he did not believe that it was possible for the blessing of God to rest upon our mission-work. This remark he was incautious enough to make, although he himself had been for years preaching to the heathen with scarcely any success whatever.

It may be gathered from a perusal of the previous

chapters, that education is an invaluable auxiliary to the Christian work of missions in India, especially in the large towns and cities. In such places it should meet the highest intellectual necessities of the people, and should nowhere fall short of the education imparted in Government institutions. Whether Christian education should be carried into the villages, is a question of considerable difficulty. In itself, it is manifest, it is as important to teach villagers Christian truth as dwellers in cities. Yet it is found in practice, that for the most part this knowledge can be better communicated to them by short earnest discourses, repeated at certain intervals, than through the agency of schools.

Education imparted in Indian cities should be of a high standard.

This brings us to the deeply interesting question of the methods in operation in preaching the gospel to the natives of India. I say methods, in the plural number, because they are not one, but several. The old plan, still pursued in many parts of the country, particularly in Northern India, and still as unsatisfactory and unproductive as ever, is that of preaching to promiscuous assemblies, whether collected in bazaars, in villages, or elsewhere. The sole good accomplished by this system is in scattering the good seed of the Word broadcast everywhere, in the hope that it may find a lodgment in some distressed and anxious soul, which it occasionally does. Undoubtedly, multitudes of persons in this way become acquainted with the first truths of Christianity, and therefore some amount of result is gained. But in regard to actual conversions—the main object which missionaries have in view—little is attained. The listening crowds are of too shifting a character, are

Preaching to promiscuous assemblies unsatisfactory.

too much engrossed in their own avocations, are too unconcerned in what they hear, understand to so small an extent the meaning of the great subjects discussed, and retain in their memories such meagre ideas respecting them, and these often distorted and mixed up with Hindoo notions, and with Hindoo interpretations of many of the religious terms employed, that although a modicum of spiritual benefit, of a very general character, accrues to the people at large, yet it is of a nature so undefined and intangible that the impression produced leads few persons to abandon their own religion, and to seek after that whose merits and features they so vaguely comprehend.

Utility of frequent and systematic preaching to the same people.

The system of preaching observed in many missions in Southern India, and in fact in all those parts of the country in which Christianity has made extensive progress among the lower castes and aboriginal tribes, is emphatically a system of concentrated effort. A very limited tract is taken in hand. Missionaries, together with their native helpers, visit all the villages in it periodically; that is, every three months or less, the gospel is preached to the same people, who gradually understand what is said, and appreciate the motives and aims of those who address them. Moreover, the missionaries come to know the faces of their hearers, and an acquaintance, often amounting to personal friendship, springs up between them. I have been told that the hardest and most unpromising soil yields to such cultivation, that the wildest and most vicious natives become tamed, and that eventually whole villages are reclaimed from heathenism to the worship of the one living and true God. The system commends itself to reason and sense, and is that followed in all the missions possessing great village communities throughout the country. As soon as the district first selected is to a certain extent evangelised, another contiguous to it is selected and worked in the same fashion; and thus mission stations multiply far and wide.

I would that all societies sending forth their agents as preachers of the gospel insisted on the observance of some such method as that now indicated; and issued a positive order prohibiting the missionaries and their native labourers from frittering away their time and strength in disjointed and tentative operations spread over unlimited regions. Although in carrying on their work missionaries need to be left in many points to themselves, yet, in the opinion of the writer, they ought not in this. He would even suggest the advisability of local committees, or the societies themselves with the aid of such committees, laying out a certain number of villages within a prescribed area, to be visited periodically so many times in the year by its foreign and native agents. This measure would doubtless restrain the liberty of not a few missionaries; but he is satisfied the restraint would be far healthier and more conducive to sound results than the present desultory methods which many are accustomed to pursue. *Importance of missionary societies directing their agents in this matter.*

Intimately connected with this question is the plan of labour in cities adopted by numerous missions. The missionary goes to his preaching-place, which may be a small room abutting on the street, or a corner of the public thoroughfare, and there delivering his message, in an hour or two returns. If this work be done conscientiously and with careful preparation, it is by *Method of preaching in cities* no means to be despised. But, at the best, it has an official aspect, and is scattering the seed by the wayside. The missionary invites his hearers to his house; but an exceedingly small number ever avail themselves of his invitation. The plan of the missionaries in Burmah is much more calculated to awaken sympathy. There they have their room open to the street as in India, where they sit, not for one hour or two, but for five or six hours in succession, and carry on conversation with all comers. As it is known that the missionaries are daily at their post for a long period, they are visited without constraint. Their room becomes the centre of attraction to many anxious persons with the burden of sin upon them, who feel that, notwithstanding the difference of religious sentiment between them and the missionaries, yet that the latter have the same longings as themselves, and perhaps, from their superior knowledge, may be able to clear away some of their doubts and difficulties. To my mind, the one system is as preferable to the other, as preaching to a few villages at frequently recurring intervals is superior to preaching to a large number at remote intervals. There is great scope for reform in this matter.

Qualifications needed in Indian missionaries.

It needs hardly to be said that missionaries in India should be men of varied gifts and talents. Religious earnestness, high enthusiasm, intense and strongly-felt piety, which no reproach or bitter speaking on the part of enemies can diminish, are absolutely necessary. Men of feeble belief, impassive and stolid, even though possessed of great mental power, are unfit for the work. So also are men who undertake it for the sake merely, or chiefly, of making it their livelihood. So likewise are timid, retiring, bashful men, who are afraid to speak the truth, or who will be cowed by opposition and discouragement. All missionaries who set foot in India should be earnest, consumed with zeal, and determined by the help of God to carry everything before them. They should be men of high-toned religious thought and feeling, feeding their faith and love by constant prayer and meditation on the Word of God. Some should be accomplished scholars; but all need not be. Provided they have other gifts already referred to, they will make useful and efficient labourers in the vineyard of the Divine Husbandman. But every man should occupy the place for which he is fitted. Great care is required here; for sometimes the most unnatural and unfortunate arrangements are made, arising perhaps from the paucity of missionaries, entailing grievous hurt and mischief on the missions to which they are attached.

Respecting the spiritual quality of men demanded in India, the Rev. T. Valpy French makes the following pregnant observations. "I should be the less careful," he remarks, "about a great influx of foreign missionaries into North India, than about the sending forth from amongst our best theological students in Europe and America a *few* men, but a few, who have grappled in personal spiritual experience with the great mysteries of faith, and have been taught the solution of many or all of them in wrestlings of soul in their closets, on their knees, with an open Bible before them; and yet who are not indifferent to the struggles of the past, so as to appreciate their moral and spiritual value,— schooled of the Spirit, even more than in the studies

The Rev. T. V. French on the spiritual quality of the men demanded.

2 H

of seats of learning, to fight the good fight of faith. Others of great force of personal character, of love and holiness, and of administrative ability, are useful, very useful also; but we crave a good and large proportion of the first. Our universities seem asleep on this point. God alone can rouse them."*

* Lahore Divinity School: Annual Letter of the Rev. T. Valpy French for 1871, p. 17.

THE END.

www.ingramcontent.com/pod-product-compliance
Lightning Source LLC
Chambersburg PA
CBHW021425300426
44114CB00010B/647